COLONIAL VOICES

Second Revised First Edition

Edited by M. L. Brillman

Foothill College

cognella® | ACADEMIC PUBLISHING

Bassim Hamadeh, CEO and Publisher
Kassie Graves, Vice President of Editorial
Jamie Giganti, Director of Academic Publishing
Natalie Piccotti, Director of Marketing
Jess Estrella, Senior Graphic Designer
Carrie Montoya, Manager, Revisions and Author Care
Kaela Martin, Project Editor
Alexa Lucido, Licensing Manager
Joyce Lue, Interior Designer
Arielle Lewis, Production Editor

3970 Sorrento Valley Blvd., Ste. 500, San Diego, CA 9212

CONTENTS

For My Parents, Jon and Diane

Introduction

Winston Churchill, Wilfrid Scawen Blunt, Leo S. Amery, Ngugi Wa Thiong'o, Simón Bolívar, Miguel Hidalgo, Salman Rushdie, Benedict Anderson, Arthur James Balfour, Túpac Amaru, Subhas Chandra Bose, Francisco Pizarro, Aimé Césaire, Cecil John Rhodes, Alexis de Tocqueville, Robert Mugabe, Jan Christian Smuts, Kwame Nkrumah, Gayatri Chakravorty Spivak, Jomo Kenyatta, Arthur Griffith, Ashis Nandy, Haile Selassie, Dadabhai Naoroji, Reginald Dyer, Robert Emmet, C. L. R. James, Daniel O'Connell, William Ewart Gladstone, Benjamin Disraeli, Queen Victoria, V. S. Naipaul, Edmund Burke, Benito Mussolini, Roger Casement, Joseph Chamberlain, Theobald Wolfe Tone, Annie Besant, King Leopold II, David Cannadine, Adam Smith, José Morelos, Sor Juana Inés de la Cruz, Emperor Lin Zexu, Wole Soyinka, Theodore Roosevelt, George Orwell, Jawaharlal Nehru, Muhammad Ali Jinnah, Bob Marley, Vo Nguyen Giap, Fela Kuti, Charles de Gaulle, Gustave de Beaumont, James and John Stuart Mill, and Margaret Thatcher.

The preceding very lengthy list contains some colonial voices that had to be omitted from this volume in the interest of space. Obviously, the assortment above is not exhaustive; a hundred more names could easily be added. Before addressing the selections that are actually included in this book, however, some terms should be defined. Students will sometimes use "imperialism" and "colonialism" interchangeably, when they are not precisely the same things. Imperialism occurs when the government of one nation controls the political, economic, or public life of another. Colonialism, by contrast, possesses the characteristics of imperialism, plus settlement. In other words, inhabitants of the metropole take up residence in the periphery. Nigeria, Egypt, and Palestine were all examples of imperialism. Canada, Haiti, and Algeria were cases of colonialism. I have attempted to use each where appropriate while avoiding as much monotony or repetition as possible.

Within this nomenclature, a further dissection is necessary. In the British context, for example, there existed different forms of colonial authority, namely crown colonies, protectorates, and spheres of influence. Crown colonies were governed directly from Westminster, especially if they had proven to be rebellious. The Indian Mutiny of 1857 and the Morant Bay rebellion in Jamaica in 1865 constituted two such episodes, and these crown colonies were under the jurisdiction of the India Office and the Colonial

Office, respectively. Protectorates were semiautonomous areas "protected" by government mandate, under which a European resident essentially oversaw law and order. Egypt exemplified a protectorate. Spheres of influence were not instances of imperialism in the traditional sense, but could have far-reaching and devastating economic effects nonetheless. European powers negotiated through "gunboat diplomacy," whereby they dictated their terms of trade with the threat of force at the ready. China and Argentina were examples of British spheres of influence in the 19th century. Victorians neither inhabited nor even occupied Peking or Buenos Aires, yet exerted tremendous pressure to the capitals' economic detriment.

French imperialism differed from that of Britain mainly in its conceptions of those over whom they governed. Natives who would have been considered mere subjects in the British Empire theoretically were granted citizenship in the French republic. How often, or to what extent, this was actually put into practice remains elusive. The trickiest part—racially, anyway—was convincing natives in Senegal or Guadeloupe that they were of the same stock and civilization as the Gauls. Britain and France became the largest beneficiaries of colonial expansion, but other powers included Germany, Italy, Belgium, the Netherlands, Spain, Portugal, Russia, Japan, and the United States. After 1871, Germany became Europe's most industrialized nation. Japan had begun its modernization process in 1868, and took the lead among Asian economies by 1900, the year in which the United States eclipsed all European nations as the world's most productive economy.

What were the reasons for imperialism and colonialism? Was there something more complex, more ambiguous, or more sinister to it all than economic exploitation pure and simple; a capitalist monopoly over an underdeveloped world? The advent of the Industrial Revolution placed enormous economic and technological demands on the state. These demands could be met by European expansion across the world; something akin to Immanuel Wallerstein's Modern World-System theory, with three distinct economic zones: the core (which dominated the world politically and economically); a semi-periphery with skilled labor; and a periphery (with unskilled, often coerced labor that contributed basic commodities such as agricultural products and raw materials).[1] Thus, along with industrialization came an increased demand for natural resources such as rubber, oil, copper, manganese, or bauxite. Europeans extracted food from subsistence farmers, forcing them to buy "imported" food that they might have previously grown themselves. Europeans—or more precisely, their colonial subjects—cut trees, dug mines, and drilled oil. In terms of infrastructure, they strung telegraph lines, laid rails, and built harbors and processing and manufacturing plants in the colonies to turn raw materials into more useful things for European and American consumers. Local industries were ruined by the competition posed by cheap Westernized machine-made products. The Indian cotton textile industry, for example, which had been pre-eminent in the 18th century, was decimated by the mills of northern English industrial cities such as Manchester and Birmingham in the 19th century, and Indians were forced to buy cloth rather than sell it as Britain opened up the subcontinent commercially. The empire, therefore, served as a web of new markets for the production of industrialized European manufactures. Colonies, moreover, provided excellent sources of cheap labor for other colonies, particularly through the transmigration of South and East Asian coolie labor to destinations such as South Africa and the Caribbean. Displaced colonials would work more cheaply than unionized European workers. These coolies often extracted, processed, and shipped resources from the colonies back to Europe.

---

1   Immanuel Wallerstein, *The Modern World-System: Capitalist Agriculture and the Origins of the European World-Economy of the Sixteenth Century* (New York: Academic Press, 1976).

There were also political and military reasons: strategic areas were sought for defense. British and Russian imperial interests, for example, clashed in the Great Game for Iran and Afghanistan because the British believed that the overland route to India could not be left unprotected. Similarly, the British wrested control of the Suez Canal, first from the French and then from the Egyptians. The canal, which opened in 1869, allowed ships to pass between Asia and Africa, cutting hundreds of miles off of these voyages. Indeed, technological advancement such as Hiram Maxim's machine gun, geopolitical military value, and the apotheosis of the military-fiscal state were all contributing factors. Wealth and power were mutually reinforcing entities. If a nation had wealth, it could obtain more power; it could pay its soldiers and sailors, it could procure mercenaries, or even bribe enemies. If a country possessed power, it could amass more wealth by aggrandizing territory; it could establish control over valuable resources, or exact revenue from the local populace.

Finally, there existed humanitarian or social impulses for the imperial mission. Colonial history reveals example upon example of irrational psychology and ingrained beliefs in Western superiority. Rudyard Kipling's phrase "the white man's burden" meant the moral obligation to spread the benefits of Western civilization to a backward and barbarous world. Nineteenth-century European ideas about progress and prosperity, as well as racist ideologies about the biological exclusivity of Caucasians, presented the bases of the colonizers' ethos. A psychological impetus for empire predicated on such Eurocentric assumptions of racial superiority complemented the other economic and political factors. Yet, this paternalistic civilizing mission illuminated something inherently hypocritical. Europeans' prejudice was, in one sense, historical in that racist or at least hierarchical mind-sets were highly prevalent as the norm of the day. In another sense, however, imperial attitudes and biases merely reflected Victorian and Edwardian feelings of inadequacy and a perpetual need for reassurance. Gazing at the colonial was really just another way of gazing at one's own navel.

The purpose of this text is to illustrate and examine what a cross-section of the colonizers and the colonized thought of each other and themselves. The pieces selected in this volume represent an amalgam of these views: a greatest hits, so to speak, of the apogee of imperialism as well as decolonization. Because of such vast geographical and chronological parameters, any attempt to acquire a complete exploration into the subject would be impossible for a primary-source document reader designed for a semester- or quarter-long course. Instead, we will survey the period as a whole by underscoring various significant events, processes, themes, and transitions that have shaped imperial and postcolonial history. What was the impact of the confluence, integration, and conflicts between cultures? Why did Europe expand, conquer, and prosper at the expense of Asia, Africa, and the Americas? The book, in effect, will encompass an overview of the political, economic, social, and technological forces, as well as the unique and strong personalities that have contributed to the making of the modern colonial and postcolonial world.

Certainly, this volume contains lacunae. Chronologically, for example, most of the entries date from the 19th and 20th centuries. There is nothing from the 17th century. Many of the writings or speeches I have chosen (16), furthermore, represent criticisms of a specific colonial situation, though proponents of empire (six) also appear. While critics of empire greatly outweigh advocates in this volume, the critiques represent a variety of attitudes. Sometimes, depending on the issue, selections of both "pros" and "antis" abut one another in the same section. Selections are largely comprised of primary sources, materials used by historians that were recorded by eye-witnesses or contemporaries (20). Primary sources can be letters, e-mails, diaries, journals, newspaper accounts, government records, poems and songs, and memoirs or autobiographies. With these last two genres, the historian must use a good deal of caution because they may have been written years after the events, and in the intervening time, the author may misremember history, aggrandize, or even minimize his or her own role.[2] History is not what happened, but a representation of what happened, and if enough people internalize it, it becomes ingrained collectively in the historical memory and imagination. Nonetheless, I have decided to include autobiographical pieces by Olaudah Equiano (1789), Chinua Achebe (1993), and Maria Rosa Luna Henson (1996) and consider them primary sources, since, despite the passage of time and the intangibles of memory, they were penned by colonial authors. This point holds ever truer for the critiques of colonialism and imperialism by J. A. Hobson (1902) and V. I. Lenin (1916), who wrote during the height of European dominance.

Secondary sources are written *post hoc* (after the fact) by historians, economists, scholars of cultural studies, and literary critics. Secondary-source authors included in *Colonial Voices* (only two) are Eric Williams (1942) and Edward Said (1978). They have become such indispensable cornerstones of colonial and postcolonial studies, however, that not only are their inclusions critical, but, in terms of their effects on historiography (the canon of published work by historians on a particular subject) and the scholarly debate they have provoked, they have evolved into kinds of primary sources in and of themselves.

The chapters in this reader have been organized thematically rather than by chronology. There are no absolute rules to the placement of the selections. The "Comfort Woman" chapter in the section on women, for example, might also go in the slavery section. I have attempted to lend structure to sometimes disparate and even fissiparous historical forces.

Colonial Voices is divided into eight sections, with two to four chapters within them. The "Initial Encounters" section deals with early contacts between Europe and the New World, beginning with the journal from the first voyage of Christopher Columbus.[3] Indeed, Columbus represented the first of those conquistadors who sought to exploit their newfound territories in the name of flag and cross. In contrast, the clergyman Bartolomé de Las Casas's *An Account, Much Abbreviated, of the Destruction of the Indies*, published in 1552, 60 years after Columbus first sailed, rejected the harsh treatment of the Indians by the Spaniards.

The section on women remains the most problematic in terms of sources. I have included four chapters on women out of 22; however, the ratio still leaves much to be desired, especially when two of the four entries were written by men. It is rather difficult to find women's voices in the colonial context because wives, particularly in the early period, rarely accompanied their husbands on their adventures. Any voices of colonial women, native or European, remain marginal and rare. Inadequate as this gap may be, for the present, the "Women" section should be viewed as a work in progress to be added to as more sources come to light. Doña Marina was instrumental in the Spanish usurpation of the Mexica Empire, yet her story has only been available through the words of contemporary male observers. Bernal Díaz del Castillo probably provided historians with the most comprehensive account of the life of Doña Marina. Similarly, in India with the case of *sati*, or widow-burning, the majority of accounts historians possess comes from British or Indian men. Presented here are two English diary entries on *sati*, one by a woman, Fanny Parks, and another by a man, James Peggs. Fortunately, I was also able to include portions of Maria Rosa Luna Henson's 1996 autobiography, *Comfort Woman: Slave of Destiny*, which chronicled her captivity and sexual, physical, and mental abuse as a sex slave of the Japanese army during the Second World War.

---

2 As George Costanza reminds us in "Seinfeld," "It's not a lie if you believe it."
3 The term New World, as opposed to the Old World (i.e., Europe) encompasses North America, Central America, South America, and the Caribbean.

The writings of Lola Rosa, as she would become known, could have seamlessly been placed in the "Slavery" section; however, given the dearth of female voices noted above, they have been placed with "Women." "Slavery," on the other hand, includes two selections. The first is an 18th-century slave narrative by Olaudah Equiano entitled *Equiano's Travels*, in which he provides an account of his life as a slave and free man in Africa, the New World, and Britain. The second selection is one of the secondary sources, and was written by the West Indian historian and politician Eric Williams from his 1942 monograph *The Negro in the Caribbean*. In his watershed thesis, Williams turned accepted wisdom on its ear by interpreting that the growth of British industry was built by slave labor, and abolition of the institution was due to economic reasons rather than humanitarian, religious, or moral ones.

Economics, in fact, truly greased the wheels of empire, and engendered forays into politics, society, and religion. Two staunch critics of empire included here are Hobson and Lenin, who, as noted above, published their anti-imperial books in 1902 and 1916, respectively. Hobson represented a Socialist viewpoint, while Lenin—Marx's pre-eminent torchbearer—presented a Communist one.

One facet of imperialism perhaps only minimally touched by the economy was literature. This section, comprised of Kipling's 1899 poem, "The White Man's Burden," and the beginning of Said's 1978 *Orientalism*, may seem to be strange bedfellows. Kipling is an obvious, perhaps gratuitous, choice as the author of empire for young and old alike *par excellence*, and again, he represents one of six chapters by champions of empire. Juxtaposed to Kipling is Said, included in the "Literature" section, not only because he was a professor of comparative literature at Columbia University, but also because his sources for *Orientalism* and for 1993's *Culture and Imperialism* came from British, French, and German Orientalist literary scholars of the Levant. After Williams, Said is the second and final example of a secondary source.

It would seem to be a foregone conclusion that Achebe, the Nigerian novelist, critic, and professor, could easily fit in "Literature;" however, his contribution to this volume, "The Education of a British-Protected Child," as the title suggests, deals with his early life in British-ruled Nigeria. His death in March 2013 marked the loss of an African literary giant, who was ever dedicated to the education and scholarly development of his country and continent's people. Just as diametrically opposed as Kipling and Said, Achebe and Lord Macaulay comprise the "Education" section; instead of native education in Indian subjects, Macaulay proposed that Indian students be steeped like Earl Grey tea in the English classics.

Douglas Hyde, an Irish-language scholar who cared much more for ancient Irish ballads than English classics, insisted that to regain its Gaelic nationhood, Ireland had to be "de-Anglicized." Gandhi had read Western intellectuals, but Indian nationalism rather than prose motivated him. His 1909 tract *Hind Swaraj*, which translates to "Indian Home Rule," philosophically confronted Indian agency in British colonialism while rejecting Western assumptions, values, and norms. Franz Fanon, every bit as gifted intellectually as Gandhi and more academic, focused on the psychology of colonialism; however, the pacifist Gandhi was 180 degrees opposed to Fanon's support for a violent brand of decolonization. The 1956 speech of Colonel Gamal Abdel Nasser concerning the nationalization of the Suez Canal is included not only as an example of an Arab League member thumbing his nose at the West, but also because it uncloaked Britain as a waning imperial power.

Finally, sovereignty is examined through the three declarations of independence of the United States of America, Haiti, and Vietnam. The historical outcomes of this trio of nations has been unequivocally different: America has been the world's post-Second-World-War superpower, Haiti has endured corrupt politicians, earthquakes, disease, and poverty, and Vietnam fought two wars with France and the United

States to secure its status as an independent Communist republic. Yet, there are similarities in these three documents, and they build cumulatively off of one another. Nelson Mandela's Rivonia Trial speech of 1964, after which he was found guilty and imprisoned for some 27 years, is also in the "Sovereignty" section, frankly because I was unsure of exactly where to place it. Mandela's was not necessarily a colonial situation because South Africa has been an independent republic since 1910; however, the policy of apartheid, or lawful racial segregation, persisted until 1994. Mandela fought against discrimination and intolerance on the basis of race. His sovereignty, therefore, translated to equality. Sadly, with the loss of Achebe in March 2013 and Mandela in December of the same year, there are no living primary-source authors in this volume. In the last analysis, it is the primary source that allows the historian to evaluate change over time through a mosaic across which historical actors have the agency to speak for themselves.

Just as this introduction began with a list of colonial voices, I would like to end with a list of acknowledgment of those voices who contributed their thoughts and insights to this project: Everyone at Cognella has been extremely helpful and patient with a tyro such as me. Very special thanks go out to Kaela Martin, Carrie Montoya, Jess Estrella, Monika Dziamka, Abbey Hastings, David Miano, Ivey Preston, Danielle Menard, Jennifer Bowen, Kate Dohe, Bassim Hamadeh, and Jessica Knott. I would also like to express my gratitude to the Department of History at Florida International University, the Steven and Dorothea Green Library at Florida International University, the National Library of Ireland Manuscripts Reading Room, Dan Brillman, Emmet Larkin, Ralph Austen, Ev Meade, Douglas Kanter, Seymour Drescher, Ronald Grigor Suny, Ani Sarkisian, Michael Stamm, Jenna Gibbs, Rebecca Friedman, Elizabeth Heath, Bianca Premo, Chantalle Verna, Maria del Mar Logroño-Narbona, Noble David Cook, Peter Reill, Darden A. Pyron, Kirsten Wood, Aurora Morcillo, Jeremy Rowan, Gwyn Davies, Gregory Camp, Susan Rosenkranz, John Kelly Babb, Eric Rivas, Jason Daniel, Ifeoluwapo Mojirayo Bandy-Toyo (Bandy), Michard Pierre, Marc-Arthur André, Byung Inn Snover, Dolly and Kuku Singh, Ranjeet and Sarjeet Singh, and Jon Brillman. Special thanks also go to Razia Saleh and the rest of the team at the Nelson Mandela Centre of Memory, part of the Nelson Mandela Foundation. Revisions would not have been possible were it not for the help of my family, the Kassab Clan: Evelyn, Raphi, Lisa, Sasha, Ashley, Jacob, Kate, Lilah, and Nora. Lastly, I give thanks for my saint and my angel, Salima and Liam. Any mistakes found in the text are mine.

—M. L. Brillman

PART I
INITIAL ENCOUNTERS

Journal of Christopher Columbus's First Voyage

In the late 15th and early 16th centuries, as Europeans traversed the globe, their continent emerged as the dominant world power. Although non-European mariners, most notably Arab and Chinese, had explored before Europeans and were highly capable navigators with much larger vessels, their efforts were ephemeral and less extensive. For Europe, however, maritime supremacy meant wealth, international prestige, and religious converts. This surge in European expansion began on the Iberian Peninsula. While England, the Netherlands, and France would also participate in the project of overseas exploration, Portugal and Spain initially led the way.

With greater European interest and knowledge about the world, demand for luxury items found in the East increased. Since the Crusades, goods from Asia such as spices, silk, and gold reached Western consumers either via the Silk Road in China through Central Asia to the Black Sea, or by caravan through the Levant. In 1453, Ottoman Turks sacked Constantinople, thereby rendering traditional overland European trade routes all the more vulnerable.

European sailors first attempted to find a direct sea route to the Orient by circumnavigating southern Africa. In terms of uninterrupted trade, the benefits were twofold: By sailing down the west coast of Africa and around the Cape of Good Hope, not only would the Turks be avoided, but also Arab, Persian, or Indian middlemen would be financially excluded. Under the sponsorship of Prince Henry the Navigator, the Portuguese made excursions along littoral Africa. Bartolomeu Dias eventually rounded the Cape of Good Hope, the southernmost part of South Africa, in 1488. Nine years later in 1497, Vasco da Gama reached Calicut on the west coast of India, and a Portuguese presence in Asia had been established. If explorers under the Portuguese flag monopolized the Indian Ocean, Spanish ships would set their courses west.

Figure 1.1. Christopher Columbus. Source: http://commons.wikimedia.org/wiki/File:Christopher_Columbus.PNG.

Christopher Columbus (born Cristóbal Colón, 1451–1506) was a Genoese sailor, who was greatly influenced by the 13th-century voyages of Marco Polo. Having moved to Spain with his son following the death of his wife, Columbus lobbied King Ferdinand and Queen Isabella of Spain for funds to lead an expedition across the Atlantic Ocean, which he believed was only hundreds of miles. Early explorers, in fact, were 15th-century versions of the free-agent athletes of today. Just as sports stars move from team to team, mariners would sail for whoever provided prospects of fortune and fame. Ferdinand Magellan, a native of Portugal, sailed for Spain. John Cabot, an explorer for the English Crown, was born Giovanni Caboto in Italy.

In 1492, having convinced the Spanish monarchs of his plan's viability, Columbus set sail westward from Granada, Spain, in early August with the *Niña*, *Pinta*, and *Santa Maria*, the flagship that was ultimately run ashore and used for lumber. In October, he and his impetuous crew reached the Bahamas and the island of Hispaniola (today Haiti and the Dominican Republic), where they began a settlement and claimed the island for Spain. Isabella and Ferdinand bestowed upon him the titles viceroy of the Indies and admiral of the ocean sea and one-tenth of any precious metals or spices he found. Prior to his death, Columbus made three more voyages eventually reaching Central and South America.

Columbus, however, was a better viceroy and admiral than he was geographer of the ocean sea: he believed China was on the other side of the Caribbean Sea. At first landfall, he mistook Cuba for Asia and called the Taino, Arawak, and Carib natives he encountered Indians. This is why we refer to the Caribbean as the West Indies. Spain had a new empire in the Western hemisphere.

The Indians were extremely generous with their goods and gave the Spaniards whatever they desired. And what the Spanish desired could be summed up in the three Gs: God, glory, and gold. When Columbus returned in 1493, he had been instructed by the Spanish monarchy to convert natives to Christianity and obtain their gold. In this entry from Columbus's diary, see if you can locate the three Gs.

Christopher Columbus's Journal from His First Voyage, 1492–3

By Christopher Columbus

PREFACE

I left the city of Granada on Saturday, 12 May 1492, and traveled to the port of Palos, where I prepared three vessels well suited for such an enterprise. I left that port, amply furnished with provisions and well crewed with seafaring men, on Friday, 3 August, sailing for Your Majesties' Canary Islands in the Ocean Sea, intending to set my course from there and to sail until I reach the Indies, where I will convey Your Majesties' embassy to those rulers and so carry out my orders. With this in mind I have resolved to set down each day full details of everything I do and see and experience on this voyage. … Moreover, My Sovereign Lord and Lady, as well as describing every night the events of the day, and recording each day the distance run in the night, I intend to make a new chart in which I will set out the whole of the Ocean Sea, with sea and land properly laid out with true positions and courses. … Above all, I must have no regard for sleep, but must concentrate on the demands of navigation; all of which will be no small task.

Sunday, 9 September

We sailed sixteen and a half leagues. I have decided to log less than our true run, so that if the voyage is long the crew will not be afraid and lose heart. In the night we sailed ninety-five miles at eight knots, making thirty-two leagues. The helmsmen steered badly, letting the ship fall off a point to W by N, and sometimes even to WNW; I had to reprimand them many times.

Saturday, 15 September

We maintained our course W, something over twenty-eight and a half leagues. Early in the night we saw a marvellous bolt of fire fall from the sky into the sea about four or five leagues away. These various things are disturbing and depressing the men, who are interpreting them as signs that we have taken a dangerous course.

Sunday, 16 September

We continued on course W. Ran about forty-own leagues; I logged only thirty-eight. … The voyage is growing long and we are far from home, and the men are beginning to complain about the length of the journey and about me for involving them in it. When they saw these great rafts of weed in the distance they began to be afraid that they were rocks or submerged ground, which made them even more impatient and outspoken in their complaints against me. Having seen the ships sailing through the weed, however, they have lost their fear somewhat, though not entirely. Everyone thought we were near some island, but I do not think it is the mainland, which by my reckoning is much further on.

Monday, 17 September

… We saw large numbers of dolphins, and they killed one from the Niña. These signs are coming from the west, where I trust that the great God in whose hands all victory lies will give us a landfall. This morning I saw a tropical bird, a white bird which does not normally spend the night at sea.

Wednesday, 19 September

The *pilotos* gave me their calculated positions: the Niñas has us 466 leagues from the Canaries; the Pinta's makes it 445; my own man makes it 424. I have been going around encouraging the men, always giving them the lower figure so as not to depress their spirits. The further we sail from Spain the greater grows their distress and unrest; they complain more every hour. They have been paying more and more attention to the signs we see, and although they took some heart from the birds, now that no land has appeared they believe nothing they see, and think that the absence of signs means that we are sailing to a new world from which we will never return.

Saturday, 22 September

Sailed about thirty-two leagues, generally WNW, with some variation either way. Very little weed. We saw some petrels and another bird. I needed this contrary wind,; the crew were very restless, thinking that these waters never produce the wind to blow them back to Spain.…

Wednesday, 10 October

Sailed WSW at about eight knots, sometimes up to nine and a half, occasionally only five and a half. Sixty-two and a half leagues in the twenty-four hours; I told the men only forty-six and a half. They could contain themselves no longer, and began to complain of the length of the voyage. I encouraged them as best I could, trying to raise their hopes of the benefits they might gain from it. I also told them that it was useless to complain; having set out for the Indies I shall continue this voyage until, with God's grace, I reach them.

Thursday, 11 October

When everyone aboard was together for the *Salve Regina*, which all seamen say or sing in their fashion, I talked to the men about the grace which God had shown us by bringing us in safety, with fair winds and no obstacles, and by comforting us with signs which were more plentiful every day. … I warned them to keep a good lookout in the bows and told them that I would give a silk doublet to the man who first sighted land.…

I was on the poop deck at ten o'clock in the evening when I saw a light. It was so indistinct that I could not be sure it was land.… the light appeared once or twice more, like a wax candle rising and falling.

Then the Pinta, being faster and in the lead, sighted land and made the signal as I had ordered.... The land appeared two hours after midnight, about two leagues away. We furled all sail[s] ... and jogged off and on until Friday morning, when we came to an island. We saw naked people, and I went ashore in a boat with armed men. ... I took the royal standard, and the captains each took a banner with the Green Cross....

When we stepped ashore we saw fine green trees, streams everywhere and different kinds of fruit. I called to the two captains to jump ashore with the rest, ... asking them to bear solemn witness that in the presence of them all I was taking possession of this island for their Lord and Lady the King and Queen....

Soon many of the islanders gathered round us. I could see that they were people who would be more easily converted to our Holy Faith by love than by coercion, and wishing them to look on us with friendship I gave some of them red bonnets and glass beads which they hung around their necks, and many other things of small value, at which they were so delighted and so eager to please us that we could not believe it. Later they swam out to the boats to bring us parrots and balls of cotton thread and darts, and many other things, exchanging them for such objects as glass beads and hawk bells. They took anything, and gave willingly whatever they had.

However, the appeared to me to be a very poor people in all respects. They go about as naked as the day they were born, even the women.... They carry no weapons, and are ignorant of them; when I showed them some swords they took them by the blade and cut themselves.... I believe they would readily become Christians; it appeared to me that they have no religion. With God's will, I will take six of them with me for Your Majesties when I leave this place....

I kept my eyes open and tried to find out if there was any gold, and I saw that some of them had a little piece hanging from a hole in their nose. I gathered from their signs that if one goes south ... there is a king with great jars full of it, enormous amounts. I tried to persuade them to go there, but I saw that the idea was not to their liking.... [T]he gold they wear hanging from their noses is ... from the island, but so as not to waste time I wish to set off to see if I can reach the island of Cipango.[1]

Sunday, 14 October

I gave orders at daybreak for the small boat of the Santa Maria and the boats of the two caravels to be got ready, and went along the coast to the northeast to examine the eastward part of the island.... The people kept coming down to the beach.... Some brought us water, some food; others, seeing that I did not wish to go ashore, swam out to us, and we understood them to be asking if we had come from Heaven....

These people have little knowledge of fighting, as Your Majesties will see from the seven I have had captured to take away with us so as to teach them our language and return them, unless Your Majesties' orders are that they all be taken to Spain or held captive on the island itself, for with fifty men one could keep the whole population in subjection and make them do whatever one wanted....

The islands are very green and lush, with sweet breezes, and there may be many things here which I do not know about, because rather than lingering I wish to explore and investigate many islands in search of gold....

---

1 Japan.

Tuesday, 16 October

…. The fish here show amazing difference from our own. Some are like cocks, with the handsomest colouring in the world; blue, yellow, red, all colours; others are marked in a thousand different ways. No man could look at them without amazement and delight, the colours are so beautiful.

Friday, 19 October

At daybreak I weighed anchor and sent the caravel Pinta off to the ESE and the Niña SSE, and I in the Santa Maria steered SE. I gave orders than they should stay on these courses until noon and then come about and sail back to rejoin me. After less than three hours' sailing we sighted an island to the E…. I have named it Isabela…. I have called the cape here at the western end Cabo Hermoso…. for beautiful it is … so green and fair, like all the land and everything else on these islands; I do not know where to go first, and my eyes never weary of seeing such marvellous vegetation, so different from our own.

I have not doubt there must be many plants and trees which would be valuable in Spain for tinctures and medicinal spices, but I am very sorry to say that I am unfamiliar with them. As we neared this cape we were met by the soft, balmy smell of the trees and flowers ashore, the sweetest fragrance in the world.

Before I sail tomorrow I shall go ashore to see what there is on the cape. The village is not here, but further inland; the men I have with me say the king lives there, and wears a lot of gold…. I do not wish to explore too much in detail, for I could not do it in fifty years; I wish to see and discover as much as I can, so as to return to Your Majesties, with God's grace, in April. If I find any quantity of gold or spices, I shall, of course, linger until I have gathered as much as I can; at present I can only keep moving until I come across them.

Sunday, 21 October

I reached this headland of the islet at ten o'clock and dropped anchor…. I should like to fill all our water containers while we are here, and the, if I have time, I shall set off to sail round this island until I find and talk to the king, and see if I may obtain from him some of the sold which I am told he wears. Then I shall set off for another, very large island which I think must be Cipango, judging by the indications given me by these Indians I have on board…. But I am still determined to continue to the mainland, to the city of Quinsay, and to give Your Majesties' letters to the Great Khan and return with his reply.

Sunday, 28 October

I sailed SSW for the nearest point of the island of Cuba…. I never saw a lovelier sight: trees everywhere, lining the river, green and beautiful. They are not like our own, and each has its own flowers and fruit. Numerous birds, large and small, singing away sweetly…. It is a joy to see all the woods and greenery, and it is difficult to give up watching all the birds and come away. It is the most beautiful island ever seen….

The Indians tell me that there are gold mines and pearls on this island, and I saw a likely spot for pearls, with clams, which are a sign of them. I understand that large vessels belonging to the Great Khan come here, and that the passage to the mainland takes ten days. I have called this river and harbour San Salvador.

Sunday, 4 November

Immediately after daybreak I went ashore in the boat to catch some of the birds I saw yesterday. On my return Martin Alonso Pinzon brought me two pieces of cinnamon, and told me that a Portuguese sailor on his ship had seen an Indian with two big bundles of it…. but when I went to look I found that they were not….

I … showed [the Indians] gold and pearls, and some of the old ones told me that in a place called Bohio there are endless quantities of gold, and the people wear it around their necks and arms and legs and in their ears, and pearls too. I also understood them to say that there are large ships and a trade in goods, all to the SE, and that a long way away there are men with one eye, and others with noses like dogs who eat human flesh; when they capture someone they cut his throat and drink his blood and cut off his private parts.

Monday, 12 November

….Yesterday … I thought it a good idea to take some of the people from the river to convey them to Your Majesties, so that they may learn our language and tell us what there is in their country, and learn our customs and matters of the Faith, and interpret for our people when they return, for I can see from my own observations that these people have no religion, nor are they idolators. They are gentle, and do not know the meaning of evil, nor killing, nor taking prisoners; they have no weapons and are so timid that one of our men can frighten away a hundred of them, just as a joke, They are ready to believe; they acknowledge that there is a God in Heaven, and are convinced that that is where we have come from, and they are quick to recite any prayer we tell them to say, and to make the sign of the cross.

Your Majesties should therefore determine to convert them to Christianity, for I believe that once this is begun a host of peoples will soon be converted to our Holy Faith, and great domains and their wealth and all their peoples will be won for Spain, for there is no doubt that these lands hold enormous quantities of gold….

On the river Mares, which I left last night, there is certainly a great amount of mastic, and it could be increased if more were wanted, for these trees take easily if re-planted and there are plenty of them … One could also obtain great quantities of cotton, which I think could very well be sold here (rather than taking it to Spain) in the cities of the Great Khan….

A canoe came alongside us yesterday with six young men. Five of them came aboard, and I ordered them to be seized and have brought them away with me. I then sent men to a house on the west side of the river, and they brought back seven females, some young and some adult. … I did this because men behave better in Spain when they have women of their own land with them than when they are deprived of them. Men have often been taken from Guinea to Portugal to learn the language, and given good treatment and gifts, and when they were taken back with a view to employing them in their own country they went ashore and were never seen again….

Friday, 16 November

I am leaving a cross planted everywhere I land in these island and territories. I therefore went ashore in the boat at the channel leading into these harbours, and on a spit of land I found two large timbers, one longer than the other, lying across one another in the shape of a cross, as precisely as any carpenter could have placed them. We knelt before them in prayer, and I have ordered a great high cross to be made using the two timbers.

Saturday, 17 November

Today the two eldest of the six young men I captured on the river Mares escaped. I had transferred them to the Niña.

Tuesday, 20 November

Today Martin Alonso Pinzon has sailed away on his own in the Pinta without my permission, moved by greed. He believes that an Indian I ordered him to take aboard his ship will give him a lot of gold. He went without waiting, not through stress of weather but because he chose to. He has gone against me in word and deed many times before.

Tuesday, 27 November

…. After sailing half a league across the bay I sighted a most excellent harbour…. We anchored, and … [g]oing in the boats to the south of the harbour mouth, I found a river which a galley could row into comfortably…. The beauty and freshness of the river, so clear that we could see the sand on the bottom; all the various sorts of palm tree, taller and more beautiful than any I have encountered before; the endless variety of other trees, so tall and green; the birds; the greenness of the level ground—all this made me want to stay here forever.

The loveliness of this country, Your Majesties, is so marvellous; it surpasses all others in amenity and beauty as daylight exceeds night. I have said repeatedly to my men that, whatever efforts I make to tell Your Majesties about it, my tongue could not tell the whole truth, or my hand set it down. Truly, I was dumbfounded by the sight of so much beauty, and find myself unable to describe it adequately. I have already written everything I could about the other places, their trees and fruits, their plants, their harbours and all their splendours, without doing them justice. Everyone has said that nowhere else could be more beautiful. I will write no more now; I hope that other men will see it and wish to describe it in writing, and do rather better….

I have written earlier of the site for a town and fortress on the river Mares, with its fine harbour and surroundings. All that I said was true enough, but there is no comparing the river Mares or the Mar de Nuestra Señora with this place. There must be large settlements inland here, with hosts of people, and things of great profit. For if Christendom is to enter into trade with all the places I have discovered so far, and hope to find before I return home, how much more, I say, must Spain, to whom it must all be subject. And Your Majesties, in my opinion, should not allow any foreigner to do business or gain a foothold here, but only Catholic Christians, for that is the beginning and end of the whole enterprise; it should be for the growth and glory of the Christian faith, and you should allow no one but good Christians to come here….

Monday, 3 December

…. I made the men row the boat to the shore where the Indians were standing, a great crowd of them, all painted red and as naked as the day they were born, some of them with plumes on their heads, and other feathers, and all carrying bunches of assegais. I went up to them and gave them a few scraps of bread and little brass ring to others, a few small beads to others. In this way I calmed them down and they all came down to the boats and gave us everything they had in exchange for whatever we chose to give them. The sailors had killed a turtle and the shell was in pieces in the boat, and the ship's boys were giving a piece the size of a fingernail and receiving a handful of spears from the Indians.

They are like the other people I have seen, with the same beliefs; the thought we had come from Heaven. They will give you whatever they have, straight away, in exchange for anything at all, never saying that it is not enough, and I think they would do the same with spices and gold if they had them….

Sunday, 16 December

.... Rest assured that this island and all the others are as firmly in your possession as Castile; whatever you wish. I, with my small company, could walk all over these islands unmolested, for I have already seen three of my seamen go ashore and a whole multitude of Indians flee from them without being threatened. They have no weapons or fighting skills, and all of them are naked. They are very timid; three men could put a thousand of them to flight, so they could easily be commanded and made to work, to sow, and to do whatever might be needed, to build towns and be taught to wear clothes and adopt our ways....

Friday, 21 December

I explored the harbour with the boats. I have never seen a harbour to equal it. I have said such fine things about the earlier ones that it is difficult to find words to convey the excellence of this one properly, and I fear I may be condemned for exaggerating things beyond the truth. In my defence, I have old sailors in my company who say the same and will confirm it, and any seafarer will agree: my fine descriptions of the earlier harbours were true, and it is also true that this one is much better than all the rest. I have been a seafarer for twenty-three years, never staying ashore for any length of time worth mentioning; I have seen all the Levant[2] and all the countries of the west; I have made passages north to England and south to the Guinea coast, and nowhere in all those lands could a man find harbours as perfect as on these islands, where we have found every one better than the last....

These people ... are naked as the day they were born, men and women alike. Elsewhere, on Juana and some of the other islands, the women wear a little cotton ting in front to cover up their private part, the size of the flap on a man's breeches, especially when they are over twelve years old, but here neither girls nor women wear anything. Also, in the other places the men hide their women from us because of jealousy, but not here, and some of the women are very fine-bodied, and they were the first to come and give thanks to Heaven for our arrival and to bring us whatever they had.... I have given the men orders not to take anything from them against their will, so they have paid them for everything. I cannot believe that any man has ever met a people so goodhearted and generous, so gentle that they did their utmost to give us everything they had, and ran to bring it to us as soon as we arrived....

Saturday, 22 December

Set sail at daybreak to pursue my course in search of the islands which the Indians tell me are rich in gold, some being more gold than earth.... Before setting sail ... I sent six men to a very large village three leagues away to the west, the chief of which came yesterday and told me he had certain pieces of gold. When the men arrived the chief took my secretary by the hand. I had sent my secretary to prevent the rest from doing anything untoward to the Indians, for they are so generous and my men so extremely greedy that they are not satisfied with getting whatever they want from the Indians for a lace end or even a piece of glass or pottery or other useless thing, but want to get everything with no payment at all, which I have always forbidden; though with the exception of the gold much of what they get is of trifling value. Considering the generosity of heart of the Indians, who would and do give a piece of gold for half a dozen glass beads, I have given orders that nothing shall be accepted without some payment....

---

2   The Mediterranean and the Middle East.

Tuesday, 25 December: Christmas Day

Last night, while sailing in light breezes from the sea of Santo Tomas to Punta Santa, and with my ship a league off the point at the end of the first watch, around eleven o'clock, I decided to lie down to sleep, for I had not slept for two days and a night. Seeing it was calm, the helmsman gave the helm to an apprentice seaman and went off to sleep....

It was the Lord's will that at midnight, knowing that I had lain down to sleep, and seeing that the sea was like water in a bowl, a dead calm, everyone lay down to sleep and the helm was left to the boy, and the currents took the ship very gently onto one of the banks, which could be heard and seen a good league away even at night. The boy, feeling the rudder grounding and hearing the noise of the sea, cried out, and I heard him and got up before anyone else had realized that we were aground. Then the master, who was officer of the watch, came on deck. I told him and the others to get into a boat we were towing, take an anchor and drop it astern. He jumped into the boat with a crowd of others, and I thought they were obeying my orders, but all they did was row off to the caravel half a league to windward.

When I saw my own men fleeing in the boat, the sea falling and the ship now in danger, I had no alternative but to cut away the mainmast and lighten ship as much as we could to see if we could float her off. However, with the tide ebbing all the time there was no help for her; she took a list, her seams began to open, and she filled up from below the waterline.

Seeing no way of saving her, I transferred to the caravel, taking all the men with me for their safety. There was still a light offshore wind and much of the night was already gone, so not knowing our way out of the banks I sailed off and on until daybreak, when I returned to the ship along the landward side of the reef. Before that I had sent ... the Marshal of the Fleet ... to tell the king what was happening and to say that because of my wish to accept his invitation to go to his harbour to visit him, as he requested last Saturday, I had lost my ship on a reef on my way to his village, a league and a half away.

He burst into tears when he heard the news of our misfortune, and sent all his people from the village in numerous large canoes. With their help we began to unload everything from the ship. We received such help from the king that she was unloaded and everything cleared from the decks in no time. He supervised things himself with his brothers and relatives, both on the ship and in guarding what was taken ashore, making sure that all was safe. From time to time he sent one of his relatives to me in tears to console me and tell me not to be distressed or downcast, for he would give me everything he had.

I sweat to Your Majesties that nowhere in Castile could everything have been better looked after; not a lace point went missing. The kind had all our things put together beside his palace while they cleared several of the houses which he wanted to give us to store everything under guard, and he ordered two armed men to keep watch all night.

The king and all his people kept weeping as if deeply affected by our loss. They are of such a loving disposition, free from greed, friendly and willing to do anything; I swear to Your Majesties, I believe there can be no better people, nor a better land, anywhere on earth. They love their neighbours as themselves, and their speech is as gentle and kindly as can be, always with a smile. Men and women, it is true, go about as naked as they were born, but I assure Your Majesties that their behaviour among themselves is above reproach. The king is held in great majesty, and has a stateliness of bearing delightful to see. They remember things well, and are eager to learn about everything; their curiosity makes them ask about this and that, to find the cause and effect of it all.

Wednesday, 26 December

The king came to the Niña at daybreak to look, and almost in tears told me not to be downhearted, because he would give me everything he had. He told me he had given the men ashore two large houses and would give them more if necessary, and as many canoes as I might want to load and unload the ship and ferry people ashore, as indeed he did yesterday without a crumb of bread or anything else being lost, for these people are so loyal and uncovetous, especially this most virtuous king.

As I was talking to him a canoe arrived from another village with some pieces of gold which they wanted to barter for a hawk bell, for they love the bells above all else. Even before the canoe was alongside they were holding up pieces of gold and shouting chuque chuque, which is what they call the bells; they go almost mad for them. Afterwards, when the canoes from the other places were leaving for home, they called me and asked me to have a bell kept for them for another day, for they would bring me four pieces of gold as big as a man's hand....

These people look on things made of brass as more valuable than anything else, so for a lace end they will readily give whatever they have in their hands. They call it turey, meaning 'from Heaven,' for turey is their word for sky. They sniff it as soon as they take it, as if they know by the smell that it comes from Heaven, and by the smell they value it very highly....

The king was very pleased to see me in better spirits, and saw my interest in gold. He told me by signs that he knows a place near here where there is a large quantity, and that I should be of good cheer, for he will give me all the gold I want.... He stayed aboard to eat with me, and then we went ashore together, where he treated me with great honour and gave me a feast....

After our meal he took me to the beach. I sent for a Turkish bow and a handful of arrows and ordered a good archer from among the ship's company to do some shooting. Not knowing about weapons, since they neither use nor possess them, the king was most impressed. This arose out of our conversation about the Caniba people, whom they call 'Caribs', who come to capture them with bows and arrows. Their arrows are not tipped with iron. None of these lands seems to have any knowledge of iron or steel, or of any other metal except gold and copper; not that I have seen much copper. I used sign language to the king that the King and Queen of Castile would send men to destroy the Caribs and hand them all over to him with their hands tied.

I ordered a lombard and spingard to be fired. The king was astonished by their power and penetration, and when the people heard the noise they all fell down. They brought me a great mask with large pieces of gold in the ears and eyes and elsewhere; the king gave it to me, and he also put some other golden decorations on my head and round my neck. He gave many similar things to the men I had with me.

The sight of all these things was a great joy and comfort to me, and my misery at losing the ship has been somewhat tempered. I can see that Our Lord caused her to go aground with the purpose of establishing us here, for various things have come together so handily that it has been a piece of good fortune rather than a disaster. Certainly, if we had not run aground I should have gone on my way without anchoring ... and I should not have left anyone here on this voyage. Even if I had wanted to leave them, I should not have been able to leave them so well found nor with so much equipment and stores and materials to build a fort. Truth to tell, many of the men I am leaving here had asked me, directly or through another, to give them permission to stay.

I have decided to build a fort.... This tower should be built, and built properly, being so far away from Your Majesties, to show the people the skills and abilities of your subjects, so that the people will love, fear and obey you....

Not a thing from the ship has been lost ... not a single plank or nail.... And I trust in the Lord that when I return from Castile, as is my intention, I shall find a great barrel of gold for which the people I am leaving here will have bartered, and that they will have found the gold mine and the spices, and all in such quantities that Your Majesties will be able to make your preparations to go to recover the Holy Sepulchre, for Your Majesties may remember my request to you that all the proceeds of this voyage of mine should be used for the conquest of Jerusalem. Your Majesties laughed and agreed, and told me that such was your ambition in any case.

Wednesday, 2 January

I went ashore this morning to take my leave of King Guacanagari[3] and to depart in the name of God....

I have left thirty-nine men in the fort on this island of Española.... I have left them all the barter goods which Your Majesties ordered me to buy ... so they can exchange them and barter for gold.... They have biscuits for a whole year, wine, and plenty of artillery....

When I was ready to leave I gathered them all together and addressed them. I told them first that they should consider the great mercies which God has granted them and me so far, for which they should always give thanks; that they should put their trust firmly in His goodness and mercy, taking care not to offend Him....

Secondly, I asked them and commanded them in Your Majesties' name, as I trusted in their goodness and loyalty, to obey their [new] captain as they would obey me.

Thirdly, I told them to pay great attention and reverence to King Guacanagari, his caciques and ... lesser dignitaries, and to avoid like death committing any annoyance or grievance towards them, considering all we owe to him and to them, and how important it is to keep them happy, remaining as the men are in his country and under his rule; that they should, indeed, make every effort to earn his goodwill by pleasant and honest conversation and to preserve his love and friendship....

Fourthly, I ordered and begged them not to cause offence or injury to any of the Indians, male or female, and not to take anything against their will. I especially told them to avoid committing any insult or violence against the women which might cause outrage, or give a bad example, or bring us into disrepute among the Indians, who are sure that we have all come from Heaven and are ambassadors of the heavenly virtues.

Friday, 4 January

At sunrise I weighed anchor in a light breeze [and set off for Spain].

Note: When the Spanish returned to the island, they found the fort at Navidad destroyed and all the men within it slaughtered.

[translation of Columbus's Journal taken from John Cummins, *The Voyage of Christopher Columbus: Columbus' Own Journal of Discovery Newly Restored and Translated* (New York: St. Martin's Press, 1992)]

---

3   Guacanagari was one of the five caciques or leaders of Hispaniola at the time of the arrival of the Spanish.

STUDY QUESTIONS

1. What factors led to European exploration?

2. Discuss the references to the three Gs in the journal.

3. What does his journal tell us about the type of leader Columbus was?

An Account, Much Abbreviated, of the Destruction of the Indies

The three Gs remained the paramount motivations behind the building of New Spain. Exploration constituted a method of procuring revenue for the coffers of the Spanish treasury. Enriched by gold and silver, precious metals also known as bullion or specie, and emboldened by territorial aggrandizement, Spain solidified itself as Europe's dominant nation-state for much of the 16th century, particularly in the Americas. Although gold and glory reigned supreme, the third constituent part—the all-important component of God—became more problematic.

In terms of religion, Catholic Spain strove steadfastly to proselytize or convert any non-Christians they encountered. Some within the Catholic Church, however, became convinced that the exploitative practices of the *encomienda* system, the forced labor of indigenous peoples, were too harsh and began to protest to Madrid. Many conquistadors deemed Indians not only a source of labor, but also savage heathens unworthy of spiritual uplifting. A more pious viewpoint reconsidered the Aristotelian model that some humans were naturally slaves, and instead held that Indians were like children, ignorant yet educable if taught the right and moral way to live as true Christians.

Bartolomé de Las Casas (circa 1484–1566) was one such priest, who spoke out zealously against forced labor, torture, and murder. Born in Seville, as a boy, Las Casas witnessed a parade to honor Columbus's return to Spain in which he espied decorated Indians, brightly colored parrots, and a rubber ball that could bounce higher than any he had ever seen. His father, who traveled with Columbus's second voyage, gave him a Taino slave. The younger Las Casas, who first traveled to New Spain in 1502, emerged as a conquistador as well as a slaveholder of means in the Caribbean and demonstrated a great penchant for material wealth. He had helped to subdue Cuba and enforced the *encomienda* system.

To their disapproval, however, Las Casas, following a religious revelation, turned against the cruel and miserly ways of his countrymen and devoted the rest of his life to the protection of and social justice for the Indians. Those few who worked to improve the condition of the Indians, such as Antonio de Montesinos and Juan Pedro Viscardo y Guzmán, were few and far between. Las Casas took holy orders

Figure 2.1. Bartolome De Las Casas. Source: http://commons.wikimedia.org/wiki/File:Bartolomedelascasas.jpg.

about 1510, became convinced of the injustices perpetrated against Indians by 1514, and for the following half-century championed the native cause on both sides of the Atlantic Ocean. He became a regular clergyman of the Dominican order in 1522, and later the bishop of Chiapas. Las Casas witnessed firsthand the brutality exacted on Indians by the Spaniards, which he recorded in his *History of the Indies*. His great exposé of Spanish abuses, entitled *An Account, Much Abbreviated, of the Destruction of the Indies*, published in 1552, renounced the *encomienda* system. So powerful was his treatise that Spain's enemies (particularly England) used his writings as propaganda. Yet the Church bolstered the conquest with thousands upon thousands of voluntary conversions. Why would the Indians do this? Their own gods had failed them, but more importantly, they were polytheistic people, who added the gods of a new religion to the panoply of their own. Las Casas, dubbed by the court of Charles V as "Protector of the Indians," viewed the natives in a paternal sense, as a father figure, who empathized with what western Europeans perceived as their child-like and primitive ways. They were nonetheless endowed with a capacity for Christ. Such enlightened campaigns by priests in the 16th and 17th centuries for the cessation of Spanish violence toward Indians demonstrated the compassion of the Catholic missionaries and facilitated the assimilation of a mestizo culture. Some refused to sacrifice humanity on the altar of avarice.

An Account, Much Abbreviated, of the Destruction of the Indies

By Bartolomé de Las Casas

AN INTRODUCTION TO THE RELATION

The islands of the Indies were discovered in the year 1492. They began to be inhabited[1] by Christian Spaniards in the year following, and thus it has been but forty-nine years[2] since Spaniards in great numbers went forth to those Islands. And the first land into which they entered for the purpose of inhabitation was the large and well-favoured Island of Hispaniola, which is six hundred leagues[3] in compass. There are infinite other exceedingly large islands lying everywhere about this Hispaniola, and all of them were, and were seen by us to be, as populous and filled with native-born peoples, the Indians, as any peopled land upon the earth. Terra Firma,[4] which lies at its nearest point two hundred fifty leagues distant, or some few more, possesses a sea-coast of above ten thousand leagues discovered (and more is discovered every day), all filled as though the land were a beehive of people, at least so far as to the year 1541 has been discovered. And so it would appear that God did set down upon those lands the entire multitude, or greatest part, of the entire human lineage.

All these universal and infinite peoples *a toto genere*,[5] God created to be a simple people, altogether without subtility, malice, or duplicity, excellent in obedience, most loyal to their native lords and to the Christians whom they serve; the most humble, most patient, meekest and most pacific, slowest to take offence and most tranquil in demeanor, least quarrelous, least querulous, most lacking in rancour or hatreds or desire for vengeance of all the peoples of the earth. They are, likewise, the most delicate,

---

1 Populated, settled.

2 *Brevísima Relación* in this form was completed in 1542, though there is a kind of afterword appended that was written in 1547, and then an imprimatur that indicates a printing date of 1552.

3 This is not the standard English league, but a unit of measure used in the 15th and 16th centuries in Spain. (For all terms relating to weights, measures, and political or administrative entities, see the Table of Weights and Measures, p. 121, and following.) Here and throughout, Las Casas' distances are estimates—speculative at best, and generally exaggerated by a figure of two or more. In this case, the figure given is about double the true circumference of Hispaniola.

4 *Editor's footnote*: Solid Earth.

5 *Editor's footnote*: Of all kinds.

slender, and tender of complexion[6] and the least able to withstand hard labour, and are those who most easily die of any sort of illness or disease, for not even the children of princes and lords among us, raised with gifts and in delicate living, are more delicate than these native Indians, even those born to the lineage of labourers and those who till the fields. They are also the most impoverished of nations, those who possess and desire to possess the fewest temporal goods, and thus they are never proud, never ambitious, never covetous. Their food is such that the food of the holy fathers in the desert would seem not to have been more austere or frugal or less delightful. Their dress is generally nakedness itself, with naught but their private parts covered, or at the most, a kind of cotton shawl, which I estimate to be between a *vara* and a half and two *varas* of cloth on each side. They make their beds upon a piece of mat, or at the farthest they may sleep upon a thing they contrive which I might liken to a fishing-net drawn together at each extreme and therefrom suspended, which in the language of the island of Hispaniola they call *hamacas*.[7]

These people are among the cleanliest and most unoccupied of the inhabitants of the earth, and of a lively understanding, very apt and tractable for all fair doctrine, excellently fit to receive our holy Catholic faith and to be indued with virtuous customs, and the people with the fewest impediments to this that God has created upon the earth. And from the moment they begin to learn about the elements of the faith, they are so importunate to know it, and to enter in the sacraments of the Church and holy worship, that I say truth when I declare that the priests and friars must be graced with the most singular degree of patience in order to bear them. And finally, I have been told by many other Spaniards who have been in that place for many years (those not of the cloth, I mean to say), and many times I have heard them say it, that the goodness they see in these Indians is not to be denied: "In sooth, these peoples were the most fortunate in the world, if they but knew God."

Into and among these gentle sheep, endowed by their Maker and Creator with all the qualities afore-said, did creep the Spaniards, who no sooner had knowledge of these people than they became like fierce wolves and tigers and lions who have gone many days without food or nourishment. And no other thing have they done for forty years until this day,[8] and still today see fit to do, but dismember, slay, perturb, afflict, torment, and destroy the Indians by all manner of cruelty—new and divers and most singular manners such as never before seen or read or heard of—some few of which shall be recounted below, and they do this to such a degree that on the Island of Hispaniola, of the above three million souls that we once saw, today there be no more than two hundred of those native peoples remaining. The Island of Cuba is almost as long as from Valladolid to Rome; today it is almost devoid of population. The Island of San Juan[9] and that of Jamaica, large and well-favoured and lovely islands both, have been laid waste. On the Isles of the Lucayos[10]—which lie next the Islands of Cuba and Hispaniola on the north and of which there are above sixty that are called the Giants and other islands both large and small, the least-favoured of them being more fertile and lovely than the garden of the king in Seville, and the most healthful land

---

6 Physical constitution.

7 *Hamaca* (hammock) was one of the Caribbean Indian (Taino) words that found its way into several European languages; "hurricane" and its cognates, for example, is another.

8 I.e., since 1502, the year Las Casas first went out to the Indies with the expedition led by Nicolás de Ovando. Las Casas is, then, implying that his *Brevísima Relación* will be based on personal experience and observation. It should be noted that Las Casas did not adopt the views expressed in this account until 1514, twelve full years after he came to the Indies. He was, in fact, an *encomendero* at first, one of those who exploited the Indians, and it was not until he was exposed to the ideas of Antonio de Montesinos, a Dominican who preached that the Indians were "men," with souls, that Las Casas' eyes were opened to the brutality of the Conquest.

9 I.e., Puerto Rico.

10 The Bahamas.

upon the earth—where there were once above five hundred thousand souls, today there is not a living creature. All were killed while being brought, and because of being brought, to the Island of Hispaniola when the Spaniards saw that their stock of the natives of that latter island had come to an end. Indeed, a ship sailing among those islands for three years, seeking to find the people who once lived there, after they had been plucked off (for a good Christian man was moved by pity for those who might be found, to convert them and win them over to Christ) found but eleven persons, which number I saw myself. Another thirty islands which lie about the region of the Island of San Juan are for the same reason desert and unhabited. It would seem that all these islands, the land part of them extending for above two thousand leagues, are unhabited and despoiled of people.

As to the great Terra Firma, we are certain that our Spaniards, through their cruelties and vile acts, have laid those lands waste and depopulated them, and they are today desert and unhabited, though once filled with reasonable[11] men, above ten kingdoms of them, larger than all of Spain, though Aragon and Portugal included, and more land than there be from Sevilla to Jerusalem twice over, which is above two thousand leagues.

We hold as a thing most certain and true that in these forty years there have been above twelve million souls—men, women, and children—killed, tyrannically and unjustly, on account of the tyrannical actions and infernal works of Christians; and in truth I do believe, without thinking to deceive myself, that they were above fifteen million.

Two principal and general customs have been employed by those, calling themselves Christians, who have passed this way, in extirpating and striking from the face of the earth those suffering nations. The first being unjust, cruel, bloody, and tyrannical warfare. The other—after having slain all those who might yearn toward or suspire after or think of freedom, or consider escaping from the torments that they are made to suffer, by which I mean all the native-born lords and adult males, for it is the Spaniards' custom in their wars to allow only young boys and females to live—being to oppress them with the hardest, harshest, and most heinous bondage to which men or beasts might ever be bound into. To these two forms of infernal tyranny, as though to genuses,[12] may be reduced or subsumed or made subordinate all the other divers and several ways, which indeed are infinite, of laying waste to those peoples.

The cause for which the Christians have slain and destroyed so many and such infinite numbers of souls, has been simply to get, as their ultimate end, the Indians' gold of them, and to stuff themselves with riches in a very few days, and to raise themselves to high estates—without proportion to their birth or breeding, it should be noted—owing to the insatiable greed and ambition that they have had, which has been greater than any the world has ever seen before. For those lands were so favoured and so rich, and the people thereupon so humble, so patient, and so easy to subject, yet the Christians have had no more respect for them, nor have had for them no more account or estimation (I speak truly, for I know and have seen the entire time) than—I would not say for beasts, for pray God that being beasts, the Christians might have respected them and treated them with some gentleness and esteem—but less than the dungheaps of the towns. And so it is in that wise that they have seen fit to cure their souls and their bodies, wherefore all the numbers and millions aforesaid have died without the faith and without the sacraments of the church. And it is a very well known and well attested fact, which all persons, however tyrannous and murderous they may be, do know and confess: That all the Indians of all the Indies never

---

11 Rational, endowed with reason; not today's sense of "sensible, having sound judgment."
12 A simile from logic, not biology; the concept of biological genuses still lay in the future.

once did aught hurt or wrong to Christians, but rather held them to be descended from heaven, from the sky, until many times they or their neighbours first received from the Christians many acts of wrongful harm, theft, murder, violence, and vexation.

ON THE ISLAND HISPANIOLA

On the island Hispaniola, which was the first, as we said, wherein the Christians entered and began the devastations and perditions of these nations, and first destroyed them and wiped the land clean of inhabitants, these Christians began to take the women and children of the Indians to serve them and use them ill, and they would eat their victuals that issued from the sweat of their brow and their hard work, and yet still were not content with what the Indians gave them willingly, according to the ability that each one had, which is not ever much, for they seldom have more than that which they have most immediate need of and can produce with little labour. And in truth, what suffices for three houses of ten persons each for a month, a Christian will eat and destroy in one day, and these Christians did them many other acts of compulsion and violence and vexation.

The Indians, at this treatment, began to see that those men must not have come down from the sky, or heaven, and some hid their victuals, others their women and children, while others fled into the wilderness to remove themselves from men of such hard and terrible conversation.[13] The Christians would smite them with their hands and strike them with their fists and beat them with sticks and cudgels, until they finally laid hands upon the lords of the villages. And this practice came to such great temerity and shamelessness and ignominy that a Christian captain did violate the wife of the greatest king, the lord of all the island.[14] And at that, the Indians began to seek ways to cast the Christians from their lands; they took up arms, which are but weak and petty things, of little offence and resistance and even less defence (for which reason, all their wars are little more than what would be games with wooden swords here in this land, or even children's games), and at that, the Christians with their horses and swords and pikes and lances began to wreak slaughters and singular cruelties upon them.

They would enter into the villages and spare not children, or old people, or pregnant women, or women with suckling babes, but would open the woman's belly and hack the babe to pieces, as though they were butchering lambs shut up in their pen. They would lay wagers who might slice open the belly of a man with one stroke of their blade, or cut off a man's head with one swift motion of their pike, or spill out his entrails. They would snatch babes from their mother's breasts and take them by their feet and dash their heads against the rocks. Others would fling them over their shoulders into the rivers, laughing and jeering, and as they tell into the water they would call out: "Thrash, you little bugger!."; other babes, they would run their swords through mother and child at once, and all that they came across. They would erect long gibbets, but no higher than that a man's feet might dangle just above the ground, and bind thirteen of the Indians at one time, in honour and reverence, they said, of Our Redeemer and the twelve Apostles, and put firewood around it and burn the Indians alive. Others, they would tie or bind their bodies all about with dry straw, and set fire to the straw and burn them that way. Others, and all those that they desired to let live, they would cut off both their hands but leave them hanging by the skin,

---

13   I.e., social intercourse, treatment of others.
14   Las Casas is referring to the case of the Spanish *encomendero* Francisco de Valenzuela, who raped the wife of the cacique Enriquillo. Enriquillo had been raised in the Franciscan monastery at Vera Paz, and he was in constant revolt against the Spaniards between 1519 and 1538, when Charles V ordered that a peace treaty be signed with him—the first such treaty in the New World.

and they would say to them: "Go, and take these letters," which was to say, carry the news to the people who have hidden themselves in the mountains and the wilderness. They would often slay the lords and nobles in this way: They would weave together twigs and branches, like unto a gridiron, but made of twigs, and raise it on forked poles or limbs of trees set into the ground, and tether the lords and nobles to that grate and set a slow fire below it, so that little by little, crying out and screaming from those torments, and in desperation, they would give up their souls.

I myself saw that once, four or five lords and men of high rank were being burned on grates in this way (and I even think that there may have been two or three pairs of grates on which others were also being burned), and on account of their loud cries and clamours, the captain seemed to take pity on them, or perhaps they disturbed his sleep, and he ordered them hanged; but the executioner that was burning them, who was worse than any hangman (and I know what his name is and even met certain kinsmen of his in Seville), was not content to hang them, and so with his hands he sewed their mouths shut with sticks, so that they could make no sounds, and then poked up the fire and roasted them as long as he had first desired. I vouchsafe that I did see all the things I have writ above, and infinite numbers of others. And because all those who were able to flee, did hide themselves in the wilderness and go up into the mountains to escape those men who were so inhumane,[15] so pitiless, and so savage, and such abominable destroyers and foremost enemies of the human lineage, the Spaniards taught and trained hunting hounds, fierce and savage dogs that would no sooner see an Indian than they would tear him to pieces, and would rather set upon a man and eat him than if he were a pig. These dogs wrought dreadful havoc and butcheries. And because sometimes, though seldom, the Indians would slay a Christian, though for good and just reason and in holy justice, the Spaniards made a law amongst themselves that for every one Christian that the Indians slew, the Christians would slay an hundred Indians.

ON THE KINGDOMS THAT ONCE WERE TO BE FOUND UPON THE ISLAND OF HISPANIOLA

On this island of Hispaniola there were five principal kingdoms of great extent, and five most powerful and mighty kings, whom the other lords, countless numbers of them, all obeyed—or almost all, for there were lords who ruled over some very distant provinces who recognized no

They would erect long gibbets ... and bind thirteen of the Indians at one time, in honour and reverence, they said, of Our Redeemer and the twelve Apostles, and put firewood around it and burn the Indians alive.

15 Sixteenth-century spelling for "inhuman," but still having the modern sense "lacking in all human qualities, feelings, etc." or "destitute of natural kindness, pity, etc."

They would weave together twigs and branches, like unto a gridiron … and tether the lords and nobles to that grate and set a slow fire below it, so that little by little, crying out and screaming from those torments, and in desperation, they would give up their souls.

man whatsoever over them. One kingdom was called Maguá, with the last syllable accented, which means "the kingdom of the fertile lowland plain."[16] And this plain is one of the most illustrious and remarkable things in the world, for it extends for eighty leagues from the Southern Sea to the Northern.[17] It is five leagues wide, and sometimes eight and even ten, and has highlands in one part and another. It is crossed by above thirty thousand rivers and streams, among them twelve as large as the Ebro and Duero and Guadalquivir;[18] and all of the rivers that flow down from a mountain which is to the west, which number twenty and twenty-five thousand, are most extraordinarily rich in gold. In that mountain, or mountain range, lies the province of Cibao, from which comes down that gold high in carats which is so famed here. The king and lord of this kingdom was called Guarionex, and his vassals were such great lords that one of them might bring together sixteen thousand fighting men to serve that greater lord, and I met some of them. This king Guarionex was very obedient and virtuous, and naturally peaceable and devoted to the king and queen of Castile; and in certain years his people, upon his command—each person who had a house—gave the hollow of a gourd filled with gold, and then afterward, unable to fill them to the top, they would cut the gourd in the middle and fill that half and give it, because the Indians of that island had very little or no skill for taking the gold from the mines. This cacique[19] would offer to serve the king of Castile by tilling land that extended from Isabela, which was the first town made by the Christians, to the city of Santo Domingo, which is fifty leagues or more, if they would not ask for gold, because he would say, and soothfully, that his vassals did not know how to get it. The farming that he said he would do, I know he was able to do it, and would do it with great pleasure, and I also know that it would be worth more to the king each year than three million *castellanos,* and so rich and fertile was the land on which he would farm that it would give sustenance for above fifty cities as large as Sevilla, were it used in that wise today.

16 In Spanish, "la vega"; La Vega is now the place-name of a city just south of Santiago, Dominican Republic.

17 From the Caribbean on the south to the Atlantic on the north.

18 The largest rivers in Spain.

19 "*Cacique*" is the Caribbean native peoples' word for their chief or ruler (feminine, *cacica*), and because Las Casas uses it with such familiarity and frequency it will not be italicized or otherwise indicated as "foreign" in these pages. In fact, the Spaniards adopted "cacique" as their word for native chief all over the Americas, and it has come to be used commonly today to mean "political boss" both in Latin America and in Spain.

The coin in which they repaid this good high king and lord was to dishonour him with his wife, an evil Christian captain being the man who violated her. And the lord, to buy time and bring together his people to take vengeance, resolved to flee and hide himself, alone, and if need be to die in exile from his land and estate within a province that was called the land of the Ciguayos, where lived a great lord his vassal. And when the Christians found him gone, they would not have it that he be kept from them; they went and made war on the lord who had him, where they committed great slaughters, until at last they found him and seized him, and bound him in chains and shackles, and put him into a boat to bring him to Castile. Which boat was lost at sea, and with him were drowned many Christians and a great quantity of gold, among which perished the great lump that was as large as a loaf of bread and of weight three thousand six hundred castellanos. And God did in this wise wreak His vengeance for such great injustices.

The other kingdom was called the kingdom of Marién, where Puerto Real is now, at the extreme of the plain toward the north, and larger than the kingdom of Portugal, although in truth much more rich and fertile and apt for inhabitation,[20] and containing many large mountains and rich mines of gold and copper, and its king was called Guacanagarí, with accent upon the last syllable, under whom there were many very great lords, of whom I saw and met many. And it was upon the land of Guacanagarí that the former Admiral[21] who discovered the Indies first stopped, and it was this Guacanagarí who received the Admiral the first time, when he discovered the island, and he met him with such humanity and courtesy, and all the Christians that were with him, and made them such a gentle and courteous welcome and aid and provisioning (the Admiral's ship having been lost just there), that in his own land and by his own parents the Admiral could not have been received better. And this I know from the Letter and the words of the Admiral himself. And yet this king died fleeing from the Christians' slaughters and cruelties, destroyed and stripped of his estate, wandering in the wilderness. All the other lords, his subjects, died under the tyranny and in the servitude that shall hereafter be recounted.

The third kingdom and realm was called Maguana, a land likewise admirable, healthful, and fertile, where now the most excellent sugar of the island is made. The king of this kingdom was called Caonabó, and in vigour and state and gravity, and ceremonies in his service, he exceeded all the others. He was taken[22] with great subtility and guile, while he lay, suspecting nothing, in his house. He was afterward put into a ship, to bring him to Castile, and as six ships were in port, waiting to set sail, God manifested His will against that great iniquity and injustice and many others, and sent that night a storm which sank all the ships and drowned all the Christians who were in them, and therein died Caonabó as well, laden down with chains and shackles. This lord had three or four brothers, equally as manly and vigourous as himself; and seeing the unjust capture and imprisonment of their brother and lord, and the destructions and slaughters that the Christians were then committing in the other kingdoms, they took up arms, especially from the moment that they learned that the king their brother was dead, to go and attack and have vengeance upon the Christians. The Christians went against them with a number of horse[23] (which

---

20   The reader is reminded that this means "fertile and apt for *settlement*," not simply "for living"; Las Casas is thinking of adding to Spain's wealth by true colonization rather than through mere exploitation, through agriculture as well as with hard metal.
21   Columbus, in late 1493; and "former" distinguishes Christopher from his son Diego, who succeeded him to the title. In his reports, Christopher Columbus notes his "friendship" with a king whom he does not name but who, as is clear both from Las Casas and other chroniclers and letter-writers, is indeed Guacanagarí.
22   Seized, captured.
23   Cavalry, horse*men*, of course, although in the parenthesis that follows, it is the animal *horse* that is the fearsome weapon because of its speed.

is the most pernicious weapon that there may be among the Indians) and wrought such devastation and slaughter that they laid waste and depopulated half of all that kingdom.

The fourth kingdom was called Xaraguá. This was like the kernel or marrow, or the court of all that island; in its highly polished tongue and speech, in the courtesy and most orderly and composed breeding[24] of its people, in the number of its nobility and their generosity—because there were many, a great number, of lords and nobles, and in the prettiness and beauty of all the people, it exceeded all the others. The king and lord of this kingdom was called Behechio; he had a sister who was called Anacaona. This brother and sister did great services to the king and queen of Castile and immense benefices to the Christians, freeing them from many perils of imminent death; and after king Behechio had died, his sister the lady Anacaona remained as queen. And to this kingdom there came one day the governor[25] who ruled this island, with sixty horse[26] and three hundred foot[27] or more, though those on horse be enough to lay waste to the entire island and Terra Firma. And above three hundred lords and nobles went out to him when he called them, promising them no harm, and he commanded that most of those lords be put by deceit and guile into a very large house of straw, and when they were closed up within, he ordered that the house be set a-fire and those lords and nobles be burned alive. And then they rushed upon all the others and put an infinite number of people to the sword, and the lady Anacaona, to show her the honour due her, they hanged her. And it came into some Christians' minds, either out of pity or because of greed, to take some children to raise them and not kill them, and so they put them up behind their horses, but another Spaniard came up and ran them through with his lance. Another, seeing a child lying on the ground, cut off its legs with his sword. Some of those who were able to flee this inhumane cruelty went over to a small island that is some eight leagues over the sea from there, and that same governor sentenced all those that had fled there to be made slaves, because they had fled the slaughter.

The fifth kingdom is called Higüey, and over it there was an old queen who was called Higuanama. This lady was hanged, and infinite was the number of people that I saw burned alive and hacked to pieces and tortured by divers and new ways of killing and torment, and all those taken alive were made slaves. And because there have been so many particular cases of slaughter and perdition of those people and those nations that even long recounting would not suffice to tell them (for in truth I do believe that however much is told, not a thousandth part may be explained, nor much less understood), I will conclude by saying and declaring with respect to those wars aforesaid, that by God and my conscience I am certain that for the Spaniards to commit all the acts of injustice and evil that I have told, and the others that might be told, the Indians gave them no more cause nor were any more to be blamed for it than a monastery-of good honest monks might give a man for robbing them or slaying them, and those monks who escaped the slaughters alive, putting them in perpetual bondage and servitude as slaves. And I would say further, that until at last all the many people and nations of that island had been slain and laid waste they did not commit against the Christians, so far as I can believe or conjecture, a single mortal sin punishable by man. And those sins which are reserved for punishment by God alone, such as a desire for vengeance, or the hatred and rancour that those peoples might harbor against such capital enemies as the Christians were to them, into these I believe very few Indians ever fell, and they were little more impetuous and hard, by the great experience that I have of them, than children of ten or twelve years old. And I know, too, as a sure and infallible truth, that the Indians always waged the most just and defensible war against the Christians,

---

24 Manners; cf. "a person of good breeding," implying courtesy and mannerliness.
25 Nicolás de Ovando.
26 Cavalrymen.
27 Foot soldiers, or infantrymen.

albeit the Christians never waged just war against the Indians, but rather were diabolical and infinitely unjust, and much more so in that wise than might be held or said about any tyrant in the world at any time before. And the same I do declare about all the wars that have been fought in all the Indies.

After these wars had ended, and all the men slain in them, so that there were generally left only young boys and women and children, the Spaniards parcelled them out amongst themselves, giving one thirty, another forty, another an hundred and two hundred (depending upon the grace which each one had curried with the tyrant-major, whom they called governor). And when the Indians were distributed among each Christian, the Spaniards coloured what they had done in the following way: That they would teach the Indians the things of the Catholic faith, although generally these were men who were idiots and cruel, exceedingly avaricious and filled with vice, though they set themselves as curates and priests of souls. And the care that they gave these souls was to send the men into the mines to dig out gold, which is intolerable work, and the women they set to work on their *estancias,* which are farms, to dig in the fields and till the land, which is labour not for women but for strong, robust men. They would give neither the men nor the women any food to eat, but rather grass and things of no solid substance. The milk dried up in all the mothers who were suckling their babes, and soon all the newborn babes died. And since the husbands were far off, and never saw their wives, procreation ceased among them. The men died in the mines from hard labour and starvation, and the women on the farms for the same cause, and so multitudes of men and women and children of that island died, and so all the people of the earth might have died as well. If a man were to tell the burthens they put upon them, which were three and four *arrobas,* and to be carried for an hundred and two hundred leagues,²⁸³⁷ and the Christians even had themselves borne in *hamacas,* which are like fishing-nets, on the backs of the Indians, because they always used them like beasts of burden (the Indians would have galls and sores on their shoulders and backs, from the burthens they were made to carry, like ill-used beasts), and to tell how they would whip, buffet, cudgel, and smite them, strike them with their fists, curse them, and inflict upon them a thousand other kinds of torture and torment while they were at work, then in truth within a little time there would be no paper that could bear such telling, and no man that could bear the horror.

And I pray that it be noted here as well, that the perdition of these islands and lands began to increase from the time the news came of the death of her most serene highness the Queen Doña Isabel, which was the year 1504, because until then some provinces only had been destroyed on this island by unjust wars, but not all of them, and these destructions, most of them or almost all, were kept from the knowledge of the queen. Because the queen, may she dwell in Glory, took exceedingly great care and admirable zeal for the salvation and prosperity of those peoples and those nations, as those of us know who saw and touched with our own eyes and our own hands examples of this.

And another rule should be noted in this: That in all the parts of the Indies where Christians have gone and have passed, they always wrought upon the Indians all the cruelties set forth above, and carried out their abominable slaughters and tyrannies and oppressions upon those innocent peoples. And ever would they pile on many more and greater and newer forms of torture, and*they would comport themselves ever more cruelly, for God had allowed them to fall ever lower and to hurl themselves ever deeper into accursed judgment.

28

ON NEW SPAIN, I

In the year 1517 New Spain was discovered, and in that discovery great atrocities were wrought upon the Indians and not a few deaths committed by those who did discover it. In the year 1518, those who call themselves Christians[29] went there to rob and kill, though they said they were going to make habitations. And since that year 1518 until this day, in the year 1542, all the iniquity, all the injustice, all the violence and tyranny that the Christians had done in the Indies before this time has been exceeded and overpassed, for they have utterly lost all fear of God and of the king, and have forgotten even themselves. Because so many and so terrible have been the devastations and cruelties, the slaughters and destructions, the depopulations, acts of theft, violence, and tyranny, and in so many and such great kingdoms of the great Terra Firma, that all the things that we have said before are as naught in comparison with those that were done there. But though we told them all (which are infinite in number, those we do not recount), they do not compare in number or in gravity to those that since that year 1518 have been done and perpetrated until this day and year 1542. And today, on this day[30] of the month of September, the most grave and abominable are still done and committed, proving the rule that we set down above, that since the beginning, the outrages and hellish deeds have but grown worse and greater.

And so, from the moment of their *entrada* into New Spain, which was the eighteenth day of April in that year 1518, until the year 1530, there passed twelve full years, which was the duration of the slaughters and devastations that the Spaniards' bloody hands and swords did work incessantly for almost four hundred and fifty leagues in compass about the city of México and its surroundings, in which there lay four and five great kingdoms, as large and very nigh as fertile as all of Spain. And all these lands were exceedingly populous and as filled with people as Toledo and Sevilla and Valladolid and Zaragoza, along with Barcelona, because there is not now nor has there ever been so great a population in those cities, however populous they were, as God set in all those leagues I have spoken of above, which to make a circuit of them all, one would journey above one thousand eight hundred leagues. And more than four million souls have the Spaniards slain within those twelve years within those four hundred and five hundred leagues, by knife and by lance, and burning them alive, women and children and young persons and old. And this was done so long as those that called themselves conquistadors (as the saying is) lasted, though these were not conquests but rather violent invasions by cruel tyrants, which are condemned not only by the law of God but eke[31] by all human laws, for they are much Worse than those committed by the Turks to destroy the Christian Church. And all this does not count those who have died and are slain every day in that tyrannical bondage, those vexations and daily oppressions that I have spoken of above.

To be particular, there is no possible tongue, nor could there be any human knowledge or skill, able to relate the heinous deeds which in divers and several parts, together at one time in some places, at divers and several times in others, have been done by those public adversaries and most capital enemies of the human lineage within that compass; and in truth, some further deeds, made by circumstances and qualities to be all the more heinous and abominable, could not be told even with great diligence and time and writing. But some things in some places I shall recount below, though with protestation, and a vow that I do not think I shall explain the thousandth part.

---

29   Probably Francisco Hernández de Córdoba, who arrived in Hispaniola in 1511 and explored Cozumel Island and the coastal area of Yucatán.
30   Las Casas does not specify the exact date.
31   Also.

ON NEW SPAIN, II

Among divers other slaughters, this one was done in a large city of above thirty thousand inhabitants, which is called Cholula: All the lords of the land and of that realm, and foremost all the priests with the highest priest of them all, did come out to receive the Christians in procession and with great reverence and respect, and they did carry them in their midst to lodge them in the city and in the lodging-houses of the highest lord or lords of it. And seeing this, the Spaniards resolved among themselves to make a slaughter there, or a punishment (as they call it), in order to cast and sow fear of them and of their ferocity through-out every corner of those lands.[32] For this was always the Spaniards' resolve in all the lands that they have entered, it is well to note: to wreak cruel and most singular slaughter, so that those meek lambs might tremble before them. And so for this purpose they sent first to call out all the lords and nobles of the city and of all the places that were subject to the city, with the principal lord of all. And as the Indians' lords and nobles came and entered to speak with the captain of the Spaniards, they were taken prisoner without anyone hearing, so as not to carry the news. The Spaniards had requested five or six thousand Indians of them, to carry their burthens; all these came soon after and these, they cast into the patio of the houses. To see all these Indians when they load themselves up to bear the burthens of the Spaniards is to have great compassion for them, and pity, for they come naked as the day they were born, with only their privates covered and small netting bags over their shoulder with their meagre meals, and they are all made to squat down, like meekest lambs. And when all were brought together and crowded into the courtyard with other people who were thereabout, armed Spaniards were set at the gates of the courtyard to stand guard, while the rest laid hand to their swords and put all those sheep to the sword and lance, so that not one might escape, but all were most grievously murdered. After two or three days, many Indians rose up, still alive though covered with blood, for they had hidden themselves and taken refuge under the dead (so many were they); they came to the Spaniards, weeping and pleading lor mercy, begging the Spaniards not to slay them. But for these poor souls there was no mercy or compassion, either, but rather as they came forward they were hacked to pieces. All the lords, who numbered above an hundred and were tightly bound, the captain commanded that they be burned and then taken out alive and raised on stakes set in the ground. But one lord, and perhaps the principal lord and king of that land, was able to free himself and he gathered another twenty or thirty or forty men and they went into the great temple they had by there, which was like a fortress, which they called *Cue*,[33] and there he defended himself for much of that day. But the Spaniards, from whom no man nor thing may take refuge, but especially these unarmed nations, set fire to the temple and there they burned them, though they cried out: "Oh, bad men! What have we ever done to you? Why would you kill us? Go ye to México, go, where our universal lord Motenzuma will have his vengeance on you." And they say that as the five or six thousand men were being put to death by sword there in the courtyard, the captain of the Spaniards was singing:

One flame the Roman City now destroyes,
And shrieks of people made a dismal noyse,
While *Nero* sung and, moved with delight,

---

32 Despite the frequent assertions of Las Casas that he was eyewitness to all he described, he accompanied neither Pedro Arias Dávila nor Hernán Cortés, to whom he is making reference here.
33 This is simply the Aztec word for "temple."

From *Tarpey* Hill beheld the wofull sight.[34]

Another great slaughter did they make in the city of Tepeaca, which was much larger and more populous than the first, wherein they put an infinite number of people to the sword, with great and particular acts of cruelty.

From Cholula they marched toward México, with the great king Motenzuma sending them thousands of presents and lords and people and fiestas on the way, and upon their entrance onto the great causeway[35] of México, which is two leagues long, Motenzuma sent his own brother, accompanied by many great lords and great presents of gold and silver and clothing. And at the entrance to the city, he himself came out in person upon litters of gold, with all his great court, to receive them, and he accompanied them to the palaces in which he ordered that they be lodged, that same day, as I have been told by some who were there present. But with some feigning, Motenzuma having no idea of treachery, the Spaniards took this great king and set eighty men to guard him, and afterward they put him in irons.

But setting all this aside, in which there might be great, and many, things to tell, I wish to tell of one singular thing that those tyrants did. The captain of the Spaniards going to the harbour to take as his prisoner another certain captain[36] who was coming against him, and leaving another certain captain,[37] I believe with an hundred or some number more men to guard the king Motenzuma, these latter Spaniards resolved to do another thing to increase the fear of them in all that land—a stratagem (as I have said) which they have often used. The Indians and the lords and people of all the city and court of Motenzuma busied themselves in naught but giving pleasure to their captive lord. And among divers other fiestas which they made for him was in the evenings to come together in all the parts and plazas of the city for great dances such as they do and is their wont, and which they call *mitotes,* as in the islands they are called *areitos.* In these celebrations they take out all their finest clothing and treasures, and all the people do take part, for it is the principal manner of their pleasure. And the noblest and most gentlemanly persons and those of most royal blood, according to their ranks, had their dances and fiestas closest to the houses wherein their lord was captive. In the part nearest to the palaces there were above two thousand lords' sons, the very cream of the nobility of all Motenzuma's kingdom. To these young men went the captain of the Spaniards with a crew of his men, and he sent other crews to all the other parts of the city where these fiestas were occurring, feigning that they were going to watch them, and he commanded that at a certain hour they all attack them. And so he went, and when they were drinking and safe-feeling in their dances, they called out: "Santiago, to them!"[38] and they began with their naked swords to rend those naked, delicate bodies and to spill that generous blood, and they left not a man alive; and the others in the other plazas did the same. This was a thing that cast all those kingdoms and nations into astonishment and grief and mourning, and filled them with bitterness and pain; and from this day until the end of the world, or the Spaniards do away with them all, they shall never

---

34 These verses are taken from the 1656 translation of Las Casas' *Brevísima Relación* by John Phillips, titled *The Tears of the Indians;* the Spanish original was a song popular at the time.

35 So called because the road ("way") was built on a "causey," or mound; Las Casas calls it a *puente,* or "bridge." The road into the Mexico City, or Tenochtitlán, was built across the lake that surrounded the city, and so was a wonder to the Spaniards who first saw it.

36 Pánfilo de Narváez.

37 Pedro de Alvarado.

38 Santiago, or Saint James, was the patron saint of Spain and the protector of the protocountry during the *Reconquista* (completed in 1492), the reconquest of Spanish land from the Moors who had conquered and occupied it for almost eight centuries. Thus, "Santiago, to them! [*Charge!*]" was the Spaniards' battle cry.

cease lamenting and singing in their areitos and dances, as in the *romances* (as we call them here[39]), that calamity and loss of the succession[40] of all their no bility, which for so many years past they had treasured and venerated.

This unjust thing, this cruelty without precedent, being seen by the Indians perpetrated upon so many guiltless innocents who had with tolerance suffered the no less unjust imprisonment of their lord (for he himself had commanded that they not attack or wage war upon the Christians), they rose up in arms throughout all the city and rushed upon them, and wounded many Spaniards, who were hard put to make their escape. But the Spaniards put a

All the lords, who numbered above an hundred and were tightly bound, the captain commanded that they be burned and then taken out alive and raised on stakes set in the ground.

knife to the breast of the prisoner Motenzuma and ordered that he send out runners and command that the Indians not attack that house, but to be pacified and at peace. Yet the Indians would not obey their lord in that, but rather held a confabulation among themselves and resolved to choose another lord and captain to direct their battles. And because now that other Spanish captain who had gone to the port was returning, victorious, and was bringing with him many more Christians, and was fast approaching, the Spaniards ceased the combat for three or four days, until he entered the city. And as he entered, with an infinite number of people gathered from all the land, the Spaniards and the Indians fought one another in such wise and for so many days, that fearing they would all die, the Spaniards resolved one night to flee the city. When the Indians learned of this, they killed a great number of Christians on the causeways[41]

39   These were chivalric romances filled with magic and enchantment; they were extraordinarily popular in Spain at this time: "The coming of printing to Spain around 1473 had given an extraordinary vogue to romances of chivalry, and *Amadis of Gaul* (1508), the most famous of them all, was known in affectionate detail by a vast body of Spaniards who, if they could not read themselves, had heard them told or read aloud" (J. H. Elliott, *Imperial Spain, 1469–1716,* London: Penguin, 1963, p. 64). When the Spaniards were entering Mexico City (Tenochtitlán), one of the soldiers in the expedition, Bernal Díaz, was amazed at what he saw, and he could only describe it in terms of the romance: "When we saw all those cities and villages built in the water, and other great towns on dry land, and that straight and level causeway leading to Mexico, we were astounded. These great towns and *cues* and buildings rising from the water, all made of stone, seemed like an enchanted vision from the tale of Amadis. Indeed, some of our soldiers asked whether it was not all a dream" (Díaz, *The Conquest of New Spain,* London: Penguin, 1963, p. 214).

40   Generations to come, transmission of the (noble) estate or title, etc.

41   These, again, are the four great causeways that connected Tenochtitlán, the "city of México," built on a lake, with dry land. Many Spaniards were indeed killed as they made their escape, but many of them were loaded down with gold and other plunder they were trying to take with them, so that many who were not killed by the Aztecs' weapons drowned when they fell off the causeway. The European mythology of the Conquest calls this "the night of sorrows," or *noche triste.*

crossing the lake, in most high and just warfare, for the most exceedingly just causes that they had, as we have said. And that these causes were just, any reasonable, fair man must acknowledge. Then, when the Christians had reformed, occurred the battle for the city in which they wrought devastations upon the admirable and wondrous Indians, slaying an infinite number of people and burning many, and great lords, too, alive.

After the most exceedingly great and abominable tyrannies that these men committed in the city of México and in the cities and much land around (ten and fifteen and twenty leagues from México, in which an infinite number of people were slain), he passed his tyrannical plague and pestilence farther on, and it did spread into and defile and lay waste to the province of Pánuco, which was a wondrous thing, the multitude of people that the province had and the devastations and slaughters that he wrought there. Then in the same wise they destroyed the province of Tututepeque, and after that the province of Ipilcingo, and afterward that of Colima, and each one of these is more land than the kingdom of León or the kingdom of Castile. To recount the devastations and deaths and cruelties that they dealt the Indians in each one of these provinces would doubtless be a thing exceedingly difficult to accomplish, and impossible to tell, and yet more tedious to hear.

It must be noted here that the title under which they made their *entradas* and by which they began to destroy all those innocents and wipe the inhabitants from those lands which with their great and infinite populace should have caused such joy and pleasure to anyone who called himself a true Christian, was to say that they came to make the Indians the subjects of the king of Spain, and to make them to obey him, and if they should not bow their knees and obey them, they were to slay them and make them slaves. And those who did not come smartly[42] to obey such unreasonable and foolish messages, and to give themselves over into the hands of such iniquitous and cruel and beastly men, the Spaniards would call them rebels who rose up against the service of Your Majesty. And so they have written and communicated it to the king our lord; and the blindness of those who ruled the Indies would not allow them to perceive or understand that which in their law is express, and clearer than any other of its principles, which is: *That no man is or may be called a rebel if he is not first a subject.* I pray all Christians who know something of God and reason, and even of human laws, to think, how may the news brought so suddenly to any person who lives upon his land and feels himself safe and secure from harm, and knows not that he owes anything to any man, and who has his own natural lords, how may these words stop the heart of any man, when they are thus suddenly spoke: "Yield thyself up to obey a foreign king, whom thou hast never seen nor heard, and if thou dost not, be advised that we shall chop thee into pieces with these swords," especially seeing by experience that they veritably do this terrible thing. And what most inspires a man's horror is that those who do indeed render obedience, they are cast into most exceedingly harsh bondage, where with incredible labour and even more long-extended tortures, in which they last some time longer than those who are put to the sword, they perish nonetheless at last, they and their women and children and all their generation. And when it is under these fears and threats that those peoples, or any other peoples in the world, are at last persuaded to obey and acknowledge the rule of that foreign king, still those men made blind and unreasonable by ambition and diabolic greed, those most inconstant and accursed *viros*, do not see that that capitulation gives them not one jot of right. For if it is truly by fears and terrors that those peoples be subjugated, then according to natural and human and divine law all the rest that these men do it is naught but air, save it be in atonement for those sins that shall cast them into the infernal fires, and likewise for the harm and

---

42   Quickly, swiftly, sharply.

offence they do the king and queen of Castile in destroying those monarchs' kingdoms and rendering naught (so far as they are able) all the right that those monarchs have to all the Indies. And these, and no others, are the services that the Spaniards have done to that king and queen in those lands, and still do this day.

With this most just and approved title, then, that tyrant of a captain sent another two tyrannical captains, much crueler and more savage than he, more evil, and with less pity and mercy, to two great and most flourishing and fertile kingdoms, filled with people and most populous, that is, the kingdom of Guatimala, which lies upon the Southern Ocean,[43] and the other Naco y Honduras or Guaimura, which lies upon the Northern Ocean,[44] bordering one another and both lying at the terminus some three hundred leagues from México to the south. One he sent by land and the other in ships by sea, each one with many horse and foot soldiers.[45]

I say true that if all that these two men did perpetrate in acts of malice, and most especially he who went to the kingdom of Guatimala, because the other soon found a hard death—if all these malicious and evil acts, I say, all the devastations, all the deaths, all the extirpations of peoples from their lands, all such savage acts of injustice that inspire horror in the centuries present and to come, were expressed and gathered together, they would make a great book indeed, for this captain exceeded all those of the past and present, both in quantity and number of abominations which he did, and in the peoples that he destroyed and lands that he laid waste and made a desert, because the number of all these is infinite.

He who went by sea and in ships wrought great acts of robbery and abuse and violent dispersion of people in the villages along the coast, some of whom came out to receive him with presents in the kingdom of Yucatán, which is on the way to the kingdom I named above, Naco y Guaimura, to which he was bound. After he had arrived there, he sent captains and many men through-out that land, and they robbed and killed and destroyed all the villages and people that were there. And there was one especially who, rising up in mutiny even against his own captain, took three hundred men and pushed inland toward Guatimala, and in this wise he made his way, destroying and burning all the villages that he came upon, and robbing and killing the people who lived in them. And he marched onward in this enterprise above an hundred and twenty leagues, so that if men were sent after him, to capture him, they would find the land laid waste and unhabited, and the Indians thereabout would slay them in revenge for the damage and destruction that the others had left. Within a few days, the Spaniards slew the principal captain who had sent them and against whom this captain had risen in rebellion, and after that there succeeded many other most exceedingly cruel and bloodthirsty tyrants, who—with heinous slaughters and acts of cruelty, and making slaves and selling them to the ships that brought them wine and clothing and other things, and with common tyrannical servitude,[46] from the year 1524 to the year 1535—laid waste to those provinces and the kingdom of Naco y Honduras, which had before seemed a true paradise of delights and were more populous than the most frequented and populous land on

---

43 The Pacific side; Guatemala is the point where Central America rightly begins, taking a sort of dogleg to the east from the southern border of Mexico. Thus Guatemala, Honduras, El Salvador, Nicaragua, Costa Rica, and Panama have "northern" (Caribbean) and "southern" (Pacific) seas.

44 The Caribbean.

45 Las Casas is referring to the expeditions of Pedro de Alvarado (1485?–1541) and Cristóbal de Olid. Alvarado was of that large noble family that sent at least five brothers to Hispaniola by 1510; he saw action in Peru and died in 1541 in Jalisco, Mexico. Not much is known of Olid.

46 That is, using the Indians as slaves in their personal service, not selling them or otherwise disposing of them.

earth. And now we have passed there and come that way, and we saw them in such devastation and so wanting in inhabitants that any person, however hard he might be, his heart would break with grief to see it. More have died in these eleven years than two million souls, and within the compass of above an hundred leagues no more than two thousand people have been left, and of these, more are being slain every day in that bondage that I have spoken of.

Turning my quill now to speak of the great tyrant of a captain who, as I have said, exceeded all those in the past and is like unto all those who live today, he went to the kingdom of Guatimala, from the provinces bordering México, which by the road he took (as he himself wrote in a letter to the principal captain who had sent him) is four hundred leagues distant from the kingdom of Guatimala, and he made his way committing slaughters and acts of robbery, burning and stealing and destroying wheresoe'er he came, all the land, with that title that I have spoken of—that is, telling the Indians that they should bow their knees to them, to these men so inhumane, unjust, and cruel, in the name of the king of Spain, who is unknown to the Indians and never heard of, and whom they no doubt deem to be much more unjust and cruel than his subjects, these unjust and cruel Spaniard conquerors. And without letting them deliberate upon it one moment, but rather almost as soon as the message had been read out, they began to kill and burn and wreak their havoc upon them.

ON THE PROVINCE AND KINGDOM OF GUATIMALA

When he came to that kingdom, as he made his *entrada* he slaughtered many people.[47] And despite this, there came out to receive him, upon litters and with trumpets and tambours and great celebrations, the principal lord with many other lords of the city of Utatlán, the chief city of the entire kingdom,[48] and they served him with all that they had, especially giving them victuals as was meet,[49] and all that they were able. As for the Spaniards, they made a camp outside the city that night, because it appeared to them strong and thus that within, there might be danger. And the day following, he called out the principal lord and many other lords, and when they had come to him like gende lambs, he laid hold of them all and told them that they were to give him so many cargas of gold. They replied that they had it not, because that land did not bear gold. And so he had them burned alive, with no further guilt or trial or sentence. And when the lords of all those provinces saw that their supreme lord and the other high lords had all been burned, and for no reason but that they would not give them gold, they all fled their villages into the wilderness, and they ordered all their people, that they go to the Spaniards and serve them as if they were their masters, but not reveal where they had gone. All the people of the land came to the Spaniards then and told them that they belonged to them and that they would serve them as their masters. This pious captain replied that he would not receive them, and indeed that he would have them all burned alive unless they revealed where their lords had gone. The Indians said that they knew not, that he was to employ them as he would, them and their wives and children, who could be found in their houses, and there they might slay or do with them as they would, and many times the Indians said this and offered this and did this. And it was a wonder to see, that the Spaniards went to the villages, where the poor people were working at their labours with their wives and children safe by, and there they ran them through with their spears and hacked them into pieces. And to a very great and powerful village they came (its people more careless

---

47 Las Casas is referring to the conquests of Pedro de Alvarado in Guatemala in 1524.
48 Utatlán was the capital of the Quiché kingdom, the largest and politically/ militarily most powerful highland Maya kingdom of the time. The "principal lord" referred to below was Tecum Uman.
49 Appropriate, fitting, etc.

than others, and thinking in their innocence that they were safe) and the Spaniards entered and in a space of two hours almost razed them to the ground, putting children and women and old persons to the sword and slaying as many as they could, who, though fleeing, did not escape.

And when the Indians saw that even with so much humility and offerings and patience and suffering they still could not break or soften such inhumane and bestial hearts, and that so without appearance or colour of reason, and indeed so perfectly contrary to it, they were hacked to pieces, and seeing that they were to die for no cause and in the very twinkling of an eye, they agreed to meet and to join together and to die in war, taking vengeance as best they could upon such cruel and hellish enemies, for they well knew that being not just unarmed, but naked, on foot, and weak, against people so fierce, on horseback, and so well armed, they could not prevail, but in the end would be destroyed. Then they invented some holes in the middle of the roads, into which the horses would fall and their innards be pierced through with sharp, fire-hardened stakes driven into the bottom of those holes, which had been covered with grass and weeds so that there might appear to be naught there. But only one time or two did horses fall into them, because the Spaniard learned to guard against them. But to take vengeance even for this, the Spaniards made it law that all the Indians of any sex and age that might be taken alive would be thrown into the holes. And thus pregnant and nursing women and children and old persons and any others that they might take, they would throw them into the holes until the pits were filled, the Indians being pierced through by the stakes, which was a sore thing to see, especially the women with their children. All the others, the Spaniards slew them with spears and lances and knives and threw them to savage dogs that tore them to pieces and ate them. And when the Spaniards came upon some lord, upon my honour they would burn him in a raging fire. They went about these inhumane slaughters for near onto seven years, from the year 1524 to the year 1530 or 1531. Judge for yourself, then, how great was the number of people that must have been consumed.

Of the infinite abominable works carried out by this wretched, ill-destined tyrant and his brothers (for they were his captains and no less wretched and insensible than he, along with the others that aided them), there was one deed that was especially remarkable. This was in the province of Cuzcatlán, where, or near by, is the city of San Salvador now, which is a most blessed land with all the coast of the Southern Sea, which extends for forty and fifty leagues. And in the city of Cuzcatlán, which was the head of the province, the Spaniards were met with the most regal welcome, and some twenty or thirty thousand Indians awaited them, bearing hens and other victuals. And when this tyrant had arrived and received the presents, he ordered that each Spaniard with him take from among that great number of people all the Indians that they would, so that for the days that they were there the Indians might serve them and be charged with bringing them all the things that they might require[50] or need. And each one took an hundred, or fifty, or the number that each one thought might be needful to be well served, and the innocent lambs were divided and portioned out among them and they served with all their strength, and there was no help but that they worship them. And meanwhile this captain bade the lords bring him great quantities of gold, for it was that that they had principally come for. The Indians replied that they would be pleased to give them all the gold they had, and they gathered together a very great number of axes (which they employ as they will) of gilt copper, which appears to be gold because it does have some. He ordered that the touchstone be brought for them, and when he saw that they were copper, he said to the Spaniards: "To the devil with this land; let's be off, for there is no gold; and each one of the Indians you have that serve you, put them in chains and have them in irons to be slaves." And so they did, and they set them in shackles with the king's

---

50   Ask for, request.

And thus pregnant and nursing women and children and old persons and any others they might take, they would throw them into the holes until the pits were filled, the Indians being pierced through by the stakes, which was a sore thing to see, especially the women with their children.

irons to be slaves, all of them that could be bound, and I saw the son of the principal lord of that city put in irons. This evil deed being seen by the Indians who were released and by the others throughout the land, the Indians began to come together and to arm themselves. The Spaniards wrought great devastation and slaughter among them, and they turned toward Guatimala, where they built a city, that same city that now, in just judgment, has been destroyed by divine justice with three deluges together, one of water and another of earth and another of stones thicker than ten and twenty oxen.

When all the lords and the men able to wage war had died, the Spaniards cast all the rest into that aforesaid hellish servitude, and by requiring slaves as tribute and being given their sons and daughters (because they have no other slaves), and sending ships filled with them to be sold in Perú, and with other slaughters and devastations which without number they carried out, they have destroyed and laid waste a kingdom of one hundred leagues on a side and above, of the happiest and most fertile and most populous that exists upon the earth. And this very tyrant wrote that it was more populous than the kingdom of México, and he said true: he and his brothers and the others have slain above four or five million souls in fifteen or sixteen years, from the year 1524 to the year 1540, and still today do slay and destroy those that remain, and will surely go on in this wise until all the rest are slain.

It was this man's custom that when he was about to make war upon some villages or provinces, he would take with him all he could of the already subject Indians, that they might wage war upon the others, and since he would not feed the ten or even twenty thousand men that he took with him, he gave them leave to eat the Indians that they captured. And thus there was in his camp the most outright and veritable butchery of human flesh, where in his presence children would be slain and cooked, and a man would be slain for his hands alone and his feet, which were considered to be a delicacy. And with these acts of inhumanity, other peoples of other lands hearing of them, they did not know where to flee, for the terror that they felt.

He killed infinite people in the building of ships. He would drive Indians from the Northern Sea to the Southern, 130 leagues, their backs bent under anchors of three and four *quintales,* with the spurs of the anchors biting into the Indians' backs and shoulders. And he sent in this wise a great deal of artillery, too, upon the shoulders of the poor naked creatures, and I saw many of them burthened with artillery staggering along the roads, despairing and exhausted. He would unmarry and steal from the married men their wives and daughters and give them to the sailors and soldiers so as to make them happy and to take them into his armadas. He swelled the ships with Indians, where all would perish of thirst and hunger. And it is true that if all the particulars of his cruelties should be related, they would make a great book that would inspire the world with horror. Two armadas he made, of many ships each one, and with them he scorched, as though by a fire rained down from heaven, all those lands. Oh! How many orphans did he make, how many fathers did he rob of their children, how many men strip of their wives, how many women leave without their husbands: how many acts of adultery and rapine and savagery was he the cause and reason of! How many persons did he deprive of their freedom, how much anguish and how many calamities did so many men and women suffer because of him! How many tears did he cause to be shed,[51] how many sighs sighed, how many moans and lamentations, how much loneliness and solitude in this world and how much damnation in the other did he cause, not just of Indians, which were infinite, but of wretched Christians as well, who in association with him engaged in such great offences, the gravest sins and most execrable abominations! And pray God that upon him mercy has been visited, and that God be content with the bad end that he at last did come to.

OF NEW SPAIN AND PÁNUCO AND JALISCO

The Spaniards having wrought the great cruelties and slaughters that we have told of, and others that we have refrained from telling, in the provinces of New Spain and the province of Pánuco, in the year 1525 there came to the province of Pánuco another insensible and cruel tyrant.[52] This man carried out many cruelties and put many into irons and made a great number of slaves in the aforesaid manner, though all were once free men, and he sent many ships laden with those unfortunates to the islands of Cuba and Hispaniola, where he was able to sell them more

And thus there was ... the most outright and veritable butchery of human flesh, where in his presence children would be slain and cooked, and a man would be slain for his hands alone and his feet, which were considered to be a delicacy.

51 It is this passage that inspired the title of one of the earliest translations of Las Casas' relation, *The Tears of the Indians (etc.)*, by one J. P. (John Phillips of London) in 1656.

52 Las Casas is referring to the conquistador Pedro Beltrán Nuño de Guzmán, the relative of Diego de Guzmán, who served in the Audience of Mexico between 1529 and 1530.

advantageously, and at last he destroyed that entire province, and once even gave for a mare eighty Indians, reasonable creatures.

From thence he was appointed to govern the city of México and all of New Spain, with other great tyrants as *oidores* and himself for the president. There, with the others, he committed such great evils, so many sins, so many cruelties, thefts, and abominations that it could not all be believed. And with these acts they put all that great land in such ultimate depopulation that if God had not restrained him through the resistance of the monks of Saint Francis, and then with the provision of a new *Audiencia Real*, which was good, and the friend of every virtue, in two years he would have left New Spain in the condition in which the island of Hispaniola is today. There was one man in the company of this tyrant who, wishing to enclose a large kitchen-plot of his with a wall, brought in eight thousand Indians to work, without paying them aught or giving them aught to eat, so that of a moment they would fall dead of starvation, and he would not even take notice.

When the principal man of this tyrant, who as I said laid waste to all of Pánuco, received those tidings of the coming of the new *Audiencia Real*, he resolved to make his way inland, to discover other lands to tyrannize, and he took by force from the province of México fifteen or twenty thousand men as bearers of burthens for both him and the Spaniards that went with him, and of this number not two hundred ever returned, and he was the cause of them all dying on the journey. When he came to the province of Mechuacam,[53] which is forty leagues from México, a land as happy and fertile and filled with people as México itself, the king and lord of that place came out to meet him, with a procession of infinite other persons, and made him a thousand gifts and obeisances. He later laid hold of this king because he was famed for being rich in gold and silver, and so that the king might give him great Treasures the tyrant began to lay upon him the following torments: He put him in the stocks by the feet and with the body extended and bound by the hands to a piece of timber, and he held burning coals to his feet, and a boy with a horsetail reed wetted with oil would from time to time sprinkle them with oil to roast the flesh the better; on one side was a cruel man with an iron crossbow pointed at his heart, and on the other, another such a one, setting on him a terrible raging dog, which in the space of a Hail Mary would have torn him to pieces; and thus they tormented and tortured him so that he would reveal to them the treasures that the captain pretended that he had, until, a certain Franciscan priest having been advised of all this, he took the poor creature from the captain's hands, although from these torments the Indian later died. And in this wise they tormented and tortured and killed many lords and caciques in those provinces so that they might give them gold and silver.

A certain tyrant at this time, going more as a visitor of the purses and possessions of the Indians, to steal them for himself, than of their souls or persons, found that certain of them had hidden their idols, for the sorry Spaniards had never shown them another, better god. He held the lords until they gave him their idols, thinking them to be of gold or silver, for which he cruelly and unjustly punished them. And so that he might not be disappointed in his purpose, which was to rob and steal, he obliged the said caciques to ransom[54] the idols from him, and they purchast them of him for all the gold and silver that they could find, in order to worship them, as was their wont, as their god. These then are the works they do and the examples that they give, and the honour those reprobate Spaniards bring to God in the Indies.

---

53 Michoacán, now a state in Mexico.
54 Buy back.

This great tyrannical captain went then from the province of Mechuacam to the province of Jalisco, which was as whole and meet as a beehive of happy, populous people, for it is among the most fertile and admirable lands of all the Indies. Indeed, this province possessed one village whose population extended for almost seven leagues. And as the tyrant entered into it, the lords and people came out with gifts and joy, as all the Indians are wont to do, to welcome the newcomers. And he began to deal out the cruelties and evil deeds that were his custom, and that all they had as their custom, and many more besides, in order to obtain the end that they held as a very god, which is to acquire gold. They would burn down the villages, lay hands on the caciques, torment and torture them, and do all this to those they took as slaves. He would carry away infinite numbers bound in chains, nursing mothers so borne down with the burthens that they carried—the belongings of the evil Christians—that, unable to carry their babies for the hardness of the labour and the weakness of starvation, they would cast them down on the side of the road, where infinite numbers perished.

One evil Christian, seizing a maiden by force in order to sin with her, the girl's mother began to rebuke him, crying that he should release her, and she struggled with him; he took out a knife or a sword and cut off the mother's hand, and the maiden, because she would not consent to let him have his way with her, he stabbed her to death.

Among many others, this tyrant had put into irons as slaves, most unjustly (as they were free, like all men in those lands are), four thousand five hundred men and women and one-year-old children suckling at their mother's breast, and others two and three and four and five years old, even those coming out to welcome him in peace, and infinite others, likewise, that were never counted.

When he had waged infinite abominable and infernal wars and had carried out other countless slaughters in these lands, he cast that entire land into coarse and pestilential, tyrannical bondage, which has been the intention and the wont of all the Christian tyrants of the Indies against those peoples. And in this, he gave permission to his very overseers and all the others to carry out cruelties and torments such as never heard of before, in order to take from the Indians gold and tributes. One overseer of his killed many Indians by hanging them and burning them alive and tossing them to savage dogs and cutting off hands and feet and heads and tongues, the Indians being all this while at peace, and for no other cause or reason but to dispirit them and cause them to fear him so that they would serve him and give him gold or tributes, for they saw him and knew him to be a most excellent tyrant, over and above the great many cruel lashes and rods and smitings and other types of cruelty that were done upon them every day and every hour.

It is said of him that he destroyed eight hundred villages and burned them in that kingdom of Jalisco, which was the cause that out of desperation, and having seen all the others so cruelly and unjustly perish, the Indians thereabout rose up and went off into the wilderness and slew, very rightly and honourably, a number of Spaniards. And afterward, with the injustices and insults done them by other new-come tyrants who passed that way in order to destroy other provinces, many of these Indians joined together, gathering their strength in certain crags and precipices, in which now once again such terrible cruelties have been done that the Spaniards have almost succeeded in depopulating and laying waste to all that great land, and slaying infinite people. And the sorry blind creatures, the Spaniards, allowed by God to come to such reprobate mind, do not see the just cause, and indeed several and divers causes filled with all justice which the Indians possess by natural, divine, and human law for cutting the Spaniards to pieces, if they but had forces and arms, and for casting them from their lands, nor see that their own is a most terribly unjust cause, filled with all iniquity and evil, and condemned by all law everywhere, and that they should desist from waging yet further warfare, over and above so many insults and tyrannies and such great and inexpugnable sins that they have committed upon those poor and defenseless Indians. Instead, these Spaniards do think and say and write that the victories that they have had over the innocent Indians, to extirpate them utterly, all those victories are given them by God because their evil wars are just, since they revel and glory in them and give thanks to God for their tyrannies, like unto those thieving tyrants of whom the prophet Zacharias speaks (Chapter 11) when he says: *Pasce pecora ocisionis, quae qui occidebant non doleban sed dicebant, benedictus deus quod divites facti sumus.*[55]

---

[55] "Feed the flock of the slaughter; whose possessors slay them, and hold themselves not guilty: and they that sell them say, Blessed be the Lord, for I am rich" (Zach. 11:4–5).

STUDY QUESTIONS

1. What effects did a Spanish presence in the New World have on the Indians?

2. How does Las Casas's account compare with that of Columbus?

3. Why do you think Spanish missionaries had some success in converting the Indians?

PART II
WOMEN

AN INTRODUCTION TO

The True History of the Conquest of New Spain

By 1519, when the Spanish arrived in Mesoamerica, the Mexican capital, Tenochtitlan, on Lake Texcoco, was one of the largest cities in the world.[1] The Mexica, who had conquered a vast swath of neighboring territory, were enjoying the apex of an empire of their own under their ruler, Moctezuma, and did not initially perceive the Spaniards as a threat.[2] The conquistadors, led by Hernán Cortés, capitalized on this and subdued the superior numbers of the Mexica with more advanced weaponry and alliances with their indigenous enemies. Under Spanish control, villages were replaced by the *encomienda* system by which Indians, and later Africans, were coerced into labor on plantations or silver mines. The paramount decimator of Indian populations, however, was by far epidemic and pandemic disease, namely smallpox. Indians did not possess the immunity to fight sickness brought from Europe. The population of Mexico, 25 million in 1519, was reduced to less than two million less than a century later. The natives of the Caribbean islands were completely exterminated by outbreaks.

There is a myth surrounding the Spanish conquest of Mexico. Mexica legend predicted that a god, Quetzalcoatl, the feathered serpent with jaguar teeth, would return as a bearded, white-skinned man. Moctezuma thought that the Spanish were such gods, and that Cortés must be Quetzalcoatl, whom the Mexica calendar foretold would return in 1519, on a floating island that carried the deities, who had white skin and beards and sticks that belched fire.

When they marched on Tenochtitlan, the conquistadors were in awe of the magnitude of the city and its architecture. Yet they were even more shocked when they viewed the racks of skulls, thousands upon thousands, at the stairs of the temples—for the Mexica paid tribute to their gods in the form of human

---

1 The Mexica are usually referred to as the Aztecs, a term popularized by the 19th-century German historian Alexander von Humboldt. Tenochtitlan was near modern-day Mexico City.

2 Moctezuma, or sometimes Motecuhzoma II, is also commonly referred to as Montezuma, especially regarding U.S. Marine songs and gastrointestinal revenge.

sacrifice. Rather than heed his advisers, Moctezuma allowed the Spaniards to enter the city and pay their respects to him while they stayed at the royal palace. He even sacrificed a couple of victims for them. The Spanish took Moctezuma prisoner and he ordered more and more gold, silver, and flowers be brought to placate them, which proved an immense error. Moctezuma felt that such lavish gifts underscored not only his generosity, but also his power. The Mexica quickly found out that the Spaniards sought to control that wealth and power. Immediately after they had been greeted with such grace, they put Moctezuma under house arrest, and he was eventually killed attempting to calm a mob of his own people. The Spanish crudely ripped the ornate feathers off of the Mexica gold, and melted it down into ingots.

Military alliances proved a key element to Cortés's success, particularly with the Tlaxcalans, who had been absorbed into the Mexica Empire. Cortés also had the help of Doña Marina, La Malinche, who was his interpreter and later his mistress and mother of a son. Although she is a central figure in any narrative of the conquest, her appearance in primary sources is limited. Few as they are, the most extensive surviving firsthand accounts come from 16th-century chroniclers Bernal Díaz del Castillo, Francisco López de Gómara, and Cortés himself.

Their narratives record that Malinche was a Nahua-speaking young woman, who had been sold into slavery and learned Maya. Eventually coming into the service of Cortés, she was baptized as Marina and learned Spanish from a Maya-speaking shipwrecked Spaniard who had been marooned on the Yucután Peninsula. She would be the Spaniards' translator throughout the conquest, even interpreting between Cortés and Moctezuma. As the Spanish brought the Mexica to submission by 1522, Malinche bore a son by Cortés named Martin. Yet, two years later, on an expedition to Honduras, Cortés coerced Marina to marry one of his subordinates, Juan Jaramillo de Salvatierra, with whom she had a daughter. Malinche was granted land and an *encomienda*, but died about a decade after the Spanish arrival.

There are problems with Díaz del Castillo as a source. First, his account was discovered and published posthumously. Second, Díaz del Castillo spent much of his chronicle refuting the claims of López de Gómara. Some scholars have even hypothesized that Díaz del Castillo might never have existed and was an exercise in propaganda, or even a figment of Cortés's imagination. In any case, no matter who told the story, Marina was represented through the eyes of men because we have no sources directly from her.

Marina, thus, represents an active agent of the conquest rather than a passive witness. Her story, however, constitutes a complicated one in that through oral, written, and pictorial representations, Malinche has been alternatively lauded or reviled by Spanish or Mexica commentators, respectively, as well as subsequent generations of historians. On the one hand, she directly helped the Spanish to conquer and prosper; on the other, she is a traitor who sold out her people to foreigners by her cunning and sexuality.

Figure 3.1. Doña Marina with Cortes and Moctezuma. Source: http://en.wikipedia.org/wiki/File:Cortez_%26_La_ Malinche.jpg.

The True History of the Conquest of New Spain

By Bernal Diaz del Castillo

[XXXVI]

The next morning, the fifteenth of March, 1519, many caciques and chieftains from that town of Tabasco and other towns came, showing all of us much respect, and they brought a present of gold, including four diadems, several small lizards, something like two small dogs, ear pieces, five ducks, two images of Indian faces, two golden soles like the ones on their own sandals, and other things of little value, whose worth I no longer remember. They also brought cloaks of the kind they make, very coarse, because those who know something of that province will already have heard that the ones they have in that country are of very little value. This present was nothing compared with the twenty women, and among them a particularly excellent woman who came to be called doña Marina after becoming Christian. Cortés received that present with pleasure, and he withdrew to talk with all the caciques and Aguilar the interpreter. He told them he was very grateful for what they brought, but he had one request: They should immediately order all their men, women, and children to settle that town, and he would like to see it settled within two days; if they did this, he would know there would be true peace. The caciques immediately sent for all the men, and, with their children and women, the town was settled in two days. The other thing he ordered was that they give up their idols and sacrifices, and they replied that they would do so. We made known to them through Aguilar, as best Cortés could, things touching our holy faith, how we were Christians and worshipped one sole, true God, and Cortés showed them a most venerable image of Our Lady with her precious son in her arms, and he told them that we worship that holy image because she is in heaven and she is Mother of Our Lord God. The caciques, said that the great *tecleciguata,* which is what they call the great women in those lands, seemed very good and that they would like to have her in their town. Cortés said that, yes, he would give it to them, and he ordered them to make a proper altar, well constructed, which they immediately did. The next morning, he ordered two of our finish carpenters, Alonso Yáñez and Álvaro López, to make a very tall cross, and after ordering all this, he asked the caciques why they were attacking us when we had asked for peace three times. They answered that they had already asked and received pardon for it. The cacique said that his brother, the cacique of Chanpoton, had advised it so that he would not be regarded as cowardly. He had already been reproached and dishonored because he did not attack us when the other captain came with four ships, and it seems he meant Juan de Grijalva. Further, he said that the Indian we brought as an interpreter and who had fled one night advised him to attack us day and night. Cortés then ordered them to bring Melchorejo to him no matter what the circumstances, and they told Cortés that when Melchorejo saw that the battle was not going well for them, he fled, and even though they had looked for him, they did not know where he was. We learned later that they sacrificed him because his advice cost them so much. Cortés also asked them from where they brought the gold and those little jewels. They replied that they came from where the sun set, and they said "Culua"[1] and "Mexico," but because we knew neither what Mexico nor Culua was, we ignored it. We brought another interpreter there, Francisco, whom we got during the Grijalva expedition, but he understood nothing of the Tabascan language, but that of Culua, which is the Mexican language. Partly using signs, he said to Cortés that Culua was much farther on, and he said Mexico, but we did not understand.

With this, the discussion stopped until the next day when we put on the altar the holy image of Our Lady and the cross, which we all worshipped, and fray Bartolomé de Olmedo said mass. All the caciques and chieftains were present, and that town was named Santa Maria de la Victoria, and the town of Tabasco has that name today. The same friar, with our interpreter Aguilar, preached many good things about our holy faith to the twenty Indian women they had given us and told them not to believe in their idols, that they were evil and not gods, nor should they sacrifice to the idols anymore because the idols deceived them, but instead they should worship Our Lord Jesus Christ. They were then baptized, and the name doña Marina was given to that Indian woman they had given us there, and she was truly a great *cacica,* daughter of great caciques and mistress over vassals, which clearly showed in her person. Further on I will talk about how and in what way she was brought there. I do not remember well the names of all the other women, nor is it relevant to name them. But these were the first Christian women in New Spain, and Cortés gave each captain his own. This doña Marina, because she was of good appearance, curious about things, and uninhibited, he gave to Alonso Hernández Puerto Carrero, who as I have said was a very fine gentleman, cousin of the Count of Medellín; when he left for Castile, doña Marina was with Cortés and he had a son by her, who was named don Martín Cortés.

We stayed in that town five days, as much to let wounds heal as for those who had kidney ailments, which went away there. Because Cortés was always trying to win over the caciques with good words, he told how the emperor our lord, whose vassals we are, has many great lords at his command, that they should pledge obedience to him, and that whatever they might need, whether assistance from us or anything else, he will come to help them. All the caciques gave him thanks, and there they declared themselves vassals of our great emperor. These were the first vassals in New Spain who pledged obedience to His Majesty.

Cortés then ordered that the next day, Palm Sunday, very early in the morning, they should come to the altar with their children and women to worship the holy image of Our Lady and the cross. He also ordered that six Indian carpenters should come then and go with our carpenters into the town of Cintla, where it pleased Our Lord God to give us victory in the past battle, as I have mentioned. He told them to cut a cross in the wood of a large tree that was called a ceiba, and they made the cross so that it would last a long time, because the cross will always be distinguished by bark that renews itself. When this was

---

1   Bernal Díaz consistently uses "Culua" to designate *Colhua,* a term associated with Colhuacan, Tenochtitlan's parent state from where its royal line first came. *Colhua* means "one with grandfathers," with a long line of forebearers, specifically the old Toltecs.

done, Cortés ordered them to prepare all the canoes they had to help us embark, because we wanted to set sail immediately on that holy day and also because two pilots came just then to tell Cortés that the ships were at great risk because of the north wind, which would strike them sideways. Early the next morning, all the caciques and chieftains came with all the canoes and their women and children, and they were already in the courtyard where we had the church and cross and many small cut branches for our procession. When we saw that all the caciques were gathered, Cortés, the captains, and everyone else walked together in a very pious procession with great devotion, and the Mercedarian father and Juan Díaz, the secular priest, in their vestments, mass was said, and we worshipped and kissed the holy cross, the caciques and Indians watching us. When we had completed our solemn fiesta, in accord with the season, the chieftains brought Cortés some ten hens and fish and vegetables. We took our leave of them and Cortés, continuing to commend the holy image and holy crosses to them, told them to keep them very clean, swept, and decorated with branches, and, if they honored the holy image and crosses, they would have health and good harvests. Because it was already late, we embarked; we set sail the next morning with fortunate navigation, and we followed the course to San Juan de Ulúa, always staying close to land.

Sailing along in good weather, those of us who knew the course said to Cortés, "Sir, there's the Rambla," which in the Indians' language is called *Ayagualulco*.[2] When we arrived at the site of Tonala, which is called San Antón, we pointed it out. Further on, we showed him the great Río de Guazacualco.[3] He saw the very high snowy mountains and, later, the mountain range of San Martín. Farther on we showed him the split rock, which is made up of some large rocks that jut out into the sea, and they had a landmark on top, something like a seat. Farther on, we showed him the Río de Alvarado, which is where Pedro de Alvarado entered during Grijalva's expedition. Then we showed him the Rio de Banderas, which was where we had bartered for the sixteen thousand pesos,[4] and then we showed him the Isla Blanca, and we told him also where the Isla Verde lay. Close to land he saw the Isla de Sacrificios, where we had found the altars during Grijalva's expedition and the sacrificed Indians. Then, with good fortune, we arrived at San Juan de Ulúa on Holy Thursday, after midday. I remember that a gentleman named Alonso Hernández Puertocarrero came and said to Cortés, "It seems to me, sir, that these gentlemen who have come two other times to these lands are saying to you, 'Behold France, Montesinos; / Behold Paris, the city; / Behold the waters of the Duero / where they go down to the sea.' And I tell you now to look at the rich lands around you, and know how to conduct yourself." By now Cortés well understood what the aim of these verses had been, and so he answered: "God give us the same good fortune in battle that he gave to the paladin Roldan;[5] as for the rest, with you and the other gentlemen as my masters, I'll know what to do."[6] This is what happened, and Cortés did not enter the Río de Alvarado like Gómara says.

---

2   *Ayahualolco*, which means "where the water goes around."

3   *Coatzacualco*, which means "place of the serpent pyramid."

4   In Chapter VII, not included here, Bernal Díaz reports that the Grijalva expedition traded for sixteen thousand pesos worth of low-grade gold items of diverse craftsmanship.

5   "Roldan" refers to the hero of the epic poem *Cantar de Roldan (Song of Roland)*, the nephew of Cha.rlemagne who was killed in the Battle of Ronceville in 778.

6   See David A. Borouchoff, "Beyond Utopia and Paradise: Cortés, Bernal Díaz and the Rhetoric of Consecration," *MLN* 106, no. 2, Hispanic issue (March 1991): 333.

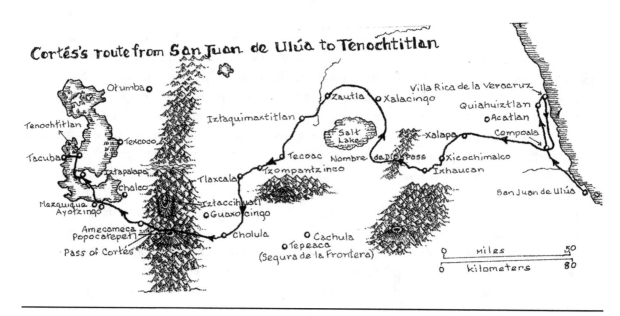

Cortés's route from San Juan de Ulua to Tenochtitlan.

DOÑA MARINA, THEY SPREAD IT AROUND THAT SHE HAD DIED

[XXXVII] Before dealing with the great Montezuma and his great Mexico and Mexicans, I want to talk about doña Marina, how from childhood she was a great lady and cacica over towns and vassals. Here is her story: Her father and mother were lords and caciques of a town, Painala, eight leagues from the town of Guazacualco, and other towns were subject to it. Her father died when she was a very small child, and her mother married another young cacique with whom she had a son and, it seemed, they loved him very much, and the father and mother agreed that he should become cacique after their deaths. To avoid any obstacles, one night they gave the child, doña Marina, to some Indians from Xicalango so she would not be seen. At that same time, the child of one of their Indian slaves died, and they announced that the one who had died was the heiress doña Marina. The people of Xicalango gave doña Marina to the people of Tabasco, and the Tabascans gave her to Cortés. I met her mother and the son of this old woman, doña Marina's half-brother, who was now a man and commanded the town jointly with his mother, because the old woman's last husband was dead. After becoming Christian, the old woman was named Marta and the son Lázaro. I know this very well because in 1523, after the conquest of Mexico and other provinces, and when Cristóbal de Olid had rebelled in Honduras, Cortés went there and passed through Guazacualco. We were with him on that entire journey as was the greater part of the citizens of the town. As doña Marina was such an excellent woman and good interpreter in all the wars of New Spain, Tlaxcala, and Mexico,

Cortés always had her with him. During that journey a gentleman named Juan Jaramillo married her in the town of Orizaba, before certain witnesses, one of them named Aranda, a former citizen of Tabasco. He spoke of the marriage, and it is not as the chronicler Gómara tells it. Doña Marina had a great presence and commanded absolutely among all the Indians in New Spain.

In the town of Guazacualco, Cortés sent for all the caciques in that province in order to address them about the holy doctrine and about their good treatment, and doña Marina's mother and half-brother, Lázaro, came with other caciques. Some days earlier doña Marina told me that she came from that province and was the mistress over vassals, and the captain Cortés knew it well, as did Aguilar the interpreter. When the mother and her son, the brother, came, they recognized one another, and clearly doña Marina was her daughter because she looked very much like her They were afraid of her, believing that she had sent for them to find and kill them, and they cried. When doña Marina saw this, she consoled them and said they should not be afraid, that when they gave her to the people from Xicalango, they did not know what they were doing, and she forgave them, gave them many golden jewels and clothes, and said they could return to their town. She said that God had done her a great favor in getting her to give up idol worship and become a Christian, to have a son by her master and lord Cortés, and to be married to a gentleman like her husband Juan Jaramillo. Even were they to make her cacica of all the provinces in New Spain, she said she would not want to be that, but would rather serve her husband and Cortés than anything else in the world. I know this with absolute certainty, and it seems to me to resemble what happened to Joseph with his brothers in Egypt, who, in the matter of the wheat, fell into Joseph's hands.[7]

This is what happened and not the account that Gómara gave, and he also says other things I am ignoring. Returning to our topic, doña Marina knew the language of Guazacualco, which is the language of Mexico, and she also knew that of Tabasco, and Jerónimo Aguilar also knew the language of Yucatan and Tabasco, which is the same; they understood each other well, and Aguilar translated everything into Castilian for Cortés. It was a great beginning for our conquest, and thus things turned out for us, praise God, very fortunately. I wanted to talk about this, because without doña Marina we could not have understood the language of New Spain and Mexico.

---

7 In the Bible, the book of Genesis, when Joseph was governor over Egypt, during the famine years, his father sent his brothers to secure wheat, and Joseph, recognizing his brothers, who had long before sold him into slavery, tested them, but eventually, through mercy, he provided them with the wheat they sought.

STUDY QUESTIONS

1. Why were the Spanish able to defeat the Mexica?

2. Discuss the role of gender in Doña Marina's prominence in the history of Mexico. Does the fact that she is a woman make her more or less powerful?

3. In what ways is Malinche a victim of history? Can she be viewed as an agent of historical change? Should she be considered a heroine or a villainess?

Wanderings of a Pilgrim in Search of the Picturesque

Not only is society in India extremely hierarchical—there are some 2,000 Hindu castes and subcastes—it is also patriarchal; in nearly every aspect of public life, males supersede females in status and importance. When I traveled to Tamil Nadu in southern India with university students in 2010, we visited an orphanage for special-needs children. To the children and the nuns who cared for them, we presented toys and money we had brought from the United States. Many of the children had disabilities, and as we spent the day playing with them, it became clear that the girls overwhelmingly outnumbered the boys. Even some nonhandicapped girls had been left there—one such child had been found inside a suitcase on the beach. Indeed, in India, as in some other cultures, male children are more highly prized than their female counterparts. Across demographic indices, some Indians even use practices such as abortion to select a baby's sex. In 2013, Indian law and society have been scrutinized by world opinion after the gang rape and murder of a 23-year-old Indian student (in September of that year, the four perpetrators were sentenced to death by hanging, and one subsequently committed suicide), followed by, over the course of the next couple of years, rape of tourists and the rapes and assaults of Indian girls no more than a few years old. Nonetheless, the majority of rapes in India remain unreported, and the authorities have been slow to adopt stronger measures for those that are reported—multiple times per hour nationwide. At one point, the Indian government even banned a documentary about the 2013 case entitled *India's Daughter*. The point of all this is that not only must Indian police—and indeed, the subcontinent as a whole—eradicate and criminalize all forms of misogyny and violence against women, but in order to understand the problem more fully, one must to some extent contextualize its historical precedents. Among those Indian customs concerning women and girls that were questioned by British governors included female infanticide, child brides, and *sati*.

As the British colonized India throughout the 18th and 19th centuries, the practice of widow immolation or burning (also known as *sati*, or by Britons as *suttee*) became a controversial issue. Cremation is a facet of Hindu burial ritual, and it was believed that a widow, prohibited from remarrying, should commit an incendiary suicide by throwing herself on her deceased husband's funeral pyre because she could not possibly carry on in life without him. As a pious Hindu wife, furthermore, she should want to subordinate herself to her husband by following him in death.

It was supposed to be a voluntary action, but as one might imagine, this was not always the case. Widows were at times coerced or even drugged before acquiescing in their fate. Were these women solely victims, or people with some degree of agency? Indeed, reasons other than grief and spousal fealty added to the decision to commit *sati*. Future financial uncertainty and trepidation of being ostracized by family constituted legitimate concerns.

Sati was mainly a practice among high-caste Hindus and was viewed as an act of spousal devotion by a loyal wife. Brahmin widows underwent *sahamarana*, or *sati*, along with their husbands, whereas women of other castes could also immolate themselves by *anumarana*, or death by fire, at a subsequent date along with an article belonging to the husband.[1] Toward the end of the 18th century and for the first three decades of the 19th, contentious debates on *sati* raged between imperial administrators, missionaries, and native male elites—the pundits who instructed Raj officials on the issue—all of whom muted the widows' voices. The issue also mobilized public opinion in India and Britain alike. Despite the fact that instances of *sati* were predominantly to be found among Brahmins, and only seldom then, they were nevertheless interpreted by the West as a representative metaphor for the subjugation of *all* Indian women. In Bengal, for example, the hundreds of cases of *sati* each year relatively had little effect in a province with a population in the millions. Though by no means ubiquitous, an increase in the prevalence of *sati* in the early 19th century, however, did provide the issue with greater exposure in Parliament, while Britons held public meetings and signed petitions for its abolition.

The problem was compounded by the widespread assertion that there existed a liturgical justification for *sati* in Vedic scripture, despite regional variations in terms of how it was performed. Some Hindu reformers, however, opposed *sati* and argued that scripture did not, in fact, condone the act. Horrified as the British were by the practice of widow-burning and convinced that the colonial state knew what was best for its subjects, they also remained tolerant of *sati*, ever cognizant not to impose too fervently on time-honored Hindu religious traditions. Accounts or engravings of *sati* certainly informed the tenor of the debate. Most representations were by men, but women occasionally commented.

Although few wives of East India Company officials accompanied their husbands to the subcontinent, Fanny Parks, who lived in India between 1822 and 1845, proved to be an exception to the rule. In her diary, Parks described a *sati* ritual witnessed by her husband Charles, a Company clerk, in 1828, a year before the practice was banned. James Peggs had served as a missionary in Orissa, near Calcutta. Living in England later, Peggs supported the abolition of *sati*. An author as well as a clergyman, Peggs, in his book on Hindu culture, included an eye-witness account from 1826.

In their artwork, many Britons depicted a romanticized scene in which a grieving wife embodied self-sacrifice. Such perspectives, however, appalled and outraged the British, who had documented cases of *sati* among children as young as twelve. Official presence became standard at funerals and data was recorded. In 1812–1813, legislation prohibiting the practice for girls less than 16 years of age, pregnant women, or mothers with children under the age of three was enacted, and the new governor-general, William Bentinck, abolished *sati* for all women in 1829. The prohibition of *sati* constituted an effort by the British to assert moral superiority over what they perceived as barbarity.

---

1   Niall Ferguson, Empire: How Britain Made the Modern World (London: Penguin Books, 2003), p. 139.

Wanderings of a Pilgrim in Search of the Picturesque

By Fanny Parks

From 1600 to the early 1800s, few officials of the English East Indian Company lived with English wives in India. This practice began to change as transportation became easier with the development of steamships. Born in 1794, Fanny Archer married Charles Parks, a writer (clerk) with the Company, in March 1822 and arrived in Calcutta in November 1822. She and her husband lived in India until 1845, mostly in and around Allahabad at the confluence of the Jumna and Ganges Rivers. Fanny Parks wrote her diary as a record for her mother in England and included descriptions of her daily activities and her observations of Indian religion, society, and customs. She never saw a sati ritual but described and commented on a sati cremation that her husband witnessed in Allahabad on November 7, 1828, when sati was legal if voluntary. Consider the similarities and differences in her account of the sati and that which Francois Bernier made in his 1667 letter, and whether gender or the time period in which each was writing made any difference in their attitudes toward the ritual of sati and the Hindu widows who performed sati.

THE SUTTEE

A rich buniya [merchant], a corn chandler, whose house was near the gate of our grounds, departed this life; he was an Hindoo. On the 7th of November, the natives in the bazar were making a great noise with their tom-toms, drums, and other discordant musical instruments, rejoicing that his widow had determined to perform suttee, i. e. to burn on his funeral-pile.

The magistrate sent for the woman, used every argument to dissuade her, and offered her money. Her only answer was, dashing her head on the floor, and saying, "If you will not let me burn with my husband, I will hang myself in your court of justice." The shastrus [Hindu scriptures] say, "The prayers and imprecations of a suttee are never uttered in vain; the great gods themselves cannot listen to them unmoved."

If a widow touch either food or water from the time her husband expires until she ascend the pile, she cannot, by Hindoo law, be burned with the body; therefore the magistrate kept the corpse forty-eight

Figure 4.1. Hindu Sati Ritual. Copyright in the Public Domain.

hours, in the hope that hunger would compel the woman to eat. Guards were set over her, but she never touched any thing. My husband accompanied the magistrate to see the suttee : about 5000 people were collected together on the banks of the Ganges : the pile was then built, and the putrid body placed upon it; the magistrate stationed guards to prevent the people from approaching it. After having bathed in the river, the widow lighted a brand, walked round the pile, set it on fire, and then mounted cheerfully: the flame caught and blazed up instantly; she sat down, placing the head of the corpse on her lap, and repeated several times the usual form, "Ram, Ram, suttee; Ram, Ram, suttee;" i.e. "God, God, I am chaste."

As the wind drove the fierce fire upon her, she shook her arms and limbs as if in agony; at length she started up and approached the side to escape. An Hindoo, one of the police who had been placed near the pile to see she had fair play, and should not be burned by force, raised his sword to strike her, and the poor wretch shrank back into the flames. The magistrate seized and committed him to prison. The woman again approached the side of the blazing pile, sprang fairly out, and ran into the Ganges, which was within a few yards. When the crowd and the brothers of the dead man saw this, they called out, "Cut her down, knock her on the head with a bamboo; tie her hands and feet; and throw her in again;" and rushed down to execute their murderous intentions, when the gentlemen and the police drove them back.

The woman drank some water, and having extinguished the fire on her red garment, said she would mount the pile again and be burned.

The magistrate placed his hand on her shoulder (which rendered her impure), and said, "By your own law, having once quitted the pile you cannot ascend again; I forbid it. You are now an outcast from the Hindoos, but I will take charge of you, the Company[1] will protect you, and you shall never want food or clothing."

He then sent her, in a palanquin, under a guard, to the hospital. The crowd made way, shrinking from her with signs of horror, but returned peaceably to their homes; the Hindoos annoyed at her escape, and the Mussulmans saying, "It was better that she should escape, but it was a pity we should have lost the tamasha (amusement) of seeing her burnt to death."

Had not the magistrate and the English gentlemen been present, the Hindoos would have cut her down when she attempted to quit the fire; or had she leapt out, would have thrown her in again, and have said, "She performed suttee of her own accord, how could we make her? it was the will of God." As a specimen of their religion the woman said, "I have transmigrated six times, and have been burned six times with six different husbands; if I do not burn the seventh time, it will prove unlucky for me!" "What good will burning do you?" asked a bystander. She replied, "The women of my husband's family have all been suttees, why should I bring disgrace upon them? I shall go to heaven, and afterwards re-appear

---

1   *Editor's note*: East India Company

on earth, and be married to a very rich man." She was about twenty or twenty-five years of age, and possessed of some property, for the sake of which her relatives wished to put her out of the world.

If every suttee were conducted in this way, very few would take place in India. The woman was not much burned, with the exception of some parts on her arms and legs. Had she performed suttee, they would have raised a little cenotaph, or a mound of earth by the side of the river, and every Hindoo who passed the place returning from bathing would have made salam to it; a high honour to the family.

India's Cries to British Humanity

By James Peggs

Toward the end of the 1700s, the evangelical movement in Britain argued that one's commitment to Christ should be reflected in action, primarily the effort to end slavery in the British empire and to proselytize or seek converts among the "heathen." Initially, the English East India Company had prohibited Christian missionaries from living within their territories and seeking Indian converts in order to prevent any unrest or opposition to the Company's trade and political control. In 1813, when the British Parliament was considering the renewal of the charter that authorized the Company's trade and political control in India, members of Parliament who were committed evangelical Christians, mainly Baptists and Methodists, forced the Company to permit missionaries to settle in their territory. Once in India, Protestant missionaries criticized Hindu religious practices such as the use of images in worship and social customs such as early marriage and sati as superstitious and barbaric.

James Peggs (1793-1850) had been a missionary at Cuttack, Orissa, south of Calcutta, and published this edition of his book in 1832 when Parliament was again reviewing the charter of the Company. Then residing in England, he sought to influence Parliament to give firm instructions to the Company to exert greater control over Hindu social customs and religious practices that he considered evil. Peggs claimed that self-immolation continued among Hindu widows, and that the Company must take more vigorous measures to enforce the prohibition on sati.

In this book, Peggs includes a description of a sati witnessed by Rev. J. England of Bangalore, in the princely state of Mysore (now the state of Karnataka in which the dominant language is Kannada or Carnatic) in south India, in June 1826. Although Company law, which permitted sati if it were voluntary, did not extend to a princely state, England is still concerned to indicate whether or not the widow was coerced to commit self-immolation. Peggs stated that his image of "Burning a Hindoo Widow" was a representation of that sati.[1]

---

1   "Introduction," *Nonfiction*, James Peggs. Copyright © by Roy Rosenzweig Center for History and New Media (CC BY-SA 3.0) at http://chnm.gmu.edu/wwh/modules/lesson5/lesson5.php?menu=1&s=5

James Peggs, India's Cries to British Humanity, Relative to Infanticide, British Connection with Idolatry, Ghau Murders, Suttee, Slavery, and Colonization in India, 1832.

THE ACCOUNT OF THE SUTTEE REPRESENTED IN THE ENGRAVING, IS FROM THE PEN OF REV. J. ENGLAND, OF BANGALORE, UNDER THE MADRAS PRESIDENCY, IN JUNE 1826.

I received a note from a gentleman that a Suttee was about to take place near his house. On hastening to the spot, I found the preparations considerably advanced, and a large concourse of spectators assembled. On my left stood the horrid pile; it was an oblong bed of dry cow-dung cakes, about ten feet long, seven wide, and three high. At each corner of it, a rough stake, about eight feet in length, was driven into the ground, and about a foot from the top of these supporters was fastened, by cords, a frame of the same dimensions as the bad, and forming a canopy. This frame must have been of considerable weight; it was covered with very dry small faggots, which the officiating Brahmuns continued to throw upon it, till they rose two feet above the frame-work. On my right, sat the poor deluded widow, who was to be the victim of this heart-rending display of Hindoo purity and gentleness; she was attended by a dozen or more Brahmuns; her mother, sister, and son (an interesting boy of about three years of age), and other relatives were also with her. Her own infant, now twelve months old,[2] was craftily kept from her by the Brahmuns. She had already performed a number of preparatory ceremonies; one of which was washing herself in a strong decoction of saffron, which is supposed to have a purifying effect. It imparted to her a horrid ghastliness; —her eyes indicated a degree of melancholy wildness; an unnatural smile now and then played on her countenance: and everything about her person and her conduct indicated that narcotics had been administered in no small quantities. Close by me stood the Fousdar, a native officer, who, besides regulating the police, is the chief military officer of the station. So heartily did he engage in this murderous work, that he gave the poor widow twenty pagodas (between six and seven pounds sterling), to confirm her resolution to be burned!

The Rev. Mr. Campbell addressed her in the Carnatic language, but the effect of his address was counteracted by the influence of the Brahmuns. The pile being completed, a quantity of straw as spread on the top. An increase of activitiy was soon visible among the men, whose 'feet are swift to shed blood.' Muntrams having been repeated over the pile, and the woman and every thing being in readiness, the hurdle to which the corpse of the husband had been fastened was now raised by six of the officiating Brahmuns; the end of a cord about two yards long, attached at the other end to the head of the bier, was taken by the widow, and the whole moved slowly towards the pile. The corpse was laid on the right side, and four men furnished with sharp swords, one stationed at each corner, now drew them from their scabbards. The trembling, ghastly offering to the Moloch of Hindoism, then began her seven circuits round the fatal pile, and finally halted opposite to her husband's corpse, at the let side of it, where she was evidently greatly agitated. Five or six Brahmuns began to talk to her with much vehemence, till, in a paroxysm of desperation, assisted by the Brahmuns, the hapless widow ascended the bed of destruction. Her mother and her sister stood by, weeping and agonized; but all was in vain—the blood-thirsty men prevailed. The devoted woman then proceeded to disengage the rings from her fingers, wrists, and ears; her murderers streaching out their greedy hands to receive them: afterwards all her trinkets, &c., were distributed among the same relentless and rapacious priests. While in the act of taking a ring from her ear, her mother and sister, unable any longer to sustain the extremity of their anguish, went up to the side of the pile, and entreated that the horrid purpose might be abandoned; but the woman fearing the encounter, without uttering a word, or even casting a parting glance at her supplicating parent and sister,

---

2   *Editor's Note:* It is strange, given that this event took place in 1826, that the widow was said to have had a one-year old child. Legislation passed in 1812-1813 dictated that practitioners of sati be mothers of children above the age of three.

threw herself down on the pile, and clasped the half-putrid corpse in her arms. Straw in abundance was heaped on the dead and the living; guns, resin, and other inflammable substances were thrown upon the straw which covered the bodies, while muntrams were prepeated at their head; six or eight pieces of kindled cow-dung were introduced among the straw, at different parts of the pile; ghee and inflammable materials were applied, and the whole blazed in as many places. The men with swords at each corner then hacked the cords, which supported the canopy of faggots—it fell and covered the lifeless corpse and the living woman! A piercing sound caught my ear; I listened a few seconds, and, notwithstanding the noise of the multitude, heard the shrieks of misery which issued from the burning pile. In an agony of feeling, we directed the attention of the Brahumns to this; and while so doing, again—still louder and more piercing than before—the burning woman rent the air with her shrieks! Several of the Brahmuns called out to the half-consumed, still conscious and imploring widow, TO COMFORT HER! The pile was now enveloped in flames, and so intense was the heat, that, as by one consent, the Brahmuns and spectators retreated several paces; they then sang a Sanscrit hymn; the hymn ended, but not the shrieks and groans of the agonized sufferer; they still pierced our ears, and almost rent our hearts! Scarcely conscious of what I did, I left this fiendish barbarity.

STUDY QUESTIONS

1. The British were appalled by *sati*. Discuss cultural relativity (or lack thereof) with respect to a Eurocentric mentality imposed upon the colonized.

2. As we asked of Doña Marina, were women who performed *sati* victims of the ritual, or active participants with agency?

3. Or can this be considered a case for false consciousness, by which Hindu widows acquiesced in their fates because they knew no alternative?

4. What were some of the reasons a Hindu family might support *sati*?

5. How are Brahmins portrayed in the accounts?

AN INTRODUCTION TO

Comfort Woman: A Filipina's Story of Prostitution and Slavery Under the Japanese Military

One of the uglier episodes of history took place during the era of Japanese imperial expansion between 1931 and 1945. This was the institutionalization by the Japanese army of the abduction and sexual enslavement of about 200,000 Asian women in this period. Most of the victims came from Korea, China, and the Philippines, though others were Indonesian, Thai, Burmese, Taiwanese, and Indochinese (Vietnamese). Even hundreds of Dutch women from Batavia, the Netherlands' name for Indonesia, were forced into the role of "comfort women." With false promises of opportunities for wartime employment in factories, many young women and girls were lured into the "comfort stations." Others were simply kidnapped and sent to various places around Japanese-occupied East Asia, often confined in captivity for years. All were physically and psychologically traumatized by systematic and continuous beatings, rapes, and torture.

Reasons for the establishment of the "comfort stations" were twofold. First, Japanese top brass believed that they would serve as a deterrent to rapes of civilians, and hence would minimize subsequent reactionary antagonism from the local populace. Second, regulation of sexual intercourse by the military and forced medical examinations of the women meant fewer cases of venereal disease. By this logic, the Japanese established what basically amounted to brothels, minus the remuneration, plus rampant violence. Some women were forced to service as many as 40 Japanese soldiers per day, some at the same time. As the Pacific theater drew to a close, thousands of "comfort women" were executed. About 60,000, less than half, survived the war, and just as so many veterans of the Second World War are passing away, so, too, are the former "comfort women."

Many "comfort women" hid their secrets out of a sense of shame for decades. Many had difficulty reintegrating into their former lives, either because of exclusion by their communities or self-imposed exile. Only recently in the past couple of decades have some come forward to tell their stories. Their plights did not merely affect them during their internment, but in most cases, for the remainder of their lives. Unfortunately, despite international pressure, the Japanese government has remained as reluctant to apologize for these acts, or even acknowledge that these past crimes of sexual violence occurred, as the women have been reticent to come forward. Top leaders such as Prime Minister Shinzo Abe have maintained that evidence of coercion is inconclusive and Japanese reparations for World War Two have been made to the Philippines. In 2013, Toru Hashimoto, the mayor of Osaka, made the ridiculous statement that "comfort women" played an important role in the Japanese war effort. "When soldiers are risking their lives by running through storms of bullets," Hashimoto explained in May, "and you want to give these emotionally charged soldiers a rest somewhere, it's clear that you need a comfort-women system."[1] United States military personnel stationed in the region, he added, should seek brothels to mitigate instances of sexual crimes against Japanese women. Despite obstacles from the Japanese establishment, by seeking justice, the women have been able to transform feelings of shame into those of strength. At long last, by the end of 2015, South Korean and Japanese officials met, and the Abe administration not only promised some $8.3 million to fund elderly "comfort women," but also accepted responsibility.

One such former sex slave, Maria Rosa Luna Henson (1928–1997), better known as Lola Rosa, told the story of her ordeal in 1992, half a century after her captivity and rapes occurred. Lola Rosa was illegitimate; her father was a rich landlord. She excelled in Catholic school until seventh grade, when the Second World War broke out in the Pacific. She was first raped by Japanese soldiers while gathering firewood. Her mother moved her for safety, and eventually, Lola Rosa joined Filipino guerrillas, serving as a courier of food, medicine, and arms. On one mission, a Japanese soldier transported her by force to a hospital, which had been turned into a base and "comfort station." At the age of 16, for nine months she was raped every day until Filipino guerrillas rescued her.

For nearly 50 years, Lola Rosa kept her story a secret to all but her mother. She took different menial jobs. Her husband, who abandoned the family, never knew. Her children only found out with the rest of the world in 1992. Her autobiography, entitled *Comfort Woman: Slave of Destiny*, published in 1996, was the first of its kind. She exemplified the most profound courage in the face of living with unspeakable horrors. She passed away in 1997, but opened the door for other "comfort women" to share their stories of pain and healing.

---

1 *Miami Herald*, May 14, 2013.

Comfort Woman: A Filipina's Story of Prostitution and Slavery Under the Japanese Military

By Maria Rosa Henson

COMFORT WOMAN

One morning in April 1943, I was asked by my Huk[1] comrades to collect some sacks of dried corn from the nearby town of Magalang. I went with two others in a cart pulled by a carabao. One comrade sat with me in the cart, the other rode on the carabao's back. It was the height of the dry season. The day was very hot.

We loaded the sacks of corn into the cart and made our way back to our barrio. As we approached the Japanese checkpoint near the town hospital of Angeles, the man beside me whispered, "Be careful, there are some guns and ammunition hidden in the sacks of corn." I froze. I did not know till then that what we were sitting on were guns. I became very nervous, fearing that if the Japanese soldiers discovered the weapons, we would all get killed.

I got off the cart and showed the sentry our passes. At that time, everyone in the barrio needed to have a pass to show that he or she lived there. The sentry looked at the sacks of corn, touching here and pressing there without saying anything.

Finally, he allowed us to pass, but after we had gone thirty meters from the checkpoint he whistled and signaled us to return. We looked at each other and turned pale. If he emptied the sack, he would surely find the guns and kill us instantly. The soldier raised his hands and signaled that I was the only one to come back, and my companions were allowed to go. I walked to the

Figure 6.1 Smuggling guns and ammunition in sacks of corn past the Japanese checkpoint. I wore a salakot to protect me from the sun's heat.

---

1   *Editor's note*: Huk: Hukbalahap, Filipino resistance fighters against the Japanese and later the government.

checkpoint, thinking the guns were safe but I would be in danger. I thought that maybe they would rape me.

The guard led me at gunpoint to the second floor of the building that used to be the town hospital. It had been turned into the Japanese headquarters and garrison. I saw six other women there. I was given a small room with a bamboo bed. The room had no door, only a curtain. Japanese soldiers kept watch in the hall outside. That night, nothing happened to me.

The following day was hell. Without warning, a Japanese soldier entered my room and pointed his bayonet at my chest. I thought he was going kill me, but he used his bayonet to slash my dress and tear it open. I was too frightened to scream. And then he raped me. When he was done, other soldiers came into my room, and they took turns raping me.

Twelve soldiers raped me in quick succession, after which I was given half an hour to rest. Then twelve more soldiers followed. They all lined up outside the room waiting for their turn. I bled so much and was in such pain, I could not even stand up. The next morning, I was too weak to get up. A woman brought me a cup of tea and breakfast of rice and dried fish. I wanted to ask her some questions, but the guard in the hall outside stopped us from saying anything to each other.

I could not eat. I felt much pain, and my vagina was swollen. I cried and cried, calling my mother. I could not resist the soldiers because they might kill me. So what else could I do? Every day, from two in the afternoon to ten in the evening, the soldiers lined up outside my room and the rooms of the six other women there. I did not even have time to wash after each assault. At the end of the day, I just closed my eyes and cried. My torn dress would be brittle from the crust that had formed from the soldiers' dried semen. I washed myself with hot water and a piece of cloth so I would be clean. I pressed the cloth to my vagina like a compress to relieve the pain and the swelling.

Every Wednesday, a Japanese doctor came to give us a check-up. Sometimes a Filipino doctor came. The other women could rest for four or five days a month while they had their period. But I had no rest because I was not yet menstruating.

The garrison did not have much food. We ate thrice a day, our meals consisting of a cup of rice, some salty black beans and thin pieces of preserved radish. On rare occasions, we had a hard-boiled egg. Sometimes there was a small piece of fried chicken. Sometimes we also had a block of brown sugar. I would suck it like candy or mix it with the rice, and I was happy. I kept the sugar in my room.

A soldier always stood in the hall outside the seven rooms where we were kept. The guard gave us tea every time we wanted some to drink. Once, he told me to wash my face with tea so that my skin would look smooth. He was kind to all the women there.

We began the day with breakfast, after which we swept and cleaned our rooms. Sometimes, the guard helped. He fixed my bed and scrubbed the floor with a wet cloth and some disinfectant. After cleaning, we went to the bathroom downstairs to wash the only dress we had and to bathe. The bathroom did not even have a door, so the

Figure 6.2 Twelve soldiers raped me in quick succession.

soldiers watched us. We were all naked, and they laughed at us, especially at me and the other young girl who did not have any pubic hair.

I felt that the six other women with me also despised the Japanese soldiers. But like me, there was nothing they could do. I never got to know them. We just looked at each other, but were not allowed to talk. Two of the women looked Chinese. They always cast their gaze downward and never met my eye.

The only time I saw them was when we were taken for our daily bath and when, twice a week, we were taken out to get some sun. After bathing, we went back to our rooms. I would hang up my dress to dry and comb my long hair. Sometimes I sat on the bamboo bed, remembering all that had been done to me. How could I escape or kill myself? The only thing that kept me from committing suicide was the thought of my mother.

Figure 6.3 The guard gives me a cube of brown sugar.

At around eleven, the guard brought each of us our lunch. He returned an hour later to collect our plates. Then a little before two in the afternoon, he brought us a basin with hot water and some pieces of cloth.

At two in the afternoon, the soldiers came. Some of them were brought by truck to the garrison. My work began, and I lay down as one by one the soldiers raped me. At six p.m., we rested for a while and ate dinner. Often I was hungry because our rations were so small. After thirty minutes, I lay down on the bed again to be raped for the next three or four hours. Every day, anywhere from ten to over twenty soldiers raped me. There were times when there were as many as thirty: they came to the garrison in truckloads. At other times, there were only a few soldiers, and we finished early.

Most of the soldiers looked so young, maybe they were only eighteen years old. Their hair was cut short, only half an inch long. Most of them were clean and good looking, but many of them were rough.

I lay on the bed with my knees up and my feet on the mat, as if I were giving birth. Once there was a soldier who was in such a hurry to come that he ejaculated even before he had entered me. He was very angry, and he grabbed my hand and forced me to fondle his genitals. But it was no use, because he could not become erect again. Another soldier was waiting for his turn outside the room and started banging on the wall. The man had no choice but to leave, but before going out, he hit my breast and pulled my hair.

It was an experience I often had. Whenever the soldiers did not feel satisfied, they vented their anger on me. Sometimes a soldier took my hand and put it around his genitals so I could guide him inside me. I soon learned that was the quickest way to satisfy the men and get the ordeal over with. But there was a soldier who did not like this. When I put my hand on his groin, he slapped me. He was very rough, poking his penis all over my genitals, even my backside, because he could not find my vagina. He kept pressing against my clitoris which got so swollen that I was in pain for three days. Even the hot water compress I made could not relieve the pain.

Figure 6.4 The soldiers watch us bathe and laugh at us.

Figure 6.5 Every day this was the scene in my room.

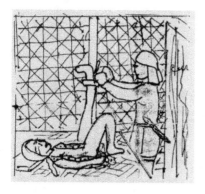

Figure 6.6 Sometimes the soldiers tied up my leg with a belt which they hung on a nail on the wall.

Some soldiers punched my legs and belly after they had ejaculated prematurely, staining their pants with their semen. One soldier raped me, and when he was finished, ordered me to fondle his genitals. He wanted to rape me a second time, but could not get an erection. So he bumped my head and legs against the wall. It was so painful. As he was hitting me, the soldiers outside started knocking impatiently on the wall. Through the thin curtain, I could see their impatient figures huddled in the hall.

Every day there were incidents of violence and humiliation. These happened not only to me, but also to the other women there. Sometimes I heard crying and the sound of someone being beaten up as there was only a partition made of woven bamboo that divided my room from those of the others.

When the soldiers raped me, I felt like a pig. Sometimes they tied up my right leg with a waist band or belt and hung it on a nail on the wall as they violated me. I was angry all the time. But there was nothing I could do. How many more days, I thought. How many more months? Someday we will be free, I thought. But how?

I thought of my guerrilla activities and my comrades. I regretted passing the sentry where the Japanese soldiers saw me. Did my comrades know that I was still alive and undergoing such horrible suffering? Maybe not. Was there anything they could do, I wondered. Sometimes I lost all hope.

I was in the hospital building for three months. Afterwards, in August of 1943, we were transferred to a big rice mill four blocks from the hospital. The mill was on Henson Road, named after my father's family, who owned the land where it stood. We found seven small rooms ready for each of us. The daily routine of rape continued. All throughout my ordeal, I kept thinking of my mother. Did she know I was still alive? How could I get in touch with her?

In December 1943, a new set of officers took over the mill. One day I saw the new captain. His face was familiar. I knew I had seen him before. Once the officer called me and asked, "Are you the girl whom I met in Fort McKinley?

I bowed my head and answered, "Yes." It was the man who had raped me two years before. He told me his name was Captain Tanaka.

The officers also demanded our services. Once they took all seven of us to a big house where they lived. That house belonged to my father, and it was where my mother worked while she was in her teens. We stayed there for an hour, and there we were raped. Tanaka was there, and so was his commanding officer, a colonel who raped me twice. We returned to the rice mill on board a truck guarded by soldiers. Sometimes we were transported to another big, old house where the other officers lived, and there we would again be raped.

Tanaka seemed to be fond of me, but I did not like him. He took pity on me. It seemed that if he could only stop the soldiers from raping me, he would. Sometimes, if the colonel was not there, he asked me to make some tea for him. He told me that he was from Osaka. He was about thirty-two years old, with eyes so small that they disappeared when he smiled.

From the time he recognized me as the girl he had raped in Fort McKinley, Tanaka became very kind to me. He could speak a little English, and he talked to me often. He asked me my name. "My name is Rosa," I answered. "Rosa means a flower, a rose."

From that time on, he called me Bara which means rose in Japanese, he said. He also asked me how old I was. I told him fifteen by making a sign with my fingers.

Many days passed. I looked at the calendar which hung in a hall outside my room. I realized Christmas was coming in a week. I remembered my mother again. I cried quietly. I missed my mother, and my father, too. Neither of them knew what had happened to me. Sometimes I stayed up all night, thinking about my parents. When morning came, it was back to the old routine.

Even the Japanese doctor who checked me every week did not spare me. Once, after the check-up, he asked me to stay behind. And then he raped me. I cried and cried because it hurt so much. His penis was very big.

Figure 6.7 I cried every night, calling my mother silently.

By now I had served thousands of soldiers. Sometimes I looked at myself in the small mirror in my room and saw that what I had been through was not etched in my face. I looked young and pretty. God, I thought, how can I escape from this hell? Please God, help me and the other girls free ourselves from here.

We were still taken regularly to the big houses where the officers stayed. The old colonel would always choose me from among the other girls and rape me twice. He did not talk to me. He just gave me a cup of tea with sugar and a big banana and signaled me to eat it.

One morning, after I had cleaned my room, bathed and washed my only dress and towel, Tanaka called me to his room. I was combing my hair. "Bara, come here," he said. I sat in front of his table.

He was writing a letter with a fountain pen which he dipped in ink. Then he held my chin. He dipped his pen in the ink and pierced me with the tip of the pen. It was painful, as if I had been pricked by a needle. To this day, that ink mark is on my chin.

I do not know why he did that. He also ran his fingers through my hair. Then, when he saw a small cockroach on the table, he swatted it and burned it with a lighted cigarette. "*Moyasu*," he said, meaning burn. Just then, we heard the sound of a vehicle coming to a halt. Tanaka stood up and told me to go back to my room. He gave me two pieces of mint candy before I left.

The colonel had arrived. He headed straight for Tanakas room. It was close to eleven a.m., and soon the guard came with my ration. It looked good—I had a piece of fried chicken, some vegetables and an egg. I kept the egg to eat before I went to sleep.

But as I was finishing my lunch, the colonel came into my room and raped me. I was scared because he looked very cruel. Afterward, he also gave me a piece of mint.

There was nothing we could do about our situation. After some time, I became very ill. I was getting chills, my fingernails were turning black, and I was always feeling thirsty. I could feel that I was going to have a malaria attack. But no matter how weak I was, the soldiers continued to rape me, and I was afraid they would hit me again even if I was very sick.

Then I developed a high fever. Tanaka found out I was ill, maybe because he could hear me crying and tossing in bed. He took me to his room and gave me a tablet for high fever. The colonel also found out. He visited me in Tanaka's room and told him that I was not to give service to the soldiers that day.

I was given my dinner in Tanaka's room, but I had no appetite. Tears just fell from my eyes. I was quiet. Tanaka looked at me sadly. I returned to my room at about ten p.m. I could not sleep the whole night, I just cried silently. I remembered my mother again and the thousands of soldiers who had raped me. I recalled their cruelty, their habit of hitting me when they were not satisfied with having raped me. I felt very weak.

I felt then that only Captain Tanaka understood my feelings. He was the only one who did not hurt me or treat me cruelly. But inside in my heart I was still very angry with him.

Sometimes, when the colonel was not in the garrison, Tanaka went to my room to talk to me, asking me if I felt better after my malaria attack. He would hold my face and look straight into my eyes. But I did not look at him. Sometimes I pitied him.

Since he understood a little English, I pleaded with him to allow me to escape. He said he could not let me go because it was against his vow. He could not do anything against the Emperor. Then he embraced me and kissed my cheeks and neck tenderly. Maybe he pitied me but could do nothing.

Figure 6.8 "Please, Tanaka, let me go."

Figure 6.9 My malaria attack. The soldier raping me thought I was fooling him and kicked me.

Even now I sometimes recall the things that Tanaka did for me. I remember the word "Bara." I have told my granddaughter about this, and she and her mother sometimes call me Lola Bara instead of Lola Rosa.

One day, at about nine in the morning, I was combing my hair and had my back to the door. Suddenly I felt someone holding my hips. I was frightened. It was Tanaka. He started kissing my hair. Then he made me lie down on the bed and raped me.

I was very angry, and I was still feeling weak from malaria. Although he was not as rough as the others, he still took advantage of me. When he finished, he said, "Arigato," and left. I understood what he meant. "Thank you," he said for the first time.

Once when a soldier was raping me, I suddenly got a malaria attack. I started shaking, and the soldier kicked me. I fell down from my bed to the floor. Maybe he thought that I was just pretending to be ill. But I kept on shivering, and I could feel that even my intestines were quivering.

The other soldiers waiting outside the room saw what happened. Captain Tanaka also noticed that something was wrong. He went to my room, picked me up from the floor and put me back on the bed. He wrapped a blanket around me and drew open the curtain that hung on my door. The soldiers waiting outside walked away.

The next day, the doctor came and confirmed that I had malaria. I was allowed to rest for a week. I was given two yellow tablets to take twice a day. But I still got malaria attacks every other day. After a week of taking the medicine, I began bleeding profusely. The Japanese doctor was not there, so Captain Tanaka found a Filipino doctor. He told me that I had a miscarriage. When I learned that I had lost a child, I began wondering how that was possible, as I had not yet begun to menstruate. And who was the father?

A week after my miscarriage, I was put back to work again. Even if I still had occasional malaria attacks, the soldiers continued to rape me. Sometimes, when the colonel was away, Captain Tanaka kept me in his room and hung up the curtain in my room so I could rest. When they saw the curtain up, the soldiers thought I was away. Captain Tanaka told them that I was in the hospital because I was sick. The captain did not rape or touch me while I was in his office.

One late morning, Tanaka asked me to bring two cups of tea to his room. On my way there, I overheard him and the colonel talking.

By now, I could understand some Japanese although I could not speak it. I heard the two men say that they were planning to conduct a zoning operation in Pampang, our barrio, because many of the residents there were guerrillas. Our soldiers had captured guerrillas from there, and they were in the garrison downstairs, said the colonel.

Figure 6.10 Tied up, along with guerrilla captives, for torture.

At that point, I walked calmly into the room and put the two cups of tea on the table. As I was walking out, I heard the colonel say, "We will set fire to Pampang." I understood because he used the word *moyasu* which, I had learned from Tanaka, meant burn. I was crying in my heart. The first thought that came to my mind was my mother who lived there. Pampang was just six kilometers from the rice mill where I was held captive. How could I get word to my mother that the entire barrio would be burned?

I knew how cruel the Japanese Imperial Army could be. When they burned down a village, they had their machine guns ready to shoot at anybody fleeing the fire, especially if they found guerrillas there. Even rats and cats were killed.

Two o'clock came, and my daily or-deal with the soldiers began. That night I could not sleep. In the morning, as the sun rose, the soldiers went for their daily exercise. *"Miyo tokai kono sorakete!"* they shouted. When the routine was over, they shouted *"Banzai!"* three times.

I was in luck that day because the guards took us downstairs so we could have some sunshine. The seven of us went down to the open field where the soldiers had their exercises. The field fronted the street, but the Japanese had fenced it off with barbed wire so no one could escape. The three guards with us were laughing and joking. I walked close to the street and saw an old man pass by. His face looked familiar to me, and I knew that he lived in our barrio.

"Tonight your barrio will be burned," I whispered to him while the guards were not looking. "Get out of there." Then I quickly turned away, pretending there was nothing the matter. Later we were sent back to our rooms for our daily routine—cleaning, bathing, washing.

Figure 6.11 Beaten by the colonel.

At lunch I could hardly swallow my food. I was very tense. The soldiers lined up outside my room as usual. I finished at nine in the evening. While I was in my room resting, I noticed that the colonel and the captain were leaving the building with some soldiers. I heard their vehicles driving away. Some of the soldiers remained to guard us.

After more than an hour, I heard the colonel and Tanaka rushing up the stairs. The colonel grabbed me from my bed and slapped me hard. My eyes swelled and there was blood on my face. The colonel was very angry because when they reached Pampang, there was not a single soul there. He suspected that it was I who had frustrated their plans, as I was the only one who had heard them talking.

I was dragged downstairs to the garrison where the colonel beat me up, tied my hands with a rope and hung them on the wall. I forced my eyes open to see what was around me. I saw some guerrilla captives. They also had many bruises and, like me, their hands were tied up.

When daylight came, I was very thirsty, and my entire body was in pain from the torture that I had undergone. At noon, the colonel went down to the garrison to inspect the prisoners. He poured water on our faces. I welcomed every drop of water that reached my parched lips. My throat was dry, and I eagerly drank up the water.

Then suddenly I felt very cold. I knew that I was going to have another malaria attack. I was shivering, but my hands were still tied up. My whole body was shaking, and I wanted to lie down. I cried, "I want to die now." Then the high fever came, and I thought I could not remain standing for long. My head was aching and felt so heavy, I could barely hold it up.

Someone held up my chin. I forced my swollen eyes to open. I saw Captain Tanaka giving me a cup of tea. He held the cup to my lips, but suddenly the colonel came down shouting. He bumped my head against the corrugated iron wall of the rice mill. I passed out.

I was still unconscious when the guerrillas attacked the garrison. My mother would tell me later that the Huks assaulted the rice mill that night to free their imprisoned comrades. They found me there still chained, and they freed me as well. One guerrilla carried me with him as the Japanese soldiers pursued him. Unable to carry me any farther, the Huk dropped me in a shallow ditch on the roadside. Fortunately, it was a moonlit night, and Anna, my mother's cousin, lived nearby. She was up late preparing the *kamote* she was going to sell in the market the following day. The moon lit up the road fronting her house, and she saw me sprawled on the roadside. She informed my mother, who promptly came to get me.

The first thing I remembered when I regained consciousness was the colonel shouting and bumping my head because Captain Tanaka was giving me something to drink. I had difficulty talking, but the first thing I asked my mother was, "What happened to the six women, my companions in the garrison? Were they killed? Did they escape?" But my mother did not know.

It was January 1944. I had been held captive as a sex slave for nine months.

PAIN AND RECOVERY

I regained consciousness only two months after I was rescued from the garrison. I found myself in my mothers house. I wept when I saw my mother's face. I wanted to speak, but no words came from my mouth. I did not say a word for a long time.

My mother nursed me back to health, spoon-feeding me as if I were a baby. I could neither stand nor walk. I crawled like an infant. I could not focus my eyes well, and everything I saw was blurred.

I refused to show myself to anybody except my mother. I was always hiding in a corner of the room. Slowly, I began to remember everything that had happened to me. I could see clearly the faces of Captain Tanaka, the colonel, and the six women I was with. I cried and cried, and my mother tried to comfort me.

Every time I spoke, I began to drool, my saliva dripping from the corner of my mouth like a dog. My mother pitied me very much. I wept not only for my pain, but for hers. I tried to write so I could explain what had happened to me, but the pencil would drop from my fingers, and the words I wrote came out badly. For years, I had difficulty writing. I practiced hard to perfect my writing, but even now my pen sometimes slips, and the letters become garbled.

I stumbled when I walked, and for years afterward I would lose my balance. Sometimes I still got malaria attacks. My mother boiled some herbal medicine to help me heal.

Despite my speech difficulties, I managed to tell my mother all that had happened to me. My mother cried bitterly. She and I were very close, and I shared with her all my secrets.

One day, one of my mother's cousins came to visit. I kissed her hand to show my respect, but my saliva dripped on her hand. She looked at me with pity. "My dear niece, what kind of sickness do you have?" My mother explained that I was stricken with malaria and high fever, and that I was tortured by the soldiers. She never told them that I had been repeatedly raped.

"Maybe her brain was damaged," my aunt cried as she embraced and kissed me. I cried, too, and so did my mother. Then I went to my room, sobbing. I thought once more of the six women I was with and of the Japanese soldiers. Once again I regretted having passed the Japanese sentry the day I went out on a mission. But I had to accept my fate.

My mother kept me hidden at home for fear that if the Japanese Army found me, both of us would be killed. For years, I was constantly haunted by nightmares. I envied other girls my age who were always smiling and looked very happy, innocently enjoying the songs and the dances and the company of their friends, while I was hiding at home.

For a year, my mouth was hanging open, and my saliva was dripping down the side of my face. I had difficulty speaking. Even my hair started falling. The mere sight of men made me run and hide. I thought all men were oppressive like Japanese soldiers. I also felt unworthy because to my mind, I had become soiled and dirty from repeated rape.

On September 1,1944, my mother took me back to Pasay so I could see our family doctor. We traveled on the roof of the train because there were so many passengers. The doctor examined me as my mother narrated my ordeal. He said that I fell unconscious because of the blow to my head and the malaria fever. He told me I was lucky to have survived. "Just pray that Rosa will not lose her memory and her sanity," he told my mother. "Otherwise, she would become forgetful or worse, she might go mad."

When I heard these words from that doctors mouth, I vowed to do everything in my power so that I would not lose my sanity.

I was the center of jokes then because of my speech difficulty. My neighbors thought that I had gone mad. Even my own mother, who was the only one who knew my secrets, was beginning to think that I was crazy because I kept muttering to myself, "Why did I not escape? Because they might kill me."

I became afraid of people who I thought were against me and talking behind my back. I became ashamed of myself. I lost my self-confidence and self-respect. I felt like hiding from people all the time. I wanted to bury my head in the ground. I had to fight a constant struggle with myself to remain alive and to keep my sanity.

Then on September 21, 1944 there was an airfight. With my own eyes, I saw the planes firing at each other. By then we had run out of food. So in October we returned to Angeles on foot. There were many other people walking. It took us a week to get there.

The US and Allied forces landed in Leyte on October 22, 1944. We were thrilled with the the news that General MacArthur had fulfilled his promise to return. He came back, landing in Leyte with Allied soldiers, warships and hundreds of planes. The battles between Japanese and Allied soldiers were fierce and lasted for weeks. We were in Angeles by then. At night, we were woken by the sound of bombing. We ran to our air raid shelter to avoid the Allied bombardment.

On January 9,1945, General MacArthur made another landing, this time in Lingayen Gulf. My mother told me that somebody had given her the news. Air raids were now taking place almost every day and night. Sometimes my mother, my uncle Emil and I spent the entire day in the air raid shelter. In our area, the Japanese Imperial Army became even more strict and cruel. We heard that massacres were taking place everywhere.

Just before Christmas that year, my uncle Pedro visited us. He came with my father's permission. My mother was very happy to see him. He handed her an envelope full of Japanese money from Don Pepe. He said the landlord had asked my mother and me to always pray and to be careful.

Pedro was very sad to learn that I had been ill. He recounted that he had walked for three days because there were no more trains or cars to board. He decided not to return to where my father was staying.

The battles between the Japanese Imperial Army and the Allied forces were now taking place more and more often. One early morning, a Japanese soldier knocked on our door with his rifle. "*Tetsudai,*" he called. We understood that the word meant helper. The soldier took my two uncles and me, whom he mistook for a boy because most of my hair had fallen off, and I was dressed like a man. My mother could not do anything to stop him.

The soldiers put us in a truck with many other boys and girls. The truck proceeded to Fort Stotsenberg, passing through our barrio. We arrived in the camp after an hour. We were ordered to work there, loading boxes of food or ammunition inside a big tunnel.

They gave us lunch—a cup of rice and a piece of dried fish. But I could not swallow the food because I was very nervous and afraid, remembering my ordeal. In the afternoon, they loaded us into the truck again and took us home. We reached home at twilight. At that time, there were no lights. There was a blackout, and only the Japanese had electricity.

That night, we slept in our air raid shelter. We hid there, thinking we could evade the Japanese soldiers. But the next morning, the same soldier was there again, knocking on our air raid shelter. We could not resist, so we boarded the truck again.

But as we drove on, we encountered two US fighter planes in the middle of the road. The Japanese soldiers ordered us to remove our hats. The pilot of the American plane saw that we were Filipinos, so he let the truck pass. We expected him to shoot. The soldier who was with us already had his eyes closed, and his hands were covering his ears. The truck moved very slowly. My uncle pinched my hand, and he crawled quietly out of the truck. I crawled out, too, as did my other uncle. The truck drove away, and the soldiers did not see us escaping.

We walked through a ricefield and past tall grasses. We moved quietly until we reached our house. It was almost dark. Later, we decided to move to another house for safety.

The next morning, a man whose two sons had been in the truck with us asked my uncle where our companions were. Those people were never found. Later, one of those who had been there recounted that the Japanese soldiers killed everyone who had helped them load food and ammunition into the tunnel.

We woke up to the sound of gunfire in the early morning of January 26, 1945. Then at about seven o'clock, as my mother, my two uncles and I were eating a breakfast of boiled *kamote* and water, three Japanese Army soldiers barged into our house. One of the soldiers pointed his pistol at my uncles and held them captive in the room downstairs. The other one dragged my mother and me to the yard at the back of the house and tied our hands behind our backs.

We saw three more soldiers in the yard and witnessed them gunning down nine men at random. It was close to the end of the war, and the Japanese were on a retreat. They were getting desperate, so they were shooting people everywhere. Later we saw the men's corpses sprawled in the ricefield behind our house.

Figure 6.12 Japanese soldiers invade our house and hold us at gunpoint. They did not notice I was a girl because I wore boy's clothing and my hair had grown only half an inch since I became bald.

The soldiers were approaching us, and my mother and I knew we were the next to be shot. Suddenly two men with loads on their backs ran past us. The soldiers saw them and chased them, leaving my mother and me alone. We were praying the "Our Father" very loudly, our eyes looking up at the sky. Then I told my mother, "We must run away now." But my mother was reluctant to leave. "If the Japanese soldiers return, they will kill us," I insisted. "Maybe God is giving us a chance to escape from here."

So we ran and hid in the air raid shelter we had dug under our house. There, we untied each other's hands. After some time, my two uncles returned, and when we saw them, my mother and I cried. Thank God we were all safe.

My uncles related that the soldiers had taken them for questioning to their headquarters in the rice mill. There, a Japanese officer, a colonel, told them that if they wished to evacuate, they should not head north because American troops were already in Dagupan, Pangasinan. Miraculously, they were released.

I was scared. The colonel who had raped me was still around, I thought, and so were the soldiers. I wondered about Tanaka. Was he still there as well? My mother saw me shaking and embraced me. "Do not worry too much," she whispered.

After a while, we thought it was safe enough to leave the air raid shelter. As we were going out, we saw Anna, my mother's cousin, who lived only three houses away. She was calling out to my mother. "Julia, please help me," she said crying. She told us about her husband William, the American soldier she had married long before the war broke out. "I need your help. I want

Figure 6.13 We prayed very loudly, looking up at the sky.

to take William with me to evacuate to the forest. He might be killed if the Japanese soldiers see him here."

William, a former soldier stationed in Fort Stotsenberg, had retired from the US Army and set up his own business. He and Anna did not have children although they adopted some of Annas nephews and nieces. Soon after the war began, Anna hid William in the ceiling of their house. He had been there for three years. He was ill from the heat and the lack of exercise; he could barely walk or talk. No one except Anna knew where he was. At the start of the war, the Japanese had rounded up all the Americans and put them in prisons or concentration camps. William would have been tortured in one of those camps, too, if Anna had not hidden him.

As the months passed, things became increasingly difficult, and there was hardly anything to eat. Anna agreed to live with another man so she and William could survive. Her adopted children were married and could manage on their own. She smuggled food to her husband and kept him alive for three years.

Now, when it was no longer safe to remain in the village, she wanted our help to rescue him. My two uncles were not convinced. "We cannot be seen with William. The Japanese will kill us," they said. But we agreed to accompany Anna to her house. There we saw William crawling on the floor. He had jumped down from the ceiling.

"We cannot take him with us," my uncle said. "We'll all get killed." William tried to hold my mother and looked up at her with tears flowing from his eyes. My mother cried, and so did Anna and I. My two uncles decided to leave. But my mother was firm. " I will not leave William, I will stay here with him even if I get killed."

My uncles stopped and listened. "Maybe God saved me and Rosa from the soldiers who were about to kill both of us, so we can save Williams life," my mother said.

So my uncles made a hammock out of bed sheets and a thick bamboo pole. They put William on the hammock and covered him with pillows and kitchen utensils. We knew that we were all risking our lives. We left our village on foot, with my mother, Anna and me walking behind my two uncles carrying the hammock. We were nervous and in tears. We prayed the "Our Father" along the way.

At dusk, we passed a sentry. The Japanese soldiers halted us. One of them poked at the hammock with his bayonet. Luckily, he struck a pillow, and all the fluffy cotton inside it fell all around us. Irritated, the soldier let us go.

We walked away safe. Then my two uncles started running, carrying the hammock with them. We ran to catch up with them. It was getting dark. Along the way, the bamboo pole broke, and the five of us had to hold on to the four corners of the bed sheet, carrying poor William. We threw away the pillows and the other things to lighten our load.

When we finally reached the village where we were going to stay, we found many other evacuees there. When they saw William, they became angry. "You bring us a pest," they said. "If the Japanese find him, we might all be killed." All of them left us, even Annas adopted children who had arrived there before we did.

That night we hid. William crawled into an air raid shelter and stayed there with Anna. My mother, my two uncles and I hid in another shelter. The whole night we could not sleep because of the noise. We heard shots being fired, airplanes flying to and fro, even the crackle of houses burning. We knew that the Allied forces were driving the Japanese away.

In the morning, we ate raw *kamote*. We ventured out of the shelter which was very hot and full of mosquitoes. The village was deserted. We crawled on the ground until we reached a field of tall grass near a small river. We witnessed an air battle, and all around Japanese soldiers were burning houses and shooting people.

The allied forces reached Angeles, Pampanga, on January 27, 1945. It was a Saturday. Everyone was happy. People greeted the soldiers with a smile and a salute of "Victory Joe." Anna was very happy, too. She kissed my mother, my two uncles and me with tears of joy in her eyes.

People were returning to the village now. Annas adopted sons came, offering to take William out of the shelter. But he refused to even look at them. William crawled out of the shelter by himself and embraced my two uncles. He was in tears. He approached my mother and kissed her on the forehead. Some of the villagers who witnessed the scene were in tears themselves.

The American soldiers gave us boxes of C-rations. We were very hungry. When night fell, we moved around quietly, careful not to make any noise, lest we be the target of Japanese snipers. The Allied soldiers were sleeping all around us, and they expected that the Japanese would shoot at them. We decided to return to our own village the next day.

At about seven o'clock the following morning, my mother, my two uncles and I rode a carabao-drawn cart. We took Anna and William with us. We found a white sheet and made it fly like a banner on the cart. The road was full. People were going back to their homes.

We took Anna and William to their house and discovered that Japanese soldiers had been there. The meal Anna had cooked and left behind untouched before she left in a hurry had been eaten. We also saw two Japanese Army caps, a bayonet and a small Japanese flag. We knew instantly that if William had been left behind in that house, he would probably have been killed.

There were many American soldiers stationed in our village. Many of them visited William, who could not yet speak, so he communicated with his fingers. We found Allied soldiers in our own house, too. They gave us canned food and blankets. At night they slept outside, on hammocks covered with mosquito nets. I was still afraid of strangers then, so I hid in my room.

My two uncles worked as helpers with the Allied forces. They gave us some money and some food. My father was still in a distant town, and we had no idea what had happened to him. We received news that Manila had been liberated on February 5, 1945. Everyone was happy, it was like a feast.

I was happy, too, but I could not stop my tears. They were too late to save me from my ordeal, I thought. I was still crying in the middle of the night. My mother always came to comfort me. My hair, which had fallen off, had grown back, but it was still only half an inch long. I always covered my head with a big handkerchief so people would not see that I was bald. We had moved to Angeles from the barrio, so my mother and I could find work. We stayed in a house near the hospital where I had been held captive for three months.

At around this time, my father returned from the faraway town where he had spent most of the war years. My uncle Pedro went to see him in his big house. My father asked about my mother and me. Pedro told him that I wanted to see him. But he refused. "Not this time," he said, "because I have many things to do. Besides, my children know about Rosa now. They asked if I had a daughter with another woman. And I am troubled by their questions."

My father added, "Rosa is old enough now. She can live with her mother in whatever way they please." Pedro left, wondering about the meaning of those words.

I was sad when I heard what my father had said. I understood that he had to do what he felt was right. I knew he wanted to show his love and concern for me, but could not upset his family. My mother understood the situation, too. My father had, in effect, forsaken us. He felt that he had fulfilled his obligation to us. He gave me his name, and for years he supported not only me but also my mothers whole family. I did not expect to see him again.

We transferred to a house near the military camp in Angeles, where my mother and I could earn some money by doing the laundry for American and Filipino troops. We had no income anymore, and my mother also told me that we could no longer rely on my fathers support.

We washed the clothes with our hands. It was also my task to iron the uniforms. I would iron them with tears in my eyes because they reminded me of the Japanese soldiers who had ruined my future.

I was always sad. Even my relatives and neighbors noticed how lonely I was. I was not interested in talking to them. And I was always guarded, wondering how they would react if they knew what had happened to me. Some soldiers would come to our house to fetch their laundry. But they never saw me because I was always hiding.

One day my mother talked to me. "Rosa, I want for you to get married," she said. I told her I had no feelings toward men. I said I hated the idea of love. But my mother urged me, saying marriage could help me forget my ordeal.

"Love will develop in due course," my mother said. I do not like to be in love, I whispered to myself. Then I began to think and think. I realized my mothers advice was for my own good. I thought it might be good to have children who would be with me when I grew old. I was an only child and could rely on no one else's help and comfort. My mother said I might go mad if I did not stop recalling the past and murmuring to myself. It was true. I often muttered questions to myself. Why did I not try to escape? I kept asking myself. And I would answer, because they might kill me.

STUDY QUESTIONS

1. Why did the Japanese military create "comfort stations?"

2. Why do you think the "comfort women" were silent for so many years?

3. Why do you think the Japanese government is so reluctant to acknowledge some of the irrefutable truths of its past?

4. What can the international community do to hasten justice for the last remaining "comfort women?"

PART III
SLAVERY

AN INTRODUCTION TO

Equiano's Travels

A s an historical narrative, *Equiano's Travels* constitutes an excellent source for studying the 18th-century slave trade across three continents. Unlike most slaves, Olaudah Equiano (1745–1797) became literate, bought his freedom, authored a memoir, went on a book tour to promote abolition, and married a white Englishwoman, Susanna Cullen.[1] Yet these events, as unlikely as they were, resulted from hard work, merit, and ability—with, of course, a healthy dose of luck.

Equiano was born about 1745 in western Africa, where most people had never heard of Europeans. His home was located in modern-day Nigeria, but Africans during the trans-Atlantic slave trade identified themselves by their "nations," which were more city-states or kingdoms than modern nation-states. Instead of considering themselves African, inhabitants of Equiano's region would have called themselves Igbo (like him), Yoruba, Hausa, Fulani, Mande, Wolof, or Bambara.[2] Although their father was a village elder, Equiano and his sister experienced slavery in Africa. African slavery, however, was vastly different from its New World counterpart. In Africa, slaves were not obtained for capitalist pecuniary advantage; rather, slaves were kidnapped, war tribute, those in debt, or victims of demographic or humanitarian crises such as famine or drought. In the African context, moreover, slaves were incorporated kin, treated as family members, and might even have slaves of their own. Equiano would encounter a much harsher, more brutal form of slavery in the New World.

British trade in slaves exploded in alacrity and numbers in 1713, when Spain granted Britain the *asiento*, or the slave-trade monopoly in the Caribbean. It remains difficult to overemphasize the importance of the slave trade to the prosperity of the early British Empire. Lush profits earned from slaves

---

1   Susanna died in 1796 at the age of 36, a year before her husband. They left two daughters, four-year-old Anna Maria, who died within months of her father, and Joanna, aged two, who inherited her parents' estate at 21 in 1816. With the help of fellow abolitionist John Audley as executor, Joanna was entitled to £950 (some $100,000 today). She died in 1857 at the age of 62. Robert J. Allison ed. *The Interesting Narrative of the Life of Olaudah Equiano Written by Himself with Related Documents* 3rd ed. (Boston: Bedford/St. Martin's, 2016), 25.

2   Ibid.

Figure 7.1. Olaudah Equiano. Source: http://commons.wikimedia.org/wiki/File:Olaudah_Equiano_-_Project_Gutenberg_eText_15399.png.

and sugar spilled over into textiles, banking, insurance, shipping, and heavy industry. By the 18th century, an expansive network of slave supply had been established by Europeans and Africans. Upon arrival at the coastal "factories," which were really a combination of trading post and detention depot, slaves were examined by physicians, perhaps branded with a company logo, and marched to the ships for embarkation.

Equiano's African experiences with slavery, until he reached the ocean, had been linguistically and culturally recognizable. Sold to European slave traders by Africans, Equiano was trekked to the west coast, where he first espied the slavers and their white crewmen, whom he believed would eat him. He witnessed the despair of chained Africans, was himself beaten, and even confessed he was dumbfounded by the brutal manner in which whites treated each other. Race, at first, was the means by which he described all white people, until he humanized them.[3] Equiano described the Middle Passage, the forced migration of about ten million African slaves across the Atlantic Ocean during the 17th, 18th, and 19th centuries. He experienced firsthand the squalid conditions aboard the slave ship: sparse oxygen, water, food, and space combined with a cacophony of cries and the horrendous stenches of human waste and death. Men were shackled below decks with limited periods of open-air exercise (to mitigate muscle atrophy, which would affect future sales), while women were permitted to roam the deck as fair game for the crew. Most slavers packed their cargo like sardines in a tin, with little room and no concern for hygiene or privacy. Captains had to contend with high mortality rates and slave uprisings. After disembarking, the slaves were subject to the auction block and forced to come to grips with their status in a new society.

Upon arrival in the New World, Equiano, who was alternatively known by his masters as Michael, Jacob, and Gustavus Vassa, soon traveled to England, where he began to assimilate to European ways. He became fluent in English, learned to read, was baptized into the Protestant faith, and carried out a number of duties for his masters, from bookkeeping to hairdressing to piloting a ship safely into port. Equiano became something of an entrepreneur himself by buying goods and reselling them for a profit. One of his masters, in fact, a Quaker named Robert King, promised Equiano his freedom for the sum of 40 pounds. Amazed when he produced the sum, King ultimately kept his word, and drew up manumission papers granting Equiano his liberty.

A persistent question centers on the authenticity of the book's authorship. It is likely that Equiano's memoirs were edited because of multiple styles in the text. If he was 12 when he left Africa and was 44 when he penned the autobiography, then Equiano had 32 years to acquire enough proficiency in English to write the book. It had initially been published by subscription, through which buyers who committed

---

3   Marcus Rediker *The Slave Ship: A Human History* (New York: Penguin, 2007), 125-30.

themselves to copies actually funded its printing. In any event, the narrative was a best-seller in its day, with eight editions in Britain. John Wesley, the founder of Methodism, enjoyed the work so much he recommended it to the great abolitionist leader, William Wilberforce. Equiano traveled to Birmingham, Manchester, Nottingham, Sheffield, Belfast, Durham, Hull, and Bath between 1789 and 1793 to promote his book and speak out against the evils of the slave trade, earning a healthy sum.

His uniqueness and ubiquity (he traveled the Western world) renders his story invaluable to students of slavery because of its *sui generis* nature. One of the many questions that have arisen from a textual analysis of Equiano's writings is, what was his identity? Was he African? Was he European? Was he a hybrid of the two? The early-20th-century scholar W. E. B. Du Bois wrote about the double consciousness of a black person living simultaneously within and without white society. On the margins of society, Equiano was African by birth, but British by assimilation and choice. Although he took a certain pride in and remained ever mindful of his African roots, he adopted the dress and cultural habits, social mores and values, as well as capitalist and Protestant ideology from Britain.

Equiano's Travels

By Olaudah Equiano

INTERESTING NARRATIVE OF THE LIFE OF OLAUDAH EQUIANO, OR GUSTAVUS VASSA, THE AFRICAN. *WRITTEN BY HIMSELF.*

CHAP. II

The author's birth and parentage—His being kidnapped with his sister—Their separation—Surprise at meeting again—Are finally separated—Account of the different places and incidents the author met with till his arrival on the coast—The effect the sight of a slave ship had on him—He sails for the West Indies—Horrors of a slave ship—Arrives at Barbadoes, where the cargo is sold and dispersed.

I hope the reader will not think I have trespassed on his patience in introducing myself to him with some account of the manners and customs of my country. They had been implanted in me with great care, and made an impression on my mind, which time could not erase, and which all the adversity and variety of fortune I have since experienced served only to rivet and record; for, whether the love of one's country be real or imaginary, or a lesson of reason, or an instinct of nature, I still look back with pleasure on the first scenes of my life, though that pleasure has been for the most part mingled with sorrow.

I have already acquainted the reader with the time and place of my birth. My father, besides many slaves, had a numerous family, of which seven lived to grow up, including myself and a sister, who was the only daughter. As I was the youngest of the sons, I became, of course, the greatest favourite with my mother, and was always with her; and she used to take particular pains to form my mind. I was trained up from my earliest years in the art of war; my daily exercise was shooting and throwing javelins; and my mother adorned me with emblems, after the manner of our greatest warriors. In this way I grew up till I was turned the age of eleven, when an end was put to my happiness in the following manner:—Generally when the grown people in the neighbourhood were gone far in the fields to labour, the children assembled together in some of the neighbours' premises to play; and commonly some of us used to get up a tree to

Olaudah Equiano, "Selections," Interesting Narrative of the Life of Olaudah Equiano, or Gustavus Vassa, the African, Written by Himself, 1789.

look out for any assailant, or kidnapper, that might come upon us; for they sometimes took those opportunities of our parents' absence to attack and carry off as many as they could seize. One day, as I was watching at the top of a tree in our yard, I saw one of those people come into the yard of our next neighbour but one, to kidnap, there being many stout young people in it. Immediately on this I gave the alarm of the rogue, and he was surrounded by the stoutest of them, who entangled him with cords, so that he could not escape till some of the grown people came and secured him. But alas! ere long it was my fate to be thus attacked, and to be carried off, when none of the grown people were nigh. One day, when all our people were gone out to their works as usual, and only I and my dear sister were left to mind the house, two men and a woman got over our walls, and in a moment seized us both, and, without giving us time to cry out, or make resistance, they stopped our mouths, and ran off with us into the nearest wood. Here they tied our hands, and continued to carry us as far as they could, till night came on, when we reached a small house, where the robbers halted for refreshment, and spent the night. We were then unbound, but were unable to take any food; and, being quite overpowered by fatigue and grief, our only relief was some sleep, which allayed our misfortune for a short time. The next morning we left the house, and continued travelling all the day. For a long time we had kept the woods, but at last we came into a road which I believed I knew. I had now some hopes of being delivered; for we had advanced but a little way before I discovered some people at a distance, on which I began to cry out for their assistance: but my cries had no other effect than to make them tie me faster and stop my mouth, and then they put me into a large sack. They also stopped my sister's mouth, and tied her hands; and in this manner we proceeded till we were out of the sight of these people. When we went to rest the following night they offered us some victuals; but we refused it; and the only comfort we had was in being in one another's arms all that night, and bathing each other with our tears. But alas! we were soon deprived of even the small comfort of weeping together. The next day proved a day of greater sorrow than I had yet experienced; for my sister and I were then separated, while we lay clasped in each other's arms. It was in vain that we besought them not to part us; she was torn from me, and immediately carried away, while I was left in a state of distraction not to be described. I cried and grieved continually; and for several days I did not eat any thing but what they forced into my mouth. At length, after many days travelling, during which I had often changed masters, I got into the hands of a chieftain, in a very pleasant country. This man had two wives and some children, and they all used me extremely well, and did all they could to comfort me; particularly the first wife, who was something like my mother. Although I was a great many days journey from my father's house, yet these people spoke exactly the same language with us. This first master of mine, as I may call him, was a smith, and my principal employment was working his bellows, which were the same kind as I had seen in my vicinity. They were in some respects not unlike the stoves here in gentlemen's kitchens; and were covered over with leather; and in the middle of that leather a stick was fixed, and a person stood up, and worked it, in the same manner as is done to pump water out of a cask with a hand pump. I believe it was gold he worked, for it was of a lovely bright yellow colour, and was worn by the women on their wrists and ancles. I was there I suppose about a month, and they at last used to trust me some little distance from the house. This liberty I used in embracing every opportunity to inquire the way to my own home: and I also sometimes, for the same purpose, went with the maidens, in the cool of the evenings, to bring pitchers of water from the springs for the use of the house. I had also remarked where the sun rose in the morning, and set in the evening, as I had travelled along; and I had observed that my father's house was towards the rising of the sun. I therefore determined to seize the first opportunity of making my escape, and to shape my course for that quarter; for I was quite oppressed and weighed down by grief after my mother and friends; and my love of liberty, ever great, was strengthened by the mortifying circumstance of not daring to eat with the free-born children, although I was mostly their companion. While I was projecting my escape, one day an unlucky event happened, which quite disconcerted my plan, and put an end to my hopes. I used to be sometimes employed in assisting an elderly woman slave to cook and take care of the poultry; and one morning, while I was feeding some chickens, I happened to toss a small pebble at one of them, which hit it on the middle and directly killed it. The old slave, having soon after missed the chicken, inquired after it; and on my relating the accident (for I told her the truth, because my mother would never suffer me to tell a lie) she flew into a violent passion, threatened that I should suffer for it; and, my master being out, she immediately went and told her mistress what I had done. This alarmed me very much, and I expected an instant flogging, which to me was uncommonly dreadful; for I had seldom been beaten at home. I therefore resolved to fly; and accordingly I ran into a thicket that was hard by, and hid myself in the bushes. Soon afterwards my mistress and the slave returned, and, not seeing me, they searched all the house, but not finding me, and I not making answer when they called to me, they thought I had run away, and the whole neighbourhood was raised in the pursuit of me. In that part of the country (as in ours) the houses and villages were skirted with woods, or shrubberies, and the bushes were so thick that a man could readily conceal himself in them, so as to elude the strictest search. The neighbours continued the whole day looking for me, and several times many of them came within a few yards of the place where I lay hid. I then gave myself up for lost entirely, and expected every moment, when I heard a rustling among the trees, to be found out, and punished by my master: but they never discovered me, though they were often so near that I even heard their conjectures as they were looking about for me; and I now learned from them, that any attempt to return home would be hopeless. Most of them supposed I had fled towards home; but the distance was so great, and the way so intricate, that they thought I could never reach it, and that I should be lost in the woods. When I heard this I was seized with a violent panic, and abandoned myself to despair. Night too began to approach, and aggravated all my fears. I had before entertained hopes of getting home, and I had determined when it should be dark to make the attempt; but I was now convinced it was fruitless, and I began to consider that, if possibly I could escape all other animals, I could not those of the human kind; and that, not knowing the way, I must perish in the woods. Thus was I like the hunted deer:

—"Ev'ry leaf and ev'ry whisp'ring breathConvey'd a foe, and ev'ry foe a death."

I heard frequent rustlings among the leaves; and being pretty sure they were snakes I expected every instant to be stung by them. This increased my anguish, and the horror of my situation became now quite insupportable. I at length quitted the thicket, very faint and hungry, for I had not eaten or drank any thing all the day; and crept to my master's kitchen, from whence I set out at first, and which was an open shed, and laid myself down in the ashes with an anxious wish for death to relieve me from all my pains. I was scarcely awake in the morning when the old woman slave, who was the first up, came to light the fire, and saw me in the fire place. She was very much surprised to see me, and could scarcely believe her own eyes. She now promised to intercede for me, and went for her master, who soon after came, and, having slightly reprimanded me, ordered me to be taken care of, and not to be ill-treated.

Soon after this my master's only daughter, and child by his first wife, sickened and died, which affected him so much that for some time he was almost frantic, and really would have killed himself, had he not been watched and prevented. However, in a small time afterwards he recovered, and I was again sold. I was now carried to the left of the sun's rising, through many different countries, and a number of large woods. The people I was sold to used to carry me very often, when I was tired, either on their shoulders or on their backs. I saw many convenient well-built sheds along the roads, at proper distances, to accommodate the merchants and travellers, who lay in those buildings along with their wives, who often accompany them; and they always go well armed.

From the time I left my own nation I always found somebody that understood me till I came to the sea coast. The languages of different nations did not totally differ, nor were they so copious as those of the Europeans, particularly the English. They were therefore easily learned; and, while I was journeying thus through Africa, I acquired two or three different tongues. In this manner I had been travelling for a considerable time, when one evening, to my great surprise, whom should I see brought to the house where I was but my dear sister! As soon as she saw me she gave a loud shriek, and ran into my arms—I was quite overpowered: neither of us could speak; but, for a considerable time, clung to each other in mutual embraces, unable to do any thing but weep. Our meeting affected all who saw us; and indeed I must acknowledge, in honour of those sable destroyers of human rights, that I never met with any ill treatment, or saw any offered to their slaves, except tying them, when necessary, to keep them from running away. When these people knew we were brother and sister they indulged us together; and the man, to whom I supposed we belonged, lay with us, he in the middle, while she and I held one another by the hands across his breast all night; and thus for a while we forgot our misfortunes in the joy of being together: but even this small comfort was soon to have an end; for scarcely had the fatal morning appeared, when she was again torn from me for ever! I was now more miserable, if possible, than before. The small relief which her presence gave me from pain was gone, and the wretchedness of my situation was redoubled by my anxiety after her fate, and my apprehensions lest her sufferings should be greater than mine, when I could not be with her to alleviate them. Yes, thou dear partner of all my childish sports! thou sharer of my joys and sorrows! happy should I have ever esteemed myself to encounter every misery for you, and to procure your freedom by the sacrifice of my own. Though you were early forced from my arms, your image has been always rivetted in my heart, from which neither *time nor fortune* have been able to remove it; so that, while the thoughts of your sufferings have damped my prosperity, they have mingled with adversity and increased its bitterness. To that Heaven which protects the weak from the strong, I commit the care of your innocence and virtues, if they have not already received their full reward, and if your youth and delicacy have not long since fallen victims to the violence of the African trader, the pestilential stench of a Guinea ship, the seasoning in the European colonies, or the lash and lust of a brutal and unrelenting overseer.

I did not long remain after my sister. I was again sold, and carried through a number of places, till, after travelling a considerable time, I came to a town called Tinmah, in the most beautiful country I have yet seen in Africa. It was extremely rich, and there were many rivulets which flowed through it, and supplied a large pond in the centre of the town, where the people washed. Here I first saw and tasted cocoa-nuts, which I thought superior to any nuts I had ever tasted before; and the trees, which were loaded, were also interspersed amongst the houses, which had commodious shades adjoining, and were in the same manner as ours, the insides being neatly plastered and whitewashed. Here I also saw and tasted for the first time sugar-cane. Their money consisted of little white shells, the size of the finger nail. I was sold here for one hundred and seventy-two of them by a merchant who lived and brought me there. I had been about two or three days at his house, when a wealthy widow, a neighbour of his, came there one evening, and brought with her an only son, a young gentleman about my own age and size. Here they saw me; and, having taken a fancy to me, I was bought of the merchant, and went home with them. Her house and premises were situated close to one of those rivulets I have mentioned, and were the finest I ever saw in Africa: they were very extensive, and she had a number of slaves to attend her. The next day I was washed and perfumed, and when meal-time came I was led into the presence of my mistress, and ate and drank before her with her son. This filled me with astonishment; and I could scarce help expressing my surprise that the young gentleman should suffer me, who was bound, to eat with him who was free; and not only so, but that he would not at any time either eat or drink till I had taken first, because I was the eldest, which was agreeable to our custom. Indeed every thing here, and all their treatment of me, made me forget that I was a slave. The language of these people resembled ours so nearly, that we understood each other perfectly. They had also the very same customs as we. There were likewise slaves daily to attend us, while my young master and I with other boys sported with our darts and bows and arrows, as I had been used to do at home. In this resemblance to my former happy state I passed about two months; and I now began to think I was to be adopted into the family, and was beginning to be reconciled to my situation, and to forget by degrees my misfortunes, when all at once the delusion vanished; for, without the least previous knowledge, one morning early, while my dear master and companion was still asleep, I was wakened out of my reverie to fresh sorrow, and hurried away even amongst the uncircumcised.

Thus, at the very moment I dreamed of the greatest happiness, I found myself most miserable; and it seemed as if fortune wished to give me this taste of joy, only to render the reverse more poignant. The change I now experienced was as painful as it was sudden and unexpected. It was a change indeed from a state of bliss to a scene which is inexpressible by me, as it discovered to me an element I had never before beheld, and till then had no idea of, and wherein such instances of hardship and cruelty continually occurred as I can never reflect on but with horror.

All the nations and people I had hitherto passed through resembled our own in their manners, customs, and language: but I came at length to a country, the inhabitants of which differed from us in all those particulars. I was very much struck with this difference, especially when I came among a people who did not circumcise, and ate without washing their hands. They cooked also in iron pots, and had European cutlasses and cross bows, which were unknown to us, and fought with their fists amongst themselves. Their women were not so modest as ours, for they ate, and drank, and slept, with their men. But, above all, I was amazed to see no sacrifices or offerings among them. In some of those places the people ornamented themselves with scars, and likewise filed their teeth very sharp. They wanted sometimes to ornament me in the same manner, but I would not suffer them; hoping that I might some time be among a people who did not thus disfigure themselves, as I thought they did. At last I came to the banks of a large river, which was covered with canoes, in which the people appeared to live with their household utensils and provisions of all kinds. I was beyond measure astonished at this, as I had never before seen any water larger than a pond or a rivulet: and my surprise was mingled with no small fear when I was put into one of these canoes, and we began to paddle and move along the river. We continued going on thus till night; and when we came to land, and made fires on the banks, each family by themselves, some dragged their canoes on shore, others stayed and cooked in theirs, and laid in them all night. Those on the land had mats, of which they made tents, some in the shape of little houses: in these we slept; and after the morning meal we embarked again and proceeded as before. I was often very much astonished to see some of the women, as well as the men, jump into the water, dive to the bottom, come up again, and swim about. Thus I continued to travel, sometimes by land, sometimes by water, through different countries and various nations, till, at the end of six or seven months after I had been kidnapped, I arrived at the sea coast. It would be tedious and uninteresting to relate all the incidents which befell me during this journey, and which I have not yet forgotten; of the various hands

I passed through, and the manners and customs of all the different people among whom I lived: I shall therefore only observe, that in all the places where I was the soil was exceedingly rich; the pomkins, eadas, plantains, yams, &c. &c. were in great abundance, and of incredible size. There were also vast quantities of different gums, though not used for any purpose; and every where a great deal of tobacco. The cotton even grew quite wild; and there was plenty of redwood. I saw no mechanics whatever in all the way, except such as I have mentioned. The chief employment in all these countries was agriculture, and both the males and females, as with us, were brought up to it, and trained in the arts of war.

The first object which saluted my eyes when I arrived on the coast was the sea, and a slave ship, which was then riding at anchor, and waiting for its cargo. These filled me with astonishment, which was soon converted into terror when I was carried on board. I was immediately handled and tossed up to see if I were sound by some of the crew; and I was now persuaded that I had gotten into a world of bad spirits, and that they were going to kill me. Their complexions too differing so much from ours, their long hair, and the language they spoke, (which was very different from any I had ever heard) united to confirm me in this belief. Indeed such were the horrors of my views and fears at the moment, that, if ten thousand worlds had been my own, I would have freely parted with them all to have exchanged my condition with that of the meanest slave in my own country. When I looked round the ship too and saw a large furnace or copper boiling, and a multitude of black people of every description chained together, every one of their countenances expressing dejection and sorrow, I no longer doubted of my fate; and, quite overpowered with horror and anguish, I fell motionless on the deck and fainted. When I recovered a little I found some black people about me, who I believed were some of those who brought me on board, and had been receiving their pay; they talked to me in order to cheer me, but all in vain. I asked them if we were not to be eaten by those white men with horrible looks, red faces, and loose hair. They told me I was not; and one of the crew brought me a small portion of spirituous liquor in a wine glass; but, being afraid of him, I would not take it out of his hand. One of the blacks therefore took it from him and gave it to me, and I took a little down my palate, which, instead of reviving me, as they thought it would, threw me into the greatest consternation at the strange feeling it produced, having never tasted any such liquor before. Soon after this the blacks who brought me on board went off, and left me abandoned to despair. I now saw myself deprived of all chance of returning to my native country, or even the least glimpse of hope of gaining the shore, which I now considered as friendly; and I even wished for my former slavery in preference to my present situation, which was filled with horrors of every kind, still heightened by my ignorance of what I was to undergo. I was not long suffered to indulge my grief; I was soon put down under the decks, and there I received such a salutation in my nostrils as I had never experienced in my life: so that, with the loathsomeness of the stench, and crying together, I became so sick and low that I was not able to eat, nor had I the least desire to taste any thing. I now wished for the last friend, death, to relieve me; but soon, to my grief, two of the white men offered me eatables; and, on my refusing to eat, one of them held me fast by the hands, and laid me across I think the windlass, and tied my feet, while the other flogged me severely. I had never experienced any thing of this kind before; and although, not being used to the water, I naturally feared that element the first time I saw it, yet nevertheless, could I have got over the nettings, I would have jumped over the side, but I could not; and, besides, the crew used to watch us very closely who were not chained down to the decks, lest we should leap into the water: and I have seen some of these poor African prisoners most severely cut for attempting to do so, and hourly whipped for not eating. This indeed was often the case with myself. In a little time after, amongst the poor chained men, I found some of my own nation, which in a small degree gave ease to my mind. I inquired of these what was to be done with us; they gave me to understand we were to be carried to these white people's country to work for them. I then was a little revived, and thought, if it were no worse than working, my situation was not so desperate: but still I feared I should be put to death, the white people looked and acted, as I thought, in so savage a manner; for I had never seen among any people such instances of brutal cruelty; and this not only shewn towards us blacks, but also to some of the whites themselves. One white man in particular I saw, when we were permitted to be on deck, flogged so unmercifully with a large rope near the foremast, that he died in consequence of it; and they tossed him over the side as they would have done a brute. This made me fear these people the more; and I expected nothing less than to be treated in the same manner. I could not help expressing my fears and apprehensions to some of my countrymen: I asked them if these people had no country, but lived in this hollow place (the ship): they told me they did not, but came from a distant one. 'Then,' said I, 'how comes it in all our country we never heard of them?' They told me because they lived so very far off. I then asked where were their women? had they any like themselves? I was told they had: 'and why,' said I,'do we not see them?' they answered, because they were left behind. I asked how the vessel could go? they told me they could not tell; but that there were cloths put upon the masts by the help of the ropes I saw, and then the vessel went on; and the white men had some spell or magic they put in the water when they liked in order to stop the vessel. I was exceedingly amazed at this account, and really thought they were spirits. I therefore wished much to be from amongst them, for I expected they would sacrifice me: but my wishes were vain; for we were so quartered that it was impossible for any of us to make our escape. While we stayed on the coast I was mostly on deck; and one day, to my great astonishment, I saw one of these vessels coming in with the sails up. As soon as the whites saw it, they gave a great shout, at which we were amazed; and the more so as the vessel appeared larger by approaching nearer. At last she came to an anchor in my sight, and when the anchor was let go I and my countrymen who saw it were lost in astonishment to observe the vessel stop; and were not convinced it was done by magic. Soon after this the other ship got her boats out, and they came on board of us, and the people of both ships seemed very glad to see each other. Several of the strangers also shook hands with us black people, and made motions with their hands, signifying I suppose we were to go to their country; but we did not understand them. At last, when the ship we were in had got in all her cargo, they made ready with many fearful noises, and we were all put under deck, so that we could not see how they managed the vessel. But this disappointment was the least of my sorrow. The stench of the hold while we were on the coast was so intolerably loathsome, that it was dangerous to remain there for any time, and some of us had been permitted to stay on the deck for the fresh air; but now that the whole ship's cargo were confined together, it became absolutely pestilential. The closeness of the place, and the heat of the climate, added to the number in the ship, which was so crowded that each had scarcely room to turn himself, almost suffocated us. This produced copious perspirations, so that the air soon became unfit for respiration, from a variety of loathsome smells, and brought on a sickness among the slaves, of which many died, thus falling victims to the improvident avarice, as I may call it, of their purchasers. This wretched situation was again aggravated by the galling of the chains, now become insupportable; and the filth of the necessary tubs, into which the children often fell, and were almost suffocated. The shrieks of the women, and the groans of the dying, rendered the whole a scene of horror almost inconceivable. Happily perhaps for myself I was soon reduced so low here that it was thought necessary to keep me almost always on deck; and from my extreme youth I was not put in fetters. In this situation I expected every hour to share the fate of my companions, some of whom were almost daily brought upon deck at the point of death, which I began to hope would soon put an end to my miseries. Often did I think many of the inhabitants of the deep much more happy than myself. I envied them the freedom they enjoyed, and as often wished I could change my condition for theirs. Every circumstance I met with served only to render my state more painful, and heighten my apprehensions, and my opinion of the cruelty of the whites. One day they had taken a number of fishes; and when they had killed and satisfied themselves with as many as they thought fit, to our astonishment who were on the deck, rather than give any of them to us to eat as we expected, they tossed the remaining fish into the sea again, although we begged and prayed for some as well as we could, but in vain; and some of my countrymen, being pressed by hunger, took an opportunity, when they thought no one saw them, of trying to get a little privately; but they were discovered, and the attempt procured them some very severe floggings. One day, when we had a smooth sea and moderate wind, two of my wearied countrymen who were chained together (I was near them at the time), preferring death to such a life of misery, somehow made through the nettings and jumped into the sea: immediately another quite dejected fellow, who, on account of his illness, was suffered to be out of irons, also followed their example; and I believe many more would very soon have done the same if they had not been prevented by the ship's crew, who were instantly alarmed. Those of us that were the most active were in a moment put down under the deck, and there was such a noise and confusion amongst the people of the ship as I never heard before, to stop her, and get the boat out to go after the slaves. However two of the wretches were drowned, but they got the other, and afterwards flogged him unmercifully for thus attempting to prefer death to slavery. In this manner we continued to undergo more hardships than I can now relate, hardships which are inseparable from this accursed trade. Many a time we were near suffocation from the want of fresh air, which we were often without for whole days together. This, and the stench of the necessary tubs, carried off many. During our passage I first saw flying fishes, which surprised me very much: they used frequently to fly across the ship, and many of them fell on the deck. I also now first saw the use of the quadrant; I had often with astonishment seen the mariners make observations with it, and I could not think what it meant. They at last took notice of my surprise; and one of them, willing to increase it, as well as to gratify my curiosity, made me one day look through it. The clouds appeared to me to be land, which disappeared as they passed along. This heightened my wonder; and I was now more persuaded than ever that I was in another world, and that every thing about me was magic. At last we came in sight of the island of Barbadoes, at which the whites on board gave a great shout, and made many signs of joy to us. We did not know what to think of this; but as the vessel drew nearer we plainly saw the harbour, and other ships of different kinds and sizes; and we soon anchored amongst them off Bridge Town. Many merchants and planters now came on board, though it was in the evening. They put us in separate parcels, and examined us attentively. They also made us jump, and pointed to the land, signifying we were to go there. We thought by this we should be eaten by these ugly men, as they appeared to us; and, when soon after we were all put down under the deck again, there was much dread and trembling among us, and nothing but bitter cries to be heard all the night from these apprehensions, insomuch that at last the white people got some old slaves from the land to pacify us. They told us we were not to be eaten, but to work, and were soon to go on land, where we should see many of our country people. This report eased us much; and sure enough, soon after we were landed, there came to us Africans of all languages. We were conducted immediately to the merchant's yard, where we were all pent up together like so many sheep in a fold, without regard to sex or age. As every object was new to me every thing I saw filled me with surprise. What struck me first was that the houses were built with stories, and in every other respect different from those in Africa: but I was still more astonished on seeing people on horseback. I did not know what this could mean; and indeed I thought these people were full of nothing but magical arts. While I was in this astonishment one of my fellow prisoners spoke to a countryman of his about the horses, who said they were the same kind they had in their country. I understood them, though they were from a distant part of Africa, and I thought it odd I had not seen any horses there; but afterwards, when I came to converse with different Africans, I found they had many horses amongst them, and much larger than those I then saw. We were not many days in the merchant's custody before we were sold after their usual manner, which is this:—On a signal given, (as the beat of a drum) the buyers rush at once into the yard where the slaves are confined, and make choice of that parcel they like best. The noise and clamour with which this is attended, and the eagerness visible in the countenances of the buyers, serve not a little to increase the apprehensions of the terrified Africans, who may well be supposed to consider them as the ministers of that destruction to which they think themselves devoted. In this manner, without scruple, are relations and friends separated, most of them never to see each other again. I remember in the vessel in which I was brought over, in the men's apartment, there were several brothers, who, in the sale, were sold in different lots; and it was very moving on this occasion to see and hear their cries at parting. O, ye nominal Christians! might not an African ask you, learned you this from your God, who says unto you, Do unto all men as you would men should do unto you? Is it not enough that we are torn from our country and friends to toil for your luxury and lust of gain? Must every tender feeling be likewise sacrificed to your avarice? Are the dearest friends and relations, now rendered more dear by their separation from their kindred, still to be parted from each other, and thus prevented from cheering the gloom of slavery with the small comfort of being together and mingling their sufferings and sorrows? Why are parents to lose their children, brothers their sisters, or husbands their wives? Surely this is a new refinement in cruelty, which, while it has no advantage to atone for it, thus aggravates distress, and adds fresh horrors even to the wretchedness of slavery.

CHAP. III

The author is carried to Virginia—His distress—Surprise at seeing a picture and a watch—Is bought by Captain Pascal, and sets out for England—His terror during the voyage—Arrives in England—His wonder at a fall of snow—Is sent to Guernsey, and in some time goes on board a ship of war with his master—Some account of the expedition against Louisbourg under the command of Admiral Boscawen, in 1758.

I now totally lost the small remains of comfort I had enjoyed in conversing with my countrymen; the women too, who used to wash and take care of me, were all gone different ways, and I never saw one of them afterwards.

I stayed in this island for a few days; I believe it could not be above a fortnight; when I and some few more slaves, that were not saleable amongst the rest, from very much fretting, were shipped off in a sloop for North America. On the passage we were better treated than when we were coming from Africa, and we had plenty of rice and fat pork. We were landed up a river a good way from the sea, about Virginia county, where we saw few or none of our native Africans, and not one soul who could talk to me. I was a few weeks weeding grass, and gathering stones in a plantation; and at last all my companions were distributed different ways, and only myself was left. I was now exceedingly miserable, and thought myself worse off than any of the rest of my companions; for they could talk to each other, but I had no person to speak to that I could understand. In this state I was constantly grieving and pining, and wishing for death rather than any thing else. While I was in this plantation the gentleman, to whom I suppose the estate belonged, being unwell, I was one day sent for to his dwelling house to fan him; when I came into the room where he was I was very much affrighted at some things I saw, and the more so as I had seen a black woman slave as I came through the house, who was cooking the dinner, and the poor creature was cruelly loaded with various kinds of iron machines; she had one particularly on her head, which locked her mouth so fast that she could scarcely speak; and could not eat nor drink. I was much astonished and shocked at this contrivance, which I afterwards learned was called the iron muzzle. Soon after I had a fan put into my hand, to fan the gentleman while he slept; and so I did indeed with great fear. While he was fast asleep I indulged myself a great deal in looking about the room, which to me appeared very fine and curious. The first object that engaged my attention was a watch which hung on the chimney, and was going. I was quite surprised at the noise it made, and was afraid it would tell the gentleman any thing I might do amiss: and when I immediately after observed a picture hanging in the room, which appeared constantly to look at me, I was still more affrighted, having never seen such things as these before. At one time I thought it was something relative to magic; and not seeing it move I thought it might be some way the whites had to keep their great men when they died, and offer them libation as we used to do to our friendly spirits. In this state of anxiety I remained till my master awoke, when I was dismissed out of the room, to my no small satisfaction and relief; for I thought that these people were all made up of wonders. In this place I was called Jacob; but on board the African snow I was called Michael. I had been some time in this miserable, forlorn, and much dejected state, without having any one to talk to, which made my life a burden, when the kind and unknown hand of the Creator (who in very deed leads the blind in a way they know not) now began to appear, to my comfort; for one day the captain of a merchant ship, called the Industrious Bee, came on some business to my master's house. This gentleman, whose name was Michael Henry Pascal, was a lieutenant in the royal navy, but now commanded this trading ship, which was somewhere in the confines of the county many miles off. While he was at my master's house it happened that he saw me, and liked me so well that he made a purchase of me. I think I have often heard him say he gave thirty or forty pounds sterling for me; but I do not now remember which. However, he meant me for a present to some of his friends in England: and I was sent accordingly from the house of my then master, one Mr. Campbell, to the place where the ship lay; I was conducted on horseback by an elderly black man, (a mode of travelling which appeared very odd to me). When I arrived I was carried on board a fine large ship, loaded with tobacco, &c. and just ready to sail for England. I now thought my condition much mended; I had sails to lie on, and plenty of good victuals to eat; and every body on board used me very kindly, quite contrary to what I had seen of any white people before; I therefore began to think that they were not all of the same disposition. A few days after I was on board we sailed for England. I was still at a loss to conjecture my destiny. By this time, however, I could smatter a little imperfect English; and I wanted to know as well as I could where we were going. Some of the people of the ship used to tell me they were going to carry me back to my own country, and this made me very happy. I was quite rejoiced at the sound of going back; and thought if I should get home what wonders I should have to tell. But I was reserved for another fate, and was soon undeceived when we came within sight of the English coast. While I was on board this ship, my captain and master named me *Gustavus Vassa*. I at that time began to understand him a little, and refused to be called so, and told him as well as I could that I would be called Jacob; but he said I should not, and still called me Gustavus; and when I refused to answer to my new name, which at first I did, it gained me many a cuff; so at length I submitted, and was obliged to bear the present name, by which I have been known ever since. The ship had a very long passage; and on that account we had very short allowance of provisions. Towards the last we had only one pound and a half of bread per week, and about the same quantity of meat, and one quart of water a-day. We spoke with only one vessel the whole time we were at sea, and but once we caught a few fishes. In our extremities the captain and people told me in jest they would kill and eat me; but I thought them in earnest, and was depressed beyond measure, expecting every moment to be my last. While I was in this situation one evening they caught, with a good deal of trouble, a large shark, and got it on board. This gladdened my poor heart exceedingly, as I thought it would serve the people to eat instead of their eating me; but very soon, to my astonishment, they cut off a small part of the tail, and tossed the rest over the side. This renewed my consternation; and I did not know what to think of these white people, though I very much feared they would kill and eat me. There was on board the ship a young lad who had never been at sea before, about four or five years older than myself: his name was Richard Baker. He was a native of America, had received an excellent education, and was of a most amiable temper. Soon after I went on board he shewed me a great deal of partiality and attention, and in return I grew extremely fond of him. We at length became inseparable; and, for the space of two years, he was of very great use to me, and was my constant companion and instructor. Although this dear youth had many slaves of his own, yet he and I have gone through many sufferings together on shipboard; and we have many nights lain in each other's bosoms when we were in great distress. Thus such a friendship was cemented between us as we cherished till his death, which, to my very great sorrow, happened in the year 1759, when he was up the Archipelago, on board his majesty's ship the Preston: an event which I have never ceased to regret, as I lost at once a kind interpreter, an agreeable companion, and a faithful friend; who, at the age of fifteen, discovered a mind superior to prejudice; and who was not ashamed to notice, to associate with, and to be the friend and instructor of one who was ignorant, a stranger, of a different complexion, and a slave! My master had lodged in his mother's house in America: he respected him very much, and made him always eat with him in the cabin. He used often to tell him jocularly that he would kill me to eat. Sometimes he would say to me—the black people were not good to eat, and would ask me if we did not eat people in my country. I said, No: then he said he would kill Dick (as he always called him) first, and afterwards me. Though this hearing relieved my mind a little as to myself, I was alarmed for Dick and whenever he was called I used to be very much afraid he was to be killed; and I would peep and watch to see if they were going to kill him: nor was I free from this consternation till we made the land. One night we lost a man overboard; and the cries and noise were so great and confused, in stopping the ship, that I, who did not know what was the matter, began, as usual, to be very much afraid, and to think they were going to make an offering with me, and perform some magic; which I still believed they dealt in. As the waves were very high I thought the Ruler of the seas was angry, and I expected to be offered up to appease him. This filled my mind with agony, and I could not any more that night close my eyes again to rest. However, when daylight appeared I was a little eased in my mind; but still every time I was called I used to think it was to be killed. Some time after this we saw some very large fish, which I afterwards found were called grampusses. They looked to me extremely terrible, and made their appearance just at dusk; and were so near as to blow the water on the ship's deck. I believed them to be the rulers of the sea; and, as the white people did not make any offerings at any time, I thought they were angry with them: and, at last, what confirmed my belief was, the wind just then died away, and a calm ensued, and in consequence of it the ship stopped going. I supposed that the fish had performed this, and I hid myself in the fore part of the ship, through fear of being offered up to appease them, every minute peeping and quaking: but my good friend Dick came shortly towards me, and I took an opportunity to ask him, as well as I could, what these fish were. Not being able to talk much English, I could but just make him understand my question; and not at all, when I asked him if any offerings were to be made to them: however, he told me these fish would swallow any body; which sufficiently alarmed me. Here he was called away by the captain, who was leaning over the quarter-deck railing and looking at the fish; and most of the people were busied in getting a barrel of pitch to light, for them to play with. The captain now called me to him, having learned some of my apprehensions from Dick; and having diverted himself and others for some time with my fears, which appeared ludicrous enough in my crying and trembling, he dismissed me. The barrel of pitch was now lighted and put over the side into the water: by this time it was just dark, and the fish went after it; and, to my great joy, I saw them no more.

However, all my alarms began to subside when we got sight of land; and at last the ship arrived at Falmouth, after a passage of thirteen weeks. Every heart on board seemed gladdened on our reaching the shore, and none more than mine. The captain immediately went on shore, and sent on board some fresh provisions, which we wanted very much: we made good use of them, and our famine was soon turned into feasting, almost without ending. It was about the beginning of the spring 1757 when I arrived in England, and I was near twelve years of age at that time. I was very much struck with the buildings and the pavement of the streets in Falmouth; and, indeed, any object I saw filled me with new surprise. One morning, when I got upon deck, I saw it covered all over with the snow that fell over-night: as I had never seen any thing of the kind before, I thought it was salt; so I immediately ran down to the mate and desired him, as well as I could, to come and see how somebody in the night had thrown salt all over the deck. He, knowing what it was, desired me to bring some of it down to him: accordingly I took up a handful of it, which I found very cold indeed; and when I brought it to him he desired me to taste it. I did so, and I was surprised beyond measure. I then asked him what it was; he told me it was snow: but I could not in anywise understand him. He asked me if we had no such thing in my country; and I told him, No. I then asked him the use of it, and who made it; he told me a great man in the heavens, called God: but here again I was to all intents and purposes at a loss to understand him; and the more so, when a little after I saw the air filled with it, in a heavy shower, which fell down on the same day. After this I went to church; and having never been at such a place before, I was again amazed at seeing and hearing the service. I asked all I could about it; and they gave me to understand it was worshipping God, who made us and all things. I was still at a great loss, and soon got into an endless field of inquiries, as well as I was able to speak and ask about things. However, my little friend Dick used to be my best interpreter; for I could make free with him, and he always instructed me with pleasure: and from what I could understand by him of this God, and in seeing these white people did not sell one another, as we did, I was much pleased; and in this I thought they were much happier than we Africans. I was astonished at the wisdom of the white people in all things I saw; but was amazed at their not sacrificing, or making any offerings, and eating with unwashed hands, and touching the dead. I likewise could not help remarking the particular slenderness of their women, which I did not at first like; and I thought they were not so modest and shamefaced as the African women.

I had often seen my master and Dick employed in reading; and I had a great curiosity to talk to the books, as I thought they did; and so to learn how all things had a beginning: for that purpose I have often taken up a book, and have talked to it, and then put my ears to it, when alone, in hopes it would answer me; and I have been very much concerned when I found it remained silent.

My master lodged at the house of a gentleman in Falmouth, who had a fine little daughter about six or seven years of age, and she grew prodigiously fond of me; insomuch that we used to eat together, and had servants to wait on us. I was so much caressed by this family that it often reminded me of the treatment I had received from my little noble African master. After I had been here a few days, I was sent on board of the ship; but the child cried so much after me that nothing could pacify her till I was sent for again. It is ludicrous enough, that I began to fear I should be betrothed to this young lady; and when my master asked me if I would stay there with her behind him, as he was going away with the ship, which had taken in the tobacco again, I cried immediately, and said I would not leave her. At last, by stealth, one night I was sent on board the ship again; and in a little time we sailed for Guernsey, where she was in part owned by a merchant, one Nicholas Doberry. As I was now amongst a people who had not their faces scarred, like some of the African nations where I had been, I was very glad I did not let them ornament me in that manner when I was with them. When we arrived at Guernsey, my master placed me to board and lodge with one of his mates, who had a wife and family there; and some months afterwards he went to England, and left me in care of this mate, together with my friend Dick: This mate had a little daughter, aged about five or six years, with whom I used to be much delighted. I had often observed that when her mother washed her face it looked very rosy; but when she washed mine it did not look so: I therefore tried oftentimes myself if I could not by washing make my face of the same colour as my little play-mate (Mary), but it was all in vain; and I now began to be mortified at the difference in our complexions. This woman behaved to me with great kindness and attention; and taught me every thing in the same manner as she did her own child, and indeed in every respect treated me as such. I remained here till the summer of the year 1757; when my master, being appointed first lieutenant of his majesty's ship the Roebuck, sent for Dick and me, and his old mate: on this we all left Guernsey, and set out for England in a sloop bound for London. As we were coming up towards the Nore, where the Roebuck lay, a man of war's boat came alongside to press our people; on which each man ran to hide himself. I was very much frightened at this, though I did not know what it meant, or what to think or do. However I went and hid myself also under a hencoop. Immediately afterwards the press-gang came on board with their swords drawn, and searched all about, pulled the people out by force, and put them into the boat. At last I was found out also: the man that found me held me up by the heels while they all made their sport of me, I roaring and crying out all the time most lustily: but at last the mate, who was my conductor, seeing this, came to my assistance, and did all he could to pacify me; but all to very little purpose, till I had seen the boat go off. Soon afterwards we came to the Nore, where the Roebuck lay; and, to our great joy, my master came on board to us, and brought us to the ship. When I went on board this large ship, I was amazed indeed to see the quantity of men and the guns. However my surprise began to diminish as my knowledge increased; and I ceased to feel those apprehensions and alarms which had taken such strong possession of me when I first came among the Europeans, and for some time after. I began now to pass to an opposite extreme; I was so far from being afraid of any thing new which I saw, that, after I had been some time in this ship, I even began to long for a battle. My griefs too, which in young minds are not perpetual, were now wearing away; and I soon enjoyed myself pretty well, and felt tolerably easy in my present situation. There was a number of boys on board, which still made it more agreeable; for we were always together, and a great part of our time was spent in play. I remained in this ship a considerable time, during which we made several cruises, and visited a variety of places: among others we were twice in Holland, and brought over several persons of distinction from it, whose names I do not now remember. On the passage, one day, for the diversion of those gentlemen, all the boys were called on the quarter-deck, and were paired proportionably, and then made to fight; after which the gentleman gave the combatants from five to nine shillings each. This was the first time I ever fought with a white boy; and I never knew what it was to have a bloody nose before. This made me fight most desperately; I suppose considerably more than an hour: and at last, both of us being weary, we were parted. I had a great deal of this kind of sport afterwards, in which the captain and the ship's company used very much to encourage me. Sometime afterwards the ship went to Leith in Scotland, and from thence to the Orkneys, where I was surprised in seeing scarcely any night: and from thence we sailed with a great fleet, full of soldiers, for England. All this time we had never come to an engagement, though we were frequently cruising off the coast of France: during which we chased many vessels, and took in all seventeen prizes. I had been learning many of the manoeuvres of the ship during our cruise; and I was several times made to fire the guns. One evening, off Havre de Grace, just as it was growing dark, we were standing off shore, and met with a fine large French-built frigate. We got all things immediately ready for fighting; and I now expected I should be gratified in seeing an engagement, which I had so long wished for in vain. But the very moment the word of command was given to fire we heard those on board the other ship cry 'Haul down the jib;' and in that instant she hoisted English colours. There was instantly with us an amazing cry of—Avast! or stop firing; and I think one or two guns had been let off, but happily they did no mischief. We had hailed them several times; but they not hearing, we received no answer, which was the cause of our firing. The boat was then sent on board of her, and she proved to be the Ambuscade man of war, to my no small disappointment. We returned to Portsmouth, without having been in any action, just at the trial of Admiral Byng (whom I saw several times during it): and my master having left the ship, and gone to London for promotion, Dick and I were put on board the Savage sloop of war, and we went in her to assist in bringing off the St. George man of war, that had ran ashore somewhere on the coast. After staying a few weeks on board the Savage, Dick and I were sent on shore at Deal, where we remained some short time, till my master sent for us to London, the place I had long desired exceedingly to see. We therefore both with great pleasure got into a waggon, and came to London, where we were received by a Mr. Guerin, a relation of my master. This gentleman had two sisters, very amiable ladies, who took much notice and great care of me. Though I had desired so much to see London, when I arrived in it I was unfortunately unable to gratify my curiosity; for I had at this time the chilblains to such a degree that I could not stand for several months, and I was obliged to be sent to St. George's Hospital. There I grew so ill, that the doctors wanted to cut my left leg off at different times, apprehending a mortification; but I always said I would rather die than suffer it; and happily (I thank God) I recovered without the operation. After being there several weeks, and just as I had recovered, the small-pox broke out on me, so that I was again confined; and I thought myself now particularly unfortunate. However I soon recovered again; and by this time my master having been promoted to be first lieutenant of the Preston man of war of fifty guns, then new at Deptford, Dick and I were sent on board her, and soon after we went to Holland to bring over the late Duke of——to England.—While I was in this ship an incident happened, which, though trifling, I beg leave to relate, as I could not help taking particular notice of it, and considering it then as a judgment of God. One morning a young man was looking up to the fore-top, and in a wicked tone, common on shipboard, d——d his eyes about something. Just at the moment some small particles of dirt fell into his left eye, and by the evening it was very much inflamed. The next day it grew worse; and within six or seven days he lost it. From this ship my master was appointed a lieutenant on board the Royal George. When he was going he wished me to stay on board the Preston, to learn the French horn; but the ship being ordered for Turkey I could not think of leaving my master, to whom I was very warmly attached; and I told him if he left me behind it would break my heart. This prevailed on him to take me with him; but he left Dick on board the Preston, whom I embraced at parting for the last time. The Royal George was the largest ship I had ever seen; so that when I came on board of her I was surprised at the number of people, men, women, and children, of every denomination; and the largeness of the guns, many of them also of brass, which I had never seen before. Here were also shops or stalls of every kind of goods, and people crying their different commodities about the ship as in a town. To me it appeared a little world, into which I was again cast without a friend, for I had no longer my dear companion Dick. We did not stay long here. My master was not many weeks on board before he got an appointment to be sixth lieutenant of the Namur, which was then at Spithead, fitting up for Vice-admiral Boscawen, who was going with a large fleet on an expedition against Louisburgh. The crew of the Royal George were turned over to her, and the flag of that gallant admiral was hoisted on board, the blue at the maintop-gallant mast head. There was a very great fleet of men of war of every description assembled together for this expedition, and I was in hopes soon to have an opportunity of being gratified with a sea-fight. All things being now in readiness, this mighty fleet (for there was also Admiral Cornish's fleet in company, destined for the East Indies) at last weighed anchor, and sailed. The two fleets continued in company for several days, and then parted; Admiral Cornish, in the Lenox, having first saluted our admiral in the Namur, which he returned. We then steered for America; but, by contrary winds, we were driven to Teneriffe, where I was struck with its noted peak. Its prodigious height, and its form, resembling a sugar-loaf, filled me with wonder. We remained in sight of this island some days, and then proceeded for America, which we soon made, and got into a very commodious harbour called St. George, in Halifax, where we had fish in great plenty, and all other fresh provisions. We were here joined by different men of war and transport ships with soldiers; after which, our fleet being increased to a prodigious number of ships of all kinds, we sailed for Cape Breton in Nova Scotia. We had the good and gallant General Wolfe on board our ship, whose affability made him highly esteemed and beloved by all the men. He often honoured me, as well as other boys, with marks of his notice; and saved me once a flogging for fighting with a young gentleman. We arrived at Cape Breton in the summer of 1758: and here the soldiers were to be landed, in order to make an attack upon Louisbourgh. My master had some part in superintending the landing; and here I was in a small measure gratified in seeing an encounter between our men and the enemy. The French were posted on the shore to receive us, and disputed our landing for a long time; but at last they were driven from their trenches, and a complete landing was effected. Our troops pursued them as far as the town of Louisbourgh. In this action many were killed on both sides. One thing remarkable I saw this day:—A lieutenant of the Princess Amelia, who, as well as my master, superintended the landing, was giving the word of command, and while his mouth was open a musquet ball went through it, and passed out at his cheek. I had that day in my hand the scalp of an indian king, who was killed in the engagement: the scalp had been taken off by an Highlander. I saw this king's ornaments too, which were very curious, and made of feathers.

Our land forces laid siege to the town of Louisbourgh, while the French men of war were blocked up in the harbour by the fleet, the batteries at the same time playing upon them from the land. This they did with such effect, that one day I saw some of the ships set on fire by the shells from the batteries, and I believe two or three of them were quite burnt. At another time, about fifty boats belonging to the English men of war, commanded by Captain George Balfour of the Ætna fire-ship, and another junior captain, Laforey, attacked and boarded the only two remaining French men of war in the harbour. They also set fire to a seventy-gun ship, but a sixty-four, called the Bienfaisant, they brought off. During my stay here I had often an opportunity of being near Captain Balfour, who was pleased to notice me, and liked me so much that he often asked my master to let him have me, but he would not part with me; and no consideration could have induced me to leave him. At last Louisbourgh was taken, and the English men of war came into the harbour before it, to my very great joy; for I had now more liberty of indulging myself, and I went often on shore. When the ships were in the harbour we had the most beautiful procession on the water I ever saw. All the admirals and captains of the men of war, full dressed, and in their barges, well ornamented with pendants, came alongside of the Namur. The vice-admiral then went on shore in his barge, followed by the other officers in order of seniority, to take possession, as I suppose, of the town and fort. Some time after this the French governor and his lady, and other persons of note, came on board our ship to dine. On this occasion our ships were dressed with colours of all kinds, from the topgallant-mast head to the deck; and this, with the firing of guns, formed a most grand and magnificent spectacle.

As soon as every thing here was settled Admiral Boscawen sailed with part of the fleet for England, leaving some ships behind with Rear-admirals Sir Charles Hardy and Durell. It was now winter; and one evening, during our passage home, about dusk, when we were in the channel, or near soundings, and were beginning to look for land, we descried seven sail of large men of war, which stood off shore. Several people on board of our ship said, as the two fleets were (in forty minutes from the first sight) within hail of each other, that they were English men of war; and some of our people even began to name some of the ships. By this time both fleets began to mingle, and our admiral ordered his flag to be hoisted. At that instant the other fleet, which were French, hoisted their ensigns, and gave us a broadside as they passed by. Nothing could create greater surprise and confusion among us than this: the wind was high, the sea rough, and we had our lower and middle deck guns housed in, so that not a single gun on board was ready to be fired at any of the French ships. However, the Royal William and the Somerset being our sternmost ships, became a little prepared, and each gave the French ships a broadside as they passed by. I afterwards heard this was a French squadron, commanded by Mons. Conflans; and certainly had the Frenchmen known our condition, and had a mind to fight us, they might have done us great mischief. But we were not long before we were prepared for an engagement. Immediately many things were tossed overboard; the ships were made ready for fighting as soon as possible; and about ten at night we had bent a new main sail, the old one being split. Being now in readiness for fighting, we wore ship, and stood after the French fleet, who were one or two ships in number more than we. However we gave them chase, and continued pursuing them all night; and at daylight we saw six of them, all large ships of the line, and an English East Indiaman, a prize they had taken. We chased them all day till between three and four o'clock in the evening, when we came up with, and passed within a musquet shot of, one seventy-four gun ship, and the Indiaman also, who now hoisted her colours, but immediately hauled them down again. On this we made a signal for the other ships to take possession of her; and, supposing the man of war would likewise strike, we cheered, but she did not; though if we had fired into her, from being so near, we must have taken her. To my utter surprise the Somerset, who was the next ship astern of the Namur, made way likewise; and, thinking they were sure of this French ship, they cheered in the same manner, but still continued to follow us. The French Commodore was about a gun-shot ahead of all, running from us with all speed; and about four o'clock he carried his foretopmast overboard. This caused another loud cheer with us; and a little after the topmast came close by us; but, to our great surprise, instead of coming up with her, we found she went as fast as ever, if not faster. The sea grew now much smoother; and the wind lulling, the seventy-four gun ship we had passed came again by us in the very same direction, and so near, that we heard her people talk as she went by; yet not a shot was fired on either side; and about five or six o'clock, just as it grew dark, she joined her commodore. We chased all night; but the next day they were out of sight, so that we saw no more of them; and we only had the old Indiaman (called Carnarvon I think) for our trouble. After this we stood in for the channel, and soon made the land; and, about the close of the year 1758-9, we got safe to St. Helen's. Here the Namur ran aground; and also another large ship astern of us; but, by starting our water, and tossing many things overboard to lighten her, we got the ships off without any damage. We stayed for a short time at Spithead, and then went into Portsmouth harbour to refit; from whence the admiral went to London; and my master and I soon followed, with a press-gang, as we wanted some hands to complete our complement.

CHAP. IV

The author is baptized—Narrowly escapes drowning—Goes on an expedition to the Mediterranean— Incidents he met with there—Is witness to an engagement between some English and French ships—A particular account of the celebrated engagement between Admiral Boscawen and Mons. Le Clue, off Cape Logas, in August 1759—Dreadful explosion of a French ship—The author sails for England— His master appointed to the command of a fire-ship—Meets a negro boy, from whom he experiences much benevolence—Prepares for an expedition against Belle-Isle—A remarkable story of a disaster which befel his ship—Arrives at Belle-Isle—Operations of the landing and siege—The author's danger and distress, with his manner of extricating himself—Surrender of Belle-Isle—Transactions afterwards on the coast of France—Remarkable instance of kidnapping—The author returns to England—Hears a talk of peace, and expects his freedom—His ship sails for Deptford to be paid off, and when he arrives there he is suddenly seized by his master and carried forcibly on board a West India ship and sold.

It was now between two and three years since I first came to England, a great part of which I had spent at sea; so that I became inured to that service, and began to consider myself as happily situated; for my master treated me always extremely well; and my attachment and gratitude to him were very great. From the various scenes I had beheld on shipboard, I soon grew a stranger to terror of every kind, and was, in that respect at least, almost an Englishman. I have often reflected with surprise that I never felt half the alarm at any of the numerous dangers I have been in, that I was filled with at the first sight of the Europeans, and at every act of theirs, even the most trifling, when I first came among them, and for some time afterwards. That fear, however, which was the effect of my ignorance, wore away as I began to know them. I could now speak English tolerably well, and I perfectly understood every thing that was said. I now not only felt myself quite easy with these new countrymen, but relished their society and manners. I no longer looked upon them as spirits, but as men superior to us; and therefore I had the stronger desire to resemble them; to imbibe their spirit, and imitate their manners; I therefore embraced every occasion of improvement; and every new thing that I observed I treasured up in my memory. I had long wished to be able to read and write; and for this purpose I took every opportunity to gain instruction, but had made as yet very little progress. However, when I went to London with my master, I had soon an opportunity of improving myself, which I gladly embraced. Shortly after my arrival, he sent me to wait upon the Miss Guerins, who had treated me with much kindness when I was there before; and they sent me to school.

While I was attending these ladies their servants told me I could not go to Heaven unless I was baptized. This made me very uneasy; for I had now some faint idea of a future state: accordingly I communicated my anxiety to the eldest Miss Guerin, with whom I was become a favourite, and pressed her to have me baptized; when to my great joy she told me I should. She had formerly asked my master to let me be baptized, but he had refused; however she now insisted on it; and he being under some obligation to her brother complied with her request; so I was baptized in St. Margaret's church, Westminster, in February 1759, by my present name. The clergyman, at the same time, gave me a book, called a Guide to the Indians, written by the Bishop of Sodor and Man. On this occasion Miss Guerin did me the honour to stand as godmother, and afterwards gave me a treat. I used to attend these ladies about the town, in which service I was extremely happy; as I had thus many opportunities of seeing London, which I desired of all things. I was sometimes, however, with my master at his rendezvous-house, which was at the foot of Westminster-bridge. Here I used to enjoy myself in playing about the bridge stairs, and often in the watermen's wherries, with other boys. On one of these occasions there was another boy with me in a wherry, and we went out into the current of the river: while we were there two more stout boys came to us in another wherry, and, abusing us for taking the boat, desired me to get into the other wherry-boat. Accordingly I went to get out of the wherry I was in; but just as I had got one of my feet into the other boat the boys shoved it off, so that I fell into the Thames; and, not being able to swim, I should unavoidably have been drowned, but for the assistance of some watermen who providentially came to my relief.

The Namur being again got ready for sea, my master, with his gang, was ordered on board; and, to my no small grief, I was obliged to leave my school-master, whom I liked very much, and always attended while I stayed in London, to repair on board with my master. Nor did I leave my kind patronesses, the Miss Guerins, without uneasiness and regret. They often used to teach me to read, and took great pains to instruct me in the principles of religion and the knowledge of God. I therefore parted from those amiable ladies with reluctance; after receiving from them many friendly cautions how to conduct myself, and some valuable presents.

When I came to Spithead, I found we were destined for the Mediterranean, with a large fleet, which was now ready to put to sea. We only waited for the arrival of the admiral, who soon came on board; and about the beginning of the spring 1759, having weighed anchor, and got under way, Sailed for the Mediterranean; and in eleven days, from the Land's End, we got to Gibraltar. While we were here I used to be often on shore, and got various fruits in great plenty, and very cheap.

I had frequently told several people, in my excursions on shore, the story of my being kidnapped with my sister, and of our being separated, as I have related before; and I had as often expressed my anxiety for her fate, and my sorrow at having never met her again. One day, when I was on shore, and mentioning these circumstances to some persons, one of them told me he knew where my sister was, and, if I would accompany him, he would bring me to her. Improbable as this story was I believed it immediately, and agreed to go with him, while my heart leaped for joy: and, indeed, he conducted me to a black young woman, who was so like my sister, that, at first sight, I really thought it was her: but I was quickly undeceived; and, on talking to her, I found her to be of another nation.

While we lay here the Preston came in from the Levant. As soon as she arrived, my master told me I should now see my old companion, Dick, who had gone in her when she sailed for Turkey. I was much rejoiced at this news, and expected every minute to embrace him; and when the captain came on board of our ship, which he did immediately after, I ran to inquire after my friend; but, with inexpressible sorrow, I learned from the boat's crew that the dear youth was dead! and that they had brought his chest, and all his other things, to my master: these he afterwards gave to me, and I regarded them as a memorial of my friend, whom I loved, and grieved for, as a brother.

While we were at Gibraltar, I saw a soldier hanging by his heels, at one of the moles[1]: I thought this a strange sight, as I had seen a man hanged in London by his neck. At another time I saw the master of a frigate towed to shore on a grating, by several of the men of war's boats, and discharged the fleet, which I understood was a mark of disgrace for cowardice. On board the same ship there was also a sailor hung up at the yard-arm.

After lying at Gibraltar for some time, we sailed up the Mediterranean a considerable way above the Gulf of Lyons; where we were one night overtaken with a terrible gale of wind, much greater than any I had ever yet experienced. The sea ran so high that, though all the guns were well housed, there was great reason to fear their getting loose, the ship rolled so much; and if they had it must have proved our destruction. After we had cruised here for a short time, we came to Barcelona, a Spanish sea-port, remarkable for its silk manufactures. Here the ships were all to be watered; and my master, who spoke different languages, and used often to interpret for the admiral, superintended the watering of ours. For that purpose he and the officers of the other ships, who were on the same service, had tents pitched in the bay; and the Spanish soldiers were stationed along the shore, I suppose to see that no depredations were committed by our men.

I used constantly to attend my master; and I was charmed with this place. All the time we stayed it was like a fair with the natives, who brought us fruits of all kinds, and sold them to us much cheaper than I got them in England. They used also to bring wine down to us in hog and sheep skins, which diverted me very much. The Spanish officers here treated our officers with great politeness and attention; and some of them, in particular, used to come often to my master's tent to visit him; where they would sometimes divert themselves by mounting me on the horses or mules, so that I could not fall, and setting them off at full gallop; my imperfect skill in horsemanship all the while affording them no small entertainment. After the ships were watered, we returned to our old station of cruizing off Toulon, for the purpose of intercepting a fleet of French men of war that lay there. One Sunday, in our cruise, we came off a place where there were two small French frigates lying in shore; and our admiral, thinking to take or destroy them, sent two ships in after them—the Culloden and the Conqueror. They soon came up to the Frenchmen; and I saw a smart fight here, both by sea and land: for the frigates were covered by batteries, and they played upon our ships most furiously, which they as furiously returned, and for a long time a constant firing was kept up on all sides at an amazing rate. At last one frigate sunk; but the people escaped, though not without much difficulty: and a little after some of the people left the other frigate also, which was a mere wreck. However, our ships did not venture to bring her away, they were so much annoyed from the batteries, which raked them both in going and coming: their topmasts were shot away, and they were otherwise so much shattered, that the admiral was obliged to send in many boats to tow them back to the fleet. I afterwards sailed with a man who fought in one of the French batteries during the engagement, and he told me our ships had done considerable mischief that day on shore and in the batteries.

After this we sailed for Gibraltar, and arrived there about August 1759. Here we remained with all our sails unbent, while the fleet was watering and doing other necessary things. While we were in this situation, one day the admiral, with most of the principal officers, and many people of all stations, being on shore, about seven o'clock in the evening we were alarmed by signals from the frigates stationed for that purpose; and in an instant there was a general cry that the French fleet was out, and just passing through the streights. The admiral immediately came on board with some other officers; and it is impossible to describe the noise, hurry and confusion throughout the whole fleet, in bending their sails and slipping their cables; many people and ships' boats were left on shore in the bustle. We had two captains on board of our ship who came away in the hurry and left their ships to follow. We shewed lights from the gun-whale to the main topmast-head; and all our lieutenants were employed amongst the fleet to tell the ships not to wait for their captains, but to put the sails to the yards, slip their cables and follow us; and in this confusion of making ready for fighting we set out for sea in the dark after the French fleet. Here I could have exclaimed with Ajax,

"Oh Jove! O father! if it be thy will That we must perish, we thy will obey, But let us perish by the light of day."

They had got the start of us so far that we were not able to come up with them during the night; but at daylight we saw seven sail of the line of battle some miles ahead. We immediately chased them till about four o'clock in the evening, when our ships came up with them; and, though we were about fifteen large ships, our gallant admiral only fought them with his own division, which consisted of seven; so that we were just ship for ship. We passed by the whole of the enemy's fleet in order to come at their commander, Mons. La Clue, who was in the Ocean, an eighty-four gun ship: as we passed they all fired on us; and at one time three of them fired together, continuing to do so for some time. Notwithstanding which our admiral would not suffer a gun to be fired at any of them, to my astonishment; but made us lie on our bellies on the deck till we came quite close to the Ocean, who was ahead of them all; when we had orders to pour the whole three tiers into her at once.

The engagement now commenced with great fury on both sides: the Ocean immediately returned our fire, and we continued engaged with each other for some time; during which I was frequently stunned with the thundering of the great guns, whose dreadful contents hurried many of my companions into awful eternity. At last the French line was entirely broken, and we obtained the victory, which was immediately proclaimed with loud huzzas and acclamations. We took three prizes, La Modeste, of sixty-four guns, and Le Temeraire and Centaur, of seventy-four guns each. The rest of the French ships took to flight with all the sail they could crowd. Our ship being very much damaged, and quite disabled from pursuing the enemy, the admiral immediately quitted her, and went in the broken and only boat we had left on board the Newark, with which, and some other ships, he went after the French. The Ocean, and another large French ship, called the Redoubtable, endeavouring to escape, ran ashore at Cape Logas, on the coast of Portugal; and the French admiral and some of the crew got ashore; but we, finding it impossible to get the ships off, set fire to them both. About midnight I saw the Ocean blow up, with a most dreadful explosion. I never beheld a more awful scene. In less than a minute the midnight for a certain space seemed turned into day by the blaze, which was attended with a noise louder and more terrible than thunder, that seemed to rend every element around us.

My station during the engagement was on the middle-deck, where I was quartered with another boy, to bring powder to the aftermost gun; and here I was a witness of the dreadful fate of many of my companions, who, in the twinkling of an eye, were dashed in pieces, and launched into eternity. Happily I escaped unhurt, though the shot and splinters flew thick about me during the whole fight. Towards the latter part of it my master was wounded, and I saw him carried down to the surgeon; but though I was much alarmed for him and wished to assist him I dared not leave my post. At this station my gun-mate (a partner in bringing powder for the same gun) and I ran a very great risk for more than half an hour of blowing up the ship. For, when we had taken the cartridges out of the boxes, the bottoms of many of them proving rotten, the powder ran all about the deck, near the match tub: we scarcely had water enough at the last to throw on it. We were also, from our employment, very much exposed to the enemy's shots; for we had to go through nearly the whole length of the ship to bring the powder. I expected therefore every minute to be my last; especially when I saw our men fall so thick about me; but, wishing to guard as much against the dangers as possible, at first I thought it would be safest not to go for the powder till the Frenchmen had fired their broadside; and then, while they were charging, I could go and come with my powder: but immediately afterwards I thought this caution was fruitless; and, cheering myself with the reflection that there was a time allotted for me to die as well as to be born, I instantly cast off all fear or thought whatever of death, and went through the whole of my duty with alacrity; pleasing myself with the hope, if I survived the battle, of relating it and the dangers I had escaped to the dear Miss Guerin, and others, when I should return to London.

Our ship suffered very much in this engagement; for, besides the number of our killed and wounded, she was almost torn to pieces, and our rigging so much shattered, that our mizen-mast and main-yard, &c. hung over the side of the ship; so that we were obliged to get many carpenters, and others from some of the ships of the fleet, to assist in setting us in some tolerable order; and, notwithstanding, it took us some time before we were completely refitted; after which we left Admiral Broderick to command, and we, with the prizes, steered for England. On the passage, and as soon as my master was something recovered of his wounds, the admiral appointed him captain of the Ætna fire-ship, on which he and I left the Namur, and went on board of her at sea. I liked this little ship very much. I now became the captain's steward, in which situation I was very happy: for I was extremely well treated by all on board; and I had leisure to improve myself in reading and writing. The latter I had learned a little of before I left the Namur, as there was a school on board. When we arrived at Spithead the Ætna went into Portsmouth harbour to refit, which being done, we returned to Spithead and joined a large fleet that was thought to be intended against the Havannah; but about that time the king died: whether that prevented the expedition I know not; but it caused our ship to be stationed at Cowes, in the isle of Wight, till the beginning of the year sixty-one. Here I spent my time very pleasantly; I was much on shore all about this delightful island, and found the inhabitants very civil.

While I was here, I met with a trifling incident, which surprised me agreeably. I was one day in a field belonging to a gentleman who had a black boy about my own size; this boy having observed me from his master's house, was transported at the sight of one of his own countrymen, and ran to meet me with the utmost haste. I not knowing what he was about turned a little out of his way at first, but to no purpose: he soon came close to me and caught hold of me in his arms as if I had been his brother, though we had never seen each other before. After we had talked together for some time he took me to his master's house, where I was treated very kindly. This benevolent boy and I were very happy in frequently seeing each other till about the month of March 1761, when our ship had orders to fit out again for another expedition. When we got ready, we joined a very large fleet at Spithead, commanded by Commodore Keppel, which was destined against Belle-Isle, and with a number of transport ships with troops on board to make a descent on the place. We sailed once more in quest of fame. I longed to engage in new adventures and see fresh wonders.

I had a mind on which every thing uncommon made its full impression, and every event which I considered as marvellous. Every extraordinary escape, or signal deliverance, either of myself or others, I looked upon to be effected by the interposition of Providence. We had not been above ten days at sea before an incident of this kind happened; which, whatever credit it may obtain from the reader, made no small impression on my mind.

We had on board a gunner, whose name was John Mondle; a man of very indifferent morals. This man's cabin was between the decks, exactly over where I lay, abreast of the quarter-deck ladder. One night, the 20th of April, being terrified with a dream, he awoke in so great a fright that he could not rest in his bed any longer, nor even remain in his cabin; and he went upon deck about four o'clock in the morning extremely agitated. He immediately told those on the deck of the agonies of his mind, and the dream which occasioned it; in which he said he had seen many things very awful, and had been warned by St. Peter to repent, who told him time was short. This he said had greatly alarmed him, and he was determined to alter his life. People generally mock the fears of others when they are themselves in safety; and some of his shipmates who heard him only laughed at him. However, he made a vow that he never would drink strong liquors again; and he immediately got a light, and gave away his sea-stores of liquor. After which, his agitation still continuing, he began to read the Scriptures, hoping to find some relief; and soon afterwards he laid himself down again on his bed, and endeavoured to compose himself to sleep, but to no purpose; his mind still continuing in a state of agony. By this time it was exactly half after seven in the morning: I was then under the half-deck at the great cabin door; and all at once I heard the people in the waist cry out, most fearfully—'The Lord have mercy upon us! We are all lost! The Lord have mercy upon us!'

Mr. Mondle hearing the cries, immediately ran out of his cabin; and we were instantly struck by the Lynne, a forty-gun ship, Captain Clark, which nearly ran us down. This ship had just put about, and was by the wind, but had not got full headway, or we must all have perished; for the wind was brisk. However, before Mr. Mondle had got four steps from his cabin-door, she struck our ship with her cutwater right in the middle of his bed and cabin, and ran it up to the combings of the quarter-deck hatchway, and above three feet below water, and in a minute there was not a bit of wood to be seen where Mr. Mondle's cabin stood; and he was so near being killed that some of the splinters tore his face. As Mr. Mondle must inevitably have perished from this accident had he not been alarmed in the very extraordinary way I have related, I could not help regarding this as an awful interposition of Providence for his preservation. The two ships for some time swinged alongside of each other; for ours being a fire-ship, our grappling-irons caught the Lynne every way, and the yards and rigging went at an astonishing rate. Our ship was in such a shocking condition that we all thought she would instantly go down, and every one ran for their lives, and got as well as they could on board the Lynne; but our lieutenant being the aggressor, he never quitted the ship. However, when we found she did not sink immediately, the captain came on board again, and encouraged our people to return and try to save her. Many on this came back, but some would not venture. Some of the ships in the fleet, seeing our situation, immediately sent their boats to our assistance; but it took us the whole day to save the ship with all their help. And by using every possible means, particularly frapping her together with many hawsers, and putting a great quantity of tallow below water where she was damaged, she was kept together: but it was well we did not meet with any gales of wind, or we must have gone to pieces; for we were in such a crazy condition that we had ships to attend us till we arrived at Belle-Isle, the place of our destination; and then we had all things taken out of the ship, and she was properly repaired. This escape of Mr. Mondle, which he, as well as myself, always considered as a singular act of Providence, I believe had a great influence on his life and conduct ever afterwards.

Now that I am on this subject I beg leave to relate another instance or two which strongly raised my belief of the particular interposition of Heaven, and which might not otherwise have found a place here, from their insignificance. I belonged for a few days in the year 1758 to the Jason, of fifty-four guns, at Plymouth; and one night, when I was on board, a woman, with a child at her breast, fell from the upper-deck down into the hold, near the keel. Every one thought that the mother and child must be both dashed to pieces; but, to our great surprise, neither of them was hurt. I myself one day fell headlong from the upper-deck of the Ætna down the after-hold, when the ballast was out; and all who saw me fall cried out I was killed: but I received not the least injury. And in the same ship a man fell from the mast-head on the deck without being hurt. In these, and in many more instances, I thought I could plainly trace the hand of God, without whose permission a sparrow cannot fall. I began to raise my fear from man to him alone, and to call daily on his holy name with fear and reverence: and I trust he heard my supplications, and graciously condescended to answer me according to his holy word, and to implant the seeds of piety in me, even one of the meanest of his creatures.

When we had refitted our ship, and all things were in readiness for attacking the place, the troops on board the transports were ordered to disembark; and my master, as a junior captain, had a share in the command of the landing. This was on the 8th of April. The French were drawn up on the shore, and had made every disposition to oppose the landing of our men, only a small part of them this day being able to effect it; most of them, after fighting with great bravery, were cut off; and General Crawford, with a number of others, were taken prisoners. In this day's engagement we had also our lieutenant killed.

On the 21st of April we renewed our efforts to land the men, while all the men of war were stationed along the shore to cover it, and fired at the French batteries and breastworks from early in the morning till about four o'clock in the evening, when our soldiers effected a safe landing. They immediately attacked the French; and, after a sharp encounter, forced them from the batteries. Before the enemy retreated they blew up several of them, lest they should fall into our hands. Our men now proceeded to besiege the citadel, and my master was ordered on shore to superintend the landing of all the materials necessary for carrying on the siege; in which service I mostly attended him. While I was there I went about to different parts of the island; and one day, particularly, my curiosity almost cost me my life. I wanted very much to see the mode of charging the mortars and letting off the shells, and for that purpose I went to an English battery that was but a very few yards from the walls of the citadel. There, indeed, I had an opportunity of completely gratifying myself in seeing the whole operation, and that not without running a very great risk, both from the English shells that burst while I was there, but likewise from those of the French. One of the largest of their shells bursted within nine or ten yards of me: there was a single rock close by, about the size of a butt; and I got instant shelter under it in time to avoid the fury of the shell. Where it burst the earth was torn in such a manner that two or three butts might easily have gone into the hole it made, and it threw great quantities of stones and dirt to a considerable distance. Three shot were also fired at me and another boy who was along with me, one of them in particular seemed

"Wing'd with red lightning and impetuous rage;"

for with a most dreadful sound it hissed close by me, and struck a rock at a little distance, which it shattered to pieces. When I saw what perilous circumstances I was in, I attempted to return the nearest way I could find, and thereby I got between the English and the French centinels. An English serjeant, who commanded the outposts, seeing me, and surprised how I came there, (which was by stealth along the seashore), reprimanded me very severely for it, and instantly took the centinel off his post into custody, for his negligence in suffering me to pass the lines. While I was in this situation I observed at a little distance a French horse, belonging to some islanders, which I thought I would now mount, for the greater expedition of getting off. Accordingly I took some cord which I had about me, and making a kind of bridle of it, I put it round the horse's head, and the tame beast very quietly suffered me to tie him thus and mount him. As soon as I was on the horse's back I began to kick and beat him, and try every means to make him go quick, but all to very little purpose: I could not drive him out of a slow pace. While I was creeping along, still within reach of the enemy's shot, I met with a servant well mounted on an English horse. I immediately stopped; and, crying, told him my case; and begged of him to help me, and this he effectually did; for, having a fine large whip, he began to lash my horse with it so severely, that he set off full speed with me towards the sea, while I was quite unable to hold or manage him. In this manner I went along till I came to a craggy precipice. I now could not stop my horse; and my mind was filled with apprehensions of my deplorable fate should he go down the precipice, which he appeared fully disposed to do: I therefore thought I had better throw myself off him at once, which I did immediately with a great deal of dexterity, and fortunately escaped unhurt. As soon as I found myself at liberty I made the best of my way for the ship, determined I would not be so fool-hardy again in a hurry.

We continued to besiege the citadel till June, when it surrendered. During the siege I have counted above sixty shells and carcases in the air at once. When this place was taken I went through the citadel, and in the bomb-proofs under it, which were cut in the solid rock; and I thought it a surprising place, both for strength and building: notwithstanding which our shots and shells had made amazing devastation, and ruinous heaps all around it.

After the taking of this island our ships, with some others commanded by Commodore Stanhope in the Swiftsure, went to Basse-road, where we blocked up a French fleet. Our ships were there from June till February following; and in that time I saw a great many scenes of war, and stratagems on both sides to destroy each others fleet. Sometimes we would attack the French with some ships of the line; at other times with boats; and frequently we made prizes. Once or twice the French attacked us by throwing shells with their bomb-vessels: and one day as a French vessel was throwing shells at our ships she broke from her springs, behind the isle of I de Re: the tide being complicated, she came within a gun shot of the Nassau; but the Nassau could not bring a gun to bear upon her, and thereby the Frenchman got off. We were twice attacked by their fire-floats, which they chained together, and then let them float down with the tide; but each time we sent boats with graplings, and towed them safe out of the fleet.

We had different commanders while we were at this place, Commodores Stanhope, Dennis, Lord Howe, &c. From hence, before the Spanish war began, our ship and the Wasp sloop were sent to St. Sebastian in Spain, by Commodore Stanhope; and Commodore Dennis afterwards sent our ship as a cartel to Bayonne in France[2], after which[3] we went in February in 1762 to Belle-Isle, and there stayed till the summer, when we left it, and returned to Portsmouth.

After our ship was fitted out again for service, in September she went to Guernsey, where I was very glad to see my old hostess, who was now a widow, and my former little charming companion, her daughter. I spent some time here very happily with them, till October, when we had orders to repair to Portsmouth. We parted from each other with a great deal of affection; and I promised to return soon, and see them again, not knowing what all-powerful fate had determined for me. Our ship having arrived at Portsmouth, we went into the harbour, and remained there till the latter end of November, when we heard great talk about peace; and, to our very great joy, in the beginning of December we had orders to go up to London with our ship to be paid off. We received this news with loud huzzas, and every other demonstration of gladness; and nothing but mirth was to be seen throughout every part of the ship. I too was not without my share of the general joy on this occasion. I thought now of nothing but being freed, and working for myself, and thereby getting money to enable me to get a good education; for I always had a great desire to be able at least to read and write; and while I was on shipboard I had endeavoured to improve myself in both. While I was in the Ætna particularly, the captain's clerk taught me to write, and gave me a smattering of arithmetic as far as the rule of three. There was also one Daniel Queen, about forty years of age, a man very well educated, who messed with me on board this ship, and he likewise dressed and attended the captain. Fortunately this man soon became very much attached to me, and took very great pains to instruct me in many things. He taught me to shave and dress hair a little, and also to read in the Bible, explaining many passages to me, which I did not comprehend. I was wonderfully surprised to see the laws and rules of my country written almost exactly here; a circumstance which I believe tended to impress our manners and customs more deeply on my memory. I used to tell him of this resemblance; and many a time we have sat up the whole night together at this employment. In short, he was like a father to me; and some even used to call me after his name; they also styled me the black Christian. Indeed I almost loved him with the affection of a son. Many things I have denied myself that he might have them; and when I used to play at marbles or any other game, and won a few half-pence, or got any little money, which I sometimes did, for shaving any one, I used to buy him a little sugar or tobacco, as far as my stock of money would go. He used to say, that he and I never should part; and that when our ship was paid off, as I was as free as himself or any other man on board, he would instruct me in his business, by which I might gain a good livelihood. This gave me new life and spirits; and my heart burned within me, while I thought the time long till I obtained my freedom. For though my master had not promised it to me, yet, besides the assurances I had received that he had no right to detain me, he always treated me with the greatest kindness, and reposed in me an unbounded confidence; he even paid attention to my morals; and would never suffer me to deceive him, or tell lies, of which he used to tell me the consequences; and that if I did so God would not love me; so that, from all this tenderness, I had never once supposed, in all my dreams of freedom, that he would think of detaining me any longer than I wished.

In pursuance of our orders we sailed from Portsmouth for the Thames, and arrived at Deptford the 10th of December, where we cast anchor just as it was high water. The ship was up about half an hour, when my master ordered the barge to be manned; and all in an instant, without having before given me the least reason to suspect any thing of the matter, he forced me into the barge; saying, I was going to leave him, but he would take care I should not. I was so struck with the unexpectedness of this proceeding, that for some time I did not make a reply, only I made an offer to go for my books and chest of clothes, but he swore I should not move out of his sight; and if I did he would cut my throat, at the same time taking his hanger. I began, however, to collect myself; and, plucking up courage, I told him I was free, and he could not by law serve me so. But this only enraged him the more; and he continued to swear, and said he would soon let me know whether he would or not, and at that instant sprung himself into the barge from the ship, to the astonishment and sorrow of all on board. The tide, rather unluckily for me, had just turned downward, so that we quickly fell down the river along with it, till we came among some outward-bound West Indiamen; for he was resolved to put me on board the first vessel he could get to receive me. The boat's crew, who pulled against their will, became quite faint different times, and would have gone ashore; but he would not let them. Some of them strove then to cheer me, and told me he could not sell me, and that they would stand by me, which revived me a little; and I still entertained hopes; for as they pulled along he asked some vessels to receive me, but they could not. But, just as we had got a little below Gravesend, we came alongside of a ship which was going away the next tide for the West Indies; her name was the Charming Sally, Captain James Doran; and my master went on board and agreed with him for me; and in a little time I was sent for into the cabin. When I came there Captain Doran asked me if I knew him; I answered that I did not; 'Then,' said he 'you are now my slave.' I told him my master could not sell me to him, nor to any one else. 'Why,' said he,'did not your master buy you?' I confessed he did. 'But I have served him,' said I,'many years, and he has taken all my wages and prize-money, for I only got one sixpence during the war; besides this I have been baptized; and by the laws of the land no man has a right to sell me:' And I added, that I had heard a lawyer and others at different times tell my master so. They both then said that those people who told me so were not my friends; but I replied—it was very extraordinary that other people did not know the law as well as they. Upon this Captain Doran said I talked too much English; and if I did not behave myself well, and be quiet, he had a method on board to make me. I was too well convinced of his power over me to doubt what he said; and my former sufferings in the slave-ship presenting themselves to my mind, the recollection of them made me shudder. However, before I retired I told them that as I could not get any right among men here I hoped I should hereafter in Heaven; and I immediately left the cabin, filled with resentment and sorrow. The only coat I had with me my master took away with him, and said if my prize-money had been 10,000 £. he had a right to it all, and would have taken it. I had about nine guineas, which, during my long sea-faring life, I had scraped together from trifling perquisites and little ventures; and I hid it that instant, lest my master should take that from me likewise, still hoping that by some means or other I should make my escape to the shore; and indeed some of my old shipmates told me not to despair, for they would get me back again; and that, as soon as they could get their pay, they would immediately come to Portsmouth to me, where this ship was going: but, alas! all my hopes were baffled, and the hour of my deliverance was yet far off. My master, having soon concluded his bargain with the captain, came out of the cabin, and he and his people got into the boat and put off; I followed them with aching eyes as long as I could, and when they were out of sight I threw myself on the deck, while my heart was ready to burst with sorrow and anguish.

FOOTNOTES

1. He had drowned himself in endeavouring to desert.
2. Among others whom we brought from Bayonne, two gentlemen, who had been in the West Indies, where they sold slaves; and they confessed they had made at one time a false bill of sale, and sold two Portuguese white men among a lot of slaves.
3. Some people have it, that sometimes shortly before persons die their ward has been seen; that is, some spirit exactly in their likeness, though they are themselves at other places at the same time. One day while we were at Bayonne Mr. Mondle saw one of our men, as he thought, in the gun-room; and a little after, coming on the quarter-deck, he spoke of some circumstances of this man to some of the officers. They told him that the man was then out of the ship, in one of the boats with the Lieutenant: but Mr. Mondle would not believe it, and we searched the ship, when he found the man was actually out of her; and when the boat returned some time afterwards, we found the man had been drowned at the very time Mr. Mondle thought he saw him.

STUDY QUESTIONS

1. Olaudah Equiano represented a confluence of African and European cultures. While he spent only his childhood in Africa, Equiano remained cognizant of his African heritage and tied to his cultural roots. Yet, he also embraced British culture and customs with prodigious alacrity. Equiano imbibed British ideas about liberty, commerce, the Protestant religion, and social habits and mores. In short, Equiano lionized British society and sought to emulate his white peers. How did Equiano define his identity? Was he African? Was he British? How do you explain this hybridity?

2. Equiano was baptized into the Christian faith at the age of 14 in 1759. What role did religion play in his life?

3. Equiano was familiar with two systems of slavery (Africa and New World). How did his experiences of the two compare? What was his view of slavery? Was it as simple as a one-sided condemnation, or something more complicated?

4. Autobiography is a literary genre that allows the author to recall and record events from his or her past. Intentionally or not, however, sometimes autobiographers reinvent their pasts to their advantage. Memory and interpretation can obscure what really took place. In what ways does Equiano appeal to the reader? Does he present a judicious and balanced view of his life, or is this selection an exercise in propaganda?

The Negro in the Caribbean

The thesis promulgated by Eric Williams (1911–1981), in which he established more clearly the connection between the apex and decline of slavery and the ascent of British capitalism, still remains a subject of academic debate today. Eric Eustace Williams was born in Port of Spain, Trinidad, in 1911. He won the Island Scholarship to study history at Oxford University in 1931–1932, earned his doctorate in 1938–1939, and served on the faculty of Washington, D.C.'s, Howard University from 1939 until 1948, before returning to the island.

While at Oxford, Williams questioned and rejected the Eurocentric nature of the writing of West Indian history. Intellectually speaking, he viewed himself as a West Indian who happened to have been born in Trinidad—better equipped to tell the story of the Caribbean, in any event, than any British historian. He does just that in his first book, *The Negro in the Caribbean*, published in 1942. The kernel of the Williams thesis appears in this monograph; however, in his second book, *Capitalism and Slavery* (1944), an outgrowth of his doctoral thesis, Williams challenges the conventional historiography regarding abolition, and places the West Indies prominently alongside Britain in his work. Scholars, moreover, had heretofore traditionally focused on moral, religious, and humanitarian reasons for emancipation. Williams underscores the economic relevance to the demise of slavery. The decline of the importance of Caribbean sugar to the British economy, he maintains, coupled with industrial maturity, heralded the concomitant decline of the importance of slavery.

The Atlantic Ocean in the mercantilist era, a period between the 15th and 18th centuries of economic protection and regulatory oversight, in which burgeoning nation-states manipulated the terms of trade in order to monopolize wealth, was the setting for a triangular trade between Europe, Africa, and the New World. Natural resources and raw (and refined) materials such as sugar, cotton, tobacco, and indigo went from the New World to Europe; manufactured goods such as weapons, liquor, and metal utensils traveled from Europe to Africa; and slaves, of course, were purveyed from Africa to the New World. Sugar, for example, amounted to roughly 20 percent of all British imports by the end of the 18th century.

Doctorate: Oxford 1939

Figure 8.1. Portrait of Eric Williams. Copyright ©
by Estate of Eric Eustace Williams. Reprinted with
permission.

Within this nexus of commerce, Britain ruled the waves,
and, at times, waived the rules.

Williams highlights the role of slavery in the rise
of capitalism in Britain during the 18th century and
the centrality of black labor to British industry and the
West Indian plantation complex. It is a controversial
reinterpretation, which veers from the usual paternalistic story of British abolition of the slave trade in 1807
and emancipation in 1833, and illuminates how the
commercial traffic of human beings served the economy
of Britain. As slavery became an economic millstone to
the "workshop of the world," money and machines—not
morality—caused industrial capitalists to jettison the
institution.

Within his argument, moreover, racism is a consequence of slavery, rather than the other way around.
Europeans initially enslaved Indians to work American
land and mines, but when indigenous populations died
from disease, Africa became the source of the cheapest labor. Racism, Williams contends, subsequently
emerged as a justification for slavery's economic benefits, rather than any initial impetus to procure
slaves. The trans-Atlantic human traffic trade was driven not by skin color, or even by climatic determin-
ism, but by sugar, cotton, and tobacco destined for European and colonial consumption.

Along with *The Black Jacobins*, Williams's countryman, high school teacher, and mentor, C. L.
R. James's 1938 study of the Saint-Domingue slave revolt, *Capitalism and Slavery*, became a seminal
monograph by a West Indian scholar. One criticism of Williams was that he was unable to reconcile
his accusatory tone and status as a West Indian colonial with the objective impartiality required by the
historian. Skeptics asserted he remained too impassioned and not distanced enough from his subject.
His anti-colonial posture shone clearly in his scholarship. Some historians such as Seymour Drescher
have revised Williams's revision as merely one of many reasons for capital accumulation in the early
industrial age. Drescher, in fact, has argued that sugar, rather than a commodity on the wane, continued
to boom simultaneously to abolition. Manumission, therefore, constituted a triumph of altruism over
economic considerations.[1] To be fair, Williams did not doubt the sincerity of the abolitionists, nor did
he question their humanitarian convictions. Extra-economic factors, however, remained ancillary to his
thesis. The selection here, from *The Negro in the Caribbean*, illuminates its origins.

Author of seven books and editor of two more, Williams proved to be a prolific scholar with a prodigious capacity for work; however, a passion for fighting injustice propelled him into activism and political life. Between 1945 and 1955, he had been a member of the Anglo-American Caribbean Commission,
on which he often clashed with his colleagues on matters of West Indian autonomy being obscured by
the visions of the larger powers. Just as he had as a historian, as a political figure, Williams opposed
colonialism, or what he deemed neocolonialism, particularly by a long shadow cast by the American
colossus. By 1957, he had become chief minister, head of government for Trinidad and Tobago. A

---

1   Seymour Drescher, Econocide: British Slavery in the Era of Abolition (Pittsburgh: University of Pittsburgh Press, 1977).

shrewd politician, Williams used his scholarship on the history of West Indian slavery to wrest financial aid from the British. When the islands became independent in 1962, Williams served as prime minister until his death in 1981 and welcomed Commonwealth status as a counterbalance to American regional hegemony.

The Negro in the Caribbean

By Eric William

THE SLAVERY BACKGROUND

The original inhabitants of the Caribbean islands were speedily exterminated by the Spanish conquerors, of whom it has been said that first they fell on their knees and then they fell on the aborigines. The islands were useless to their owners without a labor supply. It was to satisfy the labor requirements of the West Indian islands that the greatest migration in recorded history took place. This was the Negro slave trade.

The slave trade introduced the African Negro to the Caribbean stage. This great inhumanity of man to man had its origin not in contempt for the blacks or in any belief that the black man was destined for slavery. These were the later rationalizations invented to justify what was in its origin basically an economic question, one which can be expressed in one word—Sugar.

The establishment of the sugar industry created the demand for labor in the West Indian islands. That demand was for a constant supply of cheap labor, black, brown or white, with the emphasis on the cheapness of the labor rather than the color of the laborer. It happened that in the fifteenth and sixteenth centuries the cheapest labor was black labor. The Spanish planters discovered that one Negro was worth four Indians; the British planters, in their turn, realized that the money it would take to buy the services of a white indentured servant for ten years would buy a Negro for life. There was, in fact, in the Caribbean not only black slavery, but white and brown as well. But neither the white nor the brown men were forth-coming in sufficient quantities to supply the demand; Africa had inexhaustible human resources. The white indentured servant, too, was rewarded, after the expiry of his contract, with a small grant of land. These new freemen were too poor and their land too insignificant to afford the vast outlay of capital required for establishing a sugar plantation. The white indentured servants, too few to become a regular labor supply, were, therefore, a nuisance. The transported Negro, on the other hand, in a strange environment, handicapped by his ignorance of the white man's language, was pre-eminently fitted for continuous exploitation as he could be kept completely divorced from the land.

This, then, was the origin of the Negro slave trade and Negro slavery. It was a choice, from the sugar planter's point of view, of Negro labor or no labor at all. Sugar meant slavery; only incidentally, and by process of elimination, did it come to mean Negro slavery. Thus was the Negro introduced into his new habitat, and drawn into the orbit of Western civilization to make his contributions to that civilization. If today he is the white man's problem, he was in the sixteenth and seventeenth centuries the only solution of that problem.

The Western World is in danger of forgetting today what the Negro has contributed to Western civilization. The American continent would have had to pay a high price for the luxury of remaining a white man's country. No sugar, no Negroes; but, equally true, no Negroes, no sugar. "Someone had to pick the cotton." That was not why "darkies" were born; but it was certainly to cultivate the sugar cane and later pick the cotton that they were transported from Africa.

It was, in fact, sugar which raised these insignificant tropical islands from the status of pirates' nests to the dignity of the most precious colonies known to the Western World up to the nineteenth century. It was the Negro, without whom the islands would have remained uncultivated and might as well have been at the bottom of the sea, who made these islands into the prizes of war and diplomacy, coveted by the statesmen of all nations. These black "bundles", these "logs", as the Negroes were referred to, meant sugar together with other tropical products. Between 1640 and 1667, when sugar was introduced, the wealth of Barbados increased forty times. All the European wars between 1660 and 1815 were fought for the possession of these valuable Caribbean islands and for the privilege of supplying the "tons" of labor needed by the sugar plantations. Between 1760 and 1813 St. Lucia changed hands seven times.

Tremendous wealth was produced from an unstable economy based on a single crop, which combined the vices of feudalism and capitalism with the virtues of neither. Liverpool in England, Nantes in France, Rhode Island in America, prospered on the slave trade. London and Bristol, Bordeaux and Marseilles, Cadiz and Seville, Lisbon and New England, all waxed fat on the profits of the trade in the tropical produce raised by the Negro slave. Capitalism in England, France, Holland and colonial America received a double stimulus—from the manufacture of goods needed to exchange for slaves, woolen and cotton goods, copper and brass vessels, and the firearms, handcuffs, chains and torture instruments indispensable on the slave ship and on the slave plantation; and from the manufacture of colonial raw materials,—sugar, cotton, molasses. The tiniest British sugar island was considered more valuable than the thirteen mainland colonies combined. French Guadeloupe, with a population today of a mere 300,000, was once deemed more precious than Canada, and the Dutch cheerfully surrendered what is today New York State for a strip of the Guiana territory. These islands were the glittering gems in every imperial diadem, and Barbados, Jamaica, Saint-Domingue (today Haiti), and then Cuba were, in that order of succession, magic names which meant national prosperity and individual wealth. The wealth of the sugar barons became proverbial. Signs abounded in England and France, the "West Indians" held the highest offices and built magnificent mansions, which in Cuba, with a due sense of their importance, they called palaces. Sugar was king; without his Negro slave his kingdom would have been a desert.

This contribution of the Negro has failed to receive adequate recognition. It is more than ever necessary to remember it today. England and France, Holland, Spain and Denmark, not to mention the United States, Brazil and other parts of South America, all are indebted to Negro labor. As Mr. Winston Churchill declared four years ago: "Our possession of the West Indies, like that of India, … gave us the strength, the support, but especially the capital, the wealth, at a time when no other European nation possessed such a reserve, which enabled us to come through the great struggles of the Napoleonic Wars, the keen competition of commerce in the 18th and 19th centuries, and enabled us not only to acquire this appendage of possessions which we have, but also to lay the foundations of that commercial and financial leadership which, when the world was young, when everything outside Europe was undeveloped, enabled us to make our great position in the world."

Slavery was fundamentally the same everywhere, but it is important to notice a significant difference in the cultural pattern. As a necessary instrument of production, the Negro's condition did not vary whether his owner was Latin or Anglo-Saxon. But where the Anglo-Saxons had plantation colonies, with only the bare minimum of white owners, agents, supernumeraries and slave drivers, the Spanish colonies were home to the white immigrants, and the slaves benefited accordingly. As soon as the Spanish colonies, however, began to produce for the world market, Spanish slavery lost its patriarchal character. This happened in Cuba but not in Puerto Rico, and in Cuba relatively late as compared with the British and French colonies. Hence, possibly, the absence of the extreme racial tension characteristic of French St. Domingue and the Southern States. The Anglo-Saxon, too, was apprehensive that baptism, requiring instruction in the English tongue, would give the Negroes a common language and thereby foment sedition and revolts. The Latin, on the other hand, insisted on baptism and Christianity for his slave. Laugh at the Pope's sanction of slavery or his Catholic Majesty's prosecution of the slave trade; the cultural pattern presents a distinction of great significance. Spanish laws, and French to a lesser degree, were notoriously milder to the slave, and it is a sad commentary on the nature of early democracy that the Negro slaves were treated most harshly in the British self-governing colonies. When Trinidad, for instance, passed into British from Spanish hands, the British Government refused to abrogate the Spanish laws and to concede self-government to the planters. Popular franchises in the hands of slaveowners were the worst instruments of tyranny ever forged for the oppression of mankind. The greater percentage of whites, too, in the Spanish islands reduced the disproportion between the races which was characteristic of the British colonies, and which, after Saint-Domingue had gone up in the flames of the slave revolution, made all whites in the Caribbean fearful of slave conspiracies. It is perhaps in this fact that we are to find a partial explanation of the comparative absence of racial tension today in the former Spanish colonies.

Kind treatment and Christianity might mitigate slavery, they albne would not abolish it. If the Negro slave eventually became, at various times in the nineteenth century, a free man, the reason is to be found not only in the belated recognition of morality and Christian precepts but also in the fact that slavery, as an economic institution, had ceased to be profitable. That is why slavery in the British islands was abolished fifteen years earlier than in the French and fifty years earlier than in the Spanish islands. Emancipation of the Negro was a juridical, a social and political change. In the eyes of the law the slave, formerly the property of his master, a human beast of burden completely in the power and at the discretion of his owner, became free, with all the rights, privileges and perquisites pertaining thereto. But emancipation was not an economic change. It left the new freeman as much dependent on and at the mercy of his king sugar as he had been as a slave. It meant for him not the land, which was incompatible with the requirements of the capitalist sugar industry, but the Bible, which was not at variance with that industry. It meant a change from chattel slavery to peonage, or, as has been said in another connection, a change from the discipline of the cart-whip to the discipline of starvation. The slave was raised to the dubious dignity of a landless wage laborer, paid at the rate of twenty-five cents a day in the British islands. Sweet are the uses of emancipation! To free the Negro it was necessary not so much to destroy slavery, which was the consequence of sugar, as to alter the method of production in the sugar industry itself. This simple point is essential to an understanding of the situation of the Negro population in the Caribbean today. The black man, emancipated from above by legislation or from below by revolution, remains today the slave of sugar.

STUDY QUESTIONS

1. What was the economic impact of the trans-Atlantic slave trade?

2. How do you interpret the Williams thesis?

3. Are humanitarian and economic reasons for the demise of slavery mutually exclusive? In other words, is there room for both? Which, in your estimation, retains primacy?

PART IV
ECONOMICS

Imperialism: A Study

John Atkinson Hobson (1858–1940), a staunch opponent of British imperialism, was Britain's version of the American muckrakers such as Upton Sinclair, Ida Tarbell, or Lincoln Steffens, who also worked on progressive reform. He inherited his bent toward issues-based politics from the mid-19th-century radical parliamentarians John Bright and Richard Cobden. Hobson was a journalist, political economist, and social scientist who viewed history through a variety of disciplines, and who had an immense effect on Marxists and Socialists after the turn of the 20th century. Paradoxically, he also influenced that future savior of capitalism, John Maynard Keynes. J. A. Hobson opposed militarism and jingoism as well as nationalism, with an acute concern for foreign affairs by promoting the advocacy of international law. He wrote and lectured extensively on economy and society, forming a core set of beliefs he summed up as "economic humanism." Hobson adhered ideologically to international socialism to combat the more egregious aspects of capitalism. His solution was the welfare state in which the moral was as important as the practical.

One of Hobson's most original economic theories dealt with oversaving and underconsumption. Saving excessively within the British economy resulted in less capital stimulation (i.e., underconsumption) and underemployment. Critics deemed his hypothesis as contradictory to the long-standing Victorian value of thrift. Hobson, however, argued that his objective was an improved social distribution of wealth.

The turning point in Hobson's career, where economics and imperialism converged, was the Boer War between 1899 and 1902. This colonial war between the British and Dutch (or Boer) settlers in South Africa exemplified what Hobson meant by production outstripping consumption. In a 1902 article entitled, "The Economic Taproot of Imperialism," Hobson fleshed out what would become his seminal critique, *Imperialism: A Study*, published that same year.

In this lengthy moral indictment, Hobson addresses the relationship between capital accumulation and colonial expansion in two main parts: economic and political. The former contains the foundation

Figure 9.1. J. A. Hobson. Source: http://en.wikipedia.org/wiki/File:Ernest_William_Hobson_DMD1920.jpg.

for his arguments. Hobson rejects, for example, the commercial-value theory, which held that trade was more profitable with the empire as perpetual markets for British manufactured goods, instead positing not only that imperialism favored protection over free trade, but also that imperial maintenance was not worth its expenditure. Similarly, he attempts to disabuse his contemporaries of the notion that empire served as an overseas outlet for population. Those to whom Hobson refers as "economic parasites" included financiers, investors, merchants, shipbuilders, manufacturers, industrialists, soldiers, diplomats, and missionaries: in short, the entire imperial and capitalist cast of characters.

All of these, however, remain corollaries rather than the cause of imperialism. Therein lies the crux of Hobson's thesis: "the economic taproot" of imperialism, which was a function of overproduction and underconsumption. The misdistribution of key indices such as per capita income and standard of living was to blame because those with little saved, while those with expendable revenue turned to investment in the imperial project. Hobson's fiscal solution suggests an increase in the incomes of the working classes by taxing unearned capital accumulation.

Having reductively examined the economic cause of imperialism, Hobson then turns to its political effects. By preventing the advancement of self-governing representative bodies, Britain revealed a superiority complex that had been hidden behind masks of power. To him, pseudoscientific ideas of race as well as the "civilizing-mission" theory lack merit. Hobson, in fact, compares imperialism to an infectious disease and cannot find one redemptive quality in the entire phenomenon of cheap coolie labor for the enrichment of industrial magnates in the north of England and the financiers of the City of London. If public opinion could be swayed by exposés of exploitation and critiques of imperial culture, decolonization would ensue.

As a socialist, Hobson was not necessarily anticapitalist, and certainly not antidemocratic, but he did oppose their abuses, both real and ideological. The problem still remained that not all could prosper under capitalism, but he believed that Britons could be better, more socially conscious, capitalists. For posterity, Hobson not only altered the terms of the debates for future generations of scholars of empire, he also placed the interrelationships between economic imperialism, modern finance, and power at the center of those debates.

Imperialism: A Study

By J. A. Hobson

ECONOMIC PARASITES OF IMPERIALISM

I

Seeing that the Imperialism of the last six decades is clearly condemned as a business policy, in that at enormous expense it has procured a small, bad, unsafe increase of markets, and has jeopardised the entire wealth of the nation in rousing the strong resentment of other nations, we may ask, "How is the British nation induced to embark upon such unsound business?" The only possible answer is that the business interest of the nation as a whole are subordinated to those of certain sectional interests that usurp control of the national resources and use them for their private gain. This is no strange or monstrous charge to bring; it is the commonest disease of all forms of government. The famous words of Sir Thomas More are as true now as when he wrote them: "Everywhere do I perceive a certain conspiracy of rich men seeking their own advantage under the name and pretext of the commonwealth."

Although the new Imperialism has been bad business for the nation, it has been good business for certain classes and certain trades within the nation. The vast expenditure on armaments, the costly wars, the grave risks and embarrassments of foreign policy, the checks upon political and social reforms within Great Britain, though fraught with great injury to the nation, have served well the present business interests of certain industries and professions.

It is idle to meddle with politics unless we clearly recognise this central fact and understand what these sectional interests are which are the enemies of national safety and the commonwealth. We must put aside the merely sentimental diagnosis which explains wars or other national blunders by outbursts of patriotic animosity or errors of statecraft. Doubtless at every outbreak of war not only the man in the street but the man at the helm is often duped by the cunning with which aggressive motives and greedy purposes dress themselves in defensive clothing. There is, it may be safely asserted, no war within memory, however nakedly aggressive it may seem to the dispassionate historian, which has not been

J. A. Hobson, *Imperialism: A Study*, pp. 46-61, 71-93, University of Michigan Press, 1902.

presented to the people who were called upon to fight as a necessary defensive policy, in which the honour, perhaps the very existence, of the State was involved.

The disastrous folly of these wars, the material and moral damage inflicted even on the victor, appear so plain to the disinterested spectator that he is apt to despair of any State attaining years of discretion, and inclines to regard these natural cataclysms as implying some ultimate irrationalism in politics. But careful analysis of the existing relations between business and politics shows that the aggressive Imperialism which we seek to understand is not in the main the product of blind passions of races or of the mixed folly and ambition of politicians. It is far more rational than at first sight appears. Irrational from the standpoint of the whole nation, it is rational enough from the standpoint of certain classes in the nation. A completely socialist State which kept good books and presented regular balance-sheets of expenditure and assets would soon discard Imperialism; an intelligent *laissez-faire* democracy which gave duly proportionate weight in its policy to all economic interests alike would do the same. But a State in which certain well-organised business interests are able to outweigh the weak, diffused interest of the community is bound to pursue a policy which accords with the pressure of the former interests.

In order to explain Imperialism on this hypothesis we have to answer two questions. Do we find in Great Britain any well-organised group of special commercial and social interests which stand to gain by aggressive Imperialism and the militarism it involves? If such a combination of interests exists, has it the power to work its will in the arena of politics?

What is the direct economic outcome of Imperialism? A great expenditure of public money upon ships, guns, military and naval equipment and stores, growing and productive of enormous profits when a war, or an alarm of war, occurs; new public loans and important fluctuations in the home and foreign Bourses; more posts for soldiers and sailors and in the diplomatic and consular services; improvement of foreign investments by the substitution of the British flag for a foreign flag; acquisition of markets for certain classes of exports, and some protection and assistance for British trades in these manufactures; employment for engineers, missionaries, speculative miners, ranchers and other emigrants.

Certain definite business and professional interests feeding upon imperialistic expenditure, or upon the results of that expenditure, are thus set up in opposition to the common good, and, instinctively feeling their way to one another, are found united in strong sympathy to support every new imperialist exploit.

If the £60,000,000[1] which may now be taken as a minimum expenditure on armaments in time of peace were subjected to a close analysis, most of it would be traced directly to the tills of certain big firms engaged in building warships and transports, equipping and coaling them, manufacturing guns, rifles, ammunition, 'planes and motor vehicles of every kind, supplying horses, waggons, saddlery, food, clothing for the services, contracting for barracks, and for other large irregular needs. Through these main channels the millions flow to feed many subsidiary trades, most of which are quite aware that they are engaged in executing contracts for the services. Here we have an important nucleus of commercial Imperialism. Some of these trades, especially the shipbuilding, boilermaking, and gun and ammunition making trades, are conducted by large firms with immense capital, whose heads are well aware of the uses of political influence for trade purposes.

These men are Imperialists by conviction; a pushful policy is good for them.

With them stand the great manufacturers for export trade, who gain a living by supplying the real or artificial wants of the new countries we annex or open up. Manchester, Sheffield, Birmingham, to name three representative cases, are full of firms which compete in pushing textiles and hardware, engines,

---

1   In 1905; now, in 1938, £200,000,000.

tools, machinery, spirits, guns, upon new markets. The public debts which ripen in our colonies, and in foreign countries that come under our protectorate or influence, are largely loaned in the shape of rails, engines, guns, and other materials of civilization made and sent out by British firms. The making of railways, canals, and other public works, the establishment of factories, the development of mines, the improvement of agriculture in new countries, stimulate a definite interest in important manufacturing industries which feeds a very firm imperialist faith in their owners.

The proportion which such trade bears to the total industry of Great Britain is not great, but some of it is extremely influential and able to make a definite impression upon politics, through chambers of commerce, Parliamentary representatives, and semi-political, semi-commercial bodies like the Imperial South African Association or the China Society.

The shipping trade has a very definite interest which makes for Imperialism. This is well illustrated by the policy of State subsidies now claimed by shipping firms as a retainer, and in order to encourage British shipping for purposes of imperial safety and defence.

The services are, of course, imperialist by conviction and by professional interest, and every increase of the army, navy and air force enhances the political power they exert. The abolition of purchase in the army, by opening the profession to the upper middle classes, greatly enlarged this most direct feeder of imperial sentiment. The potency of this factor is, of course, largely due to the itch for glory and adventure among military officers upon disturbed or uncertain frontiers of the Empire. This has been a most prolific source of expansion in India. The direct professional influence of the services carries with it a less organised but powerful sympathetic support on the part of the aristocracy and the wealthy classes, who seek in the services careers for their sons.

To the military services we may add the Indian Civil Service and the numerous official and semi-official posts in our colonies and protectorates. Every expansion of the Empire is also regarded by these same classes as affording new openings for their sons as ranchers, planters, engineers, or missionaries. This point of view is aptly summarised by a high Indian official, Sir Charles Crossthwaite, in discussing British relations with Siam. " The real question was who was to get the trade with them, and how we could make the most of them, so as to find fresh markets for our goods and also employment for those superfluous articles of the present day, our boys."

From this standpoint our colonies still remain what James Mill cynically described them as being, "a vast system of outdoor relief for the upper classes."

In all the professions, military and civil, the army, diplomacy, the church, the bar, teaching and engineering, Greater Britain serves for an overflow, relieving the congestion of the home market and offering chances to more reckless or adventurous members, while it furnishes a convenient limbo for damaged characters and careers. The actual amount of profitable employment thus furnished by our recent acquisitions is inconsiderable, but it arouses that disproportionate interest which always attaches to the margin of employment. To extend this margin is a powerful motive in Imperialism.

These influences, primarily economic, though not unmixed with other sentimental motives, are particularly operative in military, clerical, academic, and Civil Service circles, and furnish an interested bias towards Imperialism throughout the educated circles.

II

By far the most important economic factor in Imperialism is the influence relating to investments. The growing cosmopolitanism of capital has been the greatest economic change of recent generations. Every advanced industrial nation has been tending to place a larger share of its capital outside the limits of its own political area, in foreign countries, or in colonies, and to draw a growing income from this source.

No exact or even approximate estimate of the total amount of the income of the British nation derived from foreign investments is possible. We possess, however, in the income tax assessments an indirect measurement of certain large sections of investments, from which we can form some judgment as to the total size of the income from foreign and colonial sources, and the rate of its growth.

These returns give us a measure of the amount and growth of the investments effected by British citizens in foreign and colonial stocks of a public or semi-public character, including foreign and colonial public securities, railways, etc. The income from these sources is computed as follows:—[2]

	£
1884	33,829,124
1888	46,978,371
1892	54,728,770
1896	54,901,079
1900	60,266,886
1903	63,828,715

From this table it appears that the period of energetic Imperialism coincided with a remarkable growth in the income for foreign investments.

These figures, however, only give the foreign income which can be identified as such. The closer estimates made by Sir R. Giffen and others warrant the belief that the actual income derived from foreign and colonial investments amounted to not less than £100,000,000, the capital value of the same reaching a sum of about £2,000,000,000.[3]

Income tax returns and other statistics descriptive of the growth of these investments indicate that the total amount of British investments abroad at the end of the nineteenth century cannot be set down at a lower figure than this. Considering that Sir R. Giffen regarded as "moderate" the estimate of £1,700,000,000 in 1892, the figure here named is probably below the truth.

Now, without placing any undue reliance upon these estimates, we cannot fail to recognise that in dealing with these foreign investments we are facing the most important factor in the economics of Imperialism. Whatever figures we take, two facts are evident. First, that the income derived as interest upon foreign investments enormously exceeded that derived as profits upon ordinary export and import trade. Secondly, that while our foreign and colonial trade, and presumably the income from it, were growing but slowly, the share of our import values representing income from foreign investments was growing very rapidly.

In a former chapter I pointed out how small a proportion of our national income appeared to be derived as profits from external trade. It seemed unintelligible that the enormous costs and risks of the new Imperialism should be undertaken for such small results in the shape of increase to external trade, especially when the size and character of the new markets acquired were taken into consideration. The statistics of foreign investments, however, shed clear light upon the economic forces which dominate

---

2   Figures for the years 1929–1933 are given in the Appendix, p. 375.
3   See Appendix, p. 375.

our policy. While the manufacturing and trading classes make little out of their new markets, paying, if they knew it, much more in taxation than they get out of them in trade, it is quite otherwise with the investor.

It is not too much to say that the modern foreign policy of Great Britain has been primarily a struggle for profitable markets of investment. To a larger extent every year Great Britain has been becoming a nation living upon tribute from abroad, and the classes who enjoy this tribute have had an ever-increasing incentive to employ the public policy, the public purse, and the public force to extend the field of their private investments, and to safeguard and improve their existing investments. This is, perhaps, the most important fact in modern politics, and the obscurity in which it is wrapped has constituted the gravest danger to our State.

What was true of Great Britain was true likewise of France, Germany, the United States, and of all countries in which modern capitalism had placed large surplus savings in the hands of a plutocracy or of a thrifty middle class. A well-recognised distinction is drawn between creditor and debtor countries. Great Britain had been for some time by far the largest creditor country, and the policy by which the investing classes used the instrument of the State for private business purposes is most richly illustrated in the history of her wars and annexations. But France, Germany, and the United States were advancing fast along the same path. The nature of these imperialist operations is thus set forth by the Italian economist Loria:

"When a country which has contracted a debt is unable, on account of the slenderness of its income, to offer sufficient guarantee for the punctual payment of interest, what happens ? Sometimes an out-and-out conquest of the debtor country follows. Thus France's attempted conquest of Mexico during the second empire was undertaken solely with the view of guaranteeing the interest of French citizens holding Mexican securities. But more frequently the insufficient guarantee of an international loan gives rise to the appointment of a financial commission by the creditor countries in order to protect their rights and guard the late of their invested capital. The appointment of such a commission literally amounts in the end, however, to a veritable conquest. We have examples of this in Egypt, which has to all practical purposes become a British province, and in Tunis, which has in like manner become a dependency of France, who supplied the greater part of the loan. The Egyptian revolt against the foreign domination issuing from the debt came to nothing, as it met with invariable opposition from capitalistic combinations, and Tel-el-Kebir's success bought with money, was the most brilliant victory wealth has ever obtained on the field of battle."[4]

But, though useful to explain certain economic facts, the terms "creditor" and "debtor," as applied to countries, obscure the most significant feature of this Imperialism. For though, as appears from the analysis given above, much, if not most, of the debts were "public," the credit was nearly always private, though sometimes, as in the case of Egypt, its owners succeeded in getting their Government to enter a most unprofitable partnership, guaranteeing the payment of the interest, but not sharing in it.

Aggressive Imperialism, which costs the taxpayer so dear, which is of so little value to the manufacturer and trader, which is fraught with such grave incalculable peril to the citizen, is a source of great gain to the investor who cannot find at home the profitable use he seeks for his capital, and insists that his Government should help him to profitable and secure investments abroad.

---

4 Loria, *The Economic Foundations of Politics*, p. 273 (George Allen & Unwin).

If, contemplating the enormous expenditure on armaments, the ruinous wars, the diplomatic audacity or knavery by which modern Governments seek to extend their territorial power, we put the plain, practical question, *Cui bono?* the first and most obvious answer is, the investor.

The annual income Great Britain derives from commissions on her whole foreign and colonial trade, import and export, was estimated by Sir R. Giffen[5] at £18,000,000 for 1899, taken at $2^1/_2$ per cent., upon a turnover of £800,000,000.

This is the whole that we are entitled to regard as profits on external trade. Considerable as this sum is, it cannot serve to yield an economic motive-power adequate to explain the dominance which business considerations exercise over our imperial policy. Only when we set beside it some £90,000,000 or £100,000,000, representing pure profit upon investments, do we understand whence the economic impulse to Imperialism is derived.

Investors who have put their money in foreign lands, upon terms which take full account of risks connected with the political conditions of the country, desire to use the resources of their Government to minimise these risks, and so to enhance the capital value and the interest of their private investments. The investing and speculative classes in general have also desired that Great Britain should take other foreign areas under her flag in order to secure new areas for profitable investments and speculation.

III

If the special interest of the investor is liable to clash with the public interest and to induce a wrecking policy, still more dangerous is the special interest of the financier, the general dealer in investments. In large measure the rank and file of the investors are, both for business and for politics, the cat'spaws of the great financial houses, who use stocks and shares not so much as investments to yield them interest, but as material for speculation in the money market. In handling large masses of stocks and shares, in floating companies, in manipulating fluctuations of values, the magnates of the Bourse find their gain. These great businesses—banking, broking, bill discounting, loan floating, company promoting—form the central ganglion of international capitalism. United by the strongest bonds of organisation, always in closest and quickest touch with one another, situated in the very heart of the business capital of every State, controlled, so far as Europe is concerned, chiefly by men of a single and peculiar race, who have behind them many centuries of financial experience, they are in a unique position to manipulate the policy of nations. No great quick direction of capital is possible save by their consent and through their agency. Does any one seriously suppose that a great war could be undertaken by any European State, or a great State loan subscribed, if the house of Rothschild and its connexions set their face against it?

Every great political act involving a new flow of capital, or a large fluctuation in the values of existing investments, must receive the sanction and the practical aid of this little group of financial kings. These men, holding their realised wealth and their business capital, as they must, chiefly in stocks and bonds, have a double stake, first as investors, but secondly and chiefly as financial dealers. As investors, their political influence does not differ essentially from that of the smaller investors, except that they usually possess a practical control of the businesses in which they invest. As speculators or financial dealers they constitute, however, the gravest single factor in the economics of Imperialism.

---

5 *Journal of the Statistical Society*, vol. xlii, p. 9.

To create new public debts, to float new companies, and to cause constant considerable fluctuations of values are three conditions of their profitable business. Each condition carries them into politics, and throws them on the side of Imperialism.

The public financial arrangements for the Philippine war put several millions of dollars into the pockets of Mr. Pierpont Morgan and his friends; the China-Japan war, which saddled the Celestial Empire for the first time with a public debt, and the indemnity which she will pay to her European invaders in connexion with the recent conflict, bring grist to the financial mills in Europe; every railway or mining concession wrung from some reluctant foreign potentate means profitable business in raising capital and floating companies. A policy which rouses fears of aggression in Asiatic states, and which fans the rivalry of commercial nations in Europe, evokes vast expenditure on armaments, and ever-accumulating public debts, while the doubts and risks accruing from this policy promote that constant oscillation of values of securities which is so profitable to the skilled financier. There is not a war, a revolution, an anarchist assassination, or any other public shock, which is not gainful to these men; they are harpies who suck their gains from every new forced expenditure and every sudden disturbance of public credit. To the financiers "in the know" the Jameson raid was a most advantageous coup, as may be ascertained by a comparison of the "holdings" of these men before and after that event; the terrible sufferings of England and South Africa in the war, which was a sequel of the raid, has been a source of immense profit to the big financiers who have best held out against the uncalculated waste, and have recouped themselves by profitable war contracts and by "freezing out" the smaller interests in the Transvaal. These men are the only certain gainers from the war, and most of their gains are made out of the public losses of their adopted country or the private losses of their fellow-countrymen.

The policy of these men, it is true, does not necessarily make for war; where war would bring about too great and too permanent a damage to the substantial fabric of industry, which is the ultimate and essential basis of speculation, their influence is cast for peace, as in the dangerous quarrel between Great Britain and the United States regarding Venezuela. But every increase of public expenditure, every oscillation of public credit short of this collapse, every risky enterprise in which public resources can be made the pledge of private speculations, is profitable to the big money-lender and speculator.

The wealth of these houses, the scale of their operations, and their cosmopolitan organisation make them the prime determinants of imperial policy. They have the largest definite stake in the business of Imperialism, and the amplest means of forcing their will upon the policy of nations.

In view of the part which the non-economic factors of patriotism, adventure, military enterprise, political ambition, and philanthropy play in imperial expansion, it may appear that to impute to financiers so much power is to take a too narrowly economic view of history. And it is true that the motor-power of Imperialism is not chiefly financial: finance is rather the governor of the imperial engine, directing the energy and determining its work: it does not constitute the fuel of the engine, nor does it directly generate the power. Finance manipulates the patriotic forces which politicians, soldiers, philanthropists, and traders generate; the enthusiasm for expansion which issues from these sources, though strong and genuine, is irregular and blind; the financial interest has those qualities of concentration and clear-sighted calculation which are needed to set Imperialism to work. An ambitious statesman, a frontier soldier, an overzealous missionary, a pushing trader, may suggest or even initiate a step of imperial expansion, may assist in educating patriotic public opinion to the urgent need of some fresh advance, but the final determination rests with the financial power. The direct influence exercised by great financial houses in "high politics" is supported by the control which they exercise over the body of public opinion through the Press, which, in every "civilised" country, is becoming more and more their obedient instrument.

While the specifically financial newspaper imposes "facts" and "opinions" on the business classes, the general body of the Press comes more and more under the conscious or unconscious domination of financiers. The case of the South African Press, whose agents and correspondents fanned the martial flames in this country, was one of open ownership on the part of South African financiers, and this policy of owning newspapers for the sake of manufacturing public opinion is common in the great European cities. In Berlin, Vienna, and Paris many of the influential newspapers have been held by financial houses, which used them, not primarily to make direct profits out of them, but in order to put into the public mind beliefs and sentiments which would influence public policy and thus affect the money market. In Great Britain this policy has not gone so far, but the alliance with finance grows closer every year, either by financiers purchasing a controlling share of newspapers, or by newspaper proprietors being tempted into finance. Apart from the financial Press, and financial ownership of the general Press, the City has notoriously exercised a subtle and abiding influence upon leading London newspapers, and through them upon the body of the provincial Press, while the entire dependence of the Press for its business profits upon its advertising columns has involved a peculiar reluctance to oppose the organised financial classes with whom rests the control of so much advertising business. Add to this the natural sympathy with a sensational policy which a cheap Press always manifests, and it becomes evident that the Press has been strongly biased towards Imperialism, and has lent itself with great facility to the suggestion of financial or political Imperialists who have desired to work up patriotism for some new piece of expansion.

Such is the array of distinctively economic forces making for Imperialism, a large loose group of trades and professions seeking profitable business and lucrative employment from the expansion of military and civil services, and from the expenditure on military operations, the opening up of new tracts of territory and trade with the same, and the provision of new capital which these operations require, all these finding their central guiding and directing force in the power of the general financier.

The play of these forces does not openly appear. They are essentially parasites upon patriotism, and they adapt themselves to its protecting colours. In the mouth of their representatives are noble phrases, expressive of their desire to extend the area of civilisation, to establish good government, promote Christianity, extirpate slavery, and elevate the lower races. Some of the business men who hold such language may entertain a genuine, though usually a vague, desire to accomplish these ends, but they are primarily engaged in business, and they are not unaware of the utility of the more unselfish forces in furthering their ends. Their true attitude of mind was expressed by Mr. Rhodes in his famous description of "Her Majesty's Flag" as "the greatest commercial asset in the world."[1]

THE ECONOMIC TAPROOT OF IMPERIALISM

No mere array of facts and figures adduced to illustrate the economic nature of the new Imperialism will suffice to dispel the popular delusion that the use of national force to secure new markets by annexing fresh tracts of territory is a sound and a necessary policy for an advanced industrial country like Great Britain.[6] It has indeed been proved that recent annexations of tropical countries, procured at great expense, have furnished poor and precarious markets, that our aggregate trade with our colonial possessions is virtually stationary, and that our most profitable and progressive trade is with rival industrial nations, whose territories we have

---

6   Written in 1905.

no desire to annex, whose markets we cannot force, and whose active antagonism we are provoking by our expansive policy.

But these arguments are not conclusive. It is open to Imperialists to argue thus: "We must have markets for our growing manufactures, we must have new outlets for the investment of our surplus capital and for the energies of the adventurous surplus of our population: such expansion is a necessity of life to a nation with our great and growing powers of production. An ever larger share of our population is devoted to the manufactures and commerce of towns, and is thus dependent for life and work upon food and raw materials from foreign lands. In order to buy and pay for these things we must sell our goods abroad. During the first three-quarters of -the nineteenth century we could do so without difficulty by a natural expansion of commerce with continental nations and our colonies, all of which were far behind us in the main arts of manufacture and the carrying trades. So long as England held a virtual monopoly of the world markets for certain important classes of manufactured goods, Imperialism was unnecessary. After 1870 this manufacturing and trading supremacy was greatly impaired: other nations, especially Germany, the United States, and Belgium, advanced with great rapidity, and while they have not crushed or even stayed the increase of our external trade, their competition made it more and more difficult to dispose of the full surplus of our manufactures at a profit. The encroachments made by these nations upon our old markets, even in our own possessions, made it most urgent that we should take energetic means to secure new markets. These new markets had to lie in hitherto undeveloped countries, chiefly in the tropics, where vast populations lived capable of growing economic needs which our manufacturers and merchants could supply. Our rivals were seizing and annexing territories for similar purposes, and when they had annexed them closed them to our trade. The diplomacy and the arms of Great Britain had to be used in order to compel the owners of the new markets to deal with us: and experience showed that the safest means of securing and developing such markets is by establishing 'protectorates' or by annexation. The value in 1905 of these markets must not be taken as a final test of the economy of such a policy; the process of educating civilized needs which we can supply is of necessity a gradual one, and the cost of such Imperialism must be regarded as a capital outlay, the fruits of which posterity would reap. The new markets might not be large, but they formed serviceable outlets for the overflow of our great textile and metal industries, and, when the vast Asiatic and African populations of the interior were reached, a rapid expansion of trade was expected to result.

"Far larger and more important is the pressure of capital for external fields of investment. Moreover, while the manufacturer and trader are well content to trade with foreign nations, the tendency for investors to work towards the political annexation of countries which contain their more speculative investments is very powerful. Of the fact of this pressure of capital there can be no question. Large savings are made which cannot find any profitable investment in this country; they must find employment elsewhere, and it is to the advantage of the nation that they should be employed as largely as possible in lands where they can be utilized in opening up markets for British trade and employment for British enterprise.

"However costly, however perilous, this process of imperial expansion may be, it is necessary to the continued existence and progress of our nation;[7] if we abandoned it we must be content to leave the development of the world to other nations, who will everywhere cut into our trade, and even impair our means of securing the food and raw materials we require to support our population. Imperialism is thus seen to be, not a choice, but a necessity."

---

7   "And why, indeed, are wars undertaken, if not to conquer colonies which permit the employment of fresh capital, to acquire commercial monopolies, or to obtain the exclusive use of certain highways of commerce?" (Loria, *Economic Foundations of Society*, p. 267).

The practical force of this economic argument in politics is strikingly illustrated by the later history of the United States. Here is a country which suddenly broke through a conservative policy, strongly held by both political parties, bound up with every popular instinct and tradition, and flung itself into a rapid imperial career for which it possessed neither the material nor the moral equipment, risking the principles and practices of liberty and equality by the establishment of militarism and the forcible subjugation of peoples which it could not safely admit to the condition of American citizenship.

Was this a mere wild freak of spread-eaglism, a burst of political ambition on the part of a nation coming to a sudden realization of its destiny ? Not at all. The spirit of adventure, the American "mission of civilization," were as forces making for Imperialism, clearly subordinate to the driving force of the economic factor. The dramatic character of the change is due to the unprecedented rapidity of the industrial revolution in the United States from the eighties onwards. During that period the United States, with her unrivalled natural resources, her immense resources of skilled and unskilled labour, and her genius for invention and organization, developed the best equipped and most productive manufacturing economy the world has yet seen. Fostered by rigid protective tariffs, her metal, textile, tool, clothing, furniture, and other manufactures shot up in a single generation from infancy to full maturity, and, having passed through a period of intense competition, attained, under the able control of great trust-makers, a power of production greater than has been attained in the most advanced industrial countries of Europe.

An era of cut-throat competition, followed by a rapid process of amalgamation, threw an enormous quantity of wealth into the hands of a small number of captains of industry. No luxury of living to which this class could attain kept pace with its rise of income, and a process of automatic saving set in upon an unprecedented scale. The investment of these savings in other industries helped to bring these under the same concentrative forces. Thus a great increase of savings seeking profitable investment is synchronous with a stricter economy of the use of existing capital. No doubt the rapid growth of a population, accustomed to a high and an always ascending standard of comfort, absorbs in the satisfaction of its wants a large quantity of new capital. But the actual rate of saving, conjoined with a more economical application of forms of existing capital, exceeded considerably the rise of the national consumption of manufactures. The power of production far outstripped the actual rate of consumption, and, contrary to the older economic theory, was unable to force a corresponding increase of consumption by lowering prices.

This is no mere theory. The history of any of the numerous trusts or combinations in the United States sets out the facts with complete distinctness. In the free competition of manufactures preceding combination the chronic condition is one of "over-production," in the sense that all the mills or factories can only be kept at work by cutting prices down towards a point where the weaker competitors are forced to close down, because they cannot sell their goods at a price which covers the true cost of production. The first result of the successful formation of a trust or combine is to close down the worse equipped or worse placed mills, and supply the entire market from the better equipped and better placed ones. This course may or may not be attended by a rise of price and some restriction of consumption: in some cases trusts take most of their profits by raising prices, in other cases by reducing the costs of production through employing only the best mills and stopping the waste of competition.

For the present argument it matters not which course is taken; the point is that this concentration of industry in "trusts," "combines," etc., at once limits the quantity of capital which can be effectively employed and increases the share of profits out of which fresh savings and fresh capital will spring. It is quite evident that a trust which is motived by cut-throat competition, due to an excess of capital, cannot normally find inside the " trusted " industry employment for that portion of the profits which the trust- makers desire to save and to invest. New inventions and other economies of production or distribution within the trade may absorb some of the new capital, but there are rigid limits to this absorption. The trust-maker in oil or sugar must find other investments for his savings: if he is early in the application of the combination principles to his trade, he will naturally apply his surplus capital to establish similar combinations in other industries, economising capital still further, and rendering it ever harder for ordinary saving men to find investments for their savings.

Indeed, the conditions alike of cut-throat competition and of combination attest the congestion of capital in the manufacturing industries which have entered the machine economy. We are not here concerned with any theoretic question as to the possibility of producing by modern machine methods more goods than can find a market. It is sufficient to point out that the manufacturing power of a country like the United States would grow so fast as to exceed the demands of the home market. No one acquainted with trade will deny a fact which all American economists assert, that this is the condition which the United States reached at the end of the century, so far, as the more developed industries are concerned. Her manufactures were saturated with capital and could absorb no more. One after another they sought refuge from the waste of competition in "combines" which secure a measure of profitable peace by restricting the quantity of operative capital. Industrial and financial princes in oil, steel, sugar, railroads, banking, etc., were faced with the dilemma of either spending more than they knew how to spend, or forcing markets outside the home area. Two economic courses were open to them, both leading towards an abandonment of the political isolation of the past and the adoption of imperialist methods in the future. Instead of shutting down inferior mills and rigidly restricting output to correspond with profitable sales in the home markets, they might employ their full productive power, applying their savings to increase their business capital, and, while still regulating output and prices for the home market, may "hustle" for foreign markets, dumping down their surplus goods at prices which would not be possible save for the profitable nature of their home market. So likewise they might employ their savings in seeking investments outside their country, first repaying the capital borrowed from Great Britain and other countries for the early development of their railroads, mines and manufactures, and afterwards becoming themselves a creditor class to foreign countries.

It was this sudden demand for foreign markets for manufactures and for investments which was avowedly responsible for the adoption of Imperialism as a political policy and practice by the Republican party to which the great industrial and financial chiefs belonged, and which belonged to them. The adventurous enthusiasm of President Theodore Roosevelt and his "manifest destiny" and "mission of civilization" party must not deceive us. It was Messrs. Rockefeller, Pierpont Morgan, and their associates who needed Imperialism and who fastened it upon the shoulders of the great Republic of the West. They needed Imperialism because they desired to use the public resources of their country to find profitable employment for their capital which otherwise would be superfluous.

It is not indeed necessary to own a country in order to do trade with it or to invest capital in it, and doubtless the United States could find some vent for their surplus goods, and capital in European countries. But these countries were for the most part able to make provision for themselves: most of them erected tariffs against manufacturing imports, and even Great Britain was urged to defend herself by reverting to Protection. The big American manufacturers and financiers were compelled to look to China and the Pacific and to South America for their most profitable chances; Protectionists by principle and practice, they would insist upon getting as close a monopoly of these markets as they can secure, and the competition of Germany, England, and other trading nations would drive them to the establishment of special political relations with the markets they most prize. Cuba, the Philippines, and Hawaii were but the *hors d'œuvre* to whet an appetite for an ampler banquet. Moreover, the powerful hold upon politics which these industrial and financial magnates possessed formed a separate stimulus, which, as we have shown, was operative in Great Britain and elsewhere; the public expenditure in pursuit of an imperial career would be a separate immense source of profit to these men, as financiers negotiating loans, shipbuilders and owners handling subsidies, contractors and manufacturers of armaments and other imperialist appliances.

The suddenness of this political revolution is due to the rapid manifestation of the need. In the last years of the nineteenth century the United States nearly trebled the value of its manufacturing export trade, and it was to be expected that, if the rate of progress of those years continued, within a decade it would overtake our more slowly advancing export trade, and stand first in the list of manufacture-exporting nations.[8]

This was the avowed ambition, and no idle one, of the keenest business men of America; and with the natural resources, the labour and the administrative talents at their disposal, it was quite likely they would achieve their object.[9] The stronger and more direct control over politics exercised in America by

Export Trade of United States, 1890–1900.

Year.				Agriculture.	Manufactures.	Miscellaneous.
				£	£	£
1890	.	.	.	125,756,000	31,435,000	13,019,000
1891	.	.	.	146,617,000	33,720,000	11,731,000
1892	.	.	.	142,508,000	30,479,000	11,660,000
1893	.	.	.	123,810,000	35,484,000	11,653,000
1894	.	.	.	114,737,000	35,557,000	11,168,000
1895	.	.	.	104,143,000	40,230,000	12,174,000
1896	.	.	.	132,992,000	50,738,000	13,639,000
1897	.	.	.	146,059,000	55,923,000	13,984,000
1898	.	.	.	170,383,000	61,585,000	14,743,000
1899	.	.	.	156,427,000	76,157,000	18,002,000
1900	.	.	.	180,931,000	88,281,000	21,389,000

business men enabled them to drive more quickly and more straightly along the line of their economic interests than in Great Britain. American Imperialism was the natural product of the economic pressure of a sudden advance of capitalism which could not find occupation at home and needed foreign markets for goods and for investments.

The same needs existed in European countries, and, as is admitted, drove Governments along the same path. Overproduction in the sense of an excessive manufacturing plant, and surplus capital which could not find sound investments within the country, forced Great Britain, Germany, Holland, France

---

8   Post-war conditions, with the immense opportunities afforded for exports of American goods and capital brought a pause and a temporary withdrawal from imperialist policy.

9   "We hold now three of the winning cards in the game for commercial greatness, to wit—iron, steel and coal. We have long been the granary of the world, we now aspire to be its workshop, then we want to be its clearing-house." (The President of the American Bankers' Association at Denver, 1898.)

to place larger and larger portions of their economic resources outside the area of their present political domain, and then stimulate a policy of political expansion so as to take in the new areas. The economic sources of this movement are laid bare by periodic trade-depressions due to an inability of producers to find adequate and profitable markets for what they can produce. The Majority Report of the Commission upon the Depression of Trade in 1885 put the matter in a nutshell. "That, owing to the nature of the times, the demand for our commodities does not increase at the same rate as formerly; that our capacity for production is consequently in excess of our requirements, and could be considerably increased at short notice; that this is due partly to the competition of the capital which is being steadily accumulated in the country." The Minority Report straightly imputed the condition of affairs to "over-production." Germany was in the early 1900's suffering severely from what is called a glut of capital and of manufacturing power: she had to have new markets; her Consuls all over the world were "hustling" for trade; trading settlements were forced upon Asia Minor; in East arid West Africa, in China and elsewhere the German Empire was impelled to a policy of colonization and protectorates as outlets for German commercial energy.

Every improvement of methods of production, every concentration of ownership and control, seems to accentuate the tendency. As one nation after another enters the machine economy and adopts advanced industrial methods, it becomes more difficult for its manufacturers, merchants, and financiers to dispose profitably of their economic resources, and they are tempted more and more to use their Governments in order to secure for their particular use some distant undeveloped country by annexation and protection.

The process, we may be told, is inevitable, and so it seems upon a superficial inspection. Everywhere appear excessive powers of production, excessive capital in search of investment. It is admitted by all business men that the growth of the powers of production in their country exceeds the growth in consumption, that more goods can be produced than can be sold at a profit, and that more capital exists than can find remunerative investment.

It is this economic condition of affairs that forms the taproot of Imperialism. If the consuming public in this country raised its standard of consumption to keep pace with every rise of productive powers, there could be no excess of goods or capital clamorous to use Imperialism in order to find markets: foreign trade would indeed exist, but there would be no difficulty in exchanging a small surplus of our manufactures for the food and raw material we annually absorbed, and all the savings that we made could find employment, if we chose, in home industries.

There is nothing inherently irrational in such a supposition. Whatever is, or can be, produced, can be consumed, for a claim upon it, as rent, profit, or wages, forms part of the real income of some member of the community, and he can consume it, or else exchange it for some other consumable with some one else who will consume it. With everything that is produced a consuming power is born. If then there are goods which cannot get consumed, or which cannot even get produced because it is evident they cannot get consumed, and if there is a quantity of capital and labour which cannot get full employment because its products cannot get consumed, the only possible explanation of this paradox is the refusal of owners of consuming power to apply that power in effective demand for commodities.

It is, of course, possible that an excess of producing power might exist in particular industries by misdirection, being engaged in certain manufactures, whereas it ought to have been engaged in agriculture or some other use. But no one can seriously contend that such misdirection explains the recurrent gluts and consequent depressions of modern industry, or that, when over-production is manifest in the leading manufactures, ample avenues are open for the surplus capital and labour in other industries. The general character of the excess of producing power is proved by the existence at such times of large bank stocks of idle money seeking any sort of profitable investment and finding none.

The root questions underlying the phenomena are clearly these: "Why is it that consumption fails to keep pace automatically in a community with power of production?" "Why does under-consumption or over-saving occur?" For it is evident that the consuming power, which, if exercised, would keep tense the reins of production, is in part withheld, or in other words is "saved" and stored up for investment. All saving for investment does not imply slackness of production; quite the contrary. Saving is economically justified, from the social standpoint, when the capital in which it takes material shape finds full employment in helping to produce commodities which, when produced, will be consumed. It is saving in excess of this amount that causes mischief, taking shape in surplus capital which is not needed to assist current consumption, and which either lies idle, or tries to oust existing capital from its employment, or else seeks speculative use abroad under the protection of the Government.

But it may be asked, "Why should there be any tendency to over-saving? Why should the owners of consuming power withhold a larger quantity for savings than can be serviceably employed?" Another way of putting the same question is this, "Why should not the pressure of present wants keep pace with every possibility of satisfying them?" The answer to these pertinent questions carries us to the broadest issue of the distribution of wealth. If a tendency to distribute income or consuming power according to needs were operative, it is evident that consumption would rise with every rise of producing power, for human needs are illimitable, and there could be no excess of saving. But it is quite otherwise in a state of economic society where distribution has no fixed relation to needs, but is determined by other conditions which assign to some people a consuming power vastly in excess of needs or possible uses, while others are destitute of consuming power enough to satisfy even the full demands of physical efficiency. The following illustration may serve to make the issue clear. "The volume of production has been constantly rising owing to the development of modern machinery. There are two main channels to carry off these products—one channel carrying off the product destined to be consumed by the workers, and the other channel carrying off the remainder to the rich. The workers' channel is in rock- bound banks that cannot enlarge, owing to the competitive wage system preventing wages rising *pro rata* with increased efficiency. Wages are based upon cost of living, and not upon efficiency of labour. The miner in the poor mine gets the same wages per day as the miner in the adjoining rich mine. The owner of the rich mine gets the advantage—not his labourer. The channel which conveys the goods destined to supply the rich is itself divided into two streams. One stream carries off what the rich 'spend' on themselves for the necessities and luxuries of life. The other is simply an 'overflow' stream carrying off their 'savings.' The channel for spending, i.e. the amount wasted by the rich in luxuries, may broaden somewhat, but owing to the small number of those rich enough to indulge in whims it can never be greatly enlarged, and at any rate it bears such a small proportion to the other channel that in no event can much hope of avoiding a flood of capital be hoped for from this division. The rich will never be so ingenious as to spend enough to prevent over-production. The great safety overflow channel which has been continuously more and more widened and deepened to carry off the ever-increasing flood of new capital is that division of the stream which carried the savings of the rich, and this is not only suddenly found to be incapable of further enlargement, but actually seems to be in the process of being dammed up."[10]

Though this presentation over-accentuates the cleavage between rich and poor and over-states the weakness of the workers, it gives forcible and sound expression to a most important and ill-recognised

10   *The Significance of the Trust*, by H. G. Wilshire.

economic truth. The "overflow" stream of savings is of course fed not exclusively from the surplus income of "the rich"; the professional and industrial middle classes, and to some slight extent the workers, contribute. But the "flooding" is distinctly due to the automatic saving of the surplus income of rich men. This is of course particularly true of America, where multi-millionaires rise quickly and find themselves in possession of incomes far exceeding the demands of any craving that is known to them. To make the metaphor complete, the overflow stream must be represented as reentering the stream of production and seeking to empty there all the "savings" that it carries. Where competition remains free, the result is a chronic congestion of productive power and of production, forcing down home prices, wasting large sums in advertising and in pushing for orders, and periodically causing a crisis followed by a collapse, during which quantities of capital and labour lie unemployed and unremunerated. The prime object of the trust or other combine is to remedy this waste and loss by substituting regulation of output for reckless over-production. In achieving this it actually narrows or even dams up the old channels of investment, limiting the overflow stream to the exact amount required to maintain the normal current of output. But this rigid limitation of trade, though required for the separate economy of each trust, does not suit the trust-maker, who is driven to compensate for strictly regulated industry at home by cutting new foreign channels as outlets for his productive power and his excessive savings. Thus we reach the conclusion that Imperialism is the endeavour of the great controllers of industry to broaden the channel for the flow of their surplus wealth by seeking foreign markets and foreign investments to take off the goods and capital they cannot sell or use at home.

The fallacy of the supposed inevitability of imperial expansion as a necessary outlet for progressive industry is now manifest. It is not industrial progress that demands the opening up of new markets and areas of investment, but mal-distribution of consuming power which prevents the absorption of commodities and capital within the country. The over-saving which is the economic root of Imperialism is found by analysis to consist of rents, monopoly profits, and other unearned or excessive elements of income, which, not being earned by labour of head or hand, have no legitimate *raison d'être*. Having no natural relation to effort of production, they impel their recipients to no corresponding satisfaction of consumption: they form a surplus wealth, which, having no proper place in the normal economy of production and consumption, tends to accumulate as excessive savings. Let any turn in the tide of politico-economic forces divert from these owners their excess of income and make it flow, either to the workers in higher wages, or to the community in taxes, so that it will be spent instead of being saved, serving in either of these ways to swell the tide of consumption—there will be no need to fight for foreign markets or foreign areas of investment.

Many have carried their analysis so far as to realise the absurdity of spending half our financial resources in fighting to secure foreign markets at times when hungry mouths, ill- clad backs, ill-furnished houses indicate countless unsatisfied material wants among our own population. If we may take the careful statistics of Mr. Rowntree[11] for our guide, we shall be aware that more than one-fourth of the population of our towns is living at a standard which is below bare physical efficiency. If, by some economic readjustment, the products which flow from the surplus saving of the rich to swell the overflow streams could be diverted so as to raise the incomes and the standard of consumption of this inefficient fourth, there would be no need for pushful Imperialism, and the cause of social reform would have won its greatest victory.

It is not inherent in the nature of things that we should spend our natural resources on militarism, war, and risky, unscrupulous diplomacy, in order to find markets for our goods and surplus capital. An

---

11   *Poverty: A Study of Town Life.*

intelligent progressive community, based upon substantial equality of economic and educational opportunities, will raise its standard of consumption to correspond with every increased power of production, and can find full employment for an unlimited quantity of capital and labour within the limits of the country which it occupies. Where the distribution of incomes is such as to enable all classes of the nation to convert their felt wants into an effective demand for commodities, there can be no over-production, no underemployment of capital and labour, and no necessity to fight for foreign markets.

The most convincing condemnation of the current economy is conveyed in the difficulty which producers everywhere experience in finding consumers for their products: a fact attested by the prodigious growth of classes of agents and middlemen, the multiplication of every sort of advertising, and the general increase of the distributive classes. Under a sound economy the pressure would be reversed: the growing wants of progressive societies would be a constant stimulus to the inventive and operative energies of producers, and would form a constant strain upon the powers of production. The simultaneous excess of all the factors of production, attested by frequently recurring periods of trade depression, is a most dramatic exhibition of the false economy of distribution. It does not imply a mere miscalculation in the application of productive power, or a brief temporary excess of that power; it manifests in an acute form an economic waste which is chronic and general throughout the advanced industrial nations, a waste contained in the divorcement of the desire to consume and the power to consume.

If the apportionment of income were such as to evoke no excessive saving, full constant employment for capital and labour would be furnished at home. This, of course, does not imply that there would be no foreign trade. Goods that could not be produced at home, or produced as well or as cheaply, would still be purchased by ordinary process of international exchange, but here again the pressure would be the wholesome pressure of the consumer anxious to buy abroad what he could not buy at home, not the blind eagerness of the producer to use every force or trick of trade or politics to find markets for his "surplus" goods.

The struggle for markets, the greater eagerness of producers to sell than of consumers to buy, is the crowning proof of a false economy of distribution. Imperialism is the fruit of this false economy; "social reform" is its remedy. The primary purpose of "social reform," using the term in its economic signification, is to raise the wholesome standard of private and public consumption for a nation, so as to enable the nation to live up to its highest standard of production. Even those social reformers who aim directly at abolishing or reducing some bad form of consumption, as in the Temperance movement, generally recognise the necessity of substituting some better form of current consumption which is more educative and stimulative of other tastes, and will assist to raise the general standard of consumption.

There is no necessity to open up new foreign markets; the home markets are capable of indefinite expansion. Whatever is produced in England can be consumed in England, provided that the "income" or power to demand commodities, is properly distributed. This only appears untrue because of the unnatural and unwholesome specialisation to which this country has been subjected, based upon a bad distribution of economic resources, which has induced an overgrowth of certain manufacturing trades for the express purpose of effecting foreign sales. If the industrial revolution had taken place in an England founded upon equal access by all classes to land, education and legislation, specialisation in manufactures would not have gone so far (though more intelligent progress would have been made, by reason of a widening of the area of selection of inventive and organising talents); foreign trade would have been less important, though more steady; the standard of life for all portions of the population would have been high, and the present rate of national consumption would probably have given full, constant, remunerative employment to a far larger quantity of private and public capital than is now employed.[12] For the over-saving or wider consumption that is traced to excessive incomes of the rich is a suicidal economy, even from the exclusive standpoint of capital; for consumption alone vitalises capital and makes it capable of yielding profits. An economy that assigns to the "possessing" classes an excess of consuming power which they cannot use, and cannot convert into really serviceable capital, is a dog-in-the-manger policy. The social reforms which deprive the possessing classes of their surplus will not, therefore, inflict upon them the real injury they dread; they can only use this surplus by forcing on their country a wrecking policy of Imperialism. The only safety of nations lies in removing the unearned increments of income from the possessing classes, and adding them to the wage-income of the working classes or to the public income, in order that they may be spent in raising the standard of consumption.

Social reform bifurcates, according as reformers seek to achieve this end by raising wages or by increasing public taxation and expenditure. These courses are not essentially contradictory, but are rather complementary. Working- class movements aim, either by private co-operation or by political pressure on legislative and administrative government, at increasing the proportion of the national income which accrues to labour in the form of wages, pensions, compensation for injuries, etc. State Socialism aims at getting for the direct use of the whole society an increased share of the "social values" which arise from the closely and essentially co-operative work of an industrial society, taxing property and incomes so as to draw into the public exchequer for public expenditure the "unearned elements" of income, leaving to individual producers those incomes which are necessary to induce them to apply in the best way their economic energies, and to private enterprises those businesses which do not breed monopoly, and which the public need not or cannot undertake. These are not, indeed, the sole or perhaps the best avowed objects of social reform movements. But for the purposes of this analysis they form the kernel.

Trade Unionism and Socialism are thus the natural enemies of Imperialism, for they take away from the "imperialist" classes the surplus incomes which form the economic stimulus of Imperialism.

This does not pretend to be a final statement of the full relations of these forces. When we come to political analysis we shall perceive that the tendency of Imperialism is to crush Trade Unionism and to "nibble" at or parasitically exploit State Socialism. But, confining ourselves for the present to the narrowly economic setting, Trade Unionism and State Socialism may be regarded as complementary forces arrayed against Imperialism, in as far as, by diverting to working-class or public expenditure elements of income which would otherwise be surplus savings, they raise the general standard of home consumption and abate the pressure for foreign markets. Of course, if the increase of working-class income were wholly or chiefly "saved," not spent, or if the taxation of unearned incomes were utilised for the relief of other taxes borne by the possessing classes, no such result as we have described would follow. There is, however, no reason to anticipate this result from trade-union or socialistic measures. Though no sufficient natural stimulus exists to force the well-to-do classes to spend in further luxuries the surplus incomes which they save, every working-class family is subject to powerful stimuli of economic needs, and a reasonably governed State would regard as its prime duty the relief of the present poverty of public life by new forms of socially useful expenditure.

---

12 The classical economists of England, forbidden by their theories of parsimony and of the growth of capital to entertain the notion of an indefinite expansion of home markets by reason of a constantly rising standard of national comfort, were early driven to countenance a doctrine of the necessity of finding external markets for the investment of capital. So J. S. Mill: "The expansion of capital would soon reach its ultimate boundary if the boundary itself did not continually open and leave more space" (*Political Economy*). And before him Ricardo (in a letter to Malthus): "If with every accumulation of capital we could take a piece of fresh fertile land to our island, profits would never fall."

But we are not here concerned with what belongs to the practical issues of political and economic policy. It is the economic theory for which we claim acceptance—a theory which, if accurate, dispels the delusion that expansion of foreign trade, and therefore of empire, is a necessity of national life.

Regarded from the standpoint of economy of energy, the same "choice of life" confronts the nation as the individual. An individual may expend all his energy in acquiring external possessions, adding field to field, barn to barn, factory to factory—may "spread himself" over the widest area of property, amassing material wealth which is in some sense "himself" as containing the impress of his power and interest. He does this by specialising upon the lower acquisitive plane of interest at the cost of neglecting the cultivation of the higher qualities and interests of his nature. The antagonism is not indeed absolute. Aristotle has said, "We must first secure a livelihood and then practise virtue." Hence the pursuit of material property as a reasonable basis of physical comfort would be held true economy by the wisest men; but the absorption of time, energy, and interest upon such quantitative expansion-at the necessary cost of starving the higher tastes and faculties is condemned as false economy. The same issue comes up in the business life of the individual: it is the question of intensive *versus* extensive cultivation. A rude or ignorant farmer, where land is plentiful, is apt to spread his capital and labour over a large area, taking in new tracts and cultivating them poorly. A skilled, scientific farmer will study a smaller patch of land, cultivate it thoroughly, and utilise its diverse properties, adapting it to the special needs of his most remunerative markets. The same is true of other businesses; even where the economy of large-scale production is greatest there exists some limit beyond which the wise business man will not go, aware that in doing so he will risk by enfeebled management what he seems to gain by mechanical economies of production and market.

Everywhere the issue of quantitative *versus* qualitative growth comes up. This is the entire issue of empire. A people limited in number and energy and in the land they occupy have the choice of improving to the utmost the political and economic management of their own land, confining themselves to such accessions of territory as are justified by the most economical disposition of a growing population; or they may proceed, like the slovenly farmer, to spread their power and energy over the whole earth, tempted by the speculative value or the quick profits of some new market, or else by mere greed of territorial acquisition, and ignoring the political and economic wastes and risks involved by this imperial career. It must be clearly understood that this is essentially a choice of alternatives; a full simultaneous application of intensive and extensive cultivation is impossible. A nation may either, following the example of Denmark or Switzerland, put brains into agriculture, develop a finely varied system of public education, general and technical, apply the ripest science to its special manufacturing industries, and so support in progressive comfort and character a considerable population upon a strictly limited area; or it may, like Great Britain, neglect its agriculture, allowing its lands to go out of cultivation and its population to grow up in towns, fall behind other nations in its methods of education and in the capacity of adapting to its uses the latest scientific knowledge, in order that it may squander its pecuniary and military resources in forcing bad markets and finding speculative fields of investment in distant corners of the earth, adding millions of square miles and of unassimilable population to the area of the Empire.

The driving forces of class interest which stimulate and support this false economy we have explained. No remedy will serve which permits the future operation of these forces. It is idle to attack Imperialism or Militarism as political expedients or policies unless the axe is laid at the economic root of the tree, and the classes for whose interest Imperialism works are shorn of the surplus revenues which seek this outlet.

STUDY QUESTIONS

1. According to Hobson, how are imperialism, economics, and politics interrelated?

2. What does Hobson mean by "the economic taproot" of imperialism?

Imperialism: The Final Stage of Capitalism

L enin carried on Karl Marx's work by adding to his view of historical materialism that the final moment of capitalism, after industrialization, had proven to be imperialism.[1] This thesis became the cornerstone of his work entitled, *Imperialism: The Highest Stage of Capitalism* in 1916.

Vladimir Ilich Ulyanov, or Lenin, as he was more commonly known, and the Bolshevik Party were in the vanguard of those Communists who opposed the "imperialist war" between 1914 and 1918, advocating instead for Marx's prediction of an international proletarian struggle against the bourgeoisie, rather than one between capitalist nation-states. Lenin's older brother was hanged for plotting to assassinate the czar in the 1880s, and as a student demonstrator in his youth, Lenin became an early convert to Marxism. He was exiled to Siberia for a time for organizing subversive "study groups" among Russian workers.

During the first three years of the First World War, however, Lenin remained in exile in Switzerland, and thus lacked any realistic opportunity to put his principles into practice. Eventually, as fighting persisted, he arrived in Petrograd (as the czarist capital, St. Petersburg, was named after the outbreak of war with Germany) in April 1917, furtively transported on a train by the Germans, who hoped that the rabble-rouser would further raze what was left of a crumbling Russian war effort. In his "April Theses," Lenin, in effect, issued a political program, which called for a handover of "all Power to the Soviets!" and advocated peace, bread, and land for the masses. He also sought the cessation of hostilities between Russian and German troops, whose other occupations as bucolic farmers and urbanized workers made them proletarian brethren.

Since March 1917, strikes and street riots had broken out on a large scale in Petrograd. Liberal members of the Duma (Russian parliament) demanded a constitutional government, and the czar dissolved it. Defiant deputies, however, decided to remain in session, and elected a committee to lead the

---

1 Marx constructed a linear idea of history, in which unequal capitalist relations had occurred in stages: ancient, feudal, Asiatic despotism, and industrialization.

Figure 10.1. V. I. Lenin. Source: http://commons.wikimedia.org/wiki/File:Lenin_V_I_1921_by_Parkhomenko.jpg.

Duma against the autocratic czar. Meanwhile, a city-wide soviet was formed by the Petrograd factory workers. The czar decided to yield, reorganized the committee of the Duma as a provisional government, and abdicated, offering the crown to his brother, who presciently refused it. The Romanov dynasty had come to an end; after the abdication, Nicholas II and his family were imprisoned and eventually executed in 1918.

The provisional government under the leadership of Alexander Kerensky relied on what remained of the army to establish order. As its members attempted to reassemble a military strategy against the Germans, the unpopularity of the front—exacerbated by effective propaganda of the Bolsheviks—further enervated the provisional government's authority. Soldiers deserted and went home in droves upon hearing rumors that land was to be redistributed to the peasantry.

In the summer of 1917, the Bolsheviks attempted to seize power, but were thwarted. Lenin and other Bolsheviks went into hiding for a few months. By the fall, the provisional government was threatened by a potential coup, this time from the extreme right under a junta of generals left over from czarist rule. It amounted to little more than a scare; however, as a result, the government fell back in with the Bolshevik faction and their militia, organized in the factories and working-class districts of Petrograd, called the Red Guards. The Bolsheviks, having been forgiven for their earlier attempts to overthrow the provisional government, came out of hiding, and soon exercised an even greater degree of influence than they had before by winning elections to soviets in Petrograd and Moscow. As the provisional government attempted to grasp at their waning influence, a second revolution took place, which unequivocally ushered the Bolsheviks to power in November 1917 (though it was known as the October Revolution).[2]

There were manifold reasons for the Bolshevik victory. Certainly, one immediate catalyst of the revolution was the Great War and its concomitant economic and military disasters. War had disrupted Russian industrial and economic progress and allowed Lenin to execute his plots and discipline the Party. Revisionist historians, however, maintain that though the seizure of power by the Bolsheviks was a carefully orchestrated success, there existed long-term social causes of the revolution, particularly the iniquity of Russia's pre–1917 agrarian order, as well as the plight of urban workers.

After waiting in vain for the German, French, and British proletariat to come to his aid, Lenin reluctantly entered into negotiations with the German government. The new revolutionary government signed an armistice with Germany, the Treaty of Brest-Litovsk, in early 1918.

Following a civil war with the White Army (Mensheviks, former army officers, foreign agents), Lenin promoted what became known as the New Economic Policy (NEP), Communism at a slowed pace with components of the free market—a combination of command economy and small-scale capitalist

2   The popular uprising that led to the disappearance of Tsarist rule after 300 years of the Romanov dynasty took place between February 24 and February 28, 1917, and is known as the February Revolution. Russia, however, still used the Julian Calendar, and according to the Gregorian Calendar, the revolt occurred between March 8 and March 12—thus it is also known as the March Revolution. Likewise, the October Revolution took place on November 7.

enterprises—serving as temporary relief measures, as well as a belief that the Communist state they sought would blossom more organically through the will of the people.

In 1923, Russia was renamed the Union of Soviet Socialist Republics; Lenin's ideals held that free discussion should prevail within the Party until a policy was officially decided. Once a decision had been made, however, every Communist was bound to follow the Party line unequivocally. By insisting on this principle, Lenin created a powerful and disciplined apparatus through which the objectives of Communist government could be achieved. As the Party bureaucracy expanded and strengthened, it was possible for it to control the soviets.

Lenin died of cerebral hemorrhage in 1924 after a series of strokes and two years of declining health. After his death, a godlike status was conferred on him, and his works were widely disseminated. The USSR established a cult of Lenin. The old capital was named Leningrad (now St. Petersburg), and until recently, his embalmed corpse lay on display. Although there was a power struggle during Lenin's illness and after his death, Josef Stalin had taken the reins of power by 1928. He would rule with an iron fist, liquidating or displacing millions of his enemies, both real and imagined, and starving the Russian people until his death in 1953.

Lenin, like Marx, was incorrect in his long-term predictions for the world order; the real problems with Lenin's writings concerning imperialism are that they do not account for pre–20th-century capitalist imperial exploitation, and assumes as a *fait accompli* the demise of capital after this highest stage has played out. While imperialism was largely driven by economics, and the Soviet Union had a good 74-year run until 1991, human nature and incentive trumped class consciousness, and global capitalism flourished.

Imperialism: The Final Stage of Capitalism

By V. I. Lenin

CRITIQUE OF IMPERIALISM

By the critique of imperialism, in the broad sense of the term, we mean the attitude of the different classes of society towards imperialist policy in connection with their general ideology.

The enormous dimensions of finance capital concentrated in a few hands and creating an extraordinarily dense and widespread network of relationships and connections which subordinates not only the small and medium, but also the very small capitalists and small masters, on the one hand, and the increasingly intense struggle waged against other national state groups of financiers for the division of the world and domination over other countries, on the other hand, cause the propertied classes to go over entirely to the side of imperialism. "General" enthusiasm over the prospects of imperialism, furious defence of it and painting it in the brightest colours—such are the signs of the times. Imperialist ideology also penetrates the working class. No Chinese Wall separates it from the other classes. The leaders of the present-day, so-called, "Social-Democratic" Party of Germany are justly called "social-imperialists", that is, socialists in words and imperialists in deeds; but as early as 1902, Hobson noted the existence in Britain of "Fabian imperialists" who belonged to the opportunist Fabian Society.

Bourgeois scholars and publicists usually come out in defence of imperialism in a somewhat veiled form; they obscure its complete, domination and its deep-going roots, strive to push specific and secondary details into the forefront and do their very best to distract attention from essentials by means of absolutely ridiculous schemes for "reform", such as police supervision of the trusts or banks, etc. Cynical and frank imperialists who are bold enough to admit the absurdity of the idea of reforming the fundamental characteristics of imperialism are a rarer phenomenon.

Here is an example. The German imperialists attempt, in the magazine *Archives of World Economy*, to follow the national emancipation movements in the colonies, particularly, of course, in colonies other than those belonging to Germany. They note the unrest and the protest movements in India, the movement in Natal (South Africa), in the Dutch East Indies, etc. One of them, commenting on an English report of a conference held on June 28–30, 1910, of representatives of various subject nations and races,

V. I. Lenin, *Imperialism: The Highest Stage of Capitalism*, pp. 109-128, 1916.

of peoples of Asia, Africa and Europe who are under foreign rule, writes as follows in appraising the speeches delivered at this conference: "We are told that we must fight imperialism; that the ruling states should recognise the right of subject peoples to independence; that an international tribunal should supervise the fulfilment of treaties concluded between the great powers and weak peoples. Further than the expression of these pious wishes they do not go. We see no trace of understanding of the fact that imperialism is inseparably bound up with capitalism in its present form and that, therefore [!!], an open struggle against imperialism would be hopeless, unless, perhaps, the fight were to be confined to protests against certain of its especially abhorrent excesses."[1] Since the reform of the basis of imperialism is a deception, a "pious wish", since the bourgeois representatives of the oppressed nations go no "further" forward, the bourgeois representative of an oppressing nation goes "further" *backward*, to servility towards imperialism under cover of the claim to be "scientific". That is also "logic"!

The questions as to whether it is possible to reform the basis of imperialism, whether to go forward to the further intensification and deepening of the antagonisms which it engenders. or backward, towards allaying these antagonisms, are fundamental questions in the critique of imperialism. Since the specific political features of imperialism are reaction everywhere and increased national oppression due to the oppression of the financial oligarchy and the elimination of free competition, a petty-bourgeois-democratic opposition to imperialism arose at the beginning of the twentieth century in nearly all imperialist countries. Kautsky not only did not trouble to oppose, was not only unable to oppose this petty-bourgeois reformist opposition, which is really reactionary in its economic basis, but became merged with it in practice, and this is precisely where Kautsky and the broad international Kautskian trend deserted Marxism.

In the United States, the imperialist war waged against Spain in 1898 stirred up the opposition of the "anti-imperialists", the last of the Mohicans of bourgeois democracy who declared this war to be "criminal", regarded the annexation of foreign territories as a violation of the Constitution, declared that the treatment of Aguinaldo, leader of the Filipinos (the Americans promised him the independence of his country, but later landed troops and annexed it), was "jingo treachery", and quoted the words of Lincoln: "When the white man governs himself, that is self-government; but when he governs himself and also governs others, it is no longer self-government; it is despotism."[2] But as long, as all this criticism shrank from recognising the inseverable bond between imperialism and the trusts, and, therefore, between imperialism and the foundations of capitalism, while it shrank from joining the forces engendered by large-scale capitalism and its development-it remained a "pious wish".

This is also the main attitude taken by Hobson in his critique of imperialism. Hobson anticipated Kautsky in protesting against the "inevitability of imperialism" argument, and in urging the necessity of "increasing the consuming capacity" of the people (under capitalism!). The petty-bourgeois point of view in the critique of imperialism, the omnipotence of the banks, the financial oligarchy, etc., is adopted by the authors I have often quoted, such as Agahd, A. Lansburgh, L. Eschwege, and among the French writers Victor Berard, author of a superficial book entitled *England and Imperialism* which appeared in 1900. All these authors, who make no claim to be Marxists, contrast imperialism with free competition and democracy, condemn the Baghdad railway scheme, which is leading to conflicts and war, utter "pious wishes" for peace, etc. This applies also to the compiler of international stock and share issue statistics, A. Neymarck, who, after calculating the thousands of millions of francs representing "international" securities, exclaimed in 1912: "Is it possible to believe that peace may be disturbed ... that, in the face of these enormous figures, anyone would risk starting a war?"[3]

Such simple-mindedness on the part of the bourgeois economists is not surprising; moreover, *it is in their interest* to pretend to be so naive and to talk "seriously" about peace under imperialism. But what remains of Kautsky's Marxism, when, in 1914, 1915 and 1916, he takes up the same bourgeois-reformist point of view and affirms that "everybody is agreed" (imperialists, pseudo-socialists and social-pacifists) on the matter of peace? Instead of an analysis of imperialism and an exposure of the depths of its contradictions, we have nothing but a reformist "pious wish" to wave them aside, to evade them.

Here is a sample of Kautsky's economic criticism of imperialism. He takes the statistics of the British export and import trade with Egypt for 1872 and 1912; it seems that this export and import trade has grown more slowly than British foreign trade as a whole. From this Kautsky concludes that "we have no reason to suppose that without military occupation the growth of British trade with Egypt would have been less, simply as a result of the mere operation of economic factors". "The urge of capital to expand ... can be best promoted, not by the violent methods of imperialism, but by peaceful democracy."[4]

This argument of Kautsky's, which is repeated in every key by his Russian armour-bearer (and Russian shielder of the social-chauvinists), Mr. Spectator,[5] constitutes the basis of Kautskian critique of imperialism, and that is why we must deal with it in greater detail. We will begin with a quotation from Hilferding, whose conclusions Kautsky on many occasions, and notably in April 1915, has declared to have been "unanimously adopted by all socialist theoreticians".

"It is not the business of the proletariat," writes Hilferding "to contrast the more progressive capitalist policy with that of the now bygone era of free trade and of hostility towards the state. The reply of the proletariat to the economic policy of finance capital, to imperialism, cannot be free trade, but socialism. The aim of proletarian policy cannot today be the ideal of restoring free competition—which has now become a reactionary ideal—but the complete elimination of competition by the abolition of capitalism."[6]

Kautsky broke with Marxism by advocating in the epoch of finance capital a "reactionary ideal", "peaceful democracy", "the mere operation of economic factors", for *objectively* this ideal drags us back from monopoly to non-monopoly capitalism, and is a reformist swindle.

Trade with Egypt (or with any other colony or semi-colony) "would have grown more" *without* military occupation, without imperialism, and without finance capital. What does this mean? That capitalism would have developed more rapidly if free competition had not been restricted by monopolies in general, or by the "connections", yoke (i.e., also the monopoly) of finance capital, or by the monopolist possession of colonies by certain countries?

Kautsky's argument can have no other meaning; and *this* "meaning" is meaningless. Let us assume that free competition, without any sort of monopoly, would have developed capitalism and trade more rapidly. But the more rapidly trade and capitalism develop, the greater is the concentration of production and capital which *gives rise* to monopoly. And monopolies have *already* arisen— precisely out of free competition! Even if monopolies have now begun to retard progress, it is not an argument in favour of free competition, which has become impossible after it has given rise to monopoly.

Whichever way one turns Kautsky's argument, one will find nothing in it except reaction and bourgeois reformism.

Even if we correct this argument and say, as Spectator says, that the trade of the colonies with Britain is now developing more slowly than their trade with other countries, it does not save Kautsky; for it *is also* monopoly, *also* imperialism that is beating Great Britain, only it is the monopoly and imperialism of another country (America, Germany). It is known that the cartels have given rise to a new and peculiar form of protective tariffs, i.e., goods suitable for export are protected (Engels noted this in Vol. III of *Capital*[7]). It is known, too, that the cartels add finance capital have a system peculiar to themselves, that of "exporting goods at cut-rate prices", or "dumping", as the English call it: within a given country the cartel sells its goods at high monopoly prices, but sells them abroad at a much lower price to undercut the competitor, to enlarge its own production to the utmost, etc. If Germany's trade with the British colonies is developing more rapidly than Great Britain's, it only proves that German imperialism is younger, stronger and better organised than British imperialism, is superior to it; but it by no means proves the "superiority" of free trade, for it is not a fight between free trade and protection and colonial dependence, but between two rival imperialisms, two monopolies, two groups of finance capital. The superiority of German imperialism over British imperialism is more potent than the wall of colonial frontiers or of protective tariffs: to use this as an "argument" in *favour* of free trade and "peaceful democracy" is banal, it means forgetting the essential features and characteristics of imperialism, substituting petty-bourgeois reformism for Marxism.

It is interesting to note that even the bourgeois economist, A. Lansburgh, whose criticism of imperialism is as petty-bourgeois as Kautsky's, nevertheless got closer to a more scientific study of trade statistics. He did not compare one single country, chosen at random, and one single colony with the other countries; he examined the export trade of an imperialist country: (1) with countries which are financially dependent upon it, and borrow money from it; and (2) with countries which are financially independent. He obtained the following results:

EXPORT TRADE OF GERMANY (000,000 marks)

To countries financially dependent on Germany	1889	1908	Per cent increase
Rumania	48.2	70.8	47
Portugal	19.0	32.8	73
Argentina	60.7	147.0	143
Brazil	48.7	84.5	73
Chile	28.3	64.0	114
Total	*234.8*	*451.5*	*92*
To countries financially independent of Germany			
Great Britain	651.8	997.4	53
France	210.2	437.9	108
Belgium	137.2	322.8	135
Switzerland	177.4	401.1	127
Australia	21.2	64.5	205
Dutch East Indies	8.8	40.7	363
Total	*1,206.6*	*2,264.4*	*87*

Lansburgh did not draw *conclusions* and therefore, strangely enough, failed to observe that if the figures prove anything at all, they prove that *he is wrong*, for the exports to countries financially dependent on Germany have grown *more rapidly*, if only slightly, than exports to the countries which are financially independent. (I emphasise the "if", for Lansburgh's figures are far from complete.)

Tracing the connection between exports and loans, Lansburgh writes:

"In 1890-91, a Rumanian loan was floated through the German banks, which had already in previous years made advances on this loan. It was used chiefly to purchase railway materials in Germany. In 1891, German exports to Rumania amounted to 55 million marks. The following year they dropped to 39.4 million marks and, with fluctuations, to 25.4 million in 1900. Only in very recent years have they regained the level of 1891, thanks to two new loans.

"German exports to Portugal rose, following the loans of 1888- to 21,100,000 (1890); then, in the two following years, they dropped to 16,200,000 and 7,400,000, and regained their former level only in 1903.

"The figures of German trade with Argentina are still more striking. Loans were floated in 1888 and 1890; German exports to Argentina reached 60,700,000 marks (1889). Two years later they amounted to only 18,600,000 marks, less than one-third of the previous figure. It was not until 1901 that they regained and surpassed the level of 1889, and then only as a result of new loans floated by the state and by municipalities, with advances to build power stations, and with other credit operations.

"Exports to Chile, as a consequence of the loan of 1889, rose to 45,200,000 marks (in 1892), and a year later dropped to 22,500,000 marks. A new Chilean loan floated by the German banks in 1906 was followed by a rise of exports to 84,700,000 marks in 1907, only to fall again to 52,400,000 marks in 1908." [6]

From these facts Lansburgh draws the amusing petty-bourgeois moral of how unstable and irregular export trade is when it is bound up with loans, how bad it is to invest capital abroad instead of "naturally" and "harmoniously" developing home industry, how "costly" are the millions in bakshish that Krupp has to pay in floating foreign loans, etc. But the facts tell us clearly: the increase in exports is connected with just *these* swindling tricks of finance capital, which is not concerned with bourgeois morality, but with skinning the ox twice—first, it pockets the profits from the loan; then it pockets other profits from the *same* loan which the borrower uses to make purchases from Krupp, or to purchase railway material from the Steel Syndicate, etc.

I repeat that I do not by any means consider Lansburgh's figures to be perfect; but I had to quote them because they are more scientific than Kautsky's and Spectator's and because Lansburgh showed the correct way to approach the question. In discussing the significance of finance capital in regard to exports, etc., one must be able to single out the connection of exports especially and solely with the tricks of the financiers, especially and solely with the sale of goods by cartels, etc. Simply to compare colonies with non-colonies, one imperialism with another imperialism, one semi-colony or colony (Egypt) with all other countries, is to evade and to obscure the very *essence* of the question.

Kautsky's theoretical critique of imperialism has nothing in common with Marxism and serves only as a preamble to propaganda for peace and unity with the opportunists and the social-chauvinists, precisely for the reason that it evades and obscures the very profound and fundamental contradictions of imperialism: the contradictions between monopoly and free competition which exists side by side with it, between the gigantic "operations" (and gigantic profits) of finance capital and "honest" trade in the free market, the contradiction between cartels and trusts, on the one hand, and non-cartelised industry, on the other, etc.

The notorious theory of "ultra-imperialism", invented by Kautsky, is just as reactionary. Compare his arguments on this subject in 1915, with Hobson's arguments in 1902.

Kautsky: "... Cannot the present imperialist policy be supplanted by a new, ultra-imperialist policy, which will introduce the joint exploitation of the world by internationally united finance capital in place of the mutual rivalries of national finance capitals? Such a new phase of capitalism is at any rate conceivable. Can it be achieved? Sufficient premises are still lacking to enable us to answer this question." [7]

Hobson: "Christendom thus laid out in a few great federal empires, each with a retinue of uncivilised dependencies, seems to many the most legitimate development of present tendencies, and one which would offer the best hope of permanent peace on an assured basis of inter-Imperialism."

Kautsky called ultra-imperialism or super-imperialism what Hobson, thirteen years earlier, described as inter- imperialism. Except for coining a new and clever catchword, replacing one Latin prefix by another, the only progress Kautsky has made in the sphere of "scientific" thought is that he gave out as

Marxism what Hobson, in effect, described as the cant of English parsons. After the Anglo-Boer War it was quite natural for this highly honourable caste to exert their main efforts to *console* the British middle class and the workers who had lost many of their relatives on the battlefields of South Africa and who were obliged to pay higher taxes in order to guarantee still higher profits for the British financiers. And what better consolation could there be than the theory that imperialism is not so bad; that it stands close to inter- (or ultra-) imperialism, which can ensure permanent peace? No matter what the good intentions of the English parsons, or of sentimental Kautsky, may have been, the only objective, i.e., real, social significance of Kautsky's "theory" is this: it is a most reactionary method of consoling the masses with hopes of permanent peace being possible under capitalism, by distracting their attention from the sharp antagonisms and acute problems of the present times, and directing it towards illusory prospects of an imaginary "ultraimperialism" of the future. Deception of the masses—that is all there is in Kautsky's "Marxist" theory.

Indeed, it is enough to compare well-known and indisputable facts to become convinced of the utter falsity of the prospects which Kautsky tries to conjure up before the German workers (and the workers of all lands). Let us consider India, Indo-China and China. It is known that these three colonial and semi-colonial countries, with a population of six to seven hundred million, are subjected to the exploitation of the finance capital of several imperialist powers: Great Britain, France, Japan, the U.S.A., etc. Let us assume that these imperialist countries form alliances against one another in order to protect or enlarge their possessions, their interests and their spheres of influence in these Asiatic states; these alliances will be "inter-imperialist", or "ultra-imperialist" alliances. Let us assume that *all* the imperialist countries conclude an alliance for the "peaceful" division of these parts of Asia; this alliance would be an alliance of "internationally united finance capital". There are actual examples of alliances of this kind in the history of the twentieth century—the attitude of the powers to China, for instance. We ask, is it "conceivable", assuming that the capitalist system remains intact— and this is precisely the assumption that Kautsky does make—that such alliances would be more than temporary, that they would eliminate friction, conflicts and struggle in every possible form?

The question has only to be presented clearly for any other than a negative answer to be impossible. This is because the only conceivable basis under capitalism for the division of spheres of influence, interests, colonies, etc., is a calculation of the *strength* of those participating, their general economic, financial, military strength, etc. And the strength of these participants in the division does not change to an equal degree, for the *even* development of different undertakings, trusts, branches of industry, or countries is impossible under capitalism. Half a century ago Germany was a miserable, insignificant country, if her capitalist strength is compared with that of the Britain of that time; Japan compared with Russia in the same way. Is it "conceivable" that in ten or twenty years' time the relative strength of the imperialist powers will have remained unchanged? It is out of the question.

Therefore, in the realities of the capitalist system, and not in the banal philistine fantasies of English parsons, or of the German "Marxist", Kautsky, "inter-imperialist" or "ultra-imperialist" alliances, no matter what form they may assume, whether of one imperialist coalition against another, or of a general alliance embracing *all* the imperialist powers, are *inevitably nothing* more than a "truce" in periods between wars. Peaceful alliances prepare the ground for wars, and in their turn grow out of wars; the one conditions the other, producing alternating forms of peaceful and non-peaceful struggle on *one and the same* basis of imperialist connections and relations within world economics and world politics. But in order to pacify the workers and reconcile them with the social-chauvinists who have deserted to the side of the bourgeoisie, over-wise Kautsky *separates* one link of a single chain from another, separates the present peaceful (and ultra-imperialist, nay, ultra-ultra-imperialist) alliance of *all* the powers for the "pacification" of China (remember the suppression of the Boxer Rebellion[8]) from the non-peaceful conflict of tomorrow, which will prepare the ground for another "peaceful" general alliance for the partition, say, of Turkey, on the day after tomorrow, *etc., etc.* Instead of showing the living connection between periods of imperialist peace and periods of imperialist war, Kautsky presents the workers with a lifeless abstraction in order to reconcile them to their lifeless leaders.

An American writer, Hill, in his *A History of the Diplomacy in the International Development of Europe* refers in his preface to the following periods in the recent history of diplomacy: (1) the era of revolution; (2) the constitutional movement; (3) the present era of "commercial imperialism".[9] Another writer divides the history of Great Britain's "world policy" since 1870 into four periods: (1) the first Asiatic period (that of the struggle against Russia's advance in Central Asia towards India); (2) the African period (approximately 1885-1902): that of the struggle against France for the partition of Africa (the "Fashoda incident" of 1898 which brought her within a hair's breadth of war with France); (3) the second Asiatic period (alliance with Japan against Russia); and (4) the "European" period, chiefly anti-German.[10] "The political patrol clashes take place on the financial field," wrote the banker, Riesser, in 1905, in showing how French finance capital operating in Italy was preparing the way for a political alliance of these countries, and how a conflict was developing between Germany and Great Britain over Persia, between all the European capitalists over Chinese loans, etc. Behold, the living reality of peaceful "ultra-imperialist" alliances in their inseverable connection with ordinary imperialist conflicts!

Kautsky's obscuring of the deepest contradictions of imperialism, which inevitably boils down to painting imperialism in bright colours, leaves its traces in this writer's criticism of the political features of imperialism. Imperialism is the epoch of finance capital and of monopolies, which introduce everywhere the striving for domination, not for freedom. Whatever the political system, the result of these tendencies is everywhere reaction and an extreme intensification of antagonisms in this field. Particularly intensified become the yoke of national oppression and the striving for annexations, i.e., the violation of national independence (for annexation is nothing but the violation of the right of nations to self-determination). Hilferding rightly notes the connection between imperialism and the intensification of national oppression. "In the newly opened-up countries," he writes, "the capital imported into them intensifies antagonisms and excites against the intruders the constantly growing resistance of the peoples who are awakening to national consciousness; this resistance can easily develop into dangerous measures against foreign capital. The old social relations become completely revolutionised, the age-long agrarian isolation of 'nations without history' is destroyed and they are drawn into the capitalist whirlpool. Capitalism itself gradually provides the subjugated with the means and resources for their emancipation and they set out to achieve the goal which once seemed highest to the European nations: the creation of a united national state as a means to economic and cultural freedom. This movement for national independence threatens European capital in its most valuable and most promising fields of exploitation, and European capital can maintain its domination only by continually increasing its military forces."[11]

To this must be added that it is not only in newly opened-up countries, but also in the old, that imperialism is leading to annexation, to increased national oppression, and, consequently, also to increasing resistance. While objecting to the intensification of political reaction by imperialism, Kautsky leaves in the shade a question that has become particularly urgent, viz., the impossibility of unity with the opportunists in the epoch of imperialism. While objecting to annexations , he presents his objections in a form that is most acceptable and least offensive to the opportunists. He addresses himself to a

German audience, yet he obscures the most topical and important point, for instance, the annexation of Alsace-Lorraine by Germany. In order to appraise this "mental aberration" of Kautsky's I shall take the following example. Let us suppose that a Japanese condemns the annexation of the Philippines by the Americans. The question is: will many believe that he does so because he has a horror of annexations as such, and not because he himself has a desire to annex the Philippines? And shall we not be constrained to admit that the "fight" the Japanese is waging against annexations can be regarded as being sincere and politically honest only if he fights against the annexation of Korea by Japan, and urges freedom for Korea to secede from Japan?

Kautsky's theoretical analysis of imperialism, as well as his economic and political critique of imperialism, are permeated *through and through* with a spirit, absolutely irreconcilable with Marxism, of obscuring and glossing over the fundamental contradictions of imperialism and with a striving to preserve at all costs the crumbling unity with opportunism in the European working-class movement.

THE PLACE OF IMPERIALISM IN HISTORY

We have seen that in its economic essence imperialism is monopoly capitalism. This in itself determines its place in history, for monopoly that grows out of the soil of free competition, and precisely out of free competition, is the transition from the capitalist system to a higher socioeconomic order. We must take special note of the four principal types of monopoly, or principal manifestations of monopoly capitalism, which are characteristic of the epoch we are examining.

Firstly, monopoly arose out of the concentration of production at a very high stage. This refers to the monopolist capitalist associations, cartels, syndicatess, and trusts. We have seen the important part these play in present-day economic life. At the beginning of the twentieth century, monopolies had acquired complete supremacy in the advanced countries, and although the first steps towards the formation of the cartels were taken by countries enjoying the protection of high tariffs (Germany, America), Great Britain, with her system of free trade, revealed the same basic phenomenon, only a little later, namely, the birth of monopoly out of the concentration of production.

Secondly, monopolies have stimulated the seizure of the most important sources of raw materials, especially for the basic and most highly cartelised industries in capitalist society: the coal and iron industries. The monopoly of the most important sources of raw materials has enormously increased the power of big capital, and has sharpened the antagonism between cartelised and non-cartelised industry.

Thirdly, monopoly has sprung from the banks. The banks have developed from modest middleman enterprises into the monopolists of finance capital. Some three to five of the biggest banks in each of the foremost capitalist countries have achieved the "personal link-up" between industrial and bank capital, and have concentrated in their hands the control of thousands upon thousands of millions which form the greater part of the capital and income of entire countries. A financial oligarchy, which throws a close network of dependence relationships over all the economic and political institutions of present-day bourgeois society without exception—such is the most striking manifestation of this monopoly.

Fourthly, monopoly has grown out of colonial policy. To the numerous "old" motives of colonial policy, finance capital has added the struggle for the sources of raw materials, for the export of capital, for spheres of influence, i.e., for spheres for profitable deals, concessions, monopoly profits and so on, economic territory in general. When the colonies of the European powers, for instance, comprised only one-tenth of the territory of Africa(as was the case in 1876), colonial policy was able to develop—by methods other than those of monopoly—by the "free grabbing" of territories, so to speak. But when nine-tenths of Africa had been seized (by 1900), when the whole world had been divided up, there was inevitably ushered in the era of monopoly possession of colonies and, consequently, of particularly intense struggle for the division and the redivision of the world.

The extent to which monopolist capital has intensified all the contradictions of capitalism is generally known. It is sufficient to mention the high cost of living and the tyranny of the cartels. This intensification of contradictions constitutes the most powerful driving force of the transitional period of history, which began from the time of the final victory of world finance capital.

Monopolies, oligarchy, the striving for domination and not for freedom, the exploitation of an increasing number of small or weak nations by a handful of the richest or most powerful nations—all these have given birth to those distinctive characteristics of imperialism which compel us to define it as parasitic or decaying capitalism. More and more prominently there emerges, as one of the tendencies of imperialism, the creation of the "rentier state", the usurer state, in which the bourgeoisie to an ever-increasing degree lives on the proceeds of capital exports and by "clipping coupons". It would be a mistake to believe that this tendency to decay precludes the rapid growth of capitalism. It does not. In the epoch of imperialism, certain branches of industry, certain strata of the bourgeoisie and certain countries betray, to a greater or lesser degree, now one and now another of these tendencies. On the whole, capitalism is growing far more rapidly than before; but this growth is not only becoming more and more uneven in general, its unevenness also manifests itself, in particular, in the decay of the countries which are richest in capital (Britain).

In regard to the rapidity of Germany's economic development, Riesser, the author of the book on the big German banks, states: "The progress of the preceding period (1848-70), which had not been exactly slow, compares with the rapidity with which the whole of Germany's national economy, and with it German banking, progressed during this period (1870-1905) in about the same way as the speed of the mail coach in the good old days compares with the speed of the present-day automobile ... which is whizzing past so fast that it endangers not only innocent pedestrians in its path, but also the occupants of the car." In its turn, this finance capital which has grown with such extraordinary rapidity is not unwilling, precisely because it has grown so quickly, to pass on to a more "tranquil" possession of colonies which have to be seized—and not only by peaceful methods—from richer nations. In the United States, economic development in the last decades has been even more rapid than in Germany, *and for this very reason*, the parasitic features of modern American capitalism have stood out with particular prominence. On the other hand, a comparison of, say, the republican American bourgeoisie with the monarchist Japanese or German bourgeoisie shows that the most pronounced political distinction diminishes to an extreme degree in the epoch of imperialism—not because it is unimportant in general, but because in all these cases we are talking about a bourgeoisie which has definite features of parasitism.

The receipt of high monopoly profits by the capitalists in one of the numerous branches of industry, in one of the numerous countries, etc., makes it economically possible for them to bribe certain sections of the workers, and for a time a fairly considerable minority of them, and win them to the side of the bourgeoisie of a given industry or given nation against all the others. The intensification of antagonisms between imperialist nations for the division of the world increases this urge. And so there is created that bond between imperialism and opportunism, which revealed itself first and most clearly in Great Britain, owing to the fact that certain features of imperialist development were observable there much earlier than in other countries. Some writers, L. Martov, for example, are prone to wave aside the connection between imperialism and opportunism in the working-class movement—a particularly glaring fact at the present time—by resorting to "official optimism" (*à la* Kautsky and Huysmans) like the following: the cause of the opponents of capitalism would be hopeless if it were progressive capitalism that led to the increase of opportunism, or, if it were the best-paid workers who were inclined towards opportunism, etc. We must have no illusions about "optimism" of this kind. It is optimism in respect of opportunism; it is optimism which serves to conceal opportunism. As a matter of fact the extraordinary rapidity and the particularly revolting character of the development of opportunism is by no means a guarantee that its victory will be durable: the rapid growth of a painful abscess on a healthy body can only cause it to burst more quickly and thus relieve the body of it. The most dangerous of all in this respect are those who do not wish to understand that the fight against imperialism is a sham and humbug unless it is inseparably bound up with the fight against opportunism.

From all that has been said in this book on the economic essence of imperialism, it follows that we must define it as capitalism in transition, or, more precisely, as moribund capitalism. It is very instructive in this respect to note that bourgeois economists, in describing modern capitalism, frequently employ catchwords and phrases like "interlocking", "absence of isolation", etc.; "in conformity with their functions and course of development", banks are "not purely private business enterprises: they are more and more outgrowing the sphere of purely private business regulation". And this very Riesser, whose words I have just quoted, declares with all seriousness that the "prophecy" of the Marxists concerning "socialisation" has "not come true"!

What then does this catchword "interlocking" express? It merely expresses the most striking feature of the process going on before our eyes. It shows that the observer counts the separate trees, but cannot see the wood. It slavishly copies the superficial, the fortuitous, the chaotic. It reveals the observer as one who is overwhelmed by the mass of raw material and is utterly incapable of appreciating its meaning and importance. Ownership of shares, the relations between owners of private property "interlock in a haphazard way". But underlying this interlocking, its very base, are the changing social relations of production. When a big enterprise assumes gigantic proportions, and, on the basis of an exact computation of mass data, organises according to plan the supply of primary raw materials to the extent of two-thirds, or three-fourths, of all that is necessary for tens of millions of people; when the raw materials are transported in a systematic and organised manner to the most suitable places of production, sometimes situated hundreds or thousands of miles from each other; when a single centre directs all the consecutive stages of processing the material right up to the manufacture of numerous varieties of finished articles; when these products are distributed according to a single plan among tens and hundreds of millions of consumers (the marketing of oil in America and Germany by the American oil trust)—then it becomes evident that we have socialisation of production, and not mere "interlocking", that private economic and private property relations constitute a shell which no longer fits its contents, a shell which must inevitably decay if its removal is artificially delayed, a shell which may remain in a state of decay for a fairly long period (if, at the worst, the cure of the opportunist abscess is protracted), but which will inevitably be removed.

The enthusiastic admirer of German imperialism, Schulze-Gaevernitz, exclaims:

"Once the supreme management of the German banks has been entrusted to the hands of a dozen persons, their activity is even today more significant for the public good than that of the majority of the Ministers of State. . . . (The "interlocking" of bankers, ministers, magnates of industry and rentiers is here conveniently forgotten.) If we imagine the development of those tendencies we have noted carried to their logical conclusion we will have: the money capital of the nation united in the banks; the banks themselves combined into cartels; the investment capital of the nation cast in the shape of securities. Then the forecast of that genius Saint-Simon will be fulfilled: 'The present anarchy of production, which corresponds to the fact that economic relations are developing without uniform regulation, must make way for organisation in production. Production will no longer be directed by isolated manufacturers, independent of each other and ignorant of man's economic needs; that will be done by a certain public institution. A central committee of management, being able to survey the large field of social economy from a more elevated point of view, will regulate it for the benefit of the whole of society, will put the means of production into suitable hands, and above all will take care that there be constant harmony between production and consumption. Institutions already exist which have assumed as part of their functions a certain organisation of economic labour, the banks.' We are still a long way from the fulfilment of Saint-Simon's forecast, but we are on the way towards it: Marxism, different from what Marx imagined, but different only in form."[12]

A crushing "refutation" of Marx indeed, which retreats a step from Marx's precise, scientific analysis to Saint-Simon's guess-work, the guess-work of a genius, but guess-work all the same.

NOTES

1. *Weltwirtschaffliches Archiv*, Bd. II, S. 193. —*Lenin*

2. J. Patouillet, *L'impérialisme américain*, Dijon, 1904, p. 272. —*Lenin*

3. *Bulletin de l'Institut International de Statistique*, T. XIX, Lvr. II, p. 225. —*Lenin*

4. Kautsky, *Nationalstaat, imperialistischer Staat und Staatenbund*, Nürnberg, 1915, S. 72, 70. — *Lenin*

5. *Finance Capital*, p. 567. —*Lenin*

6. *Die Bank*, 1909, 2, S. 819 et seq. —*Lenin*

7. *Die Neue Zeit*, April 30, 1915, S. 144. —*Lenin*

8. David Jayne Hill, *History of the Diplomacy in the International Development of Europe*, Vol. I, p. X. —*Lenin*

9. Schilder, op. cit., S. 178. —*Lenin*

10. *Finance Capital*, p. 487. —*Lenin*

11. [PLACEHOLDER.]

12. *Grundriss der Sozialökonomik*, S. 146. —*Lenin*

STUDY QUESTIONS

1. What were the causes of the Russian Revolution?

2. Why was the First World War considered by the Bolsheviks to be an imperialists' war?

3. Why, in Lenin's view, was imperialism the final stage of capitalism?

PART V
LITERATURE

The White Man's Burden

Over one hundred years ago, the writer Rudyard Kipling (1865–1936) held celebrity in the English-speaking world similar to that of J. K. Rowling and George R. R. Martin today. In his subject matter, Kipling represents the quintessential British imperial author. Well known for poetry such as "If" and fiction such as *The Jungle Book*, *Just So Stories*, and *Kim*, it was Kipling who coined the term "White Man's Burden," when he published a poem by that title in 1899. Even if East is East, West is West, and never are the twain to meet, as he famously pointed out, Kipling helped to make East more intelligible, and perhaps more exotic, to West, while expounding a jingoistic pride in empire.

Yet, lest present-mindedness interpret what may be his best-known poem solely as bygone Eurocentric hubris and condemn Kipling for being a stereotypically stalwart champion and apologist for the British Empire, it should be noted that he also demonstrated a profound affinity for India, the land of his birth, childhood, and, later, coming of age. It served not only as a deep reservoir from which to draw literary material; for while many of his counterparts in India expressed at best aloof disdain and at worst unabashed contempt for all things Indian, Kipling possessed a true appreciation of the country and its inhabitants. He would never pretend that Indians were equal to Englishmen; however, Kipling admired some natives, and, having been an outcast in his youth, in his literature he was sympathetic to the plight of common people marginalized by nation, race, and caste.

Born in Bombay in 1865, Kipling spent his earliest years in India, where his father held a government post in the education department. Following Anglo-Indian convention, as children Rudyard (who had been given the Christian name Joseph, but nicknamed for a favorite lake of his parents) and his sister Alice were minded by an Indian nanny or ayah, who spoke to them in Urdu and had to remind them to address their parents in English.[1] At four years old, young Rudyard also became fluent in Maratha.

---

1 The term Anglo-Indian originally referred to the British living in India, as in the above usage. In the 20th century, however, Anglo-Indian came to define those of mixed European and Indian ancestry (who had previously been known as Eurasians). As for Indian vernaculars, Alice was apparently even more adroit at swearing in Urdu than her brother. Charles Allen, *Kipling Sahib: India*

Figure 11.1. Rudyard Kipling. Source: http://commons.wikimedia.org/wiki/File:Rudyard_Kipling_from_John_Palmer.jpg.

At five years of age, he was sent away, and after more than an unhappy decade in England, Kipling returned to the subcontinent at the age of 16 as an assistant editor for the *Civil and Military Gazette* in Lahore. He spent the next six and a half years as a journalist in various posts throughout India. Despite becoming the spokesman for the empire, an authentic or "real" India was as important to Kipling as British India, and he chronicled and satirized both in his works. He was not afraid to criticize the way in which the government disenfranchised the majority of Indians, and he continued to study Indian languages. Nonetheless, he remained critical in his resentment of the pretensions of the Indian National Congress and belief that Indians were not prepared for self-rule.

"The White Man's Burden," published just before the turn of the 20th century, was a passing of the torch of sorts. Although Britain would maintain her empire for some 60 more years, the United States by the end of the 19th century entered the imperial scene by acquiring control over the Philippines, Puerto Rico, and Cuba in the wake of the Spanish-American War. Kipling offered advice to the Americans on the responsibilities and expectations of empire, as well as the obligations and disappointments in attempting to bring civilization to those who lived in ignorance and darkness. With a conviction in Western superiority, Europeans justified to themselves their exploits by disguising them as moral and dutiful attempts to halt native backwardness and barbarity. Indeed, Kipling's phrase openly addresses race; however, inherent in the burden of the white man was the understanding that there were temporal and spiritual reasons for colonial authority and codified customs to which all had to adhere.

and the Making of Rudyard Kipling (New York: Pegasus Books, 2009), pp. 45–46.

The White Man's Burden, 1899

By Rudyard Kipling

This famous poem, written by Britain's imperial poet, was a response to the American take over of the Phillipines after the Spanish-American War.

Take up the White Man's burden—
Send forth the best ye breed—
Go bind your sons to exile
To serve your captives' need;
To wait in heavy harness,
On fluttered folk and wild—
Your new-caught, sullen peoples,
Half-devil and half-child.

Take up the White Man's burden—
In patience to abide,
To veil the threat of terror
And check the show of pride;
By open speech and simple,
An hundred times made plain
To seek another's profit,
And work another's gain.

Take up the White Man's burden—
The savage wars of peace—
Fill full the mouth of Famine
And bid the sickness cease;
And when your goal is nearest

Rudyard Kipling, "The White Man's Burden," 1899.

The end for others sought,
Watch sloth and heathen Folly
Bring all your hopes to nought.

Take up the White Man's burden—
No tawdry rule of kings,
But toil of serf and sweeper—
The tale of common things.
The ports ye shall not enter,
The roads ye shall not tread,
Go mark them with your living,
And mark them with your dead.

Take up the White Man's burden
And reap his old reward:
The blame of those ye better,
The hate of those ye guard—
The cry of hosts ye humour
(Ah, slowly!) toward the light:—
"Why brought he us from bondage,
Our loved Egyptian night?"

Take up the White Man's burden—
Ye dare not stoop to less—
Nor call too loud on Freedom
To cloke your weariness;
By all ye cry or whisper,
By all ye leave or do,
The silent, sullen peoples
Shall weigh your gods and you.

Take up the White Man's burden—
Have done with childish days—
The lightly proferred laurel,
The easy, ungrudged praise.
Comes now, to search your manhood
Through all the thankless years
Cold, edged with dear-bought wisdom,
The judgment of your peers!

STUDY QUESTIONS

1. How do you interpret this poem?

AN INTRODUCTION TO

Orientalism

Late Columbia University comparative literature professor and Palestinian activist, Edward Said (1935–2003), published *Orientalism* in 1978, a book that has reshaped for over three decades how cultural historians approach colonialism and postcolonial studies. Historiography (the canon of published work by historians on a particular subject) has documented well the economic, political, and social exploitation wrought by the colonial project. Said added a new perspective in *Orientalism* by positing that European cultural dominance over its colonies was reinforced by the way in which the West studied and "knew" the East. Eurocentric representations were epistemological forms of authority and imperialism in and of themselves. In other words, words and ideas have power, and intellectuals can be agents of change on a level with soldiers, missionaries, and politicians. Control and comprehension went together like curry and rice.

The idea that power and knowledge were mutually reinforcing and aggrandizing entities had profound implications for colonizer and colonized alike.[1] By claiming to "know" their colonials, European imperialists could simultaneously justify their rule to themselves, reinforce the subordinate position of their subjects, and assert an air of omniscience. Natives had to be represented by Europeans because they could not represent themselves, and Orientals were not the Orientalists' intended readership. It was certainly not considered that Orientals could enter into an erudite dialogue with Orientalism. British, German, and French, Orientalist archaeologists, anthropologists, historians, philologists, novelists, and travel writers—all formulated a discourse of power in constructing the colonial Other. The Orientalists' "gaze" from afar, and as Said reminded us, from above, represented an exercise through which Europeans defined their identities, not only by what they were, but also by what they were not. Examples of the construction of difference included racial classifications of indigenous peoples or arbitrary geographical re-marking and renaming without consideration of pre-European borders or names. In today's societies,

---

1   Said's work follows the power-knowledge relationship posited by the late-20th-century philosopher Michel Foucault.

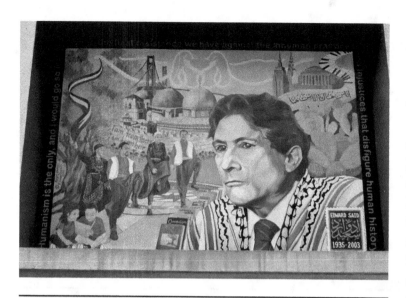

Figure 12.1. Edward W. Said. Copyright © Briantrejo (CC by 3.0) at http://commons.wikimedia.org/wiki/File:Palestinian_Cultural_Mural_Honoring_Dr._Edward_Said.jpg

the perpetuation of alterity, or otherness, affects issues such as immigration, educational and employment opportunities, and the legitimization of violence.

Orientalism is the academic specialization of the histories and languages of the East geographically (east, and south, of western Europe). The original usage of the term Orientalist specifically referred to a European scholar of the Levant or Middle East; however, the term has become widely used to encompass studies by Indologists and Africanists. The Orient constituted a mysterious locus of seduction, sensuality, and exoticism, through which many a youthful European gentleman traipsed on his Grand Tour. Said attempted to demonstrate the ways in which Orientalist thought pertained to literature and culture.

Asia, Africa, Oceania, and the Americas, therefore, were illuminated to a European readership through a cracked Eurocentric prism, which refracted upon the colonized images of themselves they accepted and internalized. By interpreting the Orient in this manner, Europeans were able to wield power through a dominant discourse, which upheld a facade of superiority with knowledge and power. *Orientalism* examines the foundations of these discursive forms of authority.

Upon release, Said's book was not bereft of controversy, and responses were varied. One criticism of *Orientalism* has charged it is anti-Western—namely, that it has categorized all Europeans who studied the East as imperialists, whose domination was inherent in their scholarship. Said has responded that while Orientalist thought and imperialism were inextricably and axiomatically connected in structure and form, that was not the only, and in some cases not even, the defining aspect of their association. While it is true that initial Western translations of Eastern languages and texts served expressly for the purposes of justifying economic, political, and military domination, epistemological appreciation and literary imagination evolved. Their work may have been funded, approved, and conducted under the aegis of imperialism, but European scholars and philologists, in spite of their superiority complexes, genuinely glorified in learning the languages they interpreted and the texts over which they pored.

Orientalism

By Edward W. Said

I

On a visit to Beirut during the terrible civil war of 1975-1976 a French journalist wrote regretfully of the gutted downtown area that "it had once seemed to belong to . . . the Orient of Chateaubriand and Nerval."[1] He was right about the place, of course, especially so far as a European was concerned. The Orient was almost a European invention, and had been since antiquity a place of romance, exotic beings, haunting memories and landscapes, remarkable experiences. Now it was disappearing; in a sense it had happened, its time was over. Perhaps it seemed irrelevant that Orientals themselves had something at stake in the process, that even in the time of Chateaubriand and Nerval Orientals had lived there, and that now it was they who were suffering; the main thing for the European visitor was a European representation of the Orient and its contemporary fate, both of which had a privileged communal significance for the journalist and his French readers.

Americans will not feel quite the same about the Orient, which for them is much more likely to be associated very differently with the Far East (China and Japan, mainly). Unlike the Americans, the French and the British—less so the Germans, Russians, Spanish, Portuguese, Italians, and Swiss—have had a long tradition of what I shall be calling *Orientalism*, a way of coming to terms with the Orient that is based on the Orient's special place in European Western experience. The Orient is not only adjacent to Europe; it is also the place of Europe's greatest and richest and oldest colonies, the source of its civilizations and languages, its cultural contestant, and one of its deepest and most recurring images of the Other. In addition, the Orient has helped to define Europe (or the West) as its contrasting image, idea, personality, experience. Yet none of this Orient is merely imaginative. The Orient is an integral part of European *material* civilization and culture. Orientalism expresses and represents that part culturally and even ideologically as a mode of discourse with supporting institutions, vocabulary, scholarship, imagery, doctrines, even colonial bureaucracies and colonial styles. In contrast, the American understanding of the Orient will seem considerably less dense, although our recent Japanese, Korean, and Indochinese adventures ought now to be creating a more sober, more realistic "Oriental" awareness. Moreover, the vastly expanded American political and economic role in the Near East (the Middle East) makes great claims on our understanding of that Orient.

It will be clear to the reader (and will become clearer still throughout the many pages that follow) that by Orientalism I mean several things, all of them, in my opinion, interdependent. The most readily accepted designation for Orientalism is an academic one, and indeed the label still serves in a number of academic institutions. Anyone who teaches, writes about, or researches the Orient—and this applies whether the person is an anthropologist, sociologist, historian, or philologist—either in its specific or its general aspects, is an Orientalist, and what he or she does is Orientalism. Compared with *Oriental studies* or *area studies,* it is true that the term *Orientalism* is less preferred by specialists today, both because it is too vague and general and because it connotes the high-handed executive attitude of nineteenth-century and early- twentieth-century European colonialism. Nevertheless books are written and congresses held with "the Orient" as their main focus, with the Orientalist in his new or old guise as their main authority. The point is that even if it does not survive as it once did, Orientalism lives on academically through its doctrines and theses about the Orient and the Oriental.

Related to this academic tradition, whose fortunes, transmigrations, specializations, and transmissions are in part the subject of this study, is a more general meaning for Orientalism. Orientalism is a style of thought based upon an ontological and epistemological distinction made between "the Orient" and ("most of the time) "the Occident." Thus a very large mass of writers, among whom are poets, novelists, philosophers, political theorists, economists, and imperial administrators, have accepted the basic distinction between East and West as the starting point for elaborate theories, epics, novels, social descriptions, and political accounts concerning the Orient, its people, customs, "mind," destiny, and so on. *This* Orientalism can accommodate Aeschylus, say, and Victor Hugo, Dante and Karl Marx. A little later in this introduction I shall deal with the methodological problems one encounters in so broadly construed a "field" as this.

The interchange between the academic and the more or less imaginative meanings of Orientalism is a constant one, and since the late eighteenth century there has been a considerable, quite disciplined—perhaps even regulated—traffic between the two. Here I come to the third meaning of Orientalism, which is something more historically and materially defined than either of the other two. Taking the late eighteenth century as a very roughly defined starting point Orientalism can be discussed and analyzed as the corporate institution for dealing with the Orient—dealing with it by making statements about it, authorizing views of it, describing it, by teaching it, settling it, ruling over it: in short, Orientalism as a Western style for dominating, restructuring, and having authority over the Orient. I have found it useful here to employ Michel Foucault's notion of a discourse, as described by him in *The Archaeology of Knowledge* and in *Discipline and Punish,* to identify Orientalism. My contention is that without examining Orientalism as a discourse one cannot possibly understand the enormously systematic discipline by which European culture was able to manage—and even produce—the Orient politically, sociologically, militarily, ideologically, scientifically, and imaginatively during the post-Enlightenment period. Moreover, so authoritative a Position did Orientalism have that I believe no one writing, thinking, or acting on the Orient could do so without taking account of the limitations on thought and action imposed by Orientalism. In brief, because of Orientalism the Orient was not (and is not) a free subject of thought or action. This is not to say that Orientalism unilaterally determines what can be said about the Orient, but that it is the whole network of interests inevitably brought to bear on (and therefore always involved in) any occasion when that peculiar entity "the Orient" is in question. How this happens is what this book tries to demonstrate. It also tries to show that European culture gained in strength and identity by setting itself off against the Orient as a sort of surrogate and even underground self.

Historically and culturally there is a quantitative as well as a qualitative difference between the Franco-British involvement in the Orient and—until the period of American ascendancy after World War II—the involvement of every other European and Atlantic power. To speak of Orientalism therefore is to speak mainly, although not exclusively, of a British and French cultural enterprise, a project whose dimensions take in such disparate realms as the imagination itself, the whole of India and the Levant, the Biblical texts and the Biblical lands, the spice trade, colonial armies and a long tradition of colonial administrators, a formidable scholarly corpus, innumerable Oriental "experts" and "hands," an Oriental professorate, a complex array of "Oriental" ideas (Oriental despotism, Oriental splendor, cruelty, sensuality), many Eastern sects, philosophies, and wisdoms domesticated for local European use—the list can be extended more or less indefinitely. My point is that Orientalism derives from a particular closeness experienced between Britain and France and the Orient, which until the early nineteenth century had really meant only India and the Bible lands. From the beginning of the nineteenth century until the end of World War II France and Britain dominated the Orient and Orientalism; since World War II America has dominated the Orient, and approaches it as France and Britain once did. Out of that closeness, whose dynamic is enormously productive even if it always demonstrates the comparatively greater strength of the Occident (British, French, or American), comes the large body of texts I call Orientalist.

It should be said at once that even with the generous number of books and authors that I examine, there is a much larger number that I simply have had to leave out. My argument, however, depends neither upon an exhaustive catalogue of texts dealing with the Orient nor upon a clearly delimited set of texts, authors, and ideas that together make up the Orientalist canon. I have depended instead upon a different methodological alternative—whose backbone in a sense is the set of historical generalizations I have so far been making in this Introduction—and it is these I want now to discuss in more analytical detail.

II

I have begun with the assumption that the Orient is not an inert fact of nature. It is not merely *there*, just as the Occident itself is not just *there* either. We must take seriously Vico's great observation that men make their own history, that what they can know is what they have made, and extend it to geography: as both geographical and cultural entities—to say nothing of historical entities—such locales, regions, geographical sectors as "Orient" and "Occident" are man-made. Therefore as much as the West itself, the Orient is an idea that has a history and a tradition of thought, imagery, and vocabulary that have given it reality and presence in and for the West. The two geographical entities thus support and to an extent reflect each other.

Having said that, one must go on to state a number of reasonable qualifications. In the first place, it would be wrong to conclude that the Orient was *essentially* an idea, or a creation with no corresponding reality. When Disraeli said in his novel *Tancred* that the East was a career, he meant that to be interested in the East was something bright young Westerners would find to be an all-consuming passion; he should not be interpreted as saying that the East was *only* a career for Westerners. There were—and are—cultures and nations whose location is in the East, and their lives, histories, and customs have a brute reality obviously greater than anything that could be said about them in the West. About that fact this study of Orientalism has very little to contribute, except to acknowledge it tacitly. But the phenomenon of Orientalism as I study it here deals principally, not with a correspondence between Orientalism and Orient, but with the internal consistency of Orientalism and its ideas about the Orient (the East as career) despite or beyond any correspondence, or lack thereof, with a "real" Orient. My point is that Disraeli's statement about the East refers mainly to that created consistency, that regular constellation of ideas as the pre-eminent thing about the Orient, and not to its mere being, as Wallace Stevens's phrase has it.

A second qualification is that ideas, cultures, and histories cannot seriously be understood or studied without their force, or more precisely their configurations of power, also being studied. To believe that the Orient was created—or, as I call it, "Orientalized"—and to believe that such things happen simply as a necessity of the imagination, is to be disingenuous. The relationship between Occident and Orient is a relationship of power, of domination, of varying degrees of a complex hegemony, and is quite accurately indicated in the title of K. M. Panikkar's classic *Asia and Western Dominance*.[2] The Orient was Orientalized not only because it was discovered to be "Oriental" in all those ways considered commonplace by an average nineteenth-century European, but also because it *could be*—that is, submitted to being—*made* Oriental. There is very little consent to be found, for example, in the fact that Flaubert's encounter with an Egyptian courtesan produced a widely influential model of the Oriental woman; she never spoke of herself, she never represented her emotions, presence, or history. *He* spoke for and represented her. He was foreign, comparatively wealthy, male, and these were historical facts of domination that allowed him not only to possess Kuchuk Hanem physically but to speak for her and tell his readers in what way she was "typically Oriental." My argument is that Flaubert's situation of strength in relation to Kuchuk Hanem was not an isolated instance. It fairly stands for the pattern of relative strength between East and West, and the discourse about the Orient that it enabled.

This brings us to a third qualification. One ought never to assume that the structure Orientalism is nothing more than a structure of lies or of myths which, were the truth about them to be told. would simply blow away. I myself believe that Orientalism is more particularly valuable as a sign of European-Atlantic power over the Orient than it is as a veridic discourse about the Orient (which is what, in its academic or scholarly form, it claims to be). Nevertheless, what we must respect and try to grasp is the sheer knitted-together strength of Orientalist discourse, its very close ties to the enabling socio-economic and political institutions, and its redoubtable durability. After all, any system of ideas that can remain unchanged as teachable wisdom (in academies, books, congresses, universities, foreign-service institutes) from the period of Ernest Renan in the late 1840s until the present in the United States must be something more formidable than a mere collection of lies. Orientalism, therefore, is not an airy European fantasy about the Orient, but a created body of theory and practice in which, for many genera-tions, there has been a considerable material investment. Continued investment made Orientalism, as a system of knowledge about the Orient, an accepted grid for filtering through the Orient into Western consciousness, just as that same investment multiplied—indeed, made truly productive—the statements proliferating out from Orientalism into the general culture.

Gramsci has made the useful analytic distinction between civil and political society in which the former is made up of voluntary (or at least rational and noncoercive) affiliations like schools, families, and unions, the latter of state institutions (the army, the police, the central bureaucracy) whose role in the polity is direct domination. Culture, of course, is to be found operating within civil society, where the influence of ideas, of institutions, and of other persons works not through domination but by what Gramsci calls consent. In any society not totalitarian, then, certain cultural forms predominate over others, just as certain ideas are more influential than others; the form of this cultural leadership is what Gramsci has identified as *hegemony,* an indispensable concept for any understanding of cultural life in the industrial West. It is hegemony, or rather the result of cultural hegemony at work, that gives Orientalism the durability and the strength I have been speaking about so far. Orientalism is never far from what Denys Hay has called the idea of Europe,[3] a collective notion identifying "us" Europeans as against all "those" non-Europeans, and indeed it can be argued that the major component in European culture is precisely what made that culture hegemonic both in and outside Europe: the idea of European identity as a superior one in comparison with all the non-European peoples and cultures. There is in addition the hegemony of European ideas about the Orient, themselves reiterating European superiority over Oriental backwardness, usually overriding the possibility that a more independent, or more skeptical, thinker might have had different views on the matter.

In a quite constant way, Orientalism depends for its strategy on this flexible *positional* superiority, which puts the Westerner in a whole series of possible relationships with the Orient without ever losing him the relative upper hand. And why should it have been otherwise, especially during the period of extraordinary European ascendancy from the late Renaissance to the present? The scientist, the scholar, the missionary, the trader, or the soldier was in, or thought about, the Orient because he *could be there*, or could think about it, with very little resistance on the Orient's part. Under the general heading of knowledge of the Orient, and within the umbrella of Western hegemony over the Orient during the period from the end of the eighteenth century, there emerged a complex Orient suitable for study in the academy, for display in the museum, for reconstruction in the colonial office, for theoretical illustration in anthropological, biological, linguistic, racial, and historical theses about mankind and the universe, for instances of economic and sociological theories of development, revolution, cultural personality, national or religious character. Additionally, the imaginative examination of things Oriental was based more or less exclusively upon a sovereign Western Consciousness out of whose unchallenged centrality an Oriental world emerged, first according to general ideas about who or what was an Oriental, then according to a detailed logic governed not simply by empirical reality but by a battery of desires, repressions, investments, and projections. If we can point to great Orientalist works of genuine scholarship like Silvestre de Sacy's *Chrestomathie arabe* or Edward William Lane's *Account of the Manners and Customs of the Modem Egyptians*, we need also to note that Renan's and Gobineau's racial ideas came out of the same impulse, as did a great many Victorian pornographic novels (see the analysis by Steven Marcus of "The Lustful Turk"[4]).

And yet, one must repeatedly ask oneself whether what matters in Orientalism is the general group of ideas overriding the mass of material—about which who could deny that they were shot through with doctrines of European superiority, various kinds of racism, imperialism, and the like, dogmatic views of "the Oriental" as a kind of ideal and unchanging abstraction?—or the much more varied work produced by almost uncountable individual writers, whom one would take up as individual instances of authors dealing with the Orient. In a sense the two alternatives, general and particular, are really two perspectives on the same material: in both instances one would have to deal with pioneers in the field like William Jones, with great artists like Nerval or Flaubert. And why would it not be possible to employ both perspectives together, or one after the other? Isn't there an obvious danger of distortion (of precisely the kind that academic Orientalism has always been prone to) if either too general or too specific a level of description is maintained systematically?

My two fears are distortion and inaccuracy, or rather the kind of inaccuracy produced by too dogmatic a generality and too positivistic a localized focus. In trying to deal with these problems I have tried to deal with three main aspects of my own contemporary reality that seem to me to point the way out of the methodological or perspectival difficulties I have been discussing, difficulties that might force one, in the first instance, into writing a coarse polemic on so unacceptably general a level of description as not to be worth the effort, or in the second instance, into writing so detailed and atomistic a series of analyses as to lose all track of the general lines of force informing the field, giving it its special cogency. How then to recognize individuality and to reconcile it with its intelligent, and by no means passive or merely dictatorial, general and hegemonic context?

III

I mentioned three aspects of my contemporary reality: I must explain and briefly discuss them now, so that it can be seen how I was led to a particular course of research and writing.

1. *The distinction between pure and political knowledge.* It is very easy to argue that knowledge about Shakespeare or Wordsworth is not political whereas-knowledge about contemporary China or the Soviet Union is. My own formal and professional designation is that of "humanist," a title which indicates the humanities as my field and therefore the unlikely eventuality that there might be anything political about what I do in that field. Of course, all these labels and terms are quite unnuanced as I use them here, but the general truth of what I am pointing to is, I think, widely held. One reason for saying that a humanist who writes about Wordsworth, or an editor whose specialty is Keats, is not involved in anything political is that what he does seems to have no direct political effect upon reality in the everyday sense. A scholar whose field is Soviet economics works in a highly charged area where there is much government interest, and what he might produce in the way of studies or proposals will be taken up by policymakers, government officials, institutional economists, intelligence experts. The distinction between "humanists" and persons whose work has policy implications, or political significance, can be broadened further by saying that the former's ideological color is a matter of incidental importance to politics (although possibly of great moment to his colleagues in the field, who may object to his Stalinism or fascism or too easy liberalism), whereas the ideology of the latter is woven directly into his material—indeed, economics, politics, and sociology in the modern academy are ideological sciences—and therefore taken for granted as being "political."

Nevertheless the determining impingement on most knowledge produced in the contemporary West (and here I speak mainly about the United States) is that it be nonpolitical, that is, scholarly, academic, impartial, above partisan or small-minded doctrinal belief. One can have no quarrel with such an ambition in theory, perhaps, but in practice the reality is much more problematic. No one has ever devised a method for detaching the scholar from the circumstances of life, from the fact of his involvement (conscious or unconscious) with a class, a set of beliefs, a social position, or from the mere activity of being a member of a society. These continue to bear on what he does professionally, even though naturally enough his research and its fruits do attempt to reach a level of relative freedom from the inhibitions and the restrictions of brute, everyday reality. For there is such a thing as knowledge that is less, rather than more, partial than the individual (with his entangling and distracting life circumstances) who produces it. Yet this knowledge is not therefore automatically nonpolitical.

Whether discussions of literature or of classical philology are fraught with—or have unmediated—political significance is a very large question that I have tried to treat in some detail elsewhere.[5] What I am interested in doing now is suggesting how the general liberal consensus that "true" knowledge is fundamentally nonpolitical (and conversely, that overtly political knowledge is not "true" knowledge) obscures the highly if obscurely organized political circumstances obtaining when knowledge is produced. No one is helped in understanding this today when the adjective "political" is used as a label to discredit any work for daring to violate the protocol of pretended suprapolitical objectivity. We may say, first, that civil society recognizes a gradation of political importance in-the various fields of knowledge. To some extent the political importance given a field comes from the possibility of its direct translation into economic terms; but to a greater extent political importance comes from the closeness of a field to ascertainable sources of power in political society. Thus an economic study of long-term Soviet energy potential and its effect on military capability is likely to be commissioned by the Defense Department, and thereafter to acquire a kind of political status impossible for a study of Tolstoi's early fiction financed in part by a foundation. Yet both works belong in what civil society acknowledges to be a similar field, Russian studies, even though one work may be done by a very conservative economist, the other by a radical literary historian. My point here is that "Russia" as a general subject matter has political priority over nicer distinctions such as "economics" and "literary history," because political society in Gramsci's sense reaches into such realms of civil society as the academy and saturates them with significance of direct concern to it.

I do not want to press all this any further on general theoretical grounds: it seems to me that the value and credibility of my case can be demonstrated by being much more specific, in the way, for example, Noam Chomsky has studied the instrumental connection between the Vietnam War and the notion of objective scholarship as it was applied to cover state-sponsored military research.[6] Now because Britain, France, and recently the United States are imperial powers, their political societies impart to their civil societies a sense of urgency, a direct political infusion as it were, where and whenever matters pertaining to their imperial interests abroad are concerned. I doubt that it is controversial, for example, to say that an Englishman in India or Egypt in the later nineteenth century took an interest in those countries that was never far from their status in his mind as British colonies. To say this may seem quite different from saying that all academic knowledge about India and Egypt is somehow tinged and impressed with, violated by, the gross political fact—and yet *that is what I am saying* in this study of Orientalism. For if it is true that no production of knowledge in the human sciences can ever ignore or disclaim its author's involvement as a human subject in his own circumstances, then it must also be true that for a European or American studying the Orient there can be no disclaiming the main circumstances of *his* actuality: that he comes up against the Orient as a European or American first, as an individual second. And to be a European or an American in such a situation is by no means an inert fact. It meant and means being aware, however dimly, that one belongs to a power with definite interests in the Orient, and more important, that one belongs to a part of the earth with a definite history of involvement in the Orient almost since the time of Homer.

Put in this way, these political actualities are still too undefined and general to be really interesting. Anyone would agree to them without necessarily agreeing also that they mattered very much, for instance, to Flaubert as he wrote *Salammbô*, or to H. A. R. Gibb as he wrote *Modern Trends in Islam*. The trouble is that there is too great a distance between the big dominating fact, as I have described it, and the details of everyday life that govern the minute discipline of a novel or a scholarly text as each is being written. Yet if we eliminate from the start any notion that "big" facts like imperial domination can be applied mechanically and deterministically to such complex matters as culture and ideas, then we will begin to approach an interesting kind of study. My idea is that European and then American interest in the Orient was political according to some of the obvious historical accounts of it that I have given here, but that it was the culture that created that interest, that acted dynamically along with brute political, economic, and military rationales to make the Orient the varied and complicated place that it obviously was in the field I call Orientalism.

Therefore, Orientalism is not a mere political subject matter or field that is reflected passively by culture, scholarship, or institutions; nor is it a large and diffuse collection of texts about the Orient; nor is it representative and expressive of some nefarious "Western" imperialist plot to hold down the "Oriental" world. It is rather a *distribution* of geopolitical awareness into aesthetic, scholarly, economic, sociological, historical, and philological texts; it is an *elaboration* not only of a basic geographical distinction (the world is made up of two unequal halves, Orient and Occident) but also of a whole series of "interests" which, by such means as scholarly discovery, philological reconstruction, psychological analysis, landscape and sociological description, it not only creates but also maintains; it *is*, rather than expresses, a certain *will* or *intention* to understand, in some cases to control, manipulate, even to incorporate, what is a manifestly different (or alternative and novel) world; it is, above all, a discourse that is by no means in direct, corresponding relationship with political power in the raw, but rather is produced and exists in an uneven exchange with various kinds of power, shaped to a degree by the exchange with power political (as with a colonial or imperial establishment), power intellectual (as with reigning sciences like comparative linguistics or anatomy, or any of the modern policy sciences), power cultural (as with orthodoxies and canons of taste, texts, values), power moral (as with ideas about what "we" do and what "they" cannot do or understand as "we" do). Indeed, my real argument is that Orientalism is—and does not simply represent—a considerable dimension of modern political-intellectural culture, and as such has less to do with the Orient than it does with "our" world.

Because Orientalism is a cultural and a political fact, then, it does not exist in some archival vacuum; quite the contrary, I think it can be shown that what is thought, said, or even done about the Orient follows (perhaps occurs within) certain distinct and intellectually knowable lines. Here too a considerable degree of nuance and elaboration can be seen working as between the broad superstructural pressures and the details of composition, the facts of textuality. Most humanistic scholars are, I think, perfectly happy with the notion that texts exist in contexts, that there is such a thing as intertextuality, that the pressures of conventions, predecessors, and rhetorical styles limit what Walter Benjamin once called the "overtaxing of the productive person in the name of . . . the principle of 'creativity,' " in which the poet is believed on his own, and out of his pure mind, to have brought forth his work.[7] Yet there is a reluctance to allow that political, institutional, and ideological constraints act in the same manner on the individual author. A humanist will believe it to be an interesting fact to any interpreter of Balzac that he was influenced in the *Comédie humaine* by the conflict between Geoffroy Saint-Hilaire and Cuvier, but the same sort of pressure on Balzac of deeply reactionary monarchism is felt in some vague way to demean his literary "genius" and therefore to be less worth serious study. Similarly—as Harry Bracken has been tirelessly showing—philosophers will conduct their discussions of Locke, Hume, and empiricism without ever taking into account that there is an explicit connection in these classic writers between their "philosophic" doctrines and racial theory, justifications of slavery, or arguments for colonial exploitation.[8] These are common enough ways by which contemporary scholarship keeps itself pure.

Perhaps it is true that most attempts to rub culture's nose in the mud of politics have been crudely iconoclastic; perhaps also the social interpretation of literature in my own field has simply not kept up with the enormous technical advances in detailed textual analysis. But there is no getting away from the fact that literary studies in general, and American Marxist theorists in particular, have avoided the effort of seriously bridging the gap between the superstructural and the base levels in textual, historical scholarship; on another occasion I have gone so far as to say that the literary-cultural establishment as a whole has declared the serious study of imperialism and culture off limits.[9] For Orientalism brings one up directly against that question—that is, to realizing that political imperialism governs an entire field of study, imagination, and scholarly institutions—in such a way as to make its avoidance an intellectual and historical impossibility. Yet there will always remain the perennial escape mechanism of saying that a literary scholar and a philosopher, for example, are trained in literature and philosophy respectively, not in politics or ideological analysis. In other words, the specialist argument can work quite effectively to block the larger and, in my opinion, the more intellectually serious perspective.

Here it seems to me there is a simple two-part answer to be given, at least so far as the study of imperialism and culture (or Orientalism) is concerned. In the first place, nearly every nineteenth-century writer (and the same is true enough of writers in earlier periods) was extraordinarily well aware of the fact of empire: this is a subject not very well studied, but it will not take a modem Victorian specialist long to admit that liberal cultural heroes like John Stuart Mill, Arnold, Carlyle, Newman, Macaulay, Ruskin, George Eliot, and even Dickens had definite views on race and imperialism, which are quite easily to be found at work in their writing. So even a specialist must deal with the knowledge that Mill, for example, made it clear in *On Liberty* and *Representative Government* that his views there could not be applied to India (he was an India Office functionary for a good deal of his life, after all) because the Indians were civilizationally, if not racially, inferior. The same kind of paradox is to be found in Marx, as I try to show in this book. In the second place, to believe that politics in the form of imperialism bears upon the production of literature, scholarship, social theory, and history writing is by no means equivalent to saying that culture is therefore a demeaned or denigrated thing. Quite the contrary: my whole point is to say that we can better understand the persistence and the durability of saturating hegemonic systems like culture when we realize that their internal constraints upon writers and thinkers were *productive*, not unilaterally inhibiting. It is this idea that Gramsci, certainly, and Foucault and Raymond Williams in their very different ways have been trying to illustrate. Even one or two pages by Williams on "the uses of the Empire" in *The Long Revolution* tell us more about nineteenth-century cultural richness than many volumes of hermetic textual analyses.[10]

Therefore I study Orientalism as a dynamic exchange between individual authors and the large political concerns shaped by the three great empires—British, French, American—in whose intellectual and imaginative territory the writing was produced. What interests me most as a scholar is not the gross political verity but the detail, as indeed what interests us in someone like Lane or Flaubert or Renan is not the (to him) indisputable truth that Occidentals are superior to Orientals, but the profoundly worked over and modulated evidence of his detailed work within the very wide space opened up by that truth. One need only remember that Lane's *Manners and Customs of the Modern Egyptians* is a classic of historical and anthropological observation because of its style, its enormously intelligent and brilliant details, not because of its simple reflection of racial superiority, to understand what I am saying here.

The kind of political questions raised by Orientalism, then, are as follows: What other sorts of intellectual, aesthetic, scholarly, and cultural energies went into the making of an imperialist tradition like the Orientalist one? How did philology, lexicography, history, biology, political and economic theory, novel-writing, and lyric poetry come to the service of Orientalism's broadly imperialist view of the world? What changes, modulations, refinements, even revolutions take place within Orientalism? What is the meaning of originality, of continuity, of individuality, in this context? How does Orientalism transmit or reproduce itself from one epoch to another? In fine, how can we treat the cultural, historical phenomenon of Orientalism as a kind of *willed human work*—not of mere unconditioned ratiocination—in all its historical complexity, detail, and worth without at the same time losing sight of the alliance between cultural work, political tendencies, the state, and the specific realities of domination? Governed by such concerns a humanistic study can responsibly address itself to politics *and* culture. But this is not to say that such a study establishes a hard-and-fast rule about the relationship between knowledge and politics. My argument is that each humanistic investigation must formulate the nature of that connection in the specific context of the study, the subject matter, and its historical circumstances.

2. *The methodological question.* In a previous book I gave a good deal of thought and analysis to the methodological importance for work in the human sciences of finding and formulating a first step, a point of departure, a beginning principle.[11]

STUDY QUESTIONS

1. In an imperial or colonial context, how can knowledge and discourse translate into dominance and power?

2. Can you think of any examples of Orientalist thought?

3. Do you think that Said's argument signifies all Orientalists as imperialists?

PART VI
EDUCATION

Minute on Education

The watchword of 19th-century Britain was progress, and the advent of railways, steamships, and the telegraph exemplified this.[1] As the first industrial nation from the late 18th century, it is no surprise that Britain, "workshop of the world," proclaimed itself the standard bearer of modernity and civilization, destined to transform its colonies for the betterment of humankind. Naturally, the idea of progress found its way into the British Raj in India in myriad ways, and Western education represented but one example of this abject essentialism.

One mode through which the British justified their civilizing mission to their colonies and to themselves was by claiming superiority in learning. In the British imperial context, Lord Thomas Babington Macaulay is probably best known for his 1835 "Minute on Education," which promulgated rigorous Anglocentric curricula in India. Macaulay asserted, for example, that the entire literary canon of the Middle East and India was not worth "a single shelf in a good European library."[2]

Macaulay was a historian who expounded his views in the Whig-leaning *Edinburgh Review* from the late 1820s. Macaulay, a classicist as well as something of a Romantic (who reputedly wept while pondering the *Iliad*), above all else represented the consummate liberal of mid-century Britain. Loyal subjects on the subcontinent, he predicted in the summer of 1833, during a parliamentary debate on India, would accept and adopt British law, government, and mores, as well as a genuine taste for European arts, literature, and sciences. If Indians imbibed Western education, Macaulay pointed out hyperbolically, and prepared for an eventuality of responsible Indian self-rule, "it will be the proudest day in English history."[3] He, his brother-in-law, Sir Charles Trevelyan, and that other reformer of *sati*, Lord William Bentinck, all advocated the inclusion of works by authors that included William Shakespeare, Sir Francis Bacon, and Adam Smith. Macaulay, unlike other utilitarian commentators on India such as James and John Stuart Mill, actually worked there as a law expert on the Governor-General's Council, and amassed

---

1   With the incorporation of Scotland into the United Kingdom in 1707, British became a more inclusive term than English.
2   Quoted in Thomas R. Metcalf, *Ideologies of the Raj*, 5th ed. (Cambridge: Cambridge University Press, 2006), p. 34.
3   Ibid

Figure 13.1. Thomas Babington Macaulay. Source: http://commons.wikimedia.org/wiki/File:Thomas_Babington_Macaulay,_1st_Baron_Macaulay_-_Project_Gutenberg_eText_13103.jpg.

a small fortune that allowed him to sit in Parliament and devote his voice to Indian affairs. Anathema to his viewpoints were the first Orientalists such as Sir William Jones, founder of the Royal Asiatick Society, who studied, translated, and lauded Sanskrit and its epistemology.

In his writings and speeches on India, Macaulay instead proved to be a staunch proponent of colonial expansion, and would have been alive to the burgeoning contemporary pseudoscientific discourses on race and gender. Indians in the British estimation, for example, with a few exceptions, were believed to be effeminate because Hinduism, the spiritual philosophy and way of life of the majority of the population, promoted peace and passivity, feebleness and cravenness, fecklessness and meekness, idolatry to female deities, and vegetarianism.[4] Britons, by contrast, were considered manly because they were bellicose, strong and brave, resolute, Christian, and carnivorous. Climatic conditions, moreover, were thought to have played a role; the heat and humidity rendered Indians languid, lazy, and prone to indulgences in sensuality. The British wore topees and retreated to the cooler hill stations, where they attempted to recreate little Britains. Most contemptuous of all were the effete and sleek Bengali *babus*, clerks and lower-echelon bureaucrats, who fawned over the British, emulating their ways almost to perfection, yet were scorned in their obsequious mimicry and ultimately separated by their race. Indians, therefore, should be reshaped in the image of Englishmen, "in taste, in opinions, in morals and in intellect," but only to an ambivalent extent.[5] By emasculating Indians, Britons could further assert their authority and power.

Macaulay's "Minute" encouraged the passage of the English Education Act of 1835, making English in schools compulsory, and was followed in 1837 by the highly chauvinist statement that any Hindu who had received an English education, could not sincerely remain a follower of Hinduism. As snide a comment as this may have been, it remained entirely commensurate with British contemporary attitudes.

In a larger sense, this was the conception of how Indians, but for their skin color, might be transformed into liberal Englishmen. The agent for this metamorphosis was British education, ready to usher India into the future in the mold championed by Macaulay. Although during his life and after, Urdu and Hindi thrived as court languages, along with some 200 subsidiary vernaculars, he would have been pleased that the real *lingua franca* in India eventually became English. Precisely because he desired Indians to emulate liberal Britons, Macaulay promoted fairness in the courts and freedom of the press. He even sincerely imagined that, on some distant day, the peoples of India might be emancipated, ready for self-government, and claim a share of the British ideas of freedom and democracy for themselves. In teaching them this, a piece of the British Raj ever would exist.

---

4   The exceptions to the rule were known as the "martial races," and included Muslims, Sikhs, Pathans, Rajputs, Marathas, Jats, and Afghanis.

5   Quoted in Amitava Kumar, "Passport Photos," in Bill Ashcroft, Gareth Griffiths, and Helen Tiffin, eds., *The Post-Colonial Studies Reader*, 2nd ed. (London and New York: Routledge, 2006), p. 456.

Minute on Education

By Thomas Babington Macaulay

2nd February 1835.

As it seems to be the opinion of some of the gentlemen who compose the Committee of Public Instruction that the course which they have hitherto pursued was strictly prescribed by the British Parliament in 1813 and as, if that opinion be correct, a legislative act will be necessary to warrant a change, I have thought it right to refrain from taking any part in the preparation of the adverse statements which are now before us, and to reserve what I had to say on the subject till it should come before me as a Member of the Council of India.

It does not appear to me that the Act of Parliament can by any art of contraction be made to bear the meaning which has been assigned to it. It contains nothing about the particular languages or sciences which are to be studied. A sum is set apart "for the revival and promotion of literature, and the encouragement of the learned natives of India, and for the introduction and promotion of a knowledge of the sciences among the inhabitants of the British territories." It is argued, or rather taken for granted, that by literature the Parliament can have meant only Arabic and Sanscrit literature; that they never would have given the honourable appellation of "a learned native" to a native who was familiar with the poetry of Milton, the metaphysics of Locke, and the physics of Newton; but that they meant to designate by that name only such persons as might have studied in the sacred books of the Hindoos all the uses of cusa-grass, and all the mysteries of absorption into the Deity. This does not appear to be a very satisfactory interpretation. To take a parallel case: Suppose that the Pacha of Egypt, a country once superior in knowledge to the nations of Europe, but now sunk far below them, were to appropriate a sum for the purpose "of reviving and promoting literature, and encouraging learned natives of Egypt," would any body infer that he meant the youth of his Pachalik to give years to the study of hieroglyphics, to search into all the doctrines disguised under the fable of Osiris, and to ascertain with all possible accuracy the ritual with which cats and onions were anciently adored? Would he be justly charged with inconsistency if, instead of employing his young subjects in deciphering obelisks, he were to order them to be instructed in the English and French languages, and in all the sciences to which those languages are the chief keys?

Thomas Babington Macaulay, "Minute on Education," Selections from *Educational Records, Part I* (1781-1839), ed. H. Sharp, 1920.

The words on which the supporters of the old system rely do not bear them out, and other words follow which seem to be quite decisive on the other side. This lakh[1] of rupees is set apart not only for "reviving literature in India," the phrase on which their whole interpretation is founded, but also "for the introduction and promotion of a knowledge of the sciences among the inhabitants of the British territories"—words which are alone sufficient to authorize all the changes for which I contend.

If the Council agree in my construction no legislative act will be necessary. If they differ from me, I will propose a short act rescinding that I clause of the Charter of 1813[2] from which the difficulty arises.

The argument which I have been considering affects only the form of proceeding. But the admirers of the oriental system of education have used another argument, which, if we admit it to be valid, is decisive against all change. They conceive that the public faith is pledged to the present system, and that to alter the appropriation of any of the funds which have hitherto been spent in encouraging the study of Arabic and Sanscrit would be downright spoliation. It is not easy to understand by what process of reasoning they can have arrived at this conclusion. The grants which are made from the public purse for the encouragement of literature differ in no respect from the grants which are made from the same purse for other objects of real or supposed utility. We found a sanitarium on a spot which we suppose to be healthy. Do we thereby pledge ourselves to keep a sanitarium there if the result should not answer our expectations? We commence the erection of a pier. Is it a violation of the public faith to stop the works, if we afterwards see reason to believe that the building will be useless? The rights of property are undoubtedly sacred. But nothing endangers those rights so much as the practice, now unhappily too common, of attributing them to things to which they do not belong. Those who would impart to abuses the sanctity of property are in truth imparting to the institution of property the unpopularity and the fragility of abuses. If the Government has given to any person a formal assurance—nay, if the Government has excited in any person's mind a reasonable expectation—that he shall receive a certain income as a teacher or a learner of Sanscrit or Arabic, I would respect that person's pecuniary interests. I would rather err on the side of liberality to individuals than suffer the public faith to be called in question. But to talk of a Government pledging itself to teach certain languages and certain sciences, though those languages may become useless, though those sciences may be exploded, seems to me quite unmeaning. There is not a single word in any public instrument from which it can be inferred that the Indian Government ever intended to give any pledge on this subject, or ever considered the destination of these funds as unalterably fixed. But, had it been otherwise, I should have denied the competence of our predecessors to bind us by any pledge on such a subject. Suppose that a Government had in the last century enacted in the most solemn manner that all its subjects should, to the end of time, be inoculated for the small-pox, would that Government be bound to persist in the practice after Jenner's discovery? These promises of which nobody claims the performance, and from which nobody can grant a release, these vested rights which vest in nobody, this property without proprietors, this robbery which makes nobody poorer, may be comprehended by persons of higher faculties than mine. I consider this plea merely as a set form of words, regularly used both in England and in India, in defence of every abuse for which no other plea can be set up.

I hold this lakh of rupees to be quite at the disposal of the Governor-General in Council for the purpose of promoting learning in India in any way which may be thought most advisable. I hold his Lordship to be quite as free to direct that it shall no longer be employed in encouraging Arabic and

1 *Editor's note*: One lakh is equal to 100,000 rupees.
2 *Editor's note*: The East India Company Act of 1813, also known as the Charter Act of 1813, provided a lakh to be set aside for Indian education.

Sanscrit, as he is to direct that the reward for killing tigers in Mysore shall be diminished, or that no more public money shall be expended on the chaunting at the cathedral.

We now come to the gist of the matter. We have a fund to be employed as Government shall direct for the intellectual improvement of the people of this country. The simple question is, what is the most useful way of employing it?

All parties seem to be agreed on one point, that the dialects commonly spoken among the natives of this part of India contain neither literary nor scientific information, and are moreover so poor and rude that, until they are enriched from some other quarter, it will not be easy to translate any valuable work into them. It seems to be admitted on all sides, that the intellectual improvement of those classes of the people who have the means of pursuing higher studies can at present be affected only by means of some language not vernacular amongst them.

What then shall that language be? One-half of the committee maintain that it should be the English. The other half strongly recommend the Arabic and Sanscrit. The whole question seems to me to be— which language is the best worth knowing?

I have no knowledge of either Sanscrit or Arabic. But I have done what I could to form a correct estimate of their value. I have read translations of the most celebrated Arabic and Sanscrit works. I have conversed, both here and at home, with men distinguished by their proficiency in the Eastern tongues. I am quite ready to take the oriental learning at the valuation of the orientalists themselves. I have never found one among them who could deny that a single shelf of a good European library was worth the whole native literature of India and Arabia. The intrinsic superiority of the Western literature is indeed fully admitted by those members of the committee who support the oriental plan of education.

It will hardly be disputed, I suppose, that the department of literature in which the Eastern writers stand highest is poetry. And I certainly never met with any orientalist who ventured to maintain that the Arabic and Sanscrit poetry could be compared to that of the great European nations. But when we pass from works of imagination to works in which facts are recorded and general principles investigated, the superiority of the Europeans becomes absolutely immeasurable. It is, I believe, no exaggeration to say that all the historical information which has been collected from all the books written in the Sanscrit language is less valuable than what may be found in the most paltry abridgments used at preparatory schools in England. In every branch of physical or moral philosophy, the relative position of the two nations is nearly the same.

How then stands the case? We have to educate a people who cannot at present be educated by means of their mother-tongue. We must teach them some foreign language. The claims of our own language it is hardly necessary to recapitulate. It stands pre-eminent even among the languages of the West. It abounds with works of imagination not inferior to the noblest which Greece has bequeathed to us,—with models of every species of eloquence,—with historical composition, which, considered merely as narratives, have seldom been surpassed, and which, considered as vehicles of ethical and political instruction, have never been equaled—with just and lively representations of human life and human nature,—with the most profound speculations on metaphysics, morals, government, jurisprudence, trade,—with full and correct information respecting every experimental science which tends to preserve the health, to increase the comfort, or to expand the intellect of man. Whoever knows that language has ready access to all the vast intellectual wealth which all the wisest nations of the earth have created and hoarded in the course of ninety generations. It may safely be said that the literature now extant in that language is of greater value than all the literature which three hundred years ago was extant in all the languages of the world together. Nor is this all. In India, English is the language spoken by the ruling class. It is spoken by the higher class of natives at the seats of Government. It is likely to become the language of commerce throughout the seas of the East. It is the language of two great European communities which are rising, the one in the south of Africa, the other in Australia,—communities which are every year becoming more important and more closely connected with our Indian empire. Whether we look at the intrinsic value of our literature, or at the particular situation of this country, we shall see the strongest reason to think that, of all foreign tongues, the English tongue is that which would be the most useful to our native subjects.

The question now before us is simply whether, when it is in our power to teach this language, we shall teach languages in which, by universal confession, there are no books on any subject which deserve to be compared to our own, whether, when we can teach European science, we shall teach systems which, by universal confession, wherever they differ from those of Europe differ for the worse, and whether, when we can patronize sound philosophy and true history, we shall countenance, at the public expense, medical doctrines which would disgrace an English farrier, astronomy which would move laughter in girls at an English boarding school, history abounding with kings thirty feet high and reigns thirty thousand years long, and geography made of seas of treacle and seas of butter.

We are not without experience to guide us. History furnishes several analogous cases, and they all teach the same lesson. There are, in modern times, to go no further, two memorable instances of a great impulse given to the mind of a whole society, of prejudices overthrown, of knowledge diffused, of taste purified, of arts and sciences planted in countries which had recently been ignorant and barbarous.

The first instance to which I refer is the great revival of letters among the Western nations at the close of the fifteenth and the beginning of the sixteenth century. At that time almost everything that was worth reading was contained in the writings of the ancient Greeks and Romans. Had our ancestors acted as the Committee of Public Instruction has hitherto noted, had they neglected the language of Thucydides and Plato, and the language of Cicero and Tacitus, had they confined their attention to the old dialects of our own island, had they printed nothing and taught nothing at the universities but chronicles in Anglo-Saxon and romances in Norman French,—would England ever have been what she now is? What the Greek and Latin were to the contemporaries of More and Ascham, our tongue is to the people of India. The literature of England is now more valuable than that of classical antiquity. I doubt whether the Sanscrit literature be as valuable as that of our Saxon and Norman progenitors. In some departments—in history for example—I am certain that it is much less so.

Another instance may be said to be still before our eyes. Within the last hundred and twenty years, a nation which had previously been in a state as barbarous as that in which our ancestors were before the Crusades has gradually emerged from the ignorance in which it was sunk, and has taken its place among civilized communities. I speak of Russia. There is now in that country a large educated class abounding with persons fit to serve the State in the highest functions, and in nowise inferior to the most accomplished men who adorn the best circles of Paris and London. There is reason to hope that this vast empire which, in the time of our grandfathers, was probably behind the Punjab, may in the time of our grandchildren, be pressing close on France and Britain in the career of improvement. And how was this change effected? Not by flattering national prejudices; not by feeding the mind of the young Muscovite with the old women's stories which his rude fathers had believed; not by filling his head with lying legends about St. Nicholas[3]; not by encouraging him to study the great question, whether the world was or not created on the 13th of September; not by calling him "a learned native" when he had mastered

---

3   *Editor's note*: Russian patron saint of the weak and oppressed.

all these points of knowledge; but by teaching him those foreign languages in which the greatest mass of information had been laid up, and thus putting all that information within his reach. The languages of western Europe civilised Russia. I cannot doubt that they will do for the Hindoo what they have done for the Tartar.

And what are the arguments against that course which seems to be alike recommended by theory and by experience? It is said that we ought to secure the co-operation of the native public, and that we can do this only by teaching Sanscrit and Arabic.

I can by no means admit that, when a nation of high intellectual attainments undertakes to superintend the education of a nation comparatively ignorant, the learners are absolutely to prescribe the course which is to be taken by the teachers. It is not necessary however to say anything on this subject. For it is proved by unanswerable evidence, that we are not at present securing the cooperation of the natives. It would be bad enough to consult their intellectual taste at the expense of their intellectual health. But we are consulting neither. We are withholding from them the learning which is palatable to them. We are forcing on them the mock learning which they nauseate.

This is proved by the fact that we are forced to pay our Arabic and Sanscrit students while those who learn English are willing to pay us. All the declamations in the world about the love and reverence of the natives for their sacred dialects will never, in the mind of any impartial person, outweigh this undisputed fact, that we cannot find in all our vast empire a single student who will let us teach him those dialects, unless we will pay him.

I have now before me the accounts of the Mudrassa for one month, the month of December, 1833. The Arabic students appear to have been seventy-seven in number. All receive stipends from the public. The whole amount paid to them is above 500 rupees a month. On the other side of the account stands the following item:

Deduct amount realized from the out-students of English for the months of May, June, and July last—103 rupees.

I have been told that it is merely from want of local experience that I am surprised at these phenomena, and that it is not the fashion for students in India to study at their own charges. This only confirms me in my opinions. Nothing is more certain than that it never can in any part of the world be necessary to pay men for doing what they think pleasant or profitable. India is no exception to this rule. The people of India do not require to be paid for eating rice when they are hungry, or for wearing woollen cloth in the cold season. To come nearer to the case before us:—The children who learn their letters and a little elementary arithmetic from the village schoolmaster are not paid by him. He is paid for teaching them. Why then is it necessary to pay people to learn Sanscrit and Arabic? Evidently because it is universally felt that the Sanscrit and Arabic are languages the knowledge of which does not compensate for the trouble of acquiring them. On all such subjects the state of the market is the detective test.

Other evidence is not wanting, if other evidence were required. A petition was presented last year to the committee by several ex-students of the Sanscrit College. The petitioners stated that they had studied in the college ten or twelve years, that they had made themselves acquainted with Hindoo literature and science, that they had received certificates of proficiency. And what is the fruit of all this? "Notwithstanding such testimonials," they say, "we have but little prospect of bettering our condition without the kind assistance of your honourable committee, the indifference with which we are generally looked upon by our countrymen leaving no hope of encouragement and assistance from them." They therefore beg that they may be recommended to the Governor-General for places under the Government—not places of high dignity or emolument, but such as may just enable them to exist. "We want means," they say, "for a decent living, and for our progressive improvement, which, however, we cannot obtain without the assistance of Government, by whom we have been educated and maintained from childhood." They conclude by representing very pathetically that they are sure that it was never the intention of Government, after behaving so liberally to them during their education, to abandon them to destitution and neglect.

I have been used to see petitions to Government for compensation. All those petitions, even the most unreasonable of them, proceeded on the supposition that some loss had been sustained, that some wrong had been inflicted. These are surely the first petitioners who ever demanded compensation for having been educated gratis, for having been supported by the public during twelve years, and then sent forth into the world well furnished with literature and science. They represent their education as an injury which gives them a claim on the Government for redress, as an injury for which the stipends paid to them during the infliction were a very inadequate compensation. And I doubt not that they are in the right. They have wasted the best years of life in learning what procures for them neither bread nor respect. Surely we might with advantage have saved the cost of making these persons useless and miserable. Surely, men may be brought up to be burdens to the public and objects of contempt to their neighbours at a somewhat smaller charge to the State. But such is our policy. We do not even stand neuter in the contest between truth and falsehood. We are not content to leave the natives to the influence of their own hereditary prejudices. To the natural difficulties which obstruct the progress of sound science in the East, we add great difficulties of our own making. Bounties and premiums, such as ought not to be given even for the propagation of truth, we lavish on false texts and false philosophy.

By acting thus we create the very evil which we fear. We are making that opposition which we do not find. What we spend on the Arabic and Sanscrit Colleges is not merely a dead loss to the cause of truth. It is bounty-money paid to raise up champions of error. It goes to form a nest not merely of helpless placehunters but of bigots prompted alike by passion and by interest to raise a cry against every useful scheme of education. If there should be any opposition among the natives to the change which I recommend, that opposition will be the effect of our own system. It will be headed by persons supported by our stipends and trained in our colleges. The longer we persevere in our present course, the more formidable will that opposition be. It will be every year reinforced by recruits whom we are paying. From the native society, left to itself, we have no difficulties to apprehend. All the murmuring will come from that oriental interest which we have, by artificial means, called into being and nursed into strength.

There is yet another fact which is alone sufficient to prove that the feeling of the native public, when left to itself, is not such as the supporters of the old system represent it to be. The committee have thought fit to lay out above a lakh of rupees in printing Arabic and Sanscrit books. Those books find no purchasers. It is very rarely that a single copy is disposed of. Twenty-three thousand volumes, most of them folios and quartos, fill the libraries or rather the lumber-rooms of this body. The committee contrive to get rid of some portion of their vast stock of oriental literature by giving books away. But they cannot give so fast as they print. About twenty thousand rupees a year are spent in adding fresh masses of waste paper to a hoard which, one should think, is already sufficiently ample. During the last three years about sixty thousand rupees have been expended in this manner. The sale of Arabic and Sanscrit books during those three years has not yielded quite one thousand rupees. In the meantime, the School Book Society is selling seven or eight thousand English volumes every year, and not only pays the expenses of printing but realizes a profit of twenty per cent. on its outlay.

The fact that the Hindoo law is to be learned chiefly from Sanscrit books, and the Mahometan law from Arabic books, has been much insisted on, but seems not to bear at all on the question. We are commanded by Parliament to ascertain and digest the laws of India. The assistance of a Law Commission has been given to us for that purpose. As soon as the Code is promulgated the Shasters and the Hedaya will be useless to a moonsiff or a Sudder Ameen. I hope and trust that, before the boys who are now entering at the Mudrassa and the Sanscrit College have completed their studies, this great work will be finished. It would be manifestly absurd to educate the rising generation with a view to a state of things which we mean to alter before they reach manhood.

But there is yet another argument which seems even more untenable. It is said that the Sanscrit and the Arabic are the languages in which the sacred books of a hundred millions of people are written, and that they are on that account entitled to peculiar encouragement. Assuredly it is the duty of the British Government in India to be not only tolerant but neutral on all religious questions. But to encourage the study of a literature, admitted to be of small intrinsic value, only because that literature inculcated the most serious errors on the most important subjects, is a course hardly reconcilable with reason, with morality, or even with that very neutrality which ought, as we all agree, to be sacredly preserved. It is confined that a language is barren of useful knowledge. We are to teach it because it is fruitful of monstrous superstitions. We are to teach false history, false astronomy, false medicine, because we find them in company with a false religion. We abstain, and I trust shall always abstain, from giving any public encouragement to those who are engaged in the work of converting the natives to Christianity. And while we act thus, can we reasonably or decently bribe men, out of the revenues of the State, to waste their youth in learning how they are to purify themselves after touching an ass or what texts of the Vedas they are to repeat to expiate the crime of killing a goat?

It is taken for granted by the advocates of oriental learning that no native of this country can possibly attain more than a mere smattering of English. They do not attempt to prove this. But they perpetually insinuate it. They designate the education which their opponents recommend as a mere spelling-book education. They assume it as undeniable that the question is between a profound knowledge of Hindoo and Arabian literature and science on the one side, and superficial knowledge of the rudiments of English on the other. This is not merely an assumption, but an assumption contrary to all reason and experience. We know that foreigners of all nations do learn our language sufficiently to have access to all the most abstruse knowledge which it contains sufficiently to relish even the more delicate graces of our most idiomatic writers. There are in this very town natives who are quite competent to discuss political or scientific questions with fluency and precision in the English language. I have heard the very question on which I am now writing discussed by native gentlemen with a liberality and an intelligence which would do credit to any member of the Committee of Public Instruction. Indeed it is unusual to find, even in the literary circles of the Continent, any foreigner who can express himself in English with so much facility and correctness as we find in many Hindoos. Nobody, I suppose, will contend that English is so difficult to a Hindoo as Greek to an Englishman. Yet an intelligent English youth, in a much smaller number of years than our unfortunate pupils pass at the Sanscrit College, becomes able to read, to enjoy, and even to imitate not unhappily the compositions of the best Greek authors. Less than half the time which enables an English youth to read Herodotus and Sophocles ought to enable a Hindoo to read Hume and Milton.

To sum up what I have said. I think it clear that we are not fettered by the Act of Parliament of 1813, that we are not fettered by any pledge expressed or implied, that we are free to employ our funds as we choose, that we ought to employ them in teaching what is best worth knowing, that English is better worth knowing than Sanscrit or Arabic, that the natives are desirous to be taught English, and are not desirous to be taught Sanscrit or Arabic, that neither as the languages of law nor as the languages of religion have the Sanscrit and Arabic any peculiar claim to our encouragement, that it is possible to make natives of this country thoroughly good English scholars, and that to this end our efforts ought to be directed.

In one point I fully agree with the gentlemen to whose general views I am opposed. I feel with them that it is impossible for us, with our limited means, to attempt to educate the body of the people. We must at present do our best to form a class who may be interpreters between us and the millions whom we govern, —a class of persons Indian in blood and colour, but English in tastes, in opinions, in morals and in intellect. To that class we may leave it to refine the vernacular dialects of the country, to enrich those dialects with terms of science borrowed from the Western nomenclature, and to render them by degrees fit vehicles for conveying knowledge to the great mass of the population.

I would strictly respect all existing interests. I would deal even generously with all individuals who have had fair reason to expect a pecuniary provision. But I would strike at the root of the bad system which has hitherto been fostered by us. I would at once stop the printing of Arabic and Sanscrit books. I would abolish the Mudrassa and the Sanscrit College at Calcutta. Benares is the great seat of Brahminical learning; Delhi of Arabic learning. If we retain the Sanscrit College at Bonares and the Mahometan College at Delhi we do enough and much more than enough in my opinion, for the Eastern languages. If the Benares and Delhi Colleges should be retained, I would at least recommend that no stipends shall be given to any students who may hereafter repair thither, but that the people shall be left to make their own choice between the rival systems of education without being bribed by us to learn what they have no desire to know. The funds which would thus be placed at our disposal would enable us to give larger encouragement to the Hindoo College at Calcutta, and establish in the principal cities throughout the Presidencies of Fort William and Agra schools in which the English language might be well and thoroughly taught.

If the decision of His Lordship in Council should be such as I anticipate, I shall enter on the performance of my duties with the greatest zeal and alacrity. If, on the other hand, it be the opinion of the Government that the present system ought to remain unchanged, I beg that I may be permitted to retire from the chair of the Committee. I feel that I could not be of the smallest use there. I feel also that I should be lending my countenance to what I firmly believe to be a mere delusion. I believe that the present system tends not to accelerate the progress of truth but to delay the natural death of expiring errors. I conceive that we have at present no right to the respectable name of a Board of Public Instruction. We are a Board for wasting the public money, for printing books which are of less value than the paper on which they are printed was while it was blank—for giving artificial encouragement to absurd history, absurd metaphysics, absurd physics, absurd theology—for raising up a breed of scholars who find their scholarship an incumbrance and blemish, who live on the public while they are receiving their education, and whose education is so utterly useless to them that, when they have received it, they must either starve or live on the public all the rest of their lives. Entertaining these opinions, I am naturally desirous to decline all share in the responsibility of a body which, unless it alters its whole mode of proceedings, I must consider, not merely as useless, but as positively noxious.

T[homas] B[abington] MACAULAY
2nd February 1835.
I give my entire concurrence to the sentiments expressed in this Minute.
W[illiam] C[avendish] BENTINCK.

STUDY QUESTIONS

1. In what direction did Macaulay wish to guide Indian education?

2. How does he view Indian disciplines of study?

PART VII

NATIONALISM

On the Necessity for De-Anglicizing Ireland

I n 19th-century British politics, the "Irish Question" confounded both liberal and conservative parliamentarians alike. From 1801, when the Act of Union absorbed Ireland into the United Kingdom, legislators considered and implemented both conciliation and coercion in striking the balance between how much freedom to allot while maintaining order and stability.

There existed multiple differences between England and Ireland. The former upheld the state religion of Anglicanism, while the majority of the latter was overwhelmingly Roman Catholic. England had industrialized and urbanized. Ireland, by contrast, largely remained an agrarian-based peasant economy. Vast tracts of Irish land were owned by absentee English or Anglo-Irish landlords, who exacted rents from a tenantry who could scarcely feed their large families on subdivided plots. English lawmakers, therefore, found it exceedingly difficult to govern for Ireland.

Irish resistance to British rule took three sometimes intersecting forms: revolutionary, constitutional, and romantic. Failed attempts at armed insurrection occurred sporadically in modern Ireland (1798, 1803, 1848, 1867), culminating in the Easter Rising of the Irish Republican Brotherhood in 1916, which led to an Anglo-Irish war, a treaty with England, and an Irish civil war between those who supported the treaty and those who did not.

From 1916, while the period of revolutionary Ireland engendered eventual Irish independence in 1922, the road to Home Rule had been paved by constitutional politicians. Between the 1820s and 1840s, Daniel O'Connell politicized the Irish masses with the creation of an indigenous political system. In the 1880s, Charles Stewart Parnell crystallized that de facto political system by perfecting a strict code of unanimity within his Irish Parliamentary Party and its obstructionist tactics in the House of Commons.

Romantic nationalists, for their part, rejected English cultural norms and celebrated Irish authenticity through such diverse disciplines as language, drama, art, literature, music, athletics, and even economics by the buying of Irish goods. For them, a nation was also a cultural state of mind defined

Figure 14.1. Douglas Hyde. Source: http://commons.wikimedia.org/wiki/File:Douglas_Hyde_2.jpg.

by a common literature and history, which was infused in a collective consciousness. For some, this romantic hearkening even called for the recollection of the virtues and triumphs of ancient Ireland. Total independence could thus be achieved only through the Repeal of the Union and a regeneration of a Gaelic identity too long on the wane. Enthusiasts sought to reestablish their Irish identity through a number of voluntary organizations that promoted Irish language and culture. Most perfidious of all to the cultural nationalists were *Seoinín* (*Shoneens*) or "West Brits," those who brought English ways—and their superior airs—to Ireland.

O'Connell could speak Irish fluently, but was a shrewd enough politician to understand he need not preach to the choir; in addition to the Irish who came to witness his orations at "Monster Meetings," his other important audience was the readership of the English press. Parnell, the Cambridge-educated Protestant landlord, did not need to know Irish when conducting business with Conservatives and Liberals in the House of Commons. It was another Irishman, however, who believed that language could serve as a conduit to unity.

Douglas Hyde (1860–1949) was a Protestant from County Roscommon, who in childhood had acquired a love of Irish idiom and folklore from rural cottiers and agricultural laborers. Hyde, who in 1893 cofounded the Gaelic League with Professor Eoin MacNeill to promote Irish cultural and linguistic education, noticed an ambivalent attitude toward—and even Irish mimicry of—the English. In a lecture entitled, "The Necessity for De-Anglicizing Ireland," delivered to the Irish Literary Society in November 1892, Hyde focused on eradicating English influences, and stressed the importance of separating nationality from politics. The restoration of Gaelic civilization, he explained, should remain apolitical.[1] The Irish, furthermore, should exalt their nation with pride, shedding the 19th-century English poet Matthew Arnold's image of "the badge of a beaten race." Hyde, however, as compared to the Gaelic Leaguer and 1916 martyr, Padraig Pearse, sought an ecumenical Irishness that was based on more than mere hatred for England.[2]

Some within the fin-de-siècle Irish literary revival mocked Hyde's pastoral sentimentality as quaint and impractical. The poet, William Butler Yeats, supported Hyde's efforts, but despite delving into the mythical Irish past as subject matter in some of his writing, Yeats wrote in English. By the end of the 19th century, in fact, there were a scant six books in print in Irish, and most people in the Gaeltacht, or

---

1 The extent to which Hyde, despite his sincerity, was able to separate politics from the Gaelic League is debatable. "The facts are that at a National Schoolmaster's Banquet at Sligo [in Ireland] in April 1905, Douglas Hyde was said to have avoided the toast of the King's [Edward VII] health by leaving the room. Hyde I believe did leave the room, and said he left to fetch his cigars, and meant no disrespect to the King. The explanation was not generally accepted I believe. For myself I did not attach too much importance to the incident, for I know that the refusal to drink [to] the King's health, or uncover [one's head] when the National Anthem is played are really marks of dissatisfaction with the system of govt. & not of disloyalty." Sir Antony Patrick MacDonnell, Under Secretary for Ireland to Sir James Bryce, Chief Secretary for Ireland, April 7, 1906. Bryce Papers, National Library of Ireland, Manuscripts Reading Room, Ms. 11, 012/4.

2 Pearse edited the Gaelic League's newspaper, *An Claidheamh Soluis* (the *Sword of Light*).

Irish-speaking pockets of the island, were illiterate.[3] The Gaelic League began to publish and disseminate textbooks as class registration numbers rose. The question of whether Irish should be incorporated into curricula was debated by members of Parliament (particularly the Board of Education), professors at Trinity College Dublin (Hyde's alma mater), and the Roman Catholic clergy. Opponents alleged that literature written in Irish was at best indecent, and at worst papist or politically inflammatory. By 1906, the league had achieved the right to teach Irish in Gaeltacht schools as a legitimate subject. In 1908, Hyde, who had declined a parliamentary seat at Westminster, was appointed a chair at the National University, and Irish was made compulsory for matriculation the following year.[4]

Since the Great Famine between 1845 and 1850, during which a million people perished and a million and a half emigrated, wiping out the base of the Irish social pyramid, Irish identity was formed by Catholicism rather than Gaelic culture. In the decades after 1850, Ireland became a nation of practicing Catholics by way of a Devotional Revolution.[5] The Gael lost out to the Grail.

For his part, Hyde understood the importance of courting the bishops and priests, Protestant unionists, and any moneyed Irish Americans in support of his cause. Yet, there was a price to be paid for Hyde's ecumenism and naïveté; the Irish-Ireland movement could only remain politically aloof for so long and was eventually co-opted by more extreme nationalists. While nationalists and unionists denounced each other, the avuncular Hyde denounced no one at all. He had hoped that Gaelic culture would be a place for all Irish people to imagine a community of nonsectarianism.

Hyde broke with the league in 1915 at a conference in Dundalk; the League had become too revolutionary for his tastes. As a result, Ireland between 1916 and 1922, dominated by Sinn Féin, forgot the Gaelic League as they prioritized physical force and independence. Hyde, who had never been a Home Ruler, would become the first president of the Irish Free State, fittingly for himself a largely ceremonial office.

---

3 Declan Kiberd, *Inventing Ireland: The Literature of the Modern Nation* (Cambridge: Harvard University Press, 1995), p. 145.
4 Ibid, p. 147. In recent decades, all Irish schoolchildren have had to study Irish. While most Irish converse in English, new generations have some bilingual facility.
5 Emmet Larkin, *The Historical Dimensions of Irish Catholicism* (Washington, DC: Catholic University of America Press, 1976).

On the Necessity for De-Anglicizing Ireland

By Douglas Hyde

Delivered before the Irish National Literary Society in Dublin, 25 November 1892.

When we speak of 'The Necessity for De-Anglicising the Irish Nation', we mean it, not as a protest against imitating what is best in the English people, for that would be absurd, but rather to show the folly of neglecting what is Irish, and hastening to adopt, pell-mell, and indiscriminately, everything that is English, simply because it is English.

This is a question which most Irishmen will naturally look at from a National point of view, but it is one which ought also to claim the sympathies of every intelligent Unionist, and which, as I know, does claim the sympathy of many.

If we take a bird's eye view of our island today, and compare it with what it used to be, we must be struck by the extraordinary fact that the nation which was once, as every one admits, one of the most classically learned and cultured nations in Europe, is now one of the least so; how one of the most reading and literary peoples has become one of the least studious and most un-literary, and how the present art products of one of the quickest, most sensitive, and most artistic races on earth are now only distinguished for their hideousness.

I shall endeavour to show that this failure of the Irish people in recent times has been largely brought about by the race diverging during this century from the right path, and ceasing to be Irish without becoming English. I shall attempt to show that with the bulk of the people this change took place quite recently, much more recently than most people imagine, and is, in fact, still going on. I should also like to call attention to the illogical position of men who drop their own language to speak English, of men who translate their euphonious Irish names into English monosyllables, of men who read English books, and know nothing about Gaelic literature, nevertheless protesting as a matter of sentiment that they hate the country which at every hand's turn they rush to imitate.

Douglas Hyde, "The Necessity for De-Anglicising Ireland," 1894.

I wish to show you that in Anglicising ourselves wholesale we have thrown away with a light heart the best claim which we have upon the world's recognition of us as a separate nationality. What did Mazzini[1] say? What is Goldwin Smith[2] never tired of declaiming? What do the Spectator and Saturday Review harp on? That we ought to be content as an integral part of the United Kingdom because we have lost the notes of nationality, our language and customs.

It has always been very curious to me how Irish sentiment sticks in this half-way house —how it continues to apparently hate the English, and at the same time continues to imitate them; how it continues to clamour for recognition as a distinct nationality, and at the same time throws away with both hands what would make it so. If Irishmen only went a little farther they would become good Englishmen in sentiment also. But—illogical as it appears—there seems not the slightest sign or probability of their taking that step. It is the curious certainty that come what may Irishmen will continue to resist English rule, even though it should be for their good, which prevents many of our nation from becoming Unionists upon the spot. It is a fact, and we must face it as a fact, that although they adopt English habits and copy England in every way, the great bulk of Irishmen and Irishwomen over the whole world are known to be filled with a dull, ever-abiding animosity against her, and right or wrong—to grieve when she prospers, and joy when she is hurt. Such movements as Young Irelandism,[3] Fenianism, Land Leagueism, and Parliamentary obstruction seem always to gain their sympathy and support. It is just because there appears no earthly chance of their becoming good members of the Empire that I urge that they should not remain in the anomalous position they are in, but since they absolutely refuse to become the one thing, that they become the other; cultivate what they have rejected, and build up an Irish nation on Irish lines.

But you ask, why should we wish to make Ireland more Celtic than it is—why should we de-Anglicise it at all?

I answer because the Irish race is at present in a most anomalous position, imitating England and yet apparently hating it. How can it produce anything good in literature, art, or institutions as long as it is actuated by motives so contradictory? Besides, I believe it is our Gaelic past which, though the Irish race does not recognise it just at present, is really at the bottom of the Irish heart, and prevents us becoming citizens of the Empire, as, I think, can be easily proved.

To say that Ireland has not prospered under English rule is simply a truism; all the world admits it, England does not deny it. But the English retort is ready. You have not prospered, they say, because you would not settle down contentedly, like the Scotch, and form part of the Empire. 'Twenty years of good, resolute, grandfatherly government', said a well-known Englishman, will solve the Irish question. He possibly made the period too short, but let us suppose this. Let us suppose for a moment—which is impossible—that there were to arise a series of Cromwells in England for the space of one hundred years, able administrators of the Empire, careful rulers of Ireland, developing to the utmost our national resources, whilst they unremittingly stamped out every spark of national feeling, making Ireland a land of wealth and factories, whilst they extinguished every thought and every idea that was Irish, and left us, at last, after a hundred years of good government, fat, wealthy, and populous, but with all our characteristics gone, with every external that at present differentiates us from the English lost or dropped; all our Irish names of places and people turned into English names; the Irish language completely extinct; the O's and the Macs dropped; our Irish intonation changed, as far as possible by English schoolmasters into something English; our history no longer remembered or taught; the

---

1   *Editor's note*: Mazzini was a 19th-century Italian politician and journalist, who advocated for the unification of Italy.
2   *Editor's note*: Smith was a British journalist, historian, and professor.
3   *Editor's note*: 19th-century Irish nationalists of differing ideologies.

names of our rebels and martyrs blotted out; our battlefields and traditions forgotten; the fact that we were not of Saxon origin dropped out of sight and memory, and let me now put the question—How many Irishmen are there who would purchase material prosperity at such a price? It is exactly such a question as this and the answer to it that shows the difference between the English and Irish race. Nine Englishmen out of ten would jump to make the exchange, and I as firmly believe that nine Irishmen out of ten would indignantly refuse it.

And yet this awful idea of complete Anglicisation, which I have here put before you in all its crudity is, and has been, making silent inroads upon us for nearly a century.

Its inroads have been silent, because, had the Gaelic race perceived what was being done, or had they been once warned of what was taking place in their own midst, they would, I think, never have allowed it. When the picture of complete Anglicisation is drawn for them in all its nakedness Irish sentimentality becomes suddenly a power and refuses to surrender its birthright ...

So much for the greatest stroke of all in our Anglicisation, the loss of our language. I have often heard people thank God that if the English gave us nothing else they gave us at least their language. In this way they put a bold face upon the matter, and pretend that the Irish language is not worth knowing, and has no literature. But the Irish language is worth knowing, or why would the greatest philologists of Germany, France, and Italy be emulously studying it, and it does possess a literature, or why would a German savant have made the calculation that the books written in Irish between the eleventh and seventeenth centuries, and still extant, would fill a thousand octavo volumes.

I have no hesitation at all in saying that every Irish-feeling Irishman, who hates the reproach of West-Britonism, should set himself to encourage the efforts, which are being made to keep alive our once great national tongue. The losing of it is our greatest blow, and the sorest stroke that the rapid Anglicisation of Ireland has inflicted upon us. In order to de-Anglicise ourselves we must at once arrest the decay of the language. We must bring pressure upon our politicians not to snuff it out by their tacit discouragement merely because they do not happen themselves to understand it. We must arouse some spark of patriotic inspiration among the peasantry who still use the language, and put an end to the shameful state of feeling—a thousand-tongued reproach to our leaders and statesmen which makes young men and women blush and hang their heads when overheard speaking their own language. Maynooth[4] has at last come splendidly to the front, and it is now incumbent upon every clerical student to attend lectures in the Irish language and history during the first three years of his course. But in order to keep the Irish language alive where it is still spoken—which is the utmost we can at present aspire to—nothing less than a house-to-house visitation and exhortation of the people themselves will do, something—though with a very different purpose—analogous to the procedure that James Stephens adopted throughout Ireland when he found her like a corpse on the dissecting table. This and some system of giving medals or badges of honour to every family who will guarantee that they have always spoken Irish amongst themselves during the year. But unfortunately, distracted as we are and torn by contending factions, it is impossible to find either men or money to carry out this simple remedy, although to a dispassionate foreigner—to a Zeuss, Jubainville, Zimmer, Kuno Meyer, Windisch, or Ascoli, and the rest—this is of greater importance than whether Mr. Redmond[5] or Mr. MacCarthy lead the largest wing of the Irish party for the moment, or Mr. So-and-So succeed with his election petition. To a person taking a bird's eye view of the situation a hundred or five hundred years

---

4   *Editor's note*: Irish seminary established by the British government in 1845.
5   *Editor's note*: John Redmond was the post-Parnell leader of the reunited Irish Party in the House of Commons. Justin MacCarthy was one of his lieutenants.

hence, believe me, it will also appear of greater importance than any mere temporary wrangle, but, unhappily, our countrymen cannot be brought to see this.

We can, however, insist, and we shall insist if Home Rule be carried, that the Irish language, which so many foreign scholars of the first calibre find so worthy of study, shall be placed on a par with—or even above—Greek, Latin, and modern languages, in all examinations held under the Irish Government. We can also insist, and we shall insist, that in those baronies where the children speak Irish, Irish shall be taught, and that Irish-speaking schoolmasters, petty sessions clerks, and even magistrates be appointed in Irish-speaking districts. If all this were done, it should not be very difficult, with the aid of the foremost foreign scholars, to bring about a tone of thought which would make it disgraceful for an educated Irishman especially of the old Celtic race, MacDermotts, O'Conors, O'Sullivans, MacCarthys, O'Neills—to be ignorant of his own language—would make it at least as disgraceful as for an educated Jew to be quite ignorant of Hebrew ...

I have now mentioned a few of the principal points on which it would be desirable for us to move, with a view to de-Anglicising ourselves; but perhaps the principal point of all I have taken for granted. That is the necessity for encouraging the use of Anglo-Irish literature instead of English books, especially instead of English periodicals. We must set our face sternly against penny dreadfuls, shilling shockers, and still more, the garbage of vulgar English weeklies like Bow Bells and the Police Intelligence. Every house should have a copy of Moore and Davis.[6] In a word, we must strive to cultivate everything that is most racial, most smacking of the soil, most Gaelic, most Irish, because in spite of the little admixture of Saxon blood in the north-east corner, this island is and will ever remain Celtic at the core, far more Celtic than most people imagine, because, as I have shown you, the names of our people are no criterion of their race. On racial lines, then, we shall best develop, following the bent of our own natures; and, in order to do this, we must create a strong feeling against West-Britonism, for it—if we give it the least chance, or show it the smallest quarter—will overwhelm us like a flood, and we shall find ourselves toiling painfully behind the English at each step following the same fashions, only six months behind the English ones; reading the same books, only months behind them; taking up the same fads, after they have become stale there, following them in our dress, literature, music, games, and ideas, only a long time after them and a vast way behind. We will become, what, I fear, we are largely at present, a nation of imitators, the Japanese of Western Europe, lost to the power of native initiative and alive only to second-hand assimilation. I do not think I am overrating this danger. We are probably at once the most assimilative and the most sensitive nation in Europe. A lady in Boston said to me that the Irish immigrants had become Americanised on the journey out before ever they landed at Castle Gardens. And when I ventured to regret it, she said, shrewdly, 'If they did not at once become Americanised they would not be Irish.' I knew fifteen Irish workmen who were working in a haggard in England give up talking Irish amongst themselves because the English farmer laughed at them. And yet O'Connell used to call us the 'finest peasantry in Europe'. Unfortunately, he took little care that we should remain so. We must teach ourselves to be less sensitive, we must teach ourselves not to be ashamed of ourselves, because the Gaelic people can never produce its best before the world as long as it remains tied to the apron-strings of another race and another island, waiting for it to move before it will venture to take any step itself.

In conclusion, I would earnestly appeal to every one, whether Unionist or Nationalist, who wishes to see the Irish nation produce its best—surely whatever our politics are we all wish that—to set his face against this constant running to England for our books, literature, music, games, fashions, and ideas.

---

6   *Editor's note*: George Moore and Thomas Davis were Irish writer and nationalists.

I appeal to every one whatever his politics—for this is no political matter—to do his best to help the Irish race to develop in future upon Irish lines, even at the risk of encouraging national aspirations, because upon Irish lines alone can the Irish race once more become what it was of yore—one of the most original, artistic, literary, and charming peoples of Europe.

STUDY QUESTIONS

1. Why did Hyde consider anglicization or West-Britonism so pernicious to Gaelic culture?

2. How would you characterize Hyde's sense of nationalism?

Indian Home Rule

One would be hard pressed to discuss India in the first half of the 20th century without mentioning the name of Mohandas K. Gandhi (1869–1948). A tiny man in physical stature, he took on the British Raj with prodigious inner strength and humility, proving that true morality was more just than colonial entitlement, arms, and wealth. In 1893, Gandhi, a London-trained barrister, traveled to Durban, South Africa, for work and experienced racial discrimination when he was kicked off a train for sitting in a whites-only car. Thus, he experienced firsthand the condition of Indians in South Africa. A year later, he began a campaign against anti-Indian racial laws such as political disenfranchisement, mandatory residence in government-designated ghettos, and the compulsory carrying of identification cards. Gandhi publicly burned the cards and was beaten and jailed, which signified the emergence of an Indian political consciousness in South Africa. It was there that he organized his first *satyagraha* (roughly translated as soul force or truth force) campaign and began to publish a newspaper, Indian Opinion, in English and Gujarati, his native tongue.

In order to comprehend Gandhi—who, despite his ascetic lifestyle, was a highly complex individual—one must understand his ideological framework. First, Gandhi's conception of Indian home rule, *Hind Swaraj*, contains a dual meaning: Indians first had to master themselves, their passions, and their desires, even quotidian ones. His autobiography, entitled *My Experiments with Truth*, deals with Gandhi's own struggles with diet, sex, and family. Only when Indians mastered themselves could that mastery be translated into the broader collective national consciousness of home rule for India. Gandhi felt that every decision one made was a political decision in the form of *dharma*, or duty.

Second, Gandhi's political program of passive resistance was not only about nonviolence, or *ahimsa*, which was, of course, fundamental to his tenets. His followers in the movement had to be prepared to be struck without striking back. They had to be prepared not only to be beaten, but also to go to jail on the flimsiest of charges. Self-suffering, he believed, could morally defeat an opponent. Passive resistance, however, could be very active, and Gandhi demonstrated this through speeches and writings, boycotting British goods and using other obstructionist tactics, as well as flagrant acts of defiance to British authority

Figure 15.1. Mohandas Gandhi. Source: http://commons.wikimedia.org/wiki/ File:Gandhi_satyagrahi.jpg.

through the process of noncooperation. Gandhi's 1931 march to the sea in opposition to the salt tax is but one example. Indian salt from the Indian Ocean, he argued, should belong to Indians.

Part of his intentions was to alter Western-biased concepts of civilization and courage. If the British had their ideas of manliness à la Lord Macaulay, Gandhi adhered to a policy of *satyagraha*, in which bravery in the face of conflict constituted true strength. It was more courageous not to be in the grip of passion. The enemy must be won over rather than destroyed. He rejected the idea of beating England at its own game of war, not only because India did not posses the military and naval capabilities to do so, but also because passive resistance gave Indians moral ascendancy.

Third, Gandhi sought a reinvention of tradition by attempting to return India to a nation of self-sufficient ashrams and village communities. He felt India's peasant masses, which formed the backbone of the country, should produce their own food and spin their own cotton cloth, or *khadi*. Spinning had profound cultural implications in that it was a response to industrialization; it was, therefore, simultaneously political ritual and economic defiance. In this 1909 treatise, entitled *Hind Swaraj*, or *Indian Home Rule*, Gandhi eschewed Western civilization's infrastructure, law, and medicine in favor of simple living. Although his intellectual gurus were Western, most notably John Ruskin and Leo Tolstoy, Gandhi rejected the scientific secularism of the West because it lacked morality. Modern science, according to Gandhi, left little room for the ethical or the emotional. He was critical of technology because he feared dependence on machines would deprive people of their humanity. Though his politics were inextricably linked to his spirituality, this is one of the instances where Gandhi was naive. Yet, he tirelessly sought alternatives to modernity and industrialization, as well as imperialism.

Fourth, Gandhi stood for a pluralistic India, free from sectarian animosity and strife. He claimed that no one has a monopoly on truth and envisaged a united India, where a Hindu majority and Muslim and Sikh minorities among others could coexist and flourish. He also advocated for women's rights and the rights of the untouchables (*Sudra* or *Dalit*).

Initially, Gandhi was a supporter of the British Empire. During the Boer War between 1899 and 1902, Gandhi saw an opportunity for better conditions for Indians by helping the British. Although he believed justice to be on the side of the Dutch Boers, loyalty demonstrated worthiness, and by aiding the British, Gandhi hoped to hold them up to their best selves. His nonviolent answer was the Indian Ambulance Corps, a group of 1,100 stretcher bearers. They also served during the Zulu rebellion of 1906, administering care to British and Zulu combatants alike. Again, in August 1914, at the outbreak of World War I, Gandhi, then little known outside of South Africa, attempted to rally his countrymen to render assistance, the implication being that if India took its share of the imperial war effort, it would prove worthy of self-government. Indian troops served in large numbers in the Middle Eastern and East African theaters. Short on war materials or production, India was long on manpower. After fulfilling their duty, however, Indians wanted a piece of the political pie.

By 1919, Gandhi had lost his faith in empire. The event which led to this change of heart was the massacre at Amritsar, during which Brigadier-General Reginald Dyer ordered some 90 Sikh and Gurkha troops to open fire on a crowd of 15,000–20,000 Indians for ten minutes, reloading twice. Afterward, 379 people, including children, lay dead, and another 1,500 were wounded. By the 1920s, Gandhi turned away from imperial duty and won over many in India to *satyagraha*, or what he called the "moral equivalent to war" by sheer dominance of personality and ideas.

Ultimately, Gandhi stepped aside in favor of spinning and Hindu education and in 1947 gave way to Jawaharlal Nehru and Muhammad Ali Jinnah, first prime ministers of India and Pakistan, respectively. Sadly, the Mahatma, or Great Soul, was assassinated on January 30, 1948, in Delhi by Nathuram Godse, a Hindu extremist who felt Gandhi was too conciliatory to Muslims.

Indian Home Rule

By Mohandas K. Gandhi

DISCONTENT AND UNREST

READER: Then you consider Partition to be a cause of the awakening? Do you welcome the unrest which has resulted from it?

EDITOR: When a man rises from sleep, he twists his limbs and is restless. It takes some time before he is entirely awakened. Similarly, although the Partition has caused an awakening, the comatose has not yet disappeared. We are still twisting our limbs and still restless, and just as the state between sleep and awakening must be considered to be necessary, so may the present unrest in India be considered a necessary and, therefore, a proper state. The knowledge that there is unrest will, it is highly probable, enable us to outgrow it. Rising from sleep, we do not continue in a comatose state, but, according to our ability, sooner or later, we are completely restored to our senses. So shall we be free from the present unrest which no one likes.

READER: What is the other form of unrest?

EDITOR: Unrest is, in reality, discontent. The latter is only now described as unrest[1]. During the Congress-period it was labelled discontent; Mr. Hume[2] always said that the spread of discontent in India was necessary. This discontent is a very useful thing. So long as a man is contented with his present lot, so long is it difficult to persuade him to come out of it. Therefore it is that every reform must be preceded by discontent. We throw away things we have only when we cease to like them. Such discontent has been produced among us after reading the great works of Indians and Englishmen[3]. Discontent has led to unrest, and the latter has brought about many deaths, many imprisonments, many banishments. Such a state of

---

1 During the 1906-9 period Gandhi was following closely the course of 'discontent and unrest' in India. See for example, 'Indian unrest', *Indian Opinion*, 20 October 1906 and 'Unrest in India', *Indian Opinion*, 1 June 1907.

2 *Editor's note*: John Hume was a British Radical politician.

3 'the great works of Indians and Englishmen': these included works of Dadabhai Naoroji and R. C. Dutt, and Allan Octavian Hume.

M. K. Gandhi, "Selections," *Indian Home Rule*, 1922.

things will still continue. It must be so. All these may be considered good signs, but they may also lead to bad results.

WHAT IS SWARAJ?[4]

READER: I have now learnt what the Congress has done to make India one nation, how the Partition has caused an awakening, and how discontent and unrest have spread through the land. I would now like to know your views on Swaraj. I fear that our interpretation is not the same.

EDITOR: It is quite possible that we do not attach the same meaning to the term. You and I and all Indians are impatient to obtain Swaraj, but we are certainly not decided as to what it is. To drive the English out of India is a thought heard from many mouths, but it does not seem that many have properly considered why it should be so. I must ask you a question. Do you think that it is necessary to drive away the English[5], if we get all we want?

READER: I should ask of them only one thing that is: "Please leave our country." If after they have complied with this request, their withdrawal from India means that they are still in India, I should have no objection. Then we would understand that, in our language, the word "gone" is equivalent to "remained."

EDITOR: Well then, let us suppose that the English have retired. What will you do then?

READER: That question cannot be answered at this stage. The state after withdrawal will depend largely upon the manner of it. If, as you assume, they retire, it seems to me we shall still keep their constitution[6], and shall carry on the government. If they simply retire for the asking, we should have an army, etc. ready at hand. We should, therefore, have no difficulty in carrying on the government.

EDITOR: You may think so: I do not. But I will not discuss the matter just now. I have to answer your question, and that I can do well by asking you several questions. Why do you want to drive away the English?

READER: Because India has become impoverished by their government. They take away our money from year to year. The most important posts are reserved for themselves. We are kept in a state of slavery. They behave insolently towards us, and disregard our feelings.

EDITOR: If they do not take our money away, become gentle, and give us responsible posts, would you still consider their presence to be harmful?

READER: That question is useless. It is similar to the question whether there is any harm in associating with a tiger[7], if he changes his nature. Such a question is sheer waste of time. When a tiger changes his nature, Englishmen will change theirs. This is not possible, and to believe it to be possible is contrary to human experience.

EDITOR: Supposing we get self-government similar to what the Canadians and the South Africans have, will it be good enough?

---

4   This chapter is a critique of the prevailing notions of swaraj.

5   Here Gandhi attacks the revolutionaries' view that physical expulsion of the British from India is the necessary and sufficient condition of swaraj.

6   Here Gandhi is attacking the meaning of swaraj held by the Extremists: expel the British but keep their political, military and economic institutions.

7   One of the striking metaphors of the book, comparable to the metaphor of the lion found in Machiavelli's *The Prince*.

READER: That question also is useless. We may get it when we have the same powers; we shall then hoist our own flag. As is Japan, so must India be[8]. We must own our navy, our army, and we must have our own splendour, and then will India's voice ring through the world.

EDITOR: You have well drawn the picture. In effect it means this: that we want English rule without the Englishman. You want the tiger's nature, but not the tiger; that is to say, you would make India English, and when it becomes English, it will be called not Hindustan but Englistan. This is not the Swaraj that I want.

READER: I have placed before you my idea of Swaraj as I think it should be. If the education we have received be of any use, if the works of Spencer, Mill[9] and others be of any importance and if the English Parliament be the mother of Parliaments, I certainly think that we should copy the English people and this to such an extent that, just as they do not allow others to obtain a footing in their country, so we should not allow them or others to obtain it in ours. What they have done in their own country has not been done in any other country. It is, therefore, proper for us to import their institutions. But now I want to know your views.

EDITOR: There is need for patience. My views will develop of themselves in the course of this discourse. It is as difficult for me to understand the true nature of Swaraj as it seems to you to be easy. I shall, therefore, for the time being, content myself with endeavouring to show that what you call Swaraj is not truly Swaraj.

---

8   Gandhi rejects the Japanese model of development, to which many Indian at the turn of the century were powerfully attracted. Gandhi's own attitude towards Japan underwent a gradual evolution in the period 1903–9. As a journalist he remained a keen observer of the rise of modern Japan. In 1905 he spoke of 'the epic heroism' exhibited by the Japanese in the 1905 naval victory over Russia, comparing the latter to the British victories over the Spanish Armada and over Napoleon. The secret of the Japanese victory was

> unity, patriotism and the resolve to do or die. All the Japanese are animated by the same spirit. No one is considered greater than the other, and there is no rift of any kind between them. They think nothing else but service to the nation ... This unity and patriotic spirit together with a heroic indifference to life (or death) have created an atmosphere in Japan the like of which is nowhere to be found in the world. (*CW* 4: 467)

The explanation of the Japanese victory, he wrote, 'deserves to be inscribed in one's mind' (*CW* 5: 32). Writing in 1907, he traced a link between the Japanese sense of self-respect and their political independence; and contrasted the Japanes situation with India's state of bondage and the resulting lack of self-respect. 'When everyone in Japan, the rich as well as the poor, came to believe in self-respect, the country became free. In the same way we too need to feel the spirit of self-respect' (*CW* 6: 457). But in HS he has become sceptical of the desirability of taking Japan as a model for India.

9   'the works of Spencer, Mill': i.e., Herbert Spencer and J. S. Mill. From available data it is not possible to indicate which works of Spencer and Mill Gandhi might have read by 1909. But we do know that he disapproved of the position of S. Krishnavarma and his colleagues in India House (London) who acted as though what India needed was the philosophy of Spencer. To counteract them he used with approval a witty article by G. K. Chesterton:

> They talk about Herbert Spencer's philosophy and other similar matters. What is the good of Indian national spirit if they cannot protect themselves from Herbert Spencer? ... One of their papers is called *The Indian Sociologist*. Do the Indian youths want to pollute their ancient villages and poison their kindly homes by introducing Spencer's philosophy into them?... But Herbert Spencer is not Indian; his philosophy is not Indian philosophy; all this clatter about the science of education and other things is not Indian. I often wish it were not English either. But this is our first difficulty, that the Indian nationalist is not national. (*CW* 9: 425–7)

As for J. S. Mill, Gandhi did mention *On Liberty* by name in the 1920s. He told a university audience:

> I know that in the West there is a powerful trend towards licence. But I have no desire to see students in India take to such licence ... I want to tell you that the man who has not received education for freedom—and you may be sure this is not to be had by reading Mill on 'Liberty'—cannot be taken to be a free man. (*CW* 19: 26,103)

THE CONDITION OF ENGLAND

READER: Then from your statement, I deduce the Government of England is not desirable and not worth copying by us.

EDITOR: Your deduction is justified. The condition of England at present is pitiable. I pray to God that India may never be in that plight. That which you consider to be the Mother of Parliaments is like a sterile woman and a prostitute[10]. Both these are harsh terms, but exactly fit the case. That Parliament has not yet of its own accord done a single good thing, hence I have compared it to a sterile woman. The natural condition of that Parliament is such that, without outside pressure, it can do nothing. It is like a prostitute because it is under the control of ministers who change from time to time. To-day it is under Mr. Asquith,[11] to-morrow it may be under Mr. Balfour.

READER: You have said this sarcastically. The term "sterile woman" is not applicable. The Parliament, being elected by the people, must work under public pressure. This is its quality.

EDITOR: You are mistaken. Let us examine it a little more closely. The best men are supposed to be elected by the people. The members serve without pay[12] and, therefore, it must be assumed only for the public weal. The electors are considered to be educated and, therefore, we should assume that they would not generally make mistakes in their choice. Such a Parliament should not need the spur of petitions or any other pressure. Its work should be so smooth that its effect would be more apparent day by day. But, as a matter of fact, it is generally acknowledged that the members are hypocritical and selfish. Each thinks of his own little interest. It is fear that is the guiding motive. What is done to-day may be undone to-morrow. It is not possible to recall a single instance in which the finality can be predicted for its work. When the greatest questions are debated its members have been seen to stretch themselves and to dose[13]. Sometimes the members talk away until the listeners are disgusted. Carlyle has called it the "talking shop of the world."[14] Members vote for their party without a thought. Their so-called discipline binds them to it. If any member, by way of exception, gives an independent vote, he is considered a renegade. If the money and the time wasted by the Parliament were entrusted to a few good men, the English nation would be occupying to-day a much higher platform. The Parliament is simply a costly toy of the nation. These views are, by no means, peculiar to me. Some great English thinkers have expressed them. One of the members of the Parliament recently said that a true Christian[15] could not become

---

10   'a sterile woman and a prostitute': Gandhi was criticised by one of his English friends (Mrs Annie Beasant?) for using the metaphor of 'prostitute'; and he regretted using it (*CW* 15: 330); this was the only word he was prepared to drop from the book. The word 'prostitute' occurs again in ch. v, and the word 'prostitution' in chs. xi and xiii. Erikson (1969, 219) exaggerates the point when he writes that the word 'prostitution' is 'a word used rather often' in *HS*.

The criticism of parliament in this chapter and elsewhere may not be interpreted to mean that Gandhi was against the institution of parliament. For example, in 1920 he said that what he wanted for India was 'a parliament chosen by the people with the fullest power over the finance, the police, the military, the navy, the courts and the educational institutions' (*CW* 19: 80). In 1921 he advised the readers of HS that his corporate activity was devoted to 'the attainment of parliamentary swaraj in accordance with the wishes of the people of India' (*CW* 19: 277–8).

11   *Editor's note*: Herbert Henry Asquith was a Liberal parliamentarian, while Arthur James Balfour was a Conservative one.

12   Remuneration for British MPs was introduced only in 1911.

13   'doze': given as 'dose' in original text.

14   'the talking-shop of the world': the Gujarati text does not mention Carlyle, referring instead to 'one of their great writers'. The source of this remark is Carlyle (1907, 319) where he is discussing the inability of the Rump Parliament to give a clear answer to Cromwell: 'For three years, Cromwell says, this question had been sounded in the ears of the Parliament. They would make no answer: nothing but talk, talk. Perhaps it lies in the nature of parliamentary bodies; perhaps no Parliament could in such case make any answer but even that of talk, talk.' Professor C. N. Patel of Ahmedabad drew my attention to this passage.

15   'a true Christian': the Gujarati text has *dharmisht*, 'an ethical person'.

a member of it. Another said that it was a baby. And, if it has remained a baby after an existence of seven hundred years, when will it outgrow its babyhood?

READER: You have set me thinking; you do not expect me to accept at once all you say. You give me entirely novel views. I shall have to digest them. Will you now explain the epithet "prostitute"?

EDITOR: That you cannot accept my views at once is only right. If you will read the literature on this subject, you will have some idea of it. The Parliament is without a real master. Under the Prime Minister, its movement is not steady, but it is buffeted about like a prostitute. The Prime Minister is more concerned about his power[16] than about the welfare of the Parliament. His energy is concentrated upon securing the success of his party.[17] His care is not always that the Parliament shall do right. Prime Ministers are known to have made the Parliament do things merely for party advantage. All this is worth thinking over.

READER: Then you are really attacking the very men whom we have hitherto considered to be patriotic and honest?

EDITOR: Yes, that is true; I can have nothing against Prime Ministers, but what I have seen leads me to think that they cannot be considered really patriotic. If they are to be considered honest because they do not take what is generally known as bribery, let them be so considered, but they are open to subtler influences. In order to gain their ends, they certainly bribe people with honours. I do not hesitate to say that they have neither real honesty nor a living conscience.

READER: As you express these views about the Parliament, I would like to hear you on the English people, so that I may have your views of their Government.

EDITOR: To the English voters their newspaper is their Bible. They take cue from their newspapers, which latter are often dishonest. The same fact is differently interpreted by different newspapers, according to the party in whose interests they are edited[18]. One newspaper would consider a great Englishman to be a paragon of honesty, another would consider him dishonest. What must be the condition of the people whose newspapers are of this type?

READER: You shall describe it.

EDITOR: These people change their views frequently. It is said that they change them every seven years. These views swing like the pendulum of a clock and are never steadfast. The people would follow a powerful orator or a man who gives them parties, receptions, etc. As are the people, so is their Parliament. They have certainly one quality very strongly developed. They will never allow their country to be lost. If any person were to cast an evil eye on it, they would pluck out his eyes. But that does not mean that the nation possesses every other virtue or that it should be imitated. If India copies England, it is my firm conviction that she will be ruined.

READER: To what do you ascribe this state of England?

EDITOR: It is not due to any peculiar fault of the English people, but the condition is due to modern civilization[19]. It is a civilization only in name. Under it the nations of Europe are becoming degraded and ruined day by day.

---

16 'power': *satta*.

17 'party': i.e., political party, *paksh*.

18 The Gujarati text adds: 'One party magnifies its own importance while the other party minimises it.'

19 The distinction between 'British people' whom Gandhi admired, and 'modern' British civilisation, which Gandhi criticised, is crucial to his argument, which is that modern civilisation has corrupted a basically good people. The root of this corruption he traces back to the de-Christianisation of modern Britain.

CIVILIZATION

READER: Now you will have to explain what you mean by civilization.[20]

EDITOR: It is not a question of what I mean. Several English writers refuse to call that, civilization which passes under that name. Many books have been written upon that subject. Societies[21] have been formed to cure the nation of the evils of civilization. A great English writer[22] has written a work called "Civilization: Its Cause and Cure." Therein he has called it a disease.

READER: Why do we not know this generally?

EDITOR: The answer is very simple. We rarely find people arguing against themselves. Those who are intoxicated by modern civilization are not likely to write against it. Their care will be to find out facts and arguments in support of it, and this they do unconsciously, believing it to be true. A man, whilst he is dreaming, believes in his dream; he is undeceived only when he is awakened from his sleep. A man labouring under the bane of civilization is like a dreaming man. What we usually read are the work of defenders of modern civilization, which undoubtedly claims among its votaries very brilliant and even some very good men. Their writings hypnotise us. And so, one by one, we are drawn into the vortex.

READER: This seems to be very plausible. Now will you tell me something of what you have read and thought of this civilization.

EDITOR: Let us first consider what state of things is described by the word "civilization."[23] Its true test lies in the fact that people living in it make bodily welfare the object of life. We will take some examples. The people of Europe to-day live in better-built houses than they did a hundred years ago. This is considered an emblem of civilization, and this is also a matter to promote bodily happiness. Formerly, they wore skins, and used as their weapons spears. Now, they wear long trousers, and for embellishing their bodies they wear a variety of clothing, and, instead of spears, they carry with them revolvers containing five or more chambers. If people of a certain country, who have hitherto not been in the habit of wearing much clothing, boots, etc., adopt European clothing, they are supposed to have become civilised out of savagery. Formerly, in Europe, people ploughed their lands mainly by manual labour. Now, one man can plough a vast tract by means of steam-engines, and can thus amass great wealth. This is called a sign of civilization. Formerly, the fewest men wrote books, that were most valuable. Now, anybody writes and prints anything he likes and poisons people's minds. Formerly, men travelled in waggons; now they fly through the air, in trains at the rate of four hundred and more miles per day. This is considered the height of civilization. It has been stated that, as men progress, they shall be able to travel in airships and

---

20 The Gujarati text adds: 'According to you, [modern] civilisation [*sudharo*] is not civilisation, but barbarism[*kudharo*].' The *sudharo/kudharo* dichotomy adds colour to the Gujarati text.

21 In 1906 Gandhi made contacts with officials of the Union of Ethical Societies in London. It had then fourteen member societies in London, and nine elsewhere in England. Henry Polak and his wife Millie Graham were members of the South Place Ethical Society. Miss Florence Winterbottom, who helped Gandhi with his lobbying in London, was the Secretary of the Union of Ethical Societies (Hunt 1986, 8–10). On his 1909 visit to London Gandhi gave a lecture to the Union of Ethical Societies at the Emerson Club (*CW* 9: 473–4, 475–6). On the same visit he also visited an ex-Tolstoyan Colony at Whiteway, near Stroud (ibid., 369). Gandhi was also familiar with the activities of 'New Crusade Society', a society based on the social teachings of John Ruskin, propagating the values of country life, agriculture, handicrafts, homespun clothes, and opposing the 'increasing dependence on machinery' and 'competitive mechanical production'. The moving spirit behind this society was Godfrey Blount, author of *A New Crusade: An Appeal* (1903). This book is listed in the Appendix to HS. A brief summary of its activities was also published in *Indian Opinion* (1905).

22 Edward Carpenter

23 'Civilisation': what is meant here is the civilisation produced by the industrial revolution. 'Let it be remembered that Western civilisation is only a hundred years old, or to be more precise fifty. Within this short span the Western people appear to have been reduced to a state of cultural anarchy. We pray that India may never be reduced to the same state as Europe' (*CW* 8: 374).

reach any part of the world in a few hours. Men will not need the use of their hands and feet. They will press a button, and they will have their clothing by their side. They will press another button, and they will have their newspaper. A third, and a motor-car will be in waiting for them. They will have a variety of delicately dished up food. Everything will be done by machinery. Formerly, when people wanted to fight with one another, they measured between them their bodily strength; now it is possible to take away thousands of lives by one man working behind a gun from a hill. This is civilization. Formerly, men worked in the open air only so much as they liked. Now, thousands of workmen meet together and for the sake of maintenance work in factories or mines. Their condition is worse than that of beasts. They are obliged to work, at the risk of their lives, at most dangerous occupations, for the sake of millionaires. Formerly, men were made slaves under physical compulsion, now[24] they are enslaved by temptation of money and of the luxuries that money can buy. There are now diseases of which people never dreamt before, and an army of doctors is engaged in finding out their cures, and so hospitals have increased. This is a test of civilization. Formerly, special messengers were required and much expense was incurred in order to send letters; to-day, anyone can abuse his fellow by means of a letter for one penny. True, at the same cost, one can send one's thanks also. Formerly, people had two or three meals consisting of homemade bread and vegetables; now, they require something to eat every two hours, so that they have hardly leisure for anything else. What more need I say? All this you can ascertain from several authoritative books. These are all true tests of civilization. And, if any one speaks to the contrary,[know that he is ignorant. This civilization takes note neither of morality nor of religion[25]. Its votaries calmly state that their business is not to teach religion. Some even consider it to be a superstitious growth. Others put on the cloak of religion, and prate about morality. But, after twenty years' experience, I have come to the conclusion that immorality is often taught in the name of morality. Even a child can understand that in all I have described above there can be no inducement to morality. Civilization seeks to increase bodily comforts, and it fails miserably even in doing so.

This civilization is irreligion,[26] and it has taken such a hold on the people in Europe that those who are in it appear to be half mad. They lack real physical strength or courage. They keep up their energy by intoxication. They can hardly be happy in solitude. Women, who should be the queens of households, wander in the streets, or they slave away in factories. For the sake of a pittance, half a million women in England alone are labouring under trying circumstances in factories or similar institutions. This awful fact is one of the causes of the daily growing suffragette movement.[27]

This civilization is such that one has only to be patient and it will be self-destroyed. According to the teaching of Mahomed this would be considered a Satanic civilization. Hinduism calls it the Black

---

24 Tolstoy's *The Slavery of Our Times,* and Taylor's *White Slaves of England* (both listed in the Appendix to HS) speak of the 'slavery' created by the new industrial civilisation.

25 'neither of morality nor of religion': morality = *niti*; religion = *dharma.*

26 'irreligion': *adharma,* contrary to dharma.

27 During his 1906 and 1909 visits to London Gandhi established direct contact with the British suffragette movement. *Indian Opinion* carried reports on the arrests of Miss Cobden and Emmeline Pankhurst; while he was veiy sympathetic to their cause he disapproved of their violent tactics—the attack on the residence of Asquith, disruption of meetings addressed by Balfour and Winston Churchill, harassment of prison officials, hunger strike in jail, destruction of prison property, etc. (*CW* 9: 303, 324–5).

Age.[28] I cannot give you an adequate conception of it. It is eating into the vitals of the English nation.[29] It must be shunned.[30] Parliament are really emblems of slavery. If you will sufficiently think over this, you will entertain the same opinion, and cease to blame the English. They rather deserve our sympathy. They are a shrewd nation and I therefore believe that they will cast off the evil. They are enterprising and industrious and their mode of thought is not inherently immoral. Neither are they bad at heart. I, therefore, respect them. Civilization is not an incurable disease[31], but it should never be forgotten that the English people are at present afflicted by it.

WHY WAS INDIA LOST?

READER: You have said much about civilization—enough to make me ponder over it. I do not now know what I should adopt and what I should avoid from the nations of Europe, but one question comes to my lips immediately. If civilization is a disease, and if it has attacked England why has she been able to take India, and why is she able to retain it?

EDITOR: Your question is not very difficult to answer, and we shall presently be able to examine the true nature of Swaraj; for I am aware that I have still to answer that question. I will, however, take up your previous question. The English have not taken India; we have given it to them. They are not in India because of their strength, but because we keep them.[32] Let us now see whether these propositions can be sustained. They came to our country originally for purposes of trade. Recall the Company Bahadur. Who made it Bahadur?[33] They had not the slightest intention at the time of establishing a kingdom. Who assisted the Company's officers? Who was tempted at the sight of their silver? Who bought their goods? History testifies that we did all this. In order to become rich all at once, we welcomed the Company's officers with open arms. We assisted them. If I am in the habit of drinking Bhang and a seller thereof sells it to me, am I to blame him or myself? By blaming the seller shall I be able to avoid the habit? And, if a particular retailer is driven away, will not another take his place? A true servant of India will have to go to the root of the matter. If an excess of food has caused me indigestion, I will certainly not avoid it by blaming water. He is a true physician who probes the cause of disease and, if you pose as a physician for the disease of India, you will have to find out its true cause.

---

28 'the Black Age': *kali juga*. According to Hindu mythology the cycle of time is divided into *kalpa*, *mahayuga* and *yuga*. The four yugas—*krita, treta, dvapara,* and *kali*—constitute one *mahayuga* (supposedly 4,320,000 years); and 1,000 mahajugas constitute one *kalpa*. At the end of each *kalpa* the cycle starts again. Humankind at present lives in the *kali yuga*, the worst segment in the entire cycle of time. It is supposed to have started in 3102 BC and is supposed to last a total of 432,000 years. During the *kali yuga* the sway of dharma is the weakest, compared to the other three yugas, and humans are normally led by violence and egoism (Zimmer 1963, 13–19).

29 The Gujarati text adds: 'This civilisation is destructive, and it is itself bound to perish.'

30 The Gujarati text adds: 'That is why the British Parliament and other parliaments are ineffective against this civilisation.'

31 'Civilisation is not an incurable disease': the Gujarati text reads, 'For them [the British] this civilisation is not an incurable disease.' The metaphor of disease occurs again in chs. VII and IX.

32 'but because we keep them': one of the underlying assumptions of HS. It was first expressed in 1908, in the paraphrase of *Unto This Last*: 'The reason why they [the British] rule over us is to be found in ourselves' (*CW* 8: 373); the idea recurs in chs. xiv and xx as well. See also Seeley [1883] 1909, 197–216. Gandhi had read Seeley at least by 1903 (*CW* 3: 462).

33 'the Company Bahadur': an honorific title by which the East India Company was known among Indians. 'Bahadur' means brave, powerful, sovereign. The Company received its first charter from Queen Elizabeth I on 31 December 1600. In 1613, Jahangir, the Mogul emperor, issued a *firman*, permitting the English to establish a trading outpost at Surat, Gujarat. The real foundation of British political dominion over India is said to date from the battle of Plassey in 1757.

READER: You are right. Now, I think you will not have to argue much with me to drive your conclusions home. I am impatient to know your further views. We are now on a most interesting topic. I shall, therefore, endeavour to follow your thought, and stop you when I am in doubt.

EDITOR: I am afraid that, in spite of your enthusiasm, as we proceed further we shall have differences of opinion. Nevertheless, I shall argue only when you will stop me. We have already seen that the English merchants were able to get a footing in India because we encouraged them. When our princes fought among themselves,[34] they sought the assistance of Company Bahadur. That corporation was versed alike in commerce and war. It was unhampered by questions of morality. Its object was to increase its commerce, and to make money. It accepted our assistance, and increased the number of its warehouses. To protect the latter it employed an army which was utilised by us also. Is it not then useless to blame the English for what we did at that time? The Hindus and the Mahomedans were at daggers drawn. This, too, gave the Company its opportunity; and thus we created the circumstances that gave the Company its control over India. Hence it is truer to say that we gave India to the English than that India was lost.

READER: Will you now tell me how they are able to retain India?

EDITOR: The causes that gave them India enable them to retain it. Some Englishmen state that they took, and they hold, India by the sword. Both these statements are wrong. The sword is entirely useless for holding India. We alone keep them. Napoleon is said to have described the English as a nation of shop-keepers. It is a fitting description. They hold whatever dominions they have for the sake of their commerce. Their army and their navy are intended to protect it. When the Transvaal offered no such attractions, the late Mr. Gladstone discovered that it was not right for the English to hold it. When it became a paying proposition, resistance led to war. Mr. Chamberlain[35] soon discovered that England enjoyed a suzerainty over the Transvaal. It is related that some one asked the late President Kruger whether there was gold in the moon. He replied that it was highly unlikely, because, if there were, the English would have annexed it. Many problems can be solved by remembering that money is their God. Then it follows that we keep the English in India for our base self-interest. We like their commerce, they please us by their subtle methods, and get what they want from us. To blame them for this is to perpetuate their power. We further strengthen their hold by quarrelling amongst ourselves. If you accept the above statements, it is proved that the English entered India for the purposes of trade. They remain in it for the same purpose, and we help them to do so. Their arms and ammunition are perfectly useless. In this connection, I remind you that it is the British flag which is waving in Japan, and not the Japanese.[36] The English have a treaty with Japan for the sake of their commerce, and you will see that, if they can manage it, their commerce will greatly expand in that country. They wish to convert the whole world into a vast market for their goods. That they cannot do so is true, but the blame will not be theirs. They will leave no stone unturned to reach the goal.

THE CONDITION OF INDIA

READER: I now understand why the English hold India. I should like to know your views about the condition of our country.

---

34   The eighteenth-century internecine wars among Indians (the Moghuls, the Mahrattas and the Sikhs) are being identified as major contributing factors to the rise of British power in India.

35   *Editor's note*: Joseph Chamberlain was a Liberal Unionist parliamentarian.

36   The metaphor of the 'flag' is used here to indicate how Japan achieved modernisation: she followed the British example (*CW* 5:41).

EDITOR: It is a sad condition. In thinking of it, my eyes water and my throat get parched. I have grave doubts whether I shall be able sufficiently to explain what is in my heart. It is my deliberate opinion that India is being ground down not under the English heel but under that of modern civilization. It is groaning under the monster's terrible weight. There is yet time to escape it, but every day makes it more and more difficult. Religion is dear to me, and my first complaint is that India is becoming irreligious.[37] Here I am not thinking of the Hindu and Mahomedan or the Zoroastrian religion, but of the religion which underlies all religions.[38] We are turning away from God.

READER: How so?

EDITOR: There is a charge laid against us that we are a lazy people, and that the Europeans are industrious and enterprising. We have accepted the charge and we, therefore, wish to change our condition. Hinduism, Islamism, Zoroastrianism, Christianity and all other religions teach that we should remain passive about worldly pursuits and active about godly pursuits, that we should set a limit to our worldly ambition, and that our religious ambition should be illimitable. Our activity should be directed into the latter channel.

READER: You seem to be encouraging religious charlatanism. Many a cheat has by talking in a similar strain led the people astray.

EDITOR: You are bringing an unlawful charge against religion. Humbug there undoubtedly is about all religions. Where there is light, there is also shadow. I am prepared to maintain that humbugs in worldly matters are far worse than the humbugs in religion. The humbug of civilization that I endeavour to show to you is not to be found in religion.

READER: How can you say that? In the name of religion Hindus and Mahomedans fought against one another. For the same cause Christians fought Christians. Thousands of innocent men have been murdered, thousands have been burned and tortured in its name. Surely, this is much worse than any civilization.[39]

EDITOR: I certainly submit that the above hardships are far more bearable than those of civilization. Everybody understands that the cruelties you have named are not part of religion, although they have been practised in its name: therefore there is no aftermath to these cruelties. They will always happen so long as there are to be found ignorant and credulous people. But there is no end to the victims destroyed in the fire of civilization. Its deadly effect is that people came under its scorching flames believing it to be all good. They become utterly irreligious and, in reality, derive little advantage from the world. Civilization is like a mouse gnawing, while it is soothing us. When its full effect is realised, we will see that religious superstition is harmless compared to that of modern civilization.[40] I am not pleading for a continuance of religious superstitions. We will certainly fight them tooth and nail, but we can never do so by disregarding religion. We can only do so by appreciating and conserving the latter.

READER: Then you will contend that the Pax Britannica is a useless encumbrance?

EDITOR: You may see peace if you like; I see none.[41]

---

37 'irreligious': *dharma-bhrasht,* a people without dharma.

38 '... religion which underlies all religions': a very important concept in Gandhi's political philosophy. Throughout *HS* religion is understood in two different senses: as sect or organised religion, and as ethic, albeit one grounded in some metaphysic.

39 Gandhi takes the offensive now: today the real humbug is the modern *secular* culture.

40 Gandhi is responding to the nineteenth-century rationalist/secularist prejudice that religion promotes superstition; modernity is the superstition of the secularists.

41 Gandhi here challenges the arguments of Utilitarians such as Fitzjames Stephen that *Pax Britannica* was an unmixed blessing for India (see Stephen 1883, 541–68).

READER: You make light of the terror that Thugs, the Pindaris, the Bhils were to the country.[42]

EDITOR: If you will give the matter some thought, you will see that the terror was by no means such a mighty thing. If it had been a very substantial thing, the other people would have died away before the English advent. Moreover, the present peace is only nominal, for by it we have become emasculated and cowardly. We are not to assume that the English have changed the nature of the Pindaris and the Bhils. It is, therefore, better to suffer the Pindari peril than that some one else should protect us from it, and thus render us effeminate. I should prefer to be killed by the arrow of a Bhil than to seek unmanly protection. India without such protection was an India full of valour. Macaulay betrayed gross ignorance when he libelled Indians as being practically cowards. They never merited the charge. Cowards living in a country inhabited by hardy mountaineers, infested by wolves and tigers must surely find an early grave. Have you ever visited our fields? I assure you that our agriculturists sleep fearlessly on their farms even to-day, and the English, you and I would hesitate to sleep where they sleep. Strength lies in absence of fear, not in the quantity of flesh and muscle we may have on our bodies. Moreover, I must remind you who desire Home Rule that, after all, the Bhils, the Pindaris, the Assamese[43] and the Thugs are our own countrymen. To conquer them[44] is your and my work. So long as we fear our own brethren, we are unfit to reach the goal.

WHAT IS TRUE CIVILIZATION?

READER: You have denounced railways, lawyers and doctors. I can see that you will discard all machinery.[45] What, then, is civilization?

EDITOR: The answer to that question is not difficult. I believe that the civilization India has evolved is not to be beaten in the world. Nothing can equal the seeds sown by our ancestors. Rome went, Greece shared the same fate, the might of the Pharaohs was broken, Japan has become westernised, of China nothing can be said, but India is still, somehow or other, sound at the foundation.[46] The people of Europe learn their lessons from the writings of the men of Greece or Rome, which exist no longer in their former glory. In trying to learn from them, the Europeans imagine that they will

---

42 'the Thugs': gangs of murderers inhabiting parts of Central India who made their living by plundering and murdering travellers. They practised a corrupt mixture of Islam and Hinduism, their principal deities being Devi, Bhavani, Durga and Kali. They were suppressed by the British between 1830 and 1850.

'the Pindaris': a professional class of free-booters, inhabiting parts of Central India. Good horsemen, they made their living by looting the cattle and property of their victims; what they could not carry, they burned and destroyed. Like the Thugs, they too practised a corrupt mixture of Islam and Hinduism; suppressed by the British in the first half of the nineteenth century.

'the Bhils': an aboriginal tribe, found mostly in Gujarat and Rajasthan, numbering about 600,000 at the turn of the twentieth century. Their religious practices were borrowed from primitive nature worship and certain forms of popular Hinduism.

43 In 1921 Gandhi apologised to the Assamese for listing them among the 'uncivilised' tribes of India:

It was certainly on my part a grave injustice done to the great Assamese people, who are eveiy whit as civilised as any other part of India ... My stupidity about the Assamese rose, when about 1890 I read an account of the Manipur expedition, when the late Sir John Gorst defended the conduct of the officials towards the late Senapati, saying that governments always liked to lop off tall poppies. Being an indifferent reader of history, I retained with me the impression that the Assamese were *jungli* [uncivilised] and committed it to writing in 1908 [*sic*], (*CW* 21: 30)

44 'To conquer them': in the Gujarati text this reads 'To win them over'.

45 'machineiy': ch. XIX deals with this topic. By introducing it here Gandhi alerts, the reader to the tension that exists between 'true civilisation' and a civilisation based on machinery.

46 'India is still, somehow or other, sound at the foundation': this is the bedrock of Gandhi's defence of Indian civilisation in *HS*. That foundation is that *artha* and *kama* should be pursued within the framework of dharma. In modern civilisation *artha* and *kama,* according to Gandhi, assert their autonomy from dharma.

avoid the mistakes of Greece and Rome. Such is their pitiable condition. In the midst of all this, India remains immovable, and that is her glory. It is a charge against India that her people are so uncivilised, ignorant and stolid, that it is not possible to induce them to adopt any changes. It is a charge really against our merit. What we have tested and found true on the anvil of experience, we dare not change. Many thrust their advice upon India, and she remains steady. This is her beauty; it is the sheet-anchor of our hope.

Civilization is that mode of conduct which points out to man the path of duty. Performance of duty and observance of morality are convertible terms. To observe morality is to attain mastery over our mind and our passions. So doing, we know ourselves.[47] The Gujarati equivalent for civilization means "good conduct."[48]

If this definition be correct, then India, as so many writers[49] have shown, has nothing to learn from anybody else,[50] and this is as it should be. We notice that mind is a restless bird; the more it gets the more it wants, and still remains unsatisfied. The more we indulge our passions, the more unbridled they become. Our ancestors, therefore, set a limit to our indulgences. They saw that happiness was largely a mental condition.[51] A man is not necessarily happy because he is rich, or unhappy because he is poor. The rich are often seem to be unhappy, the poor to be happy. Millions will always remain poor. Observing all this, our ancestors dissuaded us from luxuries and pleasures. We have managed

47   In this definition of true civilisation, central to the argument of the book, Gandhi connects the notions of self-knowledge, duty (*farajj*), morality (*niti*), mastery over the mind (*man*) and the senses (*indriyo*).

48   In 1911, in response to a question as to whether it would not have been more accurate to write 'The Gujarati equivalent for civilisation is good conduct (*siidhuro*)', Gandhi wrote the following reply:

If 'is' were to be used, the meaning would change. 'Is' is implied in 'equivalent' ... the Gujarati word generally used for 'civilisation' means 'a good way of life'. That is what I had meant to say. The sentence 'The Gujarati equivalent for civilisation is *sudharo* is quite correct. But it is not what I intended to say. Were we to say, 'The Gujarati equivalent for civilisation is "good conduct"', according to the rules of grammar, 'good conduct' would have to be taken as a Gujarati phrase ... Please let me know whether it was for this reason or for any other reasons that you concluded that 'means' was the right word. (*CW* 11: 153)

49   'as so many writers': in the Gujarati text this reads: 'as so many British writers'. *See HS*, Appendix 11.

50   'India . . . has nothing to learn from anybody else': an obvious hyperbole, to be corrected by his other statements. Thus in 1911 he recommended that Chhaganlal Gandhi, his right-hand man at Phoenix Settlement, should go to London and 'imbibe' its particular atmosphere: 'My own idea was that you should live in London for a year and gather whatever experience and knowledge you could ... if you imbibe the particular kind of atmosphere that obtains there, the voyage to England will have, to my mind, fulfilled its purpose' (*CW* 10: 401–2). In 1929 he wrote: 'The "Western civilisation" which passes for civilisation is disgusting to me. I have given a rough picture of it in *Hind Swaraj*. Time has brought no change in it. It is not my purpose even to imply that eveiything Western is bad. I have learnt a lot from the West' (*CW* 40: 300). And in 1931 he wrote:

European civilisation is no doubt suited for the Europeans but it will mean ruin for India, if we endeavour to copy it. This is not to say that we may not adopt and assimilate whatever may be good and capable of assimilation by us as it does not also mean that even the Europeans will not have to part with whatever evil might have crept into it. The incessant search for comforts and their multiplication is such an evil, and I make bold to say that the Europeans themselves will have to remodel their outlook, if they are not to perish under the weight of the comforts to which they are becoming slaves. It may be that my reading is wrong, but I know that for India to run after the Golden Fleece is to court certain death. Let us engrave on our hearts the motto of a Western philosopher, 'plain living and high thinking'. (*CW* 46: 55-6)

As late as 1936, Gandhi thought of London as being 'our Mecca or Kashi [Benares]'. In a letter of recommendation for Kamalnayan Bajaj written to H. S. L. Polak, he stated the following: 'However much we may fight Great Britain, London is increasingly becoming our Mecca or Kashi. Kamalnayan is no exception. I have advised him to take up a course in the London School of Economics. Perhaps you will put him in touch with Professor Laski who may not mind guiding young Bajaj. Muriel [Lester] has undertaken to mother him', (*CW* 63: 122).

51   The psychology of the mind adumbrated here is basic to Gandhi's moral theory and is derived from *The Bhagavad Gita*. Swaraj, or self-control, means control over the *mind*. On the *Gita's* teachings on the relationship of the mind to the body and the senses, and on how one may attain control over the mind, see Zaehner 1973, 423–5.

with the same kind of plough as it existed thousands of years ago. We have retained the same kind of cottages that we had in former times, and our indigenous education remains the same as before. We have had no system of life-corroding competition.[52] Each followed his own occupation or trade,[53] and charged a regulation wage. It was not that we did not know how to invent machinery, but our forefathers knew that, if we set our hearts after such things, we would become slaves and lose our moral fibre. They, therefore, after due deliberation, decided that we should only do what we could with our hands and feet. They saw that our real happiness and health consisted in a proper use of our hands[54] and feet. They further reasoned that large cities were a snare and a useless encumbrance,[55] and that people would not be happy in them, that there would be gangs of thieves and robbers, prostitution and vice flourishing in them, and that poor men would be robbed by rich men. They were, therefore, satisfied with small villages. They saw that kings and their swords were inferior to the sword of ethics, and they, therefore, held the sovereigns of the earth to be inferior to the Rishis and the Fakirs.[56] A nation with a constitution like this is fitter to teach others than to learn from others. This nation had courts, lawyers and doctors, but they were all within bounds.[57] Everybody knew that these professions were not particularly superior; moreover, these vakils and *vaids*[58] did not rob people; they were considered people's dependents, not their masters. Justice was tolerably fair. The ordinary rule was to avoid courts. There were no touts to lure people into them. This evil, too, was noticeable only in and around capitals. The common people lived independently, and followed their agricultural occupation. They enjoyed true Home Rule.

And where this cursed modern civilization has not reached, India remains as it was before. The inhabitants of that part of India will very properly laugh at your new-fangled notions. The English do not rule over them nor will you ever rule over them. Those whose name we speak we do not know, nor do they know us. I would certainly advise you and those like you who love the motherland to go into the interior that has yet not been polluted by the railways, and to live there for six months;[59] you might then be patriotic and speak of Home Rule.

Now you see what I consider to be real civilization. Those who want to change conditions such as I have described are enemies of the country and are sinners.

---

52 'life-corroding competition': following Ruskin, Gandhi wants to *moderate* competition by introducing 'social affections' into economic relations.

53 Here Gandhi defends the 'idea' of *varna* and rejects the 'historical' institutions of caste. This quasi-'platonic' approach to *varna* has not convinced critics such as B. R. Ambedkar and the more recent Dalit elite.

54 Manual labour, extolled here, is not a valued activity according to the norms of traditional Indian civilisation. Gandhi came to appreciate it from his reading of Ruskin, Tolstoy and Bondaref. Promotion of manual labour became an integral part of the Gandhian revolution.

55 Gandhi saw in modern Indian cities a real thceatlo civilised living (*CW* 9: 476): 'Bombay, Calcutta, and the other chief cities of India are the real plague spots' (ibid., 479); 'To me the rise of the cities like Calcutta and Bombay is a matter for sorrow rather than congratulations' (ibid., 509). He idealised and romanticised the Indian village and hoped to reinstate it in a Gandhian India.

56 'Rishis and Fakirs': *rishis* are sages according to Hindu culture; *fakirs,* according to Muslim culture, are religious mendicants of great moral authority.

57 'within bounds': the bounds of dharma. This passage throws light on the real point of his earlier criticism of lawyers and doctors: modernity has 'freed' these professions from the restraints required by traditional morality.

58 'vakils and vaids': lawyers and doctors, respectively, of pre-modern Indian culture.

59 '... go into the interior ... for six months': Gandhi believed that home rule would mean something only if it improved the lot of the villagers. This is a belief that the modern Indian elite has not understood or accepted. Writing to Henry Polak from Wardha in 1936 he stated: 'I am trying to become a villager. The place where I am writing this has a population of about 600– no roads, no post-office, no shop' (*CW* 63:122).

READER: It would be all right if India were exactly as you have described it; but it is also India where there are hundreds of child-widows, where two-year-old babies are married, where twelve-year-old girls are mothers and housewives, where women practise polyandry, where the practice of Niyog[60] obtains, where, in the name of religion, girls dedicate themselves to prostitution, and where, in the name of religion, sheep and goats are killed.[61] Do you consider these also symbols of the civilization that you have described?[62]

EDITOR: You make a mistake. The defects that you have shown are defects. Nobody mistakes them for ancient civilization. They remain in spite of it. Attempts have always been made, and will be made, to remove them. We may utilise the new spirit that is born in us[63] for purging ourselves of these evils. But what I have described to you as emblems of modern civilization are accepted as such by its votaries. The Indian civilization, as described by me, has been so described by its votaries. In no part of the world, and under no civilization, have all men attained perfection. The tendency of Indian civilization is to elevate the moral being, that of the western civilization is to propagate immorality. The latter is godless, the former is based on a belief in God. So understanding and so believing, it behoves every lover of India to cling to the old Indian civilization even as a child clings to its mother's breast.

HOW CAN INDIA BECOME FREE?

READER: I appreciate your views about civilization. I will have to think over them. I cannot take in all at once. What, then, holding the views you do, would you suggest for freeing India?

EDITOR: I do not expect my views to be accepted all of a sudden. My duty is to place them before readers like yourself. Time can be trusted to do the rest. We have already examined the conditions for freeing India, but we have done so indirectly;[64] we will now do so directly. It is a world-known maxim that the removal of the cause of a disease results in the removal of the disease itself. Similarly, if the cause of India's slavery be removed, India can become free.

READER: If Indian civilization is, as you say, the best of all, how do you account for India's slavery?

EDITOR: This civilization is unquestionably the best; but it is to be observed that all civilizations have been on their trial. That civilization which is permanent outlives it. Because the sons of India were found wanting, its civilization has been placed in jeopardy. But its strength is to be seen in its ability to survive the shock. Moreover, the whole of India is not touched. Those alone who have been affected by western civilization[65] have become enslaved. We measure the universe by our own

---

60 'Niyog': a custom permitting a man to have sexual intercourse with his brother's childless widow, or with the wife of an impotent kinsman, in order to raise children, without committing the sin of incest. Children bom out of such unions were regarded as the issue of the woman's husband. Originally intended to provide legitimate heirs for childless relatives, in course of time the custom became corniced, and became part of the 'privileges' of brahmins. While in some region, brahmins claimed the right to provide the issue upon a childless widow, in others they offered their 'services' even when the woman had other children and the husband was alive. Over the centuries, Niyoga remained a great affront to the dignity of Indian women.

61 Gandhi gives a gruesome account of his 1902 visit to the Kali temple in Calcutta: 'On the way I saw a stream of sheep going to be sacrificed to Kali ... We were greeted by rivers of blood. I could not bear to stand there. I was exasperated and restless. I have never forgotten that sight' (*CW* 39: 190).

62 The social evils enumerated in this paragraph constitute the subject matter of Gandhi's critique of Indian civilisation in *HS*.

63 'the new spirit that is born in us': a very important point. Gandhi does recognise the positive contributions made by colonialism. It made Indians self-critical and creative.

64 'indirectly ... directly': an important turning point in the argument of the book. Chs. I–XIII prepare the background for understanding the more positive ideas contained in chs. XIV–XX.

65 'western civilisation': meaning *modern* Western civilisation.

miserable foot-rule. When we are slaves, we think that the whole universe is enslaved. Because we are in an abject condition, we think that the whole of India is in that condition. As a matter of fact, it is not so, but it is as well to impute our slavery to the whole of India. But if we bear in mind the above fact we can see that, if we become free, India is free. And in this thought you have a definition of Swaraj. It is Swaraj when we learn to rule ourselves.[66] It is therefore in the palm of our hands. Do not consider this Swaraj to be like a dream.[67] Hence there is no idea of sitting still. The Swaraj that I wish to picture before you and me is such that, after we have once realised it, we will endeavour to the end of our lifetime to persuade others to do likewise. But such Swaraj has to be experienced by each one for himself.[68] One drowning man will never save another. Slaves ourselves, it would be a mere pretension to think of freeing others. Now you will have seen that it is not necessary for us to have as our goal the expulsion of the English. If the English become Indianised, we can accommodate them.[69] If they wish to remain in India along with their civilization, there is no room for them. It lies with us to bring about such a state of things.

READER: It is impossible that Englishmen should ever become Indianised.

EDITOR: To say that is equivalent to saying that the English have no humanity in them. And it is really beside the point whether they become so or not. If we keep our own house in order, only those who are fit to live in it will remain. Others will leave of their own accord. Such things occur within the experience of all of us.

READER: But it has not occurred in history!

EDITOR: To believe that, what has not occurred in history will not occur at all, is to argue disbelief in the dignity of man. At any rate, it behoves us to try what appeals to our reason. All countries are not similarly conditioned. The condition of India is unique. Its strength is immeasurable. We need not, therefore, refer to the history of other countries. I have drawn attention to the fact that, when other civilizations have succumbed, the Indians has survived many a shock.

READER: I cannot follow this. There seems little doubt that we shall have to expel the English by force of arms. So long as they are in the country, we cannot rest. One of our poets[70] says that slaves cannot even dream of happiness. We are, day by day, becoming weakened owing to the presence of the English. Our greatness is gone; our people look like terrified men. The English are in the country like a blight which we must remove by every means.

EDITOR: In your excitement, you have forgotten all we have been considering. We brought the English, and we keep them. Why do you forget that our adoption of their civilization makes their

---

66 This is the first time that true swaraj has been defined in the book.

67 Swaraj, in so far as it requires self-rule, is not, and cannot be a utopia; it is something that can be achieved by the individual here and now.

68 Swaraj for Gandhi is more than an object of research; it is something that has to be experienced internally, giving rise to an internal moral transformation of the individual. Without such an experience, swaraj would remain a mere theory or doctrine; it would never become an internal principle of action in the external political sphere. 'Experience' here has the Tolstoyan meaning, as found in *What is Art?* Compare Gandhi's comment to Joan Bondurant (who was conducting *research* on *satyagraha*): 'but *satyagraha* is not a subject for research—you must experience it, use it, live by it' (Bondurant 1965, 146). Inner experience in this context involves an awareness that *artha* and *kama* should be pursued only within the framework of dharma.

69 Here Gandhi answers the question raised in ch. IV: the physical expulsion of the British from India is not of the essence of swaraj; self-transformation is. Gandhi the assimilationist is prepared to welcome 'Indianised' Britons as true Indians.

70 'One of our poets': there is no reference to poets in the Gujarati text, which only states, 'It appears that slaves cannot even dream of happiness.' The poet in question is Tulsidas; the verse, *paradheen sapnehu sukh nahin,* is taken from his famous *Ramcharitmanas* (Tulsidas 1952, 115).

presence in India at all possible?[71] Your hatred against them ought to be transferred to their civilization. But let us assume that we have to drive away the English by fighting; how is that to be done?

READER: In the same way as Italy did it. What it was possible for Mazzini and Garibaldi[72] to do, is possible for us. You cannot deny that they were very great men.

PASSIVE RESISTANCE[73]

READER: Is there any historical evidence as to the success of what you have called soul-force or truth-force? No instance seems to have happened of any nation having risen through soul-force. I still think that the evil-doers will not cease doing evil without physical punishment.

EDITOR: The poet Tulsidas has said: "Of religion, pity or love is the root, as egotism of the body. Therefore, we should not abandon pity so long as we are alive."[74] This appears to me to be a scientific truth.[75] I believe in it as much as I believe in two and two being four. The force of love is the same as the force of the soul or truth. We have evidence of its working at every step. The universe[76] would disappear without the existence of that force. But you ask for historical evidence. It is, therefore, necessary to know what history means. The Gujarati equivalent means: "It so happened." If that is the meaning of history, it is possible to give copious evidence. But if it means the doings of kings and emperors, there can be no evidence of soul-force or passive resistance in such history. You cannot expect silver-ore in a tin-mine. History, as we know it, is a record of the wars of the world, and so there is a proverb among Englishmen that a nation which has no history, that is, no wars, is a happy nation. How kings played how they become enemies of one another and how they murdered one another is found accurately recorded in history and, if this were all that had happened in the world, it would have been ended long ago. If the story of the universe had commenced with wars, not a man would have been found alive to-day. Those people who have been warred against have disappeared, as, for instance, the natives of Australia, of whom hardly a man was left alive by the intruders. Mark, please, that these natives did not use soul-force in self-defence, and it does not require much foresight to know that the Australians will share the same

---

71 This point was raised earlier in ch. VII.
72 *Editor's note*: Garibaldi, like Mazzini, sought Italian unification in the middle of the 19th century.
73 The Gujarati title of this chapter is *satyagraha-atmabal*.
74 Next to *Bhagavad Gita*, Tulsidas' *Ramayana* had the strongest influence on Gandhi's religio-ethical development. As he states in his *Autobiography*, he regarded it 'as the greatest book in all devotional literature' (*CW* 39: 32). One of the first books published by his International Press, Phoenix, Natal, was an abridged version of this work; in introducing the work to the public he wrote, 'We wish that every Indian goes devoutly through the summary which we are placing before the public, reflect over it, and assimilate the ethical principles so vividly set out in it' (*CW* 9: 98).
The couplet cited here is popularly attributed to Tulsidas. The popular version reads as follows:

> *Daya dharma ka mool hain, pap mool abhiman*
> *Tulsi daya na chandiye, jab lag ghatmen pran*

('Of dharma pity is the root, as egotism is of *sin*. Therefore, we should not abandon pity so long as we are alive.' [Editor's translation; emphasis added.])

Gandhi here either modifies the first line of the popular version by substituting *body* for *sin*, or uses another version of the couplet familiar to him. According to a letter to the present editor from Prof. T. N. Bali, professor of Hindi at Delhi University, this couplet cannot be found in any of Tulsidas' known works.
75 'scientific truth': in Gujarati, *shastra wachan*; scientific according to the science of morals, not according to the modern notion of science.
76 'The universe': i.e., the human universe. Wthout *daya*, the human universe would become as horrible as *rasatal,* one of the seven 'hells' of Hindu mythology.

fate as their victims. "Those that wield the sword shall perish by the sword."[77] With us, the proverb is that professional swimmers will find a watery grave.

The fact that there are so many men still alive in the world shows that it is based not on the force of arms but on the force of truth or love. Therefore the greatest and most unimpeachable evidence of the success of this force is to be found in the fact that, in spite of the wars of the world, it still lives on.

Thousands, indeed, tens of thousands, depend for their existence on a very active working of this force. Little quarrels of millions of families in their daily lives disappear before the exercise of this force. Hundreds of nations live in peace. History does not and cannot take note of this fact. History is really a record of every interruption of the even working of the force of love or of the soul. Two brothers quarrel: one of them repents and re-awakens the love that was lying dormant in him;[78] the two again begin to live in peace: nobody takes note of this. But if the two brothers, through the intervention of solicitors or some other reason, take up arms or go to law—which is another form of the exhibition of brute-force—their doings would be immediately noticed in the press, they would be the talk of their neighbours, and would probably go down to history. And what is true of families and communities is true of nations. There is no reason, to believe that there is one law for families, and another for nations. History, then, is a record of an interruption of the course of nature. Soul-force, being natural, is not noted in history.

READER: According to what you say, it is plain that instances of the kind of passive resistance are not to be found in history. It is necessary to understand this passive resistance more fully. It will be better, therefore, if you enlarge upon it.

EDITOR: Passive resistance is a method of securing rights by personal suffering; it is the reverse of resistance by arms. When I refuse to do a thing that is repugnant to my conscience, I use soul-force.[79] For instance, the government of the day has passed a law which is applicable to me: I do not like it, if, by using violence, I force the government to repeal the law, I am employing what may be termed body-force. If I do not obey the law and accept the penalty for its breach, I use soul-force. It involves sacrifice of self.

Everybody admits that sacrifice of self is infinitely superior to sacrifice of others. Moreover, if this kind of force is used in a cause that is unjust only the person using it suffers. He does not make others suffer for his mistakes. Men have before now done many things which were subsequently found to have been wrong. No man can claim to be absolutely in the right, or that a particular thing is wrong, because he thinks so, but it is wrong for him so long as that is his deliberate judgment. It is, therefore, meet that he should not do that which he knows to be wrong, and suffer the consequence whatever it may be. This is the key to the use of soul-force.

READER: You would then disregard laws—this is rank disloyalty. We have always been considered a law-abiding nation. You seem to be going even beyond the extremists.[80] They say that we must obey the laws that have been passed, but that, if the laws be bad, we must drive out the law-givers even by force.

EDITOR: Whether I go beyond them or whether I do not, is a matter of no consequence to either of us. We simply want to find out what is right, and to act accordingly. The real meaning of the statement that we are a law-abiding nation is that we are passive resisters. When we do not like certain laws, we

---

77   Gospel of St Matthew, ch. 26, v. 52.
78   The Gujarati text has: 'one of them practises *satyagraha* against the other.' Omitted from the English text.
79   The Gujarati version of this definition is as follows: '*Satyagraha* or soul-force is called passive resistance in English. That word is applicable to a method by which men, enduring pain, secure their rights. Its purpose is the opposite of the purpose of using force of arms (*ladaibal*). When something is not acceptable to me, I do not do that work. In so acting I use *satyagraha* or soul-force.'
80   The implication here is that *satyagraha*, though not a violent form of action, is even more revolutionary than the revolution advocated by the Reader.

do not break the heads of law-givers, but we suffer and do not submit to the laws.[81] That we should obey laws whether good or bad is a new-fangled notion.[82] There was no such thing in former days. The people disregarded those laws they did not like, and suffered the penalties for their breach. It is contrary to our manhood, if we obey laws repugnant to our conscience. Such teaching is opposed to religion[83] and means slavery. If the government were to ask us to go about without any clothing, should we do so? If I were a passive resister, I would say to them that I would have nothing to do with their law. But we have so forgotten ourselves and become so compliant, that we do not mind any degrading law.

A man who has realised his manhood, who fears only God, will fear no one else. Man-made laws[84] are not necessarily binding on him. Even the government do not expect any such thing from us. They do not say: "You must do such and such a thing," but they say: "If you do not do it, we will punish you." We are sunk so low, that we fancy that it is our duty and our religion[85] to do what the law lays down. If man will only realise that it is unmanly to obey laws that are unjust, no man's tyranny will enslave him. This is the key to self-rule or home-rule.[86]

It is a superstition and an ungodly thing to believe that an act of a majority binds a minority. Many examples can be given in which acts of majorities will be found to have been wrong, and those of minorities to have been right. All reforms owe their origin to the initiation of minorities in opposition to majorities. If among a band of robbers, a knowledge of robbing is obligatory, is a pious man to accept the obligation? So long as the superstition that men should obey unjust laws exists, so long will their slavery exist. And a passive resister alone can remove such a superstition.

To use brute-force, to use gun-powder is contrary to passive resistance; for it means that we want our opponent to do by force—that which we desire but he does not. And, if such a use of force is justifiable, surely he is entitled to do likewise by us. And so we should never come to an agreement. We may simply fancy, like the blind horse moving in a circle round a mill, that we are making progress. Those who believe that they are not bound to obey laws which are repugnant to their conscience have only the remedy of passive resistance open to them. Any other must lead to disaster.

READER: From what you say, I deduce that passive resistance is a splendid weapon of the weak[87] but that, when they are strong, they may take up arms.

EDITOR: This is gross ignorance. Passive resistance, that is, soul-force, is matchless. It is superior to the force of arms. How, then, can it be considered only a weapon of the weak? Physical force men

---

81   The Gujarati text here links *satyagraha* with the ritual of fasting: 'but in order to annul that law we observe fast'. This is the only time that *HS* links *satyagraha* and fast.

82   'a new-fangled notion'. The reference is to the utilitarian jurisprudence introduced into India in the nineteenth century. Utility replaced dharma as the ethical basis of law. For a full account of this see Stokes 1959.

83   'religion': dharma, in the sense of ethics.

84   'Man-made laws': this terminology suggests the distinction between positive law and the higher law of dharma. Note the parallel between Gandhi's legal philosophy and that branch of Western legal philosophy which distinguishes between positive law and natural law.

85   'our duty and our religion': in Gujarati, *farajj* and dharma respectively. Modern legal positivism, according to Gandhi, corrupts the notion of law in that it makes obedience to positive law a political and a moral duty, independently of the question of whether such law is in harmony with dharma or not.

86   There is thus an ethical link between courage, *satyagraha*, and the practice of dharma. Gandhi's swaraj requires that the positive legal system recognises the validity of dharma.

87   Gandhi is defending *satyagraha* against the opinion of some of his South African friends who thought that it was the same as passive resistance practised in England recently by the suffragettes and by the opponents of the Education Act of 1902. Whereas passive resistance was compatible with mild forms of physical violence, *satyagraha*, Gandhi pointed out, was not. For a full account of Gandhi's distinction between passive resistance and *satyagraha*, see *Satyagraha in South Africa*, ch. 13 (*CW* 29: 93–7).

are strangers to the courage that is requisite in a passive resister. Do you believe that a coward can ever disobey a law that he dislikes? Extremists are considered to be advocates of brute-force. Why do they, then, talk about obeying laws? I do not blame them. They can say nothing else. When they succeed in driving out the English, and they themselves become governors, they will want you and me to obey their laws. And that is a fitting thing for their constitution. But a passive resister will say he will not obey a law that is against his conscience, even though he may be blown to pieces at the mouth of a cannon.

What do you think? Wherein is courage required—in blowing others to pieces from behind a cannon or with a smiling face to approach a cannon and to be blown to pieces? Who is the true warrior—he who keeps death always as a bosom-friend or he who controls the death of others? Believe me that a man devoid of courage and manhood can never be a passive resister.

This, however, I will admit: that even a man, weak in body, is capable of offering this resistance. One man can offer it just as well as millions. Both men and women can indulge in it. It does not require the training of an army; it needs no Jiu-jitsu. Control over the mind[88] is alone necessary, and, when that is attained, man is free like the king of the forest, and his very glance withers the enemy.

Passive resistance is an all-sided sword; it can be used anyhow; it blesses him who uses it and him against whom it is used. Without drawing a drop of blood, it produces far-reaching results. It never rusts, and cannot be stolen. Competition between passive resisters does not exhaust. The sword of passive resistance does not require a scabbard. It is strange indeed that you should consider such a weapon to be a weapon merely of the weak.

READER: You have said that passive resistance is a speciality of India. Have cannons never been used in India?

EDITOR: Evidently, in your opinion, India means its few princes.[89] To me, it means its teeming millions, on whom depends the existence of its princes and our own.

Kings will always use their kingly weapons. To use force is bred in them. They want to command, but those who have to obey commands, do not want guns; and these are in a majority throughout the world. They have to learn either body-force or soul-force. Where they learn the former, both the rulers and the ruled become like so many mad men, but, where they learn soul-force, the commands of the rulers do not go beyond the point of their swords, for true men disregard unjust commands. Peasants[90] have never been subdued by the sword, and never will be. They do not know the use of the sword, and they are not frightened by the use of it by others. That nation is great which rests its head upon death as its pillow. Those who defy death are free from all fear.[91] For those who are labouring under the delusive charms of brute-force, this picture is not overdrawn. The fact is that, in India, the nation at large has generally used passive resistance in all departments of life. We cease to cooperate with our rulers when they displease us. This is passive resistance.

I remember an instance when, in a small principality, the villagers were offended by some command issued by the prince. The former immediately began vacating the village. The prince became nervous, apologised to his subjects and withdrew his command. Many such instances can be found in India.[92]

---

88   On 'mind' see chs. XIII and XX.

89   For Gandhi's critique of the Indian princes see ch. XV.

90   Peasants: *khedut*–those who actually cultivated the land. These constituted only a small percentage of the village population, and did not always include the untouchables.

91   Gandhi has terrorists like Dhingra in mind here, terrorists who are willing to die for a cause. But *satyagraha*, he implies, requires even greater courage than that required of the terrorists.

92   The reference here is to the traditional practice of *dhurna*. Joseph Doke's biography of Gandhi gives the following accounts of *dhurna*. 'The idea of passive resistance as a means of opposing evil is inherent in Indian philosophy. In old time, it was called

Real home-rule is possible only where passive resistance is the guiding force of the people. Any other rule is foreign rule.[93]

READER: Then you will say that it is not at all necessary for us to train the body?

EDITOR: I will certainly not say any such thing. It is difficult to become a passive resister, unless the body is trained. As a rule, the mind, residing in a body that has become weakened by pampering, is also weak, and where there is no strength of mind, there can be no strength of soul. We will have to improve our physique by getting rid of infant marriages and luxurious living. If I were to ask a man having a shattered body to face a cannon's mouth I would make of myself a laughing-stock.

READER: From what you say, then, it would appear that it is not a small thing to become a passive resister, and, if that is so, I would like you to explain how a man may become a passive resister.

EDITOR: To become a passive resister is easy enough, but it is also equally difficult. I have known a lad of fourteen years become a passive resister; I have known also sick people doing likewise and I have also known physically strong and otherwise happy people being unable to take up passive resistance. After a great deal of experience, it seems to me that those who want to become passive resisters for the service of the country[94] have to observe perfect chastity, adopt poverty, follow truth, and cultivate fearlessness.

Chastity is one of the greatest disciplines without which the mind cannot attain requisite firmness. A man who is unchaste loses stamina, becomes emasculated and cowardly. He whose mind is given over to animal passions is not capable of any great effort. This can be proved by innumerable instances. What, then, is a married person to do, is the question that arises naturally; and yet it need not. When a husband and wife gratify the passions, it is no less an animal indulgence on that account. Such an indulgence, except for perpetuating the race, is strictly prohibited. But a passive resister has to avoid even that very limited indulgence, because he can have no desire for progeny. A married man, therefore, can observe perfect chastity. This subject is not capable of being treated at greater length. Several questions arise:

"to sit dhurna". Sometimes a whole community would adopt this method towards their Prince. It has been so in the history of Porbandar; then trade was dislocated and force helpless before the might of passive resistance.'

Doke cites from Bishop Heber's account of *dhurna*: 'To sit dhurna, or mourning, is to remain motionless in that posture, without food, and exposed to the weather, till the person against whom it is employed consents to the request offered, and the Hindus believe that whoever dies under such a process becomes a tormenting spirit to haunt and afflict his inflexible antagonist.' Heber narrates how on one occasion 'above three hundred thousand persons' around Benares practised mass *dhurna*—'deserted their houses, shut up their shops, suspended the labour of their farms, forbore to light fires, dress victuals, many of them even to eat, and sat down with folded arms and drooping heads, like so many sheep, on the plain which surrounds Benares' (Doke 1909, 132–3). As practised traditionally, *dhurna* was a form of coercion plain and simple. Under the Indian Penal Code the practice was outlawed by the middle of the nine-tenth century (Bose 1962, 80–2; Devanesan 1969, 45).

In a *Young India* article of 2 February 1922, Gandhi severely condemned the revival of 'sitting *dhurna*' in connection with *satyagraha*, calling it an 'ancient form of barbarity'. Some students in Calcutta had used this 'crude' and 'cowardly' method to block the passage of their fellow students. Gandhi stated emphatically that *dhurna* had nothing to do with *satyagraha*.

93 'foreign rule': in Gujarati *ku-raj* (misrule).

94 'for the service of the country': Gandhi converts the four traditional *moral* virtues mentioned here into new *civic* virtues. According to tradition, these virtues were considered to be the means of *individual* self-realisation; Gandhi points out, however, that the practice of the same virtues can also become the means of national regeneration. In a letter written to his son, Manilal, on 24 November 1909 he explains how the activity of achieving individual self-realisation can contribute to national regeneration as well:

> First of all, we shall have to consider how we can realise the self and how serve our country ... For realising the self, the first essential thing is to cultivate a strong moral sense. Morality means acquisition of virtues such as fearlessness, truth, *brahmacharya* (celibacy) and so on. Service is automatically rendered to the country in this process of cultivating morality. (*CW* 10: 70)

The idea recurs in Gandhi's letter to Maganlal Gandhi (*CW* 10: 206–7).

How is one to carry one's wife with one? What are her rights, and such other questions? Yet those who wish to take part in a great work are bound to solve these puzzles.[95]

Just as there is necessity for chastity, so is there for poverty.[96] Pecuniary ambition and passive resistance cannot well go together. Those who have money are not expected to throw it away, but they are expected to be indifferent about it. They must be prepared to lose every penny rather than give up passive resistance.

Passive resistance has been described in the course of our discussion as truth-force.[97] Truth, therefore, has necessarily to be followed, and that at any cost. In this connection, academic questions such as whether a man may not lie in order to save a life, etc. arise, but these questions occur only to those who wish to justify lying. Those who want to follow truth every time are not placed in such a quandary, and, if they are, they are still saved from a false position.

Passive resistance cannot proceed a step without fearlessness.[98] Those alone can follow the path of passive resistance who are free from fear whether as to their possessions, false honour, their relatives, the government, bodily injuries, death.

These observances are not to be abandoned in the belief that they are difficult. Nature has implanted in the human breast ability to cope with any difficulty or suffering that may come to man unprovoked. These qualities are worth having, even for those who do not wish to serve the country. Let there be no mistake as those who want to train themselves in the use of arms are also obliged to have these qualities more or less.[99] Everybody does not become a warrior for the wish. A would-be warrior will have to observe chastity, and to be satisfied with poverty as his lot. A warrior without fearlessness cannot be conceived of. It may be thought that he would not need to be exactly truthful, but that quality follows real fearlessness. When a man abandons truth, he does so owing to fear in some shape or form. The above four attributes, then, need not frighten any one. It may be as well here to note that a physical-force man has to have many other useless qualities which a passive resister never needs. And you will find that whatever extra effort a swordsman needs is due to lack of fearlessness. If he is an embodiment of the latter, the sword will drop from his hand that very moment. He does not need its support. One who is free from hatred requires no sword. A man with a stick suddenly came face to face with a lion, and instinctively raised his weapon in self-defence. The man saw that he had only prated about fearlessness when there was none in him. That moment he dropped the stick, and found himself free from all fear.

---

95   In 1906 Gandhi took the vow of *brahmacharya*. The *heroic* stage of satygraha can be reached only by those who are chaste in word, deed and thought. For Gandhi's thoughts on chastity, see *Autobiography*, III, chs. 7, 8; IV, chs. 25–30 (*CW* 39: 165–71, 252–64). For a critical analysis of Gandhi's approach to *brahmacharya* see Erikson 1969; Parekh 1989b, 172–206; and Mehta 1977, 179–213. Cf. Tolstoy, who understood chastity in married life to mean abstention from adulteiy: 'The ideal [proposed by the Sermon on the Mount] is perfect chastity, even in thought. The commandment indicating the level below which it is quite possible not to descend is man's progress towards this ideal, is that of a pure married life, refraining from adultery' (Tolstoy 1935, 121).

96   'poverty': i.e., *voluntary* poverty or simplicity of life or freedom from possessiveness. Gandhi is not at all glorifying involuntary poverty here (*pace* Keer 1973, 782). What he is arguing is that, paradoxical though it may appear to some, the virtue of detachment has a great deal to contribute towards making India economically prosperous.

97   Since *satyagraha* proceeds from truth-force, it follows that a satyagrahi cannot hide the truth from his or her 'opponent'. *Satyagraha* requires frankness and openness. This point is stressed in the Gujarati text, where he takes aim at the Indian anarchists and their secret societies. The relevant Gujarati text reads as follows: 'How can anyone demonstrate the power or force of truth unless he dedicates himself to truth? Truth, therefore, is absolutely necessary. It cannot be abandoned, whatever the cost. *Truth has nothing to hide. There is no question, therefore, of satyagrahis maintaining a secret army*' (emphasis added).

98   'fearlessness': *abhayata*, lack of cowardice. Compare the virtue of courage needed for the practice of non-violence with the virtue of courage discussed in classical Western political theory.

99   Gandhi's point is that the practice of the four virtues required for *satyagraha* calls for true heroism; satyagrahis, not anarchists such as Dhingra, are the true heroes.

STUDY QUESTIONS

1. According to Gandhi, what were the reasons for the British Raj?

2. How could India break the bonds of imperial rule?

3. What did Gandhi think of Western Civilization? (He was attributed as saying he thought it would be a good idea!)

4. How would you define *satyagraha*?

The Wretched of the Earth

I n 1954, the French, having recently lost colonial Indochina to the Vietminh, were all the more staunchly opposed to granting Algeria its independence. Algeria, the French argued, was not a colony, but an essential part of France—a French department just across the Mediterranean, governed administratively from Paris like the rest of the country. Algeria also contained one million French nationals, who also believed they were living in France.

Arab Algerians, however, discovered that the Second World War had been a war for the liberation of France from Nazi Germany, but not Algeria from France. By 1945, protesters had become more vociferous in their denunciations of French rule, and demanded Algerian independence. French politicians, on the other hand, regardless of party affiliation, as well as public opinion, sided unanimously in favor of putting down the rebellion to keep Algeria French.

The Algerian rebels organized the *Front de Libération Nationale* (FLN), an anti-colonial movement whose paramount aim was Algerian independence. The FLN fought a bloody and protracted war of attrition against France between 1954 and 1962, using guerrilla warfare tactics to defeat French military forces. In a war of attrition, guerrillas, with the advantages of a defensive theater of war and sympathy with the local populace, seek to keep the struggle alive in the hopes of breaking the other side's will to persist. Atrocities, terror, and reprisals were to be found on both sides. The period has been magnificently depicted in Gillo Pontecorvo's 1966 film, *The Battle of Algiers*, shot in Algiers and Rome. Pontecorvo's portrayal of terrorism and torture are so vivid that the film has been incorporated into the training programs of the Black Panthers and the Irish Republican Army, as well as the Pentagon—albeit with different objectives in mind.

Those one million French living in Algeria, known as the *Pieds-Noirs*, or Black-Feet, perhaps because of the European dress shoes they wore in the European Quarter, somewhat insulated from, yet dwarfed by, the teeming population of the Arab casbah, demanded more protection. Military personnel increased from 50,000 troops to 400,000 (excluding the Algerians who fought with the French, who

Figure 16.1. Frantz Fanon. Copyright © (CC by 3.0) at http://commons.wikimedia.org/wiki/File:Frantzfanonpjwproductions.jpg

alone outnumbered the some 25,000 rebel combatants). Two to three million Arabs became refugees (out of a population of nine million), and perhaps one million died. Eventually, the French had to contend with the fact that Algeria would never be part of France. In July 1962, President Charles De Gaulle, his paratroopers, and the rest of France quit Algeria under opposition from the army and the French settlers in Algeria, all but 170,000 of whom left for France.

Frantz Fanon (1925–1961) was born across the Atlantic Ocean in the French colony of Martinique. Fanon had gone to France to study, and when the Second World War began, he joined the Free French Army and served in North Africa. After the war, he returned to France to study psychiatry at the University of Lyons, from which he obtained his medical degree in 1951. Soon thereafter, he was appointed to run a psychiatry department at a hospital in Algeria.

While in Saharan Africa, Fanon joined the FLN, and French officials exiled Fanon from Algeria in 1957. He continued to practice medicine and work for the FLN in neighboring Tunisia. The de facto provisional Algerian government named him ambassador to Ghana in 1961, the year he died of leukemia, missing Algerian independence by a year.

In his short life, Fanon wrote two books that serve as important critiques of colonialism: *Black Skin, White Masks* (1952) and *The Wretched of the Earth* (1961). In his writings, Fanon examines the relationship between colonialism and racism within a psychoanalytical framework, as well as the psychological duress they caused colonized and colonizer alike. He rejected the parochialism of Eurocentric psychoanalysis, antiquated and essentializing in pseudoscience that sought to attribute mental diagnoses based on assumptions and generalizations about colonized peoples. In theorizing about the damaged colonial psyche, Fanon addressed particularly those adherents to negritude, a black-consciousness movement popular in 20th-century francophone intellectual circles. Skeptical as he was, Fanon still recognized the importance of negritude as a cultural alternative to metropolitan hegemony.

In this selection from *The Wretched of the Earth*, Fanon engages in a discourse on decolonization and violence. "In short," the existentialist writer Jean-Paul Sartre explained in his preface to the 1963 edition of *Les damnés de la terre*, "the Third World finds *itself* and speaks to *itself* through his voice."[1] Fanon's work gave articulation to those marginalized voices he believed must inherit their birthright through bloodshed.

---

1   Frantz Fanon, *The Wretched of the Earth* (New York: Grove Press, 1963), p. 10.

The Wretched of the Earth

By Frantz Fanon

CONCERNING VIOLENCE

National liberation, national renaissance, the restoration of nationhood to the people, commonwealth: whatever may be the headings used or the new formulas introduced, decolonization is always a violent phenomenon. At whatever level we study it—relationships between individuals, new names for sports clubs, the human admixture at cocktail parties, in the police, on the directing boards of national or private banks—decolonization is quite simply the replacing of a certain "species" of men by another "species" of men. Without any period of transition, there is a total, complete, and absolute substitution. It is true that we could equally well stress the rise of a new nation, the setting up of a new state, its diplomatic relations, and its economic and political trends. But we have precisely chosen to speak of that kind of *tabula rasa* which characterizes at the outset all decolonization. Its unusual importance is that it constitutes, from the very first day, the minimum demands of the colonized. To tell the truth, the proof of success lies in a whole social structure being changed from the bottom up. The extraordinary importance of this change is that it is willed, called for, demanded. The need for this change exists in its crude state, impetuous and compelling, in the consciousness and in the lives of the men and women who are colonized. But the possibility of this change is equally experienced in the form of a terrifying future in the consciousness of another "species" of men and women: the colonizers.

Decolonization, which sets out to change the order of the world, is, obviously, a program of complete disorder. But it cannot come as a result of magical practices, nor of a natural shock, nor of a friendly understanding. Decolonization, as we know, is a historical process: that is to say that it cannot be understood, it cannot become intelligible nor clear to itself except in the exact measure that we can discern the movements which give it historical form and content. Decolonization is the meeting of two forces, opposed to each other by their very nature, which in fact owe their originality to that sort of substantification which results from and is nourished by the situation in the colonies. Their first encounter was marked by violence and their existence together—that is to say the exploitation of the native by the settler—was carried on by dint of a great array of bayonets and cannons. The settler and the native are old acquaintances. In fact, the settler right when he speaks of knowing "them" well. For it is the settler who perpetuates his existence. The settler owes the fact of his very existence, that is to say, his property, to the colonial system.

Decolonization never takes place unnoticed, for it influences individuals and modifies them fundamentally. It transforms spectators crushed with their inessentiality into privileged actors, with the grandiose glare of history's floodlights upon them. It brings a natural rhythm into existence, introduced by new men, and with it a new language and a new humanity. Decolonization is the veritable creation of new men. But this creation owes nothing of its legitimacy to any supernatural power; the "thing" which has been colonized becomes man during the same process by which it frees itself.

In decolonization, there is therefore the need of a complete calling in question of the colonial situation. If we wish to describe it precisely, we might find it in the well-known words: "The last shall be first and the first last." Decolonization is the putting into practice of this sentence. That is why, if we try to describe it, all decolonization is successful.

The naked truth of decolonization evokes for us the searing bullets and bloodstained knives which emanate from it. For it the last shall be first, this will only come to pass after a murderous and decisive struggle between the two protagonists. That affirmed intention to place the last at the head of things, and to make them climb at a pace (too quickly, some say) the well-known steps which characterize an organized society, can only triumph if we use all means to turn the scale, including, of course, that of violence.

You do not turn any society, however primitive it may be, upside down with such a program if you have not decided from the very beginning, that is to say from the actual formulation of that program, to overcome all the obstacles that you will come across in so doing. The native who decides to put the program into practice, and to become its moving force, is ready for violence at all times. From birth it is clear to him that this narrow world, strewn with prohibitions, can only be called in question by absolute violence.

The colonial world is a world divided into compartments. It is probably unnecessary to recall the existence of native quarters and European quarters, of schools for natives and schools for Europeans; in the same way we need not recall apartheid in South Africa. Yet, if we examine closely this system of compartments, we will at least be able to reveal the lines of force it implies. This approach to the colonial world, its ordering and its geographical layout will allow us to mark out the lines on which a decolonized society will be reorganized.

The colonial world is a world cut in two. The dividing line, the frontiers are shown by barracks and police stations. In the colonies it is the policeman and the soldier who are the official, instituted go-betweens, the spokesmen of the settler and his rule of oppression. In capitalist societies the educational system, whether lay or clerical, the structure of moral reflexes handed down from father to son, the exemplary honesty of workers who are given a medal after fifty years of good and loyal service, and the affection which springs from harmonious relations and good behavior—all these aesthetic expressions of respect for the established order serve to create around the exploited person an atmosphere of submission and of inhibition which lightens the task of policing considerably. In the capitalist countries a multitude of moral teachers, counselors and "bewilderers" separate the exploited from those in power. In the colonial countries, on the contrary, the policeman and the soldier, by their immediate presence and their frequent and direct action maintain contact with the native and advise him by means of rifle butts and napalm not to budge. It is obvious here that the agents of government speak the language of pure force intermediary does not lighten the oppression, nor seek to hide the domination; he shows them up and puts them into practice with the clear conscience of an upholder of the peace; yet he is the bringer of violence into the home and into the mind of the native.

The zone where the natives live is not complementary to the zone inhabited by the settlers. The two zones are opposed, but not in the service of a higher unity. Obedient to the rules of pure Aristotelian logic, they both follow the principle of reciprocal exclusivity. No conciliation is possible, for of the two terms, one is superfluous. The settlers' town is a strongly built town, all made of stone and steel. It is a brightly lit town; the streets are covered with asphalt, and the garbage cans swallow all the leavings, unseen, unknown and hardly thought about. The settler's feet are never visible, except perhaps in the sea; but there you're never close enough to see them. His feet are protected by strong shoes although the streets of his town are clean and even, with no holes or stones. The settler's town is a well-fed town, an easygoing town; its belly is always full of good things. The settlers' town is a town of white people, of foreigners.

The town belonging to the colonized people, or at least the native town, the Negro village, the medina, the reservation, is a place of ill fame, peopled by men of evil repute. They are born there, it matters little where or how; they die there, it matters not where, nor how. It is a world without spaciousness; men live there on top of each other, and their huts are built one on top of the other. The native town is a hungry town, starved of bread, of meat, of shoes, of coal, of light. The native town is a crouching village, a town on its knees, a town wallowing in the mire. It is a town of niggers and dirty Arabs. The look that the native turns on the settler's town is a look of lust, a look of lust, a look of envy: it expresses his dreams of possession—all manner of possession: to sit at the settler's table, to sleep in the settler's bed, with his wife is possible. The colonized man is an envious man. And this the settler knows very well; when their glances meet he ascertains bitterly, always on the defensive, "They want to take our place." It is true, for there is no native who does not dream at least once a day of setting himself up in the settler's place.

This world divided into compartments, this world cut in two is inhabited by two different species. The originality of the colonial context is that economic reality, inequality, and the immense difference of ways of life never come to mask the human realities. When you examine at close quarters the colonial context, it is evident that what parcels out the world is to begin with the fact of belonging to or not belonging to a given race, a given species. In the colonies the economic substructure is also a super-structure. The cause is the consequence; you are rich because you are white, you are white because you are rich. This is why Marxist analysis should always be slightly stretched every time we have to do with the colonial problem.

Everything up to and including the very nature of precapitalist society, so well explained by Marx, must here be thought out again. The serf is in essence different from the knight, but a reference to divine right is necessary to legitimize this statutory difference. In the colonies, the foreigner coming from another country imposed his rule by means of guns and machines. In defiance of his successful transplantation, in spite of his appropriation, the settler still remains foreigner. It is neither the act of owning factories, nor estates, nor a bank balance which distinguishes the governing classes. The governing race is first and foremost those who come from elsewhere, those who are unlike the original inhabitants, "the others."

The violence which has ruled over the ordering of the colonial world, which has ceaselessly drummed the rhythm for the destruction of native social forms and broken up without reserve the systems of reference of the economy, the customs of dress and external life, that same violence will be claimed and taken over by the native at the moment when, deciding to embody history in his own person, he surges into the forbidden quarters. To wreck the colonial world is henceforward a mental picture of action which is very clear, very easy to understand and which may be assumed by each one of the individuals which constitute the colonized people. To break up the colonial world does not mean that after the frontiers have been abolished lines of communication will be set up between the two zones. The destruction of the colonial world is no more and no less that the abolition of one zone, its burial in the depths of the earth or its expulsion from the country.

The natives' challenge to the colonial world is not a rational confrontation of points of view. It is not a treatise on the universal, but the untidy affirmation of an original idea propounded as an absolute. The colonial world is a Manichean world. It is not enough for the settler to delimit physically, that is to say with the help of the army and the police force, the place of the native. As if to show the totalitarian character of colonial exploitation the settler paints the native as a sort of quintessence of evil.* Native society is not simply described as a society lacking in values. It is not enough for the colonist to affirm that those values have disappeared from, or still better never existed in, the colonial world. The native is declared insensible to ethics; he represents not only the absence of values, but also the negation of values. He is, let us dare to admit, the enemy of values, and in this sense he is the absolute evil. He is the corrosive element, destroying all that comes near him; he is the deforming element, disfiguring all that has to do with beauty or morality; he is the depository of maleficent powers, the unconscious and irretrievable instrument of blind forces. Monsieur Meyer could thus state seriously in the French National Assembly that the Republic must not be prostituted by allowing the Algerian people to become part of it. All values, in fact, are irrevocably poisoned and diseased as soon as they are allowed in contact with the colonized race. The customs of the colonized people, their traditions, their myths—above all, their myths—are the very sign of that poverty of spirit and of their constitutional depravity. That is why we must put the DDT which destroys parasites, the bearers of disease, on the same level as the Christian religion which wages war on embryonic heresies and instincts, and on evil as yet unborn. The recession of yellow fever and the advance of evangelization form part of the same balance sheet. But the triumphant *communiqués* from the missions are in fact a source of information concerning the implantation of foreign influences in the core of the colonized people. I speak of the Christian religion, and no one need be astonished. The Church in the colonies is the white people's Church, the foreigner's Church. She does not call the native to God's ways but to the ways of the white man, of the master, of the oppressor. And as we know, in this matter many are called but few chosen.

At times this Manicheism goes to its logical conclusion and dehumanizes the native, or to speak plainly, it turns him into an animal. In fact, the terms the settler uses when he mentions the native are zoological terms. He speaks of the yellow man's reptilian motions, of the stink of the native quarter, of breeding swarms, of foulness, of spawn, of gesticulations. When the settler seeks to describe the native fully in exact terms he constantly refers to the bestiary. The European rarely hits on a picturesque style; but the native, who knows what is in the mind of the settler, guesses at once what he is thinking of. Those hordes of vital statistics, those hysterical masses, those faces bereft of all humanity, those distended bodies which are like nothing on earth, that mob without beginning or end, those children who seem to belong to nobody, that laziness stretched out in the sun, that vegetative rhythm of life—all this forms part of the colonial vocabulary. General de Gaulle speaks of "the yellow multitudes" and François Mauriac of the black, brown, and yellow masses which soon will be unleashed. The native knows all this, and laughs to himself every time he spots an allusion to the animal world in the other's words. For he knows that he is not an animal; and it is precisely at the moment he realizes his humanity that he begins sharpen the weapons with which he will secure its victory.

---

* We have demonstrated the mechanism of this Manichean world in *Black Skin, White Masks* (New York: Grove Press, 1967).

As soon as the native begins to pull on his moorings, and to cause anxiety to the settler, he is handed over to well-meaning souls who in cultural congresses point out to him the specificity and wealth of Western values. But every time Western values are mentioned they produce in the native a sort of stiffening or muscular lockjaw. During the period of decolonization, the native's reason is appealed to. He is offered definite values, he is told frequently that decolonization need not mean regression, and that he must put his trust in qualities which are well-tried, solid, and highly esteemed. But it so happens that when the native hears a speech about Western culture he pulls out his knife—or at least he makes sure it is within reach. The violence with which the supremacy of white values is affirmed and the aggressiveness which has permeated the victory of these values over the ways of life and of thought of the native mean that, in revenge, the native laughs in mockery when Western values are mentioned in front of him. In the colonial context the settler only ends his work of breaking in the native when the latter admits loudly and intelligibly the supremacy of the white man's values. In the period of decolonization, the colonized masses mock at these very values, insult them, and vomit them up.

This phenomenon is ordinarily masked because, during the period of decolonization, certain colonized intellectuals have begun a dialogue with the bourgeoisie of the colonialist country. During this phase, the indigenous population is discerned only as an indistinct mass. The few native personalities whom the colonialist bourgeois have come to know here and there have not sufficient influence on that immediate discernment to give rise to nuances. On the other hand, during the period of liberation, the colonialist bourgeoisie looks feverishly for contacts with the elite and it is with these elite that the familiar dialogue concerning values is carried on. The colonialist bourgeoisie, when it realizes that it is impossible for it to maintain its domination over the colonial countries, decides to carry out a rearguard action with regard to culture, values, techniques, and so on. Now what we must never forget is that the immense majority of colonized peoples is oblivious to these problems. For a colonized people the most essential value, because the most concrete, is first and foremost the land: the land which will bring them bread and, above all, dignity. But this dignity has nothing to do with the dignity of the human individual: for that human individual has never heard tell of it. All that the native has seen in his country is that they can freely arrest him, beat him, starve him: and no professor of ethics, no priest has ever come to be beaten in his place, nor to share their bread with him. As far as the native is concerned, morality is very concrete; it is to silence the settler's defiance, to break his flaunting violence—in a word, to put him out of the picture. The well-known principle that all men are equal will be illustrated in the colonies from the moment that the native claims that he is the equal of the settler. One step more, and he is ready to fight to be more than the settler. In fact, he has already decided to eject him and to take his place; as we see it, it is a whole material and moral universe which is breaking up. The intellectual who for his part has followed the colonialist with regard to the universal abstract will fight in order that the settler and the native may live together in peace in a new world. But the thing he does not see, precisely because he is permeated by colonialism and all its ways of thinking, is that the settler, from the moment that the colonial context disappears, has no longer any interest in remaining or in co-existing. It is not by chance that, even before any negotiation* between the Algerian and French governments has taken place, the European minority which calls itself "liberal" has already made its position clear: it demands nothing more nor less than twofold citizenship. By setting themselves apart in an abstract manner, the liberals try to force the settler into taking a very concrete jump into the unknown. Let us admit it, the settler knows perfectly well that no phraseology can be a substitute for reality.

---

* Fanon is writing in 1961.—*Trans.*

Thus the native discovers that his life, his breath, his beating heart are the same as those of the settler. He finds out that the settler's skin is not of any more value than a native's skin; and it must be said that this discovery shakes the world in a very necessary manner. All the new, revolutionary assurance of the native stems from it. For if, in fact, my life is worth as much as the settler's, his glance no longer shrivels me up nor freezes me, and his voice no longer turns me into stone. I am no longer on tenterhooks in his presence; in fact, I don't give a damn for him. Not only does his presence no longer trouble me, but I am already preparing such efficient ambushes for him that soon there will be no way out but that of flight.

We have said that the colonial context is characterized by the dichotomy which it imposes upon the whole people. Decolonization unifies that people by the radical decision to remove from it its heterogeneity, and by unifying it on a national, sometimes a racial, basis. We know the fierce words of the Senegalese patriots, referring to the maneuvers of their president, Senghor: "We have demanded that the higher posts should be given to Africans; and now Senghor is Africanizing the Europeans." That is to say that the native can see clearly and immediately if decolonization has come to pass or not, for his minimum demands are simply that the last shall be first.

But the native intellectual brings variants to this petition, and, in fact, he seems to have good reasons: higher civil servants, technicians, specialists—all seem to be needed. Now, the ordinary native interprets these unfair promotions as so many acts of sabotage, and he is often heard to declare: "It wasn't worth while, then, our becoming independent . . ."

In the colonial countries where a real struggle for freedom has taken place, where the blood of the people has flowed and where the length of the period of armed warfare has favored the backward surge of intellectuals toward bases grounded in the people, we can observe a genuine eradication of the superstructure built by these intellectuals from the bourgeois colonialist environment. The colonialist bourgeoisie, in its narcissistic dialogue, expounded by the members of its universities, had in fact deeply implanted in the minds of the colonized intellectual that the essential qualities remain eternal in spite of all the blunders men may make: the essential qualities of the West, of course. The native intellectual accepted the cogency of these ideas, and deep down in his brain you could always find a vigilant sentinel ready to defend the Greco-Latin pedestal. Now it so happens that during the struggle for liberation, at the moment that the native intellectual comes into touch again with his people, this artificial sentinel is turned into dust. All the Mediterranean values—the triumph of the human individual, of clarity, and of beauty—become lifeless, colorless knickknacks. All those speeches seem like collections of dead words; those values which seemed to uplift the soul are revealed as worthless, simply because they have nothing to do with the concrete conflict in which the people is engaged.

Individualism is the first to disappear. The native intellectual had learnt from his masters that the individual ought to express himself fully. The colonialist bourgeoisie had hammered into the native's mind the idea of a society of individuals where each person shuts himself up in his own subjectivity, and whose only wealth is individual thought. Now the native who has the opportunity to return to the people during the struggle for freedom will discover the falseness of this theory. The very forms of organization of the struggle will suggest to him a different vocabulary. Brother, sister, friend—these are words outlawed by the colonialist bourgeoisie, because for them my brother is my purse, my friend is part of my scheme for getting on. The native intellectual takes part, in a sort of auto-da-fé, in the destruction of all his idols: egoism, recrimination that springs from pride, and the childish stupidity of those who always want to have the last word. Such a colonized intellectual, dusted over by colonial culture, will in the same way discover the substance of village assemblies, the cohesion of people's committees, and the extraordinary fruitfulness of local meetings and groupments. Henceforward, the interests of one will be the interests of all, for in concrete fact *everyone* will be massacred—or *everyone* will be saved. The motto "look out for yourself," the atheist's method of salvation, is in this context forbidden.

Self-criticism has been much talked about of late, but few people realize that it is an African institution. Whether in the djemaas* of northern Africa or in the meetings of western Africa, tradition demands that the quarrels which occur in a village should be settled in public. It is communal self-criticism, of course, and with a note of humor, because everybody is relaxed, and because in the last resort we all want the same things. But the more the intellectual imbibes the atmosphere of the people, the more completely he abandons the habits of calculation, of unwonted silence, of mental reservations, and shakes off the spirit of concealment. And it is true that already at that level we can say that the community triumphs, and that it spreads its own light and its own reason.

But it so happens sometimes that decolonization occurs in areas which have not been sufficiently shaken by the struggle for liberation, and there may be found those same know-all, smart, wily intellectuals. We find intact in them the manners and forms of thought picked up during their association with the colonialist bourgeoisie. Spoilt children of yesterday's colonialism and of today's national governments, they organize the loot of whatever national resources exist. Without pity, they use today's national distress as a means of getting on through scheming and legal robbery, by import-export combines, limited liability companies, gambling on the stock exchange, or unfair promotion. They are insistent in their demands for the nationalization of commerce, that is to say the reservation of markets and advantageous bargains for nationals only. As far as doctrine is concerned, they proclaim the pressing necessity of nationalizing the robbery of the nation. In this arid phase of national life, the so-called period of austerity the success of their depredations is swift to call forth the violence and anger of the people. For this same people, poverty-stricken yet independent, comes very quickly to possess a social conscience in the African and international context of today; and this the petty individualists will quickly learn.

In order to assimilate and to experience the oppressor's culture, the native has had to leave certain of his intellectual possessions in pawn. These pledges include his adoption of the forms of thought of the colonialist bourgeoisie. This is very noticeable in the inaptitude of the native intellectual to carry on a two-sided discussion; for he cannot eliminate himself when confronted with an object or an idea. On the other hand, when once he begins to militate among the people he is struck with wonder and amazement; he is literally disarmed by their good faith and honesty. The danger that will haunt him continually is that of becoming the uncritical mouthpiece of the masses; he becomes a kind of yes-man who nods assent at every word coming from the people, which he interprets as considered judgments. Now, the *fellah*, the unemployed man, the starving native do not lay a claim to the truth, they do not *say* that they represent the truth, for they *are* the truth.

Objectively, the intellectual behaves in this phase like a common opportunist. In fact he has not stopped maneuvering. There is never fact question of his being either rejected or welcomed by the people. What they ask is simply that all resources should be pooled. The inclusion of the native intellectual in the upward surge of the masses will in this case be differentiated by a curious cult of detail. That is not to say that the people are hostile to analysis; on the contrary, they like having things explained to them, they are glad to understand a line of argument and they like to see where they are going. But at the beginning of his association with the people the native intellectual over-stresses details and thereby comes to forget that the defeat of colonialism is the real object of the struggle. Carried away by the multitudinous aspects of the fight, he tends to concentrate on local tasks, performed with enthusiasm but almost always too

---

* Village assemblies.—*Trans.*

solemnly. He fails to see the whole of the movement all the time. He introduces the idea of special disciplines, of specialized functions, of departments within the terrible stone crusher, the fierce mixing machine which a popular revolution is. He is occupied in action on a particular front, and it so happens that he lose sight of the unity of the movement. Thus, is a local defeat is inflicted, he may well be drawn into doubt, and from thence to despair. The people, on the other hand, take their stand from the start on the broad and inclusive positions of *bread and the land*: how can we obtain the land, and bread to eat? And this obstinate point of view of the masses, which may seem shrunken and limited, is in the end the most worthwhile and the most efficient mode of procedure.

The problem of truth ought also to be considered. In every age, among the people, truth is the property of the national cause. No absolute verity, no discourse on the purity of the soul, can shake this position. The native replies to the living lie of the colonial situation by an equal falsehood. His dealings with his fellow-nationals are open; they are strained and incomprehensible with regard to the settlers. Truth is that which hurries on the break-up of the colonialist regime; it is that which promotes the emergence of the nation; it is all that protects the natives, and ruins the foreigners. In this colonialist context there is no truthful behavior: and the good is quite simply that which is evil for "them."

Thus we see that the primary Manicheism which governed colonial society is preserved intact during the period of decolonization; that is to say that the settler never ceases to be the enemy, the opponent, the foe that must be overthrown. The oppressor, in his own sphere, starts the process, a process of domination, of exploitation and of pillage, and in the other sphere the coiled, plundered creature which is the native provides fodder for the process as best he can, the process which moves uninterruptedly from the banks of the colonial territory to the palaces and the docks of the mother country. In this becalmed zone the sea has a smooth surface, the palm tree stirs gently in the breeze, the waves lap against the pebbles, and raw materials are ceaselessly transported, justifying the presence of the settler: and all the while the native, bent double, more dead than alive, exists interminably in an unchanging dream. The settler makes history; his life is an epoch, an Odyssey. He is the absolute beginning: "This land was created by us"; he is the unceasing cause: "If we leave, all is lost, and the country will go back to the Middle Ages." Over against him torpid creatures, wasted by fevers, obsessed by ancestral customs, form an almost inorganic background for the innovating dynamism of colonial mercantilism.

The settler makes history and is conscious of making it. And because he constantly refers to the history of his which mother country, he clearly indicates that he himself is the extension of that mother country. Thus the history which he writes is not the history of the country which he plunders but the history of his own nation in regard to all that she skims off, all that she violates and starves.

The immobility to which the native is condemned can only be called in question if the native decides to put an end to the history of colonization—the history of pillage—and to bring into existence the history of the nation—the history of decolonization.

A world divided into compartments, a motionless, Manicheistic world, a world of statues: the statue of the general who carried out the conquest, the statue of the engineer who built the bridge; a world which is sure of itself, which crushes with its stones the backs flayed by whips: this is the colonial world. The native is a being hemmed in; apartheid is simply one form of the division into compartments of the colonial world. The first thing which the native learns is to stay in his place, and not to go beyond certain limits. This is why the dreams of the native are always of muscular prowess; his dreams are of action and of aggression. I dream I am jumping, swimming, running, climbing; I dream that I burst out laughing, that I span a river in one stride, or that I am followed by a flood of motorcars which never catch up with me. During the period of colonization, the native never stops achieving his freedom from nine in the evening until six in the morning.

The colonized man will first manifest this aggressiveness which has been deposited in his bones against his own people. This is the period when the niggers beat each other up, and the police and magistrates do not know which way to turn when faced with the astonishing waves of crime in North Africa. We shall see later how this phenomenon should be judged.* When the native is confronted with the colonial order of things, he finds he is in a state of permanent tension. The settler's world is a hostile world, which spurns the native, but at the same time it is a world of which he is envious. We have seen that the native never ceases to dream of putting himself in the place of the settler—not of becoming the settler but of substituting himself for the setter. This hostile world, ponderous and aggressive because it fends off the colonized masses with all the harshness it is capable of, represents not merely a hell from which the swiftest flight possible is desirable, but also a paradise close at hand which is guarded by terrible watchdogs.

The native is always on the alert, for since he can only make out with difficulty the many symbols of the colonial world, he is never sure whether or not he has crossed the frontier. Confronted with a world ruled by the settler, the native is always presumed guilty. But the native's guilt is never a guilt which he accepts; it is rather a kind of curse, a sort of sword of Damocles, for, in his innermost spirit, the native admits no accusation. He is overpowered but not tamed; he is treated as an inferior but he is not convinced of his inferiority. He is patiently waiting until the settler is off his guard to fly at him. The native's muscle are always tensed. You can't say that he is terrorized, even apprehensive. He is in fact ready at a moment's notice to exchange the role of the quarry for that of the hunter. The native is an oppressed person whose permanent dream is to become the persecutor. The symbols of social order—the police, the bugle calls in the barracks, military parades and the waving flags—are at one and the same time inhibitory and stimulating: for they do not convey the message "Don't dare to budge"; rather, they cry out "Get ready to attack." And, in fact, if the native had any tendency to fall asleep and to forget, the settler's hauteur and the settler's anxiety to test the strength of the colonial system would remind him at every turn that the great showdown cannot be put off indefinitely. That impulse to take the settler's place implies a tonicity of muscles the whole time; and in fact we know that in certain emotional conditions the presence of an obstacle accentuates the tendency toward motion.

The settler-native relationship is a mass relationship. The settler pits brute force against the weight of numbers? He is an exhibitionist. His preoccupation with security makes him remind the native out loud that there he alone is master. The settler keeps alive In the native an anger which he deprives of outlet; the native is trapped in the tight links of the chains of colonialism. But we have seen that inwardly the settler can only achieve a pseudo petrification. The native's muscular tension finds outlet regularly in bloodthirsty explosions—in tribal warfare, in feuds between septs, and in quarrels between individuals.

Where individuals are concerned, a positive negation of common sense is evident While the settler or the policeman has the right the livelong day to strike the native, to insult him and to make him crawl to them, you will see the native reaching for his knife at the slightest hostile or aggressive glance cast on him by another native; for the last resort of the native is to defend his personality vis-à-vis his brother. Tribal feuds only serve to perpetuate old grudges buried deep in the memory. By throwing himself with all his force into the vendetta, the native tries to persuade himself that colonialism does not exist, that everything is going on as before, that history continues. Here on the level of communal organizations

---

* See the section: "Colonial War and Mental Disorders."

we clearly discern the well-known behavior patterns of avoidance. It is as if plunging into a fraternal bloodbath allowed them to ignore the obstacle, and to put off till later the choice, nevertheless inevitable, which opens up the question of armed resistance to colonialism. Thus collective autodestruction in a very concrete form is one of the ways in which the native's muscular tension is set free. All these patterns of conduct are those of the death reflex when faced with danger, a suicidal behavior which proves to the settler (whose existence and domination is by them all the more justified) that these men are not reasonable human beings. In the same way the native manages by-pass the settler. A belief in fatality removes all blame from the oppressor; the cause of misfortunes and of poverty is attributed to God: He is Fate. In this way the individual accepts the disintegration ordained by God, bows down before the settler and his lot, and by a kind of interior restabilization acquires a stony calm.

Meanwhile, however, life goes on, and the native will strengthen the inhibitions which contain his aggressiveness by drawing on the terrifying myths which are so frequently found in underdeveloped communities. There are maleficent spirits which intervene every time a step is taken in the wrong direction, leopard-men, serpent-men, six-legged dogs, zombies—a whole series of tiny animals or giants which create around the native a world of prohibitions, of barriers and of inhibitions far more terrifying than the world of the settler. This magical superstructure which permeates native society fulfills certain well-defined functions in the dynamism of the libido. One of the characteristics of underdeveloped societies is in fact that the libido is first and foremost the concern of a group, or of the family. The feature of communities whereby a man who dreams that he has sexual relations with a woman other than his own must confess it in public and pay a fine in kind or in working days to the injured husband or family is fully described by ethnologists. We may note in passing that this proves that the so-called prehistoric societies attach great importance to the unconscious.

The atmosphere of myth and magic frightens me and so takes on an undoubted reality. By terrifying me, it integrates me in the traditions and the history of my district or of my tribe, and at the same time it reassures me, it gives me a status, as it were an identification paper. In underdeveloped countries the occult sphere is a sphere belonging to the community which is entirely under magical jurisdiction. By entangling myself in this inextricable network where actions are repeated with crystalline inevitability, I find the everlasting world which belongs to

STUDY QUESTIONS

1. How did Fanon articulate that violence is the means by which the oppressed must gain freedom?

2. Is the use of violence ever legitimate as a way toward independence or to remedy disenfranchisement and grievances?

3. Do you think that the use of terrorism by the people is the moral equivalent to the use of torture by the state?

4. How does psychoanalysis relate to colonialism?

Speech, September 15, 1956

I n Egypt in the early 1880s, a British protectorate was established, to the chagrin of the French, who had recently completed the Suez Canal in 1869 while vying for the mandate. The canal allowed ships to pass between Europe and Asia, cutting hundreds of miles off of voyages. When the *khedive*, or local ruler, had been forced to sell his shares of the canal due to bankruptcy in 1875, the British prime minister, Benjamin Disraeli, bought them up for Queen Victoria. Control of the canal by the British meant not only greater intercontinental commercial activity, but also strategic oversight over a new gateway to India. Such justifications would lead Britain to greater imperial expansion in Africa after 1882. From that year, when an anti-European movement was suppressed, the British would govern Egypt until 1922, but occupied it until 1956. It took a post–Second World War crisis in the region to reveal an empire on the wane.

Colonel Gamal Abdel Nasser (1918–1970) emerged as president of Egypt in 1956, after a coup four years earlier had ousted the monarchy. As a charter member of the Arab League, which had been founded in 1945, an independent Egypt, divested of 19th-century British and French incursions, flexed its political muscle against 20th-century British and American hegemony in the Suez Canal crisis of 1956.

The origins of the Suez crisis had to do with Soviet-procured Czechoslovakian arms that had been dealt to Egypt in 1955. Fearing the pernicious effects of Communism, Washington and London offered Nasser funding for the building of the Aswan Dam. When Nasser hesitated to accept, the offer was rescinded from the table. In retaliation, Nasser nationalized the Suez Canal on July 26, 1956, after British troops had returned home. Events escalated to the point where British, French, and Israeli troops were mobilized to Port Said by the end of the year to overthrow Nasser. Sir Anthony Eden, the British prime minister during the affair, reputedly wanted Nasser murdered. Whether that was figurative or literal language, from the United States' perspective, cooler heads should prevail, particularly in case Egypt and other Arab states ran to the arms of the Soviet Union. President Dwight D. Eisenhower and Secretary

Figure 17.1. Gamal Abdel Nasser. Source: http://commons.wikimedia.org/wiki/File:Gamal-002.jpg.

of State John Foster Dulles threatened their bellicose allies with economic deprivations, forcing their withdrawal and handover to United Nations forces. Only then did the United States support a bailout coordinated through the International Monetary Fund, which allowed Harold Macmillan, then chancellor of the exchequer, to avoid devaluing the British pound and subsequent financial catastrophe.

The Suez crisis, therefore, exemplified Britain's diminution as a colonial power as well as a world power and its increasing dependence on the United States in the era of Cold War politics, economics, and militarism. As Eden shrewdly observed, Suez illuminated certain realities. Soon after, Britain removed its presence from Jordan and Iraq in the late 1950s, and British diplomatic supremacy in Middle Eastern affairs was coming to a close. For his part, Nasser was hailed as a hero throughout the region for thwarting the foreign yoke of the imperialists in the name of Arab nationalism.

Speech, September 15, 1956

By Gamal Abdel Nasser

THE SUEZ CANAL: EGYPT'S POLICY

Delivered at Air Force Graduation, Bilbeis, Egypt, September 15, 1956:

In these decisive days in the history of mankind, these days in which truth struggles to have itself recognized in international chaos where powers of evil domination and imperialism have prevailed Egypt stands firmly to preserve her sovereignty. Your country stands solidly and stanchly to preserve her dignity against imperialistic schemes of a number of nations who have uncovered their desires for domination and supremacy.

In these days and in such circumstances Egypt has resolved to show the world that when small nations decide to preserve their sovereignty, they will do that all right and that when these small nations are fully determined to defend their rights and maintain their dignity, they will undoubtedly succeed in achieving their ends.

We are now hearing saber-rattling in Britain and France, those big powers which aim at derogating Egypt from sovereignty. I declare in the name of the Egyptian people who have smashed the fetters of foreign domination, aggression and feudalism that we are fully determined to defend our sovereign rights and preserve our dignity.

Conspiracies and threats attempted by the big powers will never intimidate us. We believe in our sovereign rights and we shall never allow imperialists to derogate them from us. These are objectives which we have proclaimed since the inception of the revolution. We shall never falter or be terrified by threats. We stick firmly to these principles and objectives and we shall defend them to the last drop of our blood.

I am speaking in the name of every Egyptian Arab and in the name of all free countries and of all those who believe in liberty and are ready to defend it. I am speaking in the name of principles

Gamal Abdel Nasser, "The Suez Canal." Published in 1956 by McMurry, Inc.

proclaimed by these countries in the Atlantic Charter.[1] But they are now violating these principles and it has become our lot to shoulder the responsibility of reaffirming and establishing them anew.

Now that we have effected complete evacuation of the British forces and purged Egyptian soil of the vestiges of foreign domination, it is our divine duty to defend our free and independent country against the conspiracies and vile desires of the imperialists.

Today we have practiced one of our sovereign rights and seen attempts made to derogate from our sovereignty.

Selwyn Lloyd[2] declared at the London conference that we are living in an age in which a sovereign country may surrender some of her rights. But I believe this can be done only by countries practicing their sovereignty as well as that of other countries. A country that wishes to be really free and independent and that will not infringe on the sovereignty of others will practice its sovereign rights by itself and will never transcend them.

Egypt is now a sovereign country which will never transgress against other countries and she is fully determined never to allow others to infringe on her sovereignty. On Aug. 2, Britain, the United States and France called for a conference which they labeled a conference on internationalization of the Suez Canal.

They alleged Egypt could derive no benefits from the canal. Previously they denied us loans and financial aid necessary for the High Dam project and they seemed bent on depriving Egypt of benefits she could derive from the canal to raise the standard of living of her people. The British Premier declared, "all our trouble is with Gamal Abdel Nasser," for naturally Eden is not interested in seeing a glorious and powerful army in Egypt.

What does all this amount to? They are determined to frustrate Egyptian attempts at progress and industrialization. Economic pressure has been applied against Egypt to stifle the progress of her people and reduce them to submission. But I am fully aware we shall never submit to pressure or threats and that we can rely on our own resources and efforts.

Then came the London conference to which certain states were invited and where a number of resolutions were laid down with the concurrence of some of the states invited. This was followed by a visit to Egypt of the five-power commission headed by [Robert Gordon] Menzies [Prime Minister of Australia] who declared he had come to reach an understanding with Egypt—an understanding under the threat of aggression and use of force.

We have tried by all possible means to cooperate with those countries which claim to assist smaller nations and which promised to collaborate with us but they demanded their fees in advance. This we refused so they started to fight with us. They said they will pay toward building the High Dam and then they withdrew their offer and cast doubts on the Egyptian economy. Are we to disclaim our sovereign right? Egypt insists her sovereignty must remain intact and refuses to give up any part of that sovereignty for the sake of money.

Egypt nationalized the Egyptian Suez Canal company. When Egypt granted the concession to de Lesseps it was stated in the concession between the Egyptian Government and the Egyptian company that the company of the Suez Canal is an Egyptian company subject to Egyptian authority. Egypt nationalized this Egyptian company and declared freedom of navigation will be preserved.

---

1   *Editor's note*: The Atlantic Charter was a 1941 statement, drafted by the United States and Great Britain, and adopted by the United Nations, which proposed policy for peace in post-war Europe.

2   *Editor's note*: Lloyd was the British Foreign Secretary.

But the imperialists became angry. Britain and France said Egypt grabbed the Suez Canal as if it were part of France or Britain. The British Foreign Secretary forgot that only two years ago he signed an agreement staring the Suez Canal is an integral part of Egypt.

Egypt declared she was ready to negotiate. But as soon as negotiations began threats and intimidations started.

Yesterday many ships arrived and for the first time in years fifty ships were piloted through the canal. The canal authority has today seventy Egyptian pilots. These Egyptian and Greek pilots who refused bribery and temptation worked day and night and were able to maintain navigation in the canal. As I speak to you now the canal, thanks to Egyptian and Greek pilots, is still open. We have succeeded in foiling a conspiracy of Britain, France and the pilots and we have proved to the world when a nation wants to preserve its freedom, it will be free.

Today in the name of the Egyptian people, in the name of each one of you, I honor those men by granting them the Egyptian Order of Merit.

Today we have won a battle of conspiracy and treachery. Today conspirators in moral and international anarchy have been defeated. Today as we win this battle through perseverance and will power we go forward to attain victories in other fields. Today we must defeat forces that are trying to mislead world public opinion.

Great powers are struck with the fever of greed, but we will nevertheless preserve our rights.

Eden stated in the House of Commons there shall be no discrimination between states using the canal. We on our part reaffirm that and declare there is no discrimination between canal users. He also said Egypt shall not be allowed to succeed because that would spell success for Arab nationalism and would be against their policy, which aims at the protection of Israel.

Today they are speaking of a new association whose main objective would be to rob Egypt of the canal and deprive her of rightful canal dues. Suggestions made by Eden in the House of Commons which have been backed by France and the United States are a clear violation of the 1888 convention, since it is impossible to have two bodies organizing navigation in the canal.

It is equally impossible for the proposed organization to remain abroad and continue to collect dues. If this were permissible we for our part would form an organization for users of the port of London—a situation which would spell international anarchy and the end of international law and relations.

We instructed our Ambassador to Washington to tell America's Foreign Secretary that America is helping Britain excite people in Egypt and engage them in a new war. The American President has been speaking of maintaining peace, so why does America support this proposal for the formation of an association which they call an association for users of the canal but which is in truth one for declaring war?

If the big powers are using threats to derogate from our independence we will have them know we happen to believe in this independence and that what we have done is purely within our sovereign rights. What users of the canal have a right to is free passage through the canal and this we guarantee.

They are threatening to use force against us. But we are fully determined never to surrender any of our rights. We shall resist any aggression and fight against those who attempt to derogate from our sovereignty.

By stating that by succeeding Abdel Nasser would weaken Britain's stand against Arab nationalism, Eden is in fact admitting his real objective is not Abdel Nasser as such but rather to defeat Arab nationalism and crush its cause. Eden speaks and finds his own answer. A month ago he let out the cry that he was after Abdel Nasser. Today the Egyptian people are fully conscious of their sovereign rights and Arab nationalism is fully awakened to its new destiny.

Then they claim they wish to apply such and such clauses of the 1888 convention. But Egypt has been executing provisions of the 1888 convention throughout past years till the present day. Between 1888 and 1956 ships have been sailing through the canal and paying dues to a body responsible for its administration. Ships had always abided by measures and regulations imposed by the canal company.

Of 8,000,000 Algerians, 10,000 are fighting half a million French soldiers. We have arms sufficient to equip those who can fight. We shall fight aggressors.

Those who attack Egypt will never leave Egypt alive. We shall fight a regular war, a total war, a guerrilla war. Those who attack Egypt will soon realize they brought disaster upon themselves. He who attacks Egypt attacks the whole Arab world. They say in their papers the whole thing will be over in forty-eight hours. They do not know how strong we really are.

We believe in international law. But we will never submit. We shall show the world how a small country can stand in the face of great powers threatening with armed might. Egypt might be a small power but she is great inasmuch as she has faith in her power and convictions. I feel quite certain every. Egyptian shares the same convictions as I do and believes in everything I am stressing now.

We shall defend our freedom and independence to the last drop of our blood. This is the stanch feeling of every Egyptian. The whole Arab nation will stand by us in our common fight against aggression and domination. Free peoples, too, people who are really free will stand by us and support us against the forces of tyranny.

Today we are victorious while we are serving every nation of the world. We are serving countries like India and Indonesia and we are victorious while we contribute toward world prosperity and development of world trade.

This we have achieved by the efforts of Egyptian citizens who are working day and night so navigation in the canal will go on uninterrupted and even better than it ever was before.

Today we are going forward armed with our belief in God, with our patriotism and with our self-confidence to attain for Egypt its dignity, freedom and honor.

STUDY QUESTIONS

1. What is the significance of Nasser's nationalization of the Suez Canal?

2. Why was his rhetoric in this speech applauded by the Arab world? What does it have to do with imperialism?

PART VIII
SOVEREIGNTY

The Declaration of Independence

W e all learned in high school that "No Taxation without Representation" was the rallying cry of the American Revolution.[1] As a result of the budgetary necessities of the French and Indian War, the colonies were prepared to contribute to the exchequer a share of their prosperity and viewed themselves fully as British subjects, yet they wanted their interests to be given greater attention in Parliament. This lack of representation made the imperial levies on goods such as paper or tea all the more egregious. Even after hostilities between the two sides had begun, soldiers in the Continental Army initially understood themselves to be fighting for their rights as free Englishmen, and eventually transformed the rebellion into a drive for severance of the ties with Great Britain.

The ideology of the American Revolution derived its origins from Europe. Freedom of the individual from tyranny of the state and the misuses of power by a monarch were fundamental themes. Radical colonists began to display disaffection with their increasingly burdensome status as British subjects, articulated by a class of urbanized professionals and an intellectual community comprised of pamphleteers and essayists such as Thomas Paine, whose tract, *Common Sense*, gave voice to their frustrations. Directly influential in shaping the political philosophy of the revolutionaries were the ideas and attitudes of 17th- and 18th-century Enlightenment thinkers. Colonial American writers cited Locke and Rousseau on natural rights and the social contract, respectively, Montesquieu on the system of checks and balances, and Voltaire on the evils of religious oppression.

Some historians have argued that the American Revolution, in contrast to the French, was not a revolution in the sense that the social and economic order was uprooted and restructured by a Third Estate, but a struggle solely for political rights. Rather than the overthrow of all elites, within this narrative, the goal of the American War of Independence was the attainment and preservation of political liberty that had been thwarted by tyranny. The abusive monarchical power of George III infringed on

---

1   What's up, Mr. Wilson!

Figure 18.1. Thomas Jefferson. Source: http://commons.wikimedia.org/wiki/File:Thomas_Jefferson_by_Mather_Brown.jpg.

those rights and that liberty across the Atlantic Ocean. Colonists opposed arbitrary and excessive taxation, a standing British army, impressment, and basically any military power unchecked by civil power.

A constitution would be one such check, by engendering a political culture of laws and institutions. The American Revolution was, in essence, a middle-class revolution of artisans, planters, merchants, and scholars—the privileged few who would run the new country—fomented by their ideas about governmental responsibility. Men such as George Washington, Thomas Jefferson, John Adams, James Madison, and Benjamin Franklin became adherents to republicanism, a system of government with no monarch and the preeminence above all else of the sovereignty of the states, vested ultimately in the people. A law-making representative body would thus be held accountable to the citizenry through the electoral process. Indeed, the Declaration excluded many; only white male citizens could vote and hold office with property qualifications. Slaves, Indians, the poor, and women were all disenfranchised. No state constitution bestowed female suffrage except New Jersey, and it was revoked shortly after the turn of the 19th century.

The Second Continental Congress, which convened in Carpenters' Hall in Philadelphia, decided to hold a referendum on the question of independence during the summer of 1776. The committee assigned to draft a document was comprised of Jefferson, Franklin, Adams, New York solicitor Robert Livingston, and Connecticut businessman Roger Sherman. As chairman, the 33-year-old Jefferson (1743–1826) was selected to write the Declaration, but he had editorial aid from Franklin, who conveniently lived a block from where the Virginian was staying in the "City of Brotherly Love." A significant change from Franklin's quill was the replacement of Jefferson's "We hold these truths to be sacred and undeniable" with, "We hold these truths to be self-evident."[2] Adams provided some amendments as well.

One of the most important pieces of writing in history, the Declaration of Independence directly addresses the king's abuse of power. Echoing Enlightenment tenets, Jefferson emphasizes that the people can only be governed with their consent. On July 2, 1776, after some debate the 13-colony Congress voted unanimously for independence (proclaimed July 4), a treasonous act against the empire. Upon hearing the Declaration read aloud a few days later, a raucous mob in New York City brought down a statue of George III and beheaded it.

---

2   Walter Isaacson, *Benjamin Franklin: An American Life* (New York: Simon & Schuster Paperbacks, 2004), 312. For other more minor alterations, see ibid.

When the chamber reviewed the slaveholding Jefferson's Declaration, entire portions were excised, including a criticism of the British slave trade. Other passages deemed verbose were removed so as not to dilute the contents' powerful message, but stung his pride all the same. If the man who would become the third president of the United States could have only known the vast extent to which his words have been embraced and immortalized by revolutionaries who have striven for liberty ever since, Jefferson's hurt feelings might have been assuaged.

The Declaration of Independence: A Transcription

By Thomas Jefferson

IN CONGRESS, July 4, 1776.

The unanimous Declaration of the thirteen united States of America,

When in the Course of human events, it becomes necessary for one people to dissolve the political bands which have connected them with another, and to assume among the powers of the earth, the separate and equal station to which the Laws of Nature and of Nature's God entitle them, a decent respect to the opinions of mankind requires that they should declare the causes which impel them to the separation.

We hold these truths to be self-evident, that all men are created equal, that they are endowed by their Creator with certain unalienable Rights, that among these are Life, Liberty and the pursuit of Happiness.—That to secure these rights, Governments are instituted among Men, deriving their just powers from the consent of the governed, —That whenever any Form of Government becomes destructive of these ends, it is the Right of the People to alter or to abolish it, and to institute new Government, laying its foundation on such principles and organizing its powers in such form, as to them shall seem most likely to effect their Safety and Happiness. Prudence, indeed, will dictate that Governments long established should not be changed for light and transient causes; and accordingly all experience hath shewn, that mankind are more disposed to suffer, while evils are sufferable, than to right themselves by abolishing the forms to which they are accustomed. But when a long train of abuses and usurpations, pursuing invariably the same Object evinces a design to reduce them under absolute Despotism, it is their right, it is their duty, to throw off such Government, and to provide new Guards for their future security.—Such has been the patient sufferance of these Colonies; and such is now the necessity which constrains them to alter their former Systems of Government. The history of the present King of Great Britain is a history of repeated injuries and usurpations, all having in direct object the establishment of an absolute Tyranny over these States. To prove this, let Facts be submitted to a candid world.

Thomas Jefferson, "The Declaration of Independence," 1776.

He has refused his Assent to Laws, the most wholesome and necessary for the public good.

He has forbidden his Governors to pass Laws of immediate and pressing importance, unless suspended in their operation till his Assent should be obtained; and when so suspended, he has utterly neglected to attend to them. He has refused to pass other Laws for the accommodation of large districts of people, unless those people would relinquish the right of Representation in the Legislature, a right inestimable to them and formidable to tyrants only.

He has called together legislative bodies at places unusual, uncomfortable, and distant from the depository of their public Records, for the sole purpose of fatiguing them into compliance with his measures.

He has dissolved Representative Houses repeatedly, for opposing with manly firmness his invasions on the rights of the people.

He has refused for a long time, after such dissolutions, to cause others to be elected; whereby the Legislative powers, incapable of Annihilation, have returned to the People at large for their exercise; the State remaining in the mean time exposed to all the dangers of invasion from without, and convulsions within.

He has endeavoured to prevent the population of these States; for that purpose obstructing the Laws for Naturalization of Foreigners; refusing to pass others to encourage their migrations hither, and raising the conditions of new Appropriations of Lands.

He has obstructed the Administration of Justice, by refusing his Assent to Laws for establishing Judiciary powers.

He has made Judges dependent on his Will alone, for the tenure of their offices, and the amount and payment of their salaries.

He has erected a multitude of New Offices, and sent hither swarms of Officers to harrass our people, and eat out their substance.

He has kept among us, in times of peace, Standing Armies without the Consent of our legislatures.

He has affected to render the Military independent of and superior to the Civil power.

He has combined with others to subject us to a jurisdiction foreign to our constitution, and unacknowledged by our laws; giving his Assent to their Acts of pretended Legislation:

For Quartering large bodies of armed troops among us:

For protecting them, by a mock Trial, from punishment for any Murders which they should commit on the Inhabitants of these States:

For cutting off our Trade with all parts of the world:

For imposing Taxes on us without our Consent:

For depriving us in many cases, of the benefits of Trial by Jury:

For transporting us beyond Seas to be tried for pretended offences

For abolishing the free System of English Laws in a neighbouring Province, establishing therein an Arbitrary government, and enlarging its Boundaries so as to render it at once an example and fit instrument for introducing the same absolute rule into these Colonies:

For taking away our Charters, abolishing our most valuable Laws, and altering fundamentally the Forms of our Governments:

For suspending our own Legislatures, and declaring themselves invested with power to legislate for us in all cases whatsoever.

He has abdicated Government here, by declaring us out of his Protection and waging War against us.

He has plundered our seas, ravaged our Coasts, burnt our towns, and destroyed the lives of our people.

He is at this time transporting large Armies of foreign Mercenaries to compleat the works of death, desolation and tyranny, already begun with circumstances of Cruelty & perfidy scarcely paralleled in the most barbarous ages, and totally unworthy the Head of a civilized nation.

He has constrained our fellow Citizens taken Captive on the high Seas to bear Arms against their Country, to become the executioners of their friends and Brethren, or to fall themselves by their Hands.

He has excited domestic insurrections amongst us, and has endeavoured to bring on the inhabitants of our frontiers, the merciless Indian Savages, whose known rule of warfare, is an undistinguished destruction of all ages, sexes and conditions.

In every stage of these Oppressions We have Petitioned for Redress in the most humble terms: Our repeated Petitions have been answered only by repeated injury. A Prince whose character is thus marked by every act which may define a Tyrant, is unfit to be the ruler of a free people.

Nor have We been wanting in attentions to our Brittish brethren. We have warned them from time to time of attempts by their legislature to extend an unwarrantable jurisdiction over us. We have reminded them of the circumstances of our emigration and settlement here. We have appealed to their native justice and magnanimity, and we have conjured them by the ties of our common kindred to disavow these usurpations, which, would inevitably interrupt our connections and correspondence. They too have been deaf to the voice of justice and of consanguinity. We must, therefore, acquiesce in the necessity, which denounces our Separation, and hold them, as we hold the rest of mankind, Enemies in War, in Peace Friends.

We, therefore, the Representatives of the united States of America, in General Congress, Assembled, appealing to the Supreme Judge of the world for the rectitude of our intentions, do, in the Name, and by Authority of the good People of these Colonies, solemnly publish and declare, That these United Colonies are, and of Right ought to be Free and Independent States; that they are Absolved from all Allegiance to the British Crown, and that all political connection between them and the State of Great Britain, is and ought to be totally dissolved; and that as Free and Independent States, they have full Power to levy War, conclude Peace, contract Alliances, establish Commerce, and to do all other Acts and Things which Independent States may of right do. And for the support of this Declaration, with a firm reliance on the protection of divine Providence, we mutually pledge to each other our Lives, our Fortunes and our sacred Honor.

The 56 signatures on the Declaration appear in the positions indicated:

Column 1
Georgia:
   Button Gwinnett
   Lyman Hall
   George Walton

Column 2
North Carolina:
   William Hooper
   Joseph Hewes
   John Penn
South Carolina:
   Edward Rutledge
   Thomas Heyward, Jr.
   Thomas Lynch, Jr.
   Arthur Middleton

Column 3
Massachusetts:
   John Hancock
Maryland:
   Samuel Chase
   William Paca
   Thomas Stone
   Charles Carroll of Carrollton
Virginia:
   George Wythe
   Richard Henry Lee
   Thomas Jefferson

Benjamin Harrison
Thomas Nelson, Jr.
Francis Lightfoot
Lee Carter Braxton

Column 4
Pennsylvania:
   Robert Morris
   Benjamin Rush
   Benjamin Franklin
   John Morton
   George Clymer
   James Smith
   George Taylor
   James Wilson
   George Ross
Delaware:
   Caesar Rodney
   George Read
   Thomas McKean

Column 5
New York:
   William Floyd
   Philip Livingston
   Francis Lewis
   Lewis Morris
New Jersey:
   Richard Stockton

John Witherspoon
Francis Hopkinson
John Hart
Abraham Clark

Column 6
New Hampshire:
Josiah Bartlett
William Whipple
Massachusetts:
Samuel Adams
John Adams
Robert Treat Paine
Elbridge Gerry
Rhode Island:
Stephen Hopkins
William Ellery
Connecticut:
Roger Sherman
Samuel Huntington
William Williams
Oliver Wolcott
New Hampshire:
Matthew Thornton

STUDY QUESTIONS

1. What is Jefferson's most poignant theme in the Declaration of Independence?

2. This document was written as a flagrant act of defiance against the colonial authority of the British. How is it universal?

3. Do you think the United States of America still takes to heart the sentiments articulated in the Declaration?

AN INTRODUCTION TO

The Haitian Declaration of Independence

S aint-Domingue was the second colony to gain independence in the Western hemisphere after the United States, but what made the republic truly unique was that the country that became Haiti in 1804 was established by former slaves. Many of the Spanish conquistadors had moved on to loot the South American continent by the end of the 16th century, and by treaty, Spanish Santo Domingo, part of the island of Hispaniola, became French Saint-Domingue before the end of the 17th century.

As a French colony, sugar production increased, and due to the labor-intensive nature of sugar cultivation and refinement, so did the importation of African slaves. Eventually, Saint-Domingue, by sugar and coffee, became the wealthiest colony in the Western Hemisphere, as well as an important remunerative boon to a French economy suffocated by revolution. By 1789, Saint-Domingue possessed 40,000 whites, half a million African slaves, and 30,000 *gens de couleur*, or people of color, those of European and African blood.[1] Some of the *gens de couleur* and *affranchis* (freedmen of pure African blood) owned land and even slaves themselves. Many served in the colonial militaries. Most, however, were not only completely disenfranchised politically and socially, but also faced severe racial discrimination.

The French Revolution essentially began in 1789 as a class struggle by the people—the Third Estate—against the clergy and the nobility. The republican mantra of liberty, equality, and brotherhood, however, ultimately would be reserved for whites. It was in the midst of the hypocrisy of racial exclusion from the revolutionary ideals of human rights for all that the Haitian Revolution became the outgrowth of a slave revolt in the early 1790s.

The slave insurrection broke out in August 1791, and within days the sugarcane fields and refineries were set on fire, while whites who could not escape were murdered. Some slaves loyally strove to protect their masters' plantations, but most decamped. The following year, the French government sent troops

---

1   Madison Smartt Bell, *Toussaint Louverture* (New York: Vintage, 2007), p. 8.

Figure 19.1. Toussaint L'Overture. Source: http://commons.wikimedia.org/wiki/File:Général_Toussaint_Louverture.jpg.

Figure 19.2. Jean-Jacques Dessalines. Source: http://commons.wikimedia.org/wiki/File:Dessalines.jpg.

to quell the disturbances when Haitian leadership organized an army. What had begun as a rebellion for the improvement of conditions for slaves rather than outright manumission grew into a revolution as well as a race war, with atrocities and reprisals on both sides.

The top two leaders of the Haitian Revolution were Toussaint Louverture (1744–1803) and Jean-Jacques Dessalines (1758–1806). The rebels allied themselves with whichever nation could best help them attain liberty. France was at war with Spain until 1795, and freed slaves in Saint-Domingue had joined the Spanish forces on the western half of the island in the hopes of obtaining their freedom. When republican France abolished slavery and granted universal citizenship to all colonial subjects in 1794, Louverture and Dessalines supported the French and began fighting the Spanish and their British allies. The United States remained anxious that an insurrection led by slaves could spread to slaveholding American states, and refused initially to recognize diplomatic relations with a newly independent Haiti.

Although Louverture and Dessalines's forces lacked training and arms, knowing the terrain, they utilized guerrilla tactics to avoid the close-fire columned combat prevalent among European troops. Instead, the rebels ambushed European enemies from higher ground, pilfering guns and ammunition. By 1801, a decade after the fighting had begun, the Haitian rebels controlled the Spanish half of Hispaniola.

Though he fervently sought emancipation for slaves and viewed himself as ruler of Haiti, Louverture stopped short of a declaration of independence out of loyalty to France and a fear of American domination of the Caribbean. Yet, it was Dessalines rather than Louverture who presided over the defeat of the French in 1803. Despite his devotion to the republic, Louverture was arrested by Napoleon and imprisoned in a remote fortress in the French Alps, where he died.

The diminutive Corsican, it would seem, quickly forgot that it was Louverture's fealty that had kept Saint-Domingue French. When Napoleon reinstituted slavery in the French empire, the flames of rebellion were reignited. Haitian troops, along with malaria and yellow fever, decimated the remnants of the French forces. Independence was declared on January 1, 1804, and Dessalines became emperor of Haiti later that year.

The Haitian Declaration of Independence 1804

By J. J. Dessalines

THE COMMANDER IN CHIEF TO THE PEOPLE OF HAITI

Citizens:

It is not enough to have expelled the barbarians who have bloodied our land for two centuries; it is not enough to have restrained those ever-evolving factions that one after another mocked the specter of liberty that France dangled before you. We must, with one last act of national authority, forever assure the empire of liberty in the country of our birth; we must take any hope of re-enslaving us away from the inhuman government that for so long kept us in the most humiliating torpor. In the end we must live independent or die.

Independence or death ... let these sacred words unite us and be the signal of battle and of our reunion.

Citizens, my countrymen, on this solemn day I have brought together those courageous soldiers who, as liberty lay dying, spilled their blood to save it; these generals who have guided your efforts against tyranny have not yet done enough for your happiness; the French name still haunts our land.

Everything revives the memories of the cruelties of this barbarous people: our laws, our habits, our towns, everything still carries the stamp of the French. Indeed! There are still French in our island, and you believe yourself free and independent of that Republic which, it is true, has fought all the nations, but which has never defeated those who wanted to be free.

What! Victims of our [own] credulity and indulgence for 14 years; defeated not by French armies, but by the pathetic eloquence of their agents' proclamations; when will we tire of breathing the air that they breathe? What do we have in common with this nation of executioners? The difference between its cruelty and our patient moderation, its color and ours the great seas that separate us, our avenging climate, all tell us plainly that they are not our brothers, that they never will be, and that if they find refuge among us, they will plot again to trouble and divide us.

Native citizens, men, women, girls, and children, let your gaze extend on all parts of this island: look there for your spouses, your husbands, your brothers, your sisters. Indeed! Look there for your children, your suckling infants, what have they become? ... I shudder to say it ... the prey of these vultures.

Instead of these dear victims, your alarmed gaze will see only their assassins, these tigers still dripping with their blood, whose terrible presence indicts your lack of feeling and your guilty slowness in avenging them. What are you waiting for before appeasing their spirits? Remember that you had wanted your remains to rest next to those of your fathers, after you defeated tyranny; will you descend into their tombs without having avenged them? No! Their bones would reject yours.

And you, precious men, intrepid generals, who, without concern for your own pain, have revived liberty by shedding all your blood, know that you have done nothing if you do not give the nations a terrible, but just example of the vengeance that must be wrought by a people proud to have recovered its liberty and jealous to maintain it let us frighten all those who would dare try to take it from us again; let us begin with the French. Let them tremble when they approach our coast, if not from the memory of those cruelties they perpetrated here, then from the terrible resolution that we will have made to put to death anyone born French whose profane foot soils the land of liberty.

We have dared to be free, let us be thus by ourselves and for ourselves. Let us imitate the grown child: his own weight breaks the boundary that has become an obstacle to him. What people fought for us? What people wanted to gather the fruits of our labor? And what dishonorable absurdity to conquer in order to be enslaved. Enslaved?... Let us leave this description for the French; they have conquered but are no longer free.

Let us walk down another path; let us imitate those people who, extending their concern into the future, and dreading to leave an example of cowardice for posterity, preferred to be exterminated rather than lose their place as one of the world's free peoples.

Let us ensure, however, that a missionary spirit does not destroy our work; let us allow our neighbors to breathe in peace; may they live quietly under the laws that they have made for themselves, and let us not, as revolutionary firebrands, declare ourselves the lawgivers of the Caribbean, nor let our glory consist in troubling the peace of the neighboring islands. Unlike that which we inhabit, theirs has not been drenched in the innocent blood of its inhabitants; they have no vengeance to claim from the authority that protects them.

Fortunate to have never known the ideals that have destroyed us, they can only have good wishes for our prosperity.

Peace to our neighbors; but let this be our cry: "Anathama to the French name! Eternal hatred of France!"

Natives of Haiti! My happy fate was to be one day the sentinel who would watch over the idol to which you sacrifice; I have watched, sometimes fighting alone, and if I have been so fortunate as to return to your hands the sacred trust you confided to me, know that it is now your task to preserve it. In fighting for your liberty, I was working for my own happiness. Before consolidating it with laws that will guarantee your free individuality, your leaders, who I have assembled here, and I, owe you the final proof of our devotion.

Generals and you, leaders, collected here close to me for the good of our land, the day has come, the day which must make our glory, our independence, eternal.

If there could exist among us a lukewarm heart, let him distance himself and tremble to take the oath which must unite us. Let us vow to ourselves, to posterity, to the entire universe, to forever renounce

France, and to die rather than live under its domination; to fight until our last breath for the independence of our country.

And you, a people so long without good fortune, witness to the oath we take, remember that I counted on your constancy and courage when I threw myself into the career of liberty to fight the despotism and tyranny you had struggled against for 14 years. Remember that I sacrificed everything to rally to your defense; family, children, fortune, and now I am rich only with your liberty; my name has become a horror to all those who want slavery. Despots and tyrants curse the day that I was born. If ever you refused or grumbled while receiving those laws that the spirit guarding your fate dictates to me for your own good, you would deserve the fate of an ungrateful people. But I reject that awful idea; you will sustain the liberty that you cherish and support the leader who commands you. Therefore vow before me to live free and independent, and to prefer death to anything that will try to place you back in chains. Swear, finally, to pursue forever the traitors and enemies of your independence.

* * * * *

Done at the headquarters of Gonaives,[1] the first day of January 1804, the first year of independence.

The Deed of independence

Native Army

Today, January 1st 1804, the general in chief of the native army, accompanied by the generals of the army, assembled in order to take measures that will insure the good of the country;

After having told the assembled generals his true intentions, to assure forever a stable government for the natives of Haiti, the object of his greatest concern, which he has accomplished in a speech which declares to foreign powers the decision to make the country independent, and to enjoy a liberty consecrated by the blood of the people of this island; and after having gathered their responses has asked that each of the assembled generals take a vow to forever renounce France, to die rather than live under its domination, and to fight for independence until their last breath.

The generals, deeply moved by these sacred principles, after voting their unanimous attachment to the declared project of independence, have all sworn to posterity, to the universe, to forever renounce France, and to die rather than to live under its domination.

---

1 *Editor's note*: A city in northern Haiti

STUDY QUESTIONS

1. How does this document compare to the American Declaration of Independence?

2. What was the significance of the Haitian Revolution?

The Declaration of Independence of the Democratic Republic of Vietnam

After being humiliated by Nazi occupation and the collaboration of the Vichy government during the Second World War, the French sought to maintain their empire at all costs. Their presence in Vietnam was established in 1858, and France colonized the kingdom by the mid-1880s, renaming it Indochina.

The hero of the Vietnamese independence movement was Ho Chi Minh (born Nguyen That Thanh, 1890–1969), who had questioned the moral and legal legitimacy to French rule over Vietnam. While living in Paris in 1919, earning his keep as a kitchen employee at the Ritz Hotel, he even appealed to the French and American delegations of the post–First World War Peace Conference. Despite his pleas for self-government, freedom of the press, amnesty for political prisoners, and the right for the Vietnamese to attain their destiny through sovereignty and self-determination, he was ignored.

By 1920, Ho had become one of the founders of the French Communist Party because he viewed the Communists as the only group in France who cared about the colonial question. Marxist ideology, therefore, would be the vehicle to break the chains of colonial bondage and realize for the Vietnamese the French revolutionary maxim of liberty, equality, and fraternity.

During the war, Ho returned home through China to a Japanese-occupied Vietnam to foment grassroots resistance under the Vietminh (Vietnamese nationalists). Now there were two foreign occupiers with which to contend. In early September 1945, following the Japanese surrender to the Allies, Ho timely declared Vietnam's independence in Hanoi's main square. As evidentiary justification for severance of colonial ties, he cited the United States' Declaration of Independence and the French Declaration of the Rights of Man. Tensions mounted over the next year and boiled over when, in November 1946, the French navy bombarded the port of Haiphong, killing thousands of civilians. The Vietminh, fearing Hanoi would suffer the same fate, launched a preemptive attack on the French garrison there, and war was declared.

Figure 20.1. Ho Chi Minh. Source: http://commons.wikimedia.org/wiki/File:Ho_Chi_Minh_1946.jpg.

At first, the Vietminh were no match for the French forces, who possessed superior weapons and numbers. The Vietminh, however, utilized guerrilla warfare—small campaigns, waged against the enemy indirectly, under the cover of jungle, and with the aid of the local population. Like the revolutions in America and Haiti, guerrillas ambushed and rapidly withdrew due to their inferior numbers and resources; their tactics not only proved effective, but actually turned the tide of war. Thus, guerrillas strike, retreat, regroup, and fight on. Their most important weapon, however, was attrition—the indefatigable will to fight. The enemy was worn down in terms of personnel and resources, as well as psychology, until prosecuting the war any longer proved more costly than exiting. By 1954, the Eisenhower administration was largely supporting France's colonial war.

When Chinese Communists came to power in 1949, Ho refused their troops, but accepted their supplies, particularly in the form of artillery. Meanwhile, French public support of the war began to wane. Unable to contend with the guerrilla campaign of the Vietminh, the French attempted to lure General Vo Nguyen Giap's army to a remote outpost near the Laotian border known as Dien Bien Phu. There, the French hoped to trap the Vietminh in a conventional battle with control of the roads and airspace. Giap obliged the French; with great effort and courtesy of the Chinese, the Vietminh brought in heavy artillery, which they had hitherto not used, by carrying it piecemeal up the mountains for reassembly. Giap totally surprised and routed the unwitting French army when he positioned his artillery on the hilltops overlooking the valley of Dien Bien Phu. The French left Vietnam in 1954 to American advisers, eventually escalating into war with the Vietcong (Vietnamese Communists) between 1965 and 1975.

The Declaration of Independence of the Democratic Republic of Vietnam*

By Ho Chi Minh

HANOI, SEPTEMBER 2, 1945

"All men are created equal. They are endowed by their Creator with certain inalienable rights, among these are Life, Liberty, and the pursuit of Happiness."

This immortal statement was made in the Declaration of Independence of the United States of America in 1776. In a broader sense, this means: All the peoples on the earth are equal from birth, all the peoples have a right to live, to be happy and free.

The Declaration of the French Revolution made in 1791 on the Rights of Man and the Citizen also states: "All men are born free and with equal rights, and must always remain free and have equal rights." Those are undeniable truths.

Nevertheless, for more than eighty years, the French imperialists, abusing the standard of Liberty, Equality, and Fraternity, have violated our Fatherland and oppressed our fellow-citizens. They have acted contrary to the ideals of humanity and justice. In the field of politics, they have deprived our people of every democratic liberty.

They have enforced inhuman laws; they have set up three distinct political regimes in the North, the Center and the South of Vietnam in order to wreck our national unity and prevent our people from being united.

They have built more prisons than schools. They have mercilessly slain our patriots-they have drowned our uprisings in rivers of blood. They have fettered public opinion; they have practised obscurantism against our people. To weaken our race they have forced us to use opium and alcohol.

In the fields of economics, they have fleeced us to the backbone, impoverished our people, and devastated our land.

Author's Note: the Democratic Republic of Vietnam has been renamed The Socialist Republic of Vietnam.

They have robbed us of our rice fields, our mines, our forests, and our raw materials. They have monopolised the issuing of bank-notes and the export trade.

They have invented numerous unjustifiable taxes and reduced our people, especially our peasantry, to a state of extreme poverty.

They have hampered the prospering of our national bourgeoisie; they have mercilessly exploited our workers.

In the autumn of 1940, when the Japanese Fascists violated Indochina's territory to establish new bases in their fight against the Allies, the French imperialists went down on their bended knees and handed over our country to them.

Thus, from that date, our people were subjected to the double yoke of the French and the Japanese. Their sufferings and miseries increased. The result was that from the end of last year to the beginning of this year, from Quang Tri province to the North of Vietnam, more than two million of our fellow-citizens died from starvation. On March 9, the French troops were disarmed by the Japanese. The French colonialists either fled or surrendered, showing that not only were they incapable of "protecting" us, but that, in the span of five years, they had twice sold our country to the Japanese.

On several occasions before March 9, the Vietminh League urged the French to ally themselves with it against the Japanese. Instead of agreeing to this proposal, the French colonialists so intensified their terrorist activities against the Vietminh members that before fleeing they massacred a great number of our political prisoners detained at Yen Bay and Cao Bang.[1]

Not withstanding all this, our fellow-citizens have always manifested toward the French a tolerant and humane attitude. Even after the Japanese putsch of March 1945, the Vietminh League helped many Frenchmen to cross the frontier, rescued some of them from Japanese jails, and protected French lives and property.

From the autumn of 1940, our country had in fact ceased to be a French colony and had become a Japanese possession.

After the Japanese had surrendered to the Allies, our whole people rose to regain our national sovereignty and to found the Democratic Republic of Vietnam.

The truth is that we have wrested our independence from the Japanese and not from the French.

The French have fled, the Japanese have capitulated, Emperor Bao Dai has abdicated. Our people have broken the chains which for nearly a century have fettered them and have won independence for the Fatherland. Our people at the same time have overthrown the monarchic regime that has reigned supreme for dozens of centuries. In its place has been established the present Democratic Republic.

For these reasons, we, members of the Provisional Government, representing the whole Vietnamese people, declare that from now on we break off all relations of a colonial character with France; we repeal all the international obligation that France has so far subscribed to on behalf of Vietnam and we abolish all the special rights the French have unlawfully acquired in our Fatherland.

The whole Vietnamese people, animated by a common purpose, are determined to fight to the bitter end against any attempt by the French colonialists to reconquer their country.

We are convinced that the Allied nations which at Tehran and San Francisco[2] have acknowledged the principles of self-determination and equality of nations, will not refuse to acknowledge the independence of Vietnam.

---

1   *Editor's note:* Places in Northern Vietnam
2   *Editor's note:* Sites of UN organizational meetings.

A people who have courageously opposed French domination for more than eighty years, a people who have fought side by side with the Allies against the Fascists during these last years, such a people must be free and independent.

For these reasons, we, members of the Provisional Government of the Democratic Republic of Vietnam, solemnly declare to the world that Vietnam has the right to be a free and independent country and in fact it is so already. The entire Vietnamese people are determined to mobilise all their physical and mental strength, to sacrifice their lives and property in order to safeguard their independence and liberty.

STUDY QUESTIONS

1. How does this document compare to the American Declaration of Independence? What irony is inherent in the juxtaposition of the two?

2. How does the Vietnamese declaration of independence compare to the Haitian declaration?

3. Is it useful to compare and contrast primary sources that were written across different chronological and spatial historical scenarios?

The Rivonia Trial Speech to the Court

I n many ways, South Africa has followed a separate path to modernity in Africa. Reconfigured as the Union of South Africa in 1910, the country had been colonized by the Dutch, known as Afrikaners or Boers (Dutch for farmer), as well as the British. Both European settler populations also fought against indigenous warriors of the Khoisan.[1]

Cape Colony was one of the few locations that was settled by whites before the Scramble for Africa began in the late 19th century. The colony had been predominantly Dutch, and when the British established a presence on the cape by 1795, they resented the imposition of Britain's usurpation. As a result, the Boers moved north during the Great Trek of 1836, where they established the Orange Free State and the Transvaal.

Both groups fought border wars against Africans, pushing the Khoisan southwest into the Kalahari Desert. Conflicts between the Boers, led by President Paul Kruger, and Uitlanders, or foreigners (i.e., the British) reemerged when huge quantities of gold and diamonds were discovered in the Boer-controlled Johannesburg area of the Transvaal in the 1880s. British industrial imperialists, led by Cecil John Rhodes, developed the environs with mines and railroads. Rhodes represented the quintessential imperialist—so much so that he even had two countries named after him in Africa, one northern and one southern. "We are the first race in the world," he boasted, "the more of the world we inhabit the better it is for the human race."[2] Through his British South Africa Company (BSAC), Rhodes had amassed a fortune in diamond and gold mining before entering politics as prime minister of Cape Colony. He supported the belief that the British Empire on the African continent should spread from the "Cape to Cairo," and envisaged a global network of colonies. Later in life, Rhodes established a scholarship at Oxford

---

1   The San and the Khoi collectively comprise the Khoisan people. Other Bantu-speaking groups that had migrated from central Africa to southern Africa over many years included the Xhosa, the Zulus, and the Sotho-Tswana.

2   Piers Brendon, *The Decline and Fall of the British Empire*, 1781–1997 (New York: Vintage Books, 2010), p. 193.

University for Americans of British heritage, so that they, too, as Rudyard Kipling implored, might bask in imperial glory.

Such actions resulted in the Boer War (1899–1902), which was eventually won by the British. Still, concessions had to be made to the Boers. The black majority could either serve as cheap labor in the mines or eke out an existence on barren reservations. The British retained the central political authority, while the Boers in the veldt received some representation, electing a majority to the colony's legislature. All of this resulted in the South African Union in 1910. Although this rendered South Africa as part of a postcolonial moment, it also constituted an aberration on the African continent because its white settler populations, Afrikaner and British, obtained self-government much earlier than its intracontinental neighbors.

Between 1948 and 1994, however, a white minority, embodied in the National Party, controlled all aspects of political, economic, and social life under a legalized policy of racial segregation known as apartheid (literally, "apartness" in Afrikaans). It was an authoritarian regime upheld by fear and force. The some 300 apartheid laws precluded instances of miscegenation (no marriage,

Figure 21.1. Nelson Mandela. Copyright © South Africa The Good News (CC by 2.0) at http://commons.wikimedia.org/wiki/File:Nelson_Mandela-2008_%28edit%29.jpg

cohabitation, or sexual relations) of people of different races, as well as other prohibitions for blacks in education, employment, and political or labor unions. Public domains such as beaches and hospitals were segregated. Prejudicial notions, based on assumptions about language, dress, and diet, informed racist discrimination. This resulted in opprobrium by world opinion and South Africa's increasing isolation.

Another component to apartheid, begun in 1959, was the establishment by the South African government of ten *Bantustans*, or "homelands," geographically about 13 percent of South Africa, for the teeming black majority. These areas were located in the hinterland beyond the white-controlled cities of Johannesburg, Cape Town, and Pretoria. Anger at this state of second-class citizenship boiled over in 1960 in Sharpeville, where 69 protesters were gunned down for demonstrating against the *Bantustans* and the compulsory carrying of an identification pass. Public agitation also took place in the Soweto ghetto of one million people. The government took the measure of banning the African National Congress (ANC).

Founded in 1912 and modeled after the Indian National Congress, 27 years its predecessor, the ANC had always adhered to nonviolent and democratic ideals; its suppression in 1960 was the result of the precarious political climate at the time. When constitutional avenues were closed to the ANC, they turned to armed struggle and sabotage by organizing *Umkhonto we Sizwe*, or the "Spear of the Nation." As an ANC leader, Nelson Mandela (1918-2013), explained, five decades of peaceful protest had only yielded harsher repression. Police arrested Mandela in 1962, and he was charged with leaving the country illegally and inciting workers to strike. At his trial the following year, Mandela defended acts of violence as responses to acts of violence perpetrated by the government against the people. While serving a five-year sentence, Mandela was again brought to trial after the raid on Liliesleaf Farm, Rivonia. It was in what became known as the "Rivonia Trial" that he made his famous speech from the dock. The Rivonia indictment charged 11 persons with over 200 acts of sabotage and the incitement of violent insurrection with the intent to overthrow the government. Subsequent charges included recruitment for guerrilla warfare and conspiracy to aid foreign militaries in a Communist revolution.[3] The court sentenced him to life imprisonment with hard labor. Mandela would be incarcerated as a political prisoner for the next 27 years.[4]

Over the decades, international pressure on South Africa mounted as vigils were held at St. Paul's Cathedral and the London University Student Union elected Mandela president. Even Cold-War giants such Leonid Brezhnev and Adlai Stevenson, enemies who mutually envisioned a free South Africa as a potential ideological proxy, sought leniency for Mandela. In 1989, a new government came to power, and Frederik W. de Klerk replaced P. W. Botha, one of apartheid's staunchest supporters. De Klerk's administration, on the other hand, constituted a sea change in South African political life. The following year, Botha's state of emergency ended, the prohibition of the ANC was lifted, and Mandela was freed from prison at 71 years of age.[5] Despite an advanced age, Mandela faced the difficult task of work to end apartheid. In addition to the problems with halting decades-long discrimination, some of the Bantustans, bastions of Zulu and Xhosa strength, were loath to be incorporated into a new South Africa. Mandela and the ANC, nonetheless, eagerly awaited the country's first multiracial elections, for black candidates and voters alike, which would unequivocally signal the transition from rule by a white minority to a black majority. As expected, Mandela was swept into office in 1994, the first nonwhite president of South Africa.

As a final step to confront the psychological damage suffered during the apartheid era, the Mandela administration organized a Truth and Reconciliation Commission in 1995. Under the chairmanship of Archbishop Desmond Tutu, the commission sought to foster national healing. Painful as it was to families of the victims, amnesty was given to those who confessed to their crimes. The point was not necessarily to punish the guilty, but to acknowledge past abuses. Sadly, since Mandela took office, South Africa has been plagued by violent crime, an AIDS epidemic, and poverty. Despite such social ills, however, Mandela will leave behind a legacy of bringing social justice and racial equality to a country that just 20 years ago possessed neither.

Although Mandela's story technically is not a colonial one, it warrants inclusion in this volume, purely on the basis of its courage and resolve in the face of racial oppression. Indeed, racism has always played a significant role in South African history, first with the Dutch and British colonists and later with Afrikaner governments. Nonetheless, despite having decolonized some half-century earlier than its African counterparts, the brutal realities of the apartheid era rendered life for blacks in South Africa scarcely distinguishable from their colonized cousins all over the continent. None felt this more acutely than Mandela, in prison cells for nearly three decades. His speech from the dock on April 20, 1964, still possesses the powerful defiance against social inequality and racial injustice.

---

3   Nelson Mandela, *Long Walk to Freedom* (New York: Little, Bowen and Company, 1995), 352-55.
4   Mandela spent 18 years on Robben Island, when he was transferred to Pollsmoor Prison in 1982. In 1988, he moved to Victor Verster Prison, from whence he was released in February 1990.
5   Mandela and de Klerk shared the 1993 Nobel Peace Prize.

The Rivonia Trial Speech to the Court, April 20, 1964

By Nelson Mandela

I AM PREPARED TO DIE

Nelson Mandela's statement from the dock at the opening of the defence case in the Rivonia Trial.

My Lord, I am the First Accused.

I hold a Bachelor's Degree in Arts and practised as an attorney in Johannesburg for a number of years in partnership with Mr. Oliver Tambo, a co-conspirator in this case. I am a convicted prisoner serving five years for leaving the country without a permit and for inciting people to go on strike at the end of May 1961.

I admit immediately that I was one of the persons who helped to form Umkhonto we Sizwe, and that I played a prominent role in its affairs until I was arrested in August 1962. In the statement which I am about to make, I shall correct certain false impressions which have been created by State witnesses; amongst other things I will demonstrate that certain of the acts referred to in the evidence were not, and could not have been committed by Umkhonto. I will also deal with the relationship between the African National Congress and with the part which I personally have played in the affairs of both organisations. I shall deal also with the part played by the Communist Party. In order to explain these matters properly, I will have to explain what Umkhonto set out to achieve; what methods it prescribed for the achievement of these objects, and why these methods were chosen. I will also have to explain how I came, I became involved in the activities of these organisations.

At the outset, I want to say that the suggestion made by the state in its opening that the struggle in South Africa is under the influence of foreigners or communists is wholly incorrect. I have done whatever I did, both as an individual and as a leader of my people, because of my experience in South Africa and my own proudly felt African background, and not because of what any outsider might have said.

In my youth in the Transkei I listened to the elders of my tribe telling stories of the old days. Amongst the tales they related to me were those of wars fought by our ancestors in defence of the fatherland.

The names of Dingane and Bambatha, Hintsa and Makana, Squngathi and Dalasile, Moshoeshoe and Sekhukhune, were praised as the pride and the glory of the entire African nation. I hoped then that life might offer me the opportunity to serve my people and make my own humble contribution to their freedom struggle. This is what has motivated me in all that I have done in relation to the charges made against me in this case.

Having said this, I must deal immediately and at some length with the question of sabotage. Some of the things so far told to the Court are true and some are untrue. I do not however, deny that I planned sabotage. I did not plan it in a spirit of recklessness, nor because I have any love for violence. I planned it as a result of a calm and sober assessment of the political situation that had arisen after many years of tyranny, exploitation, and oppression of my people by the whites.

I deny that Umkhonto was responsible for a number of acts which clearly fell outside the policy of the organisation, but which have been charged in the indictment against us. I do not know what justification there was for these acts, or who committed them, but to demonstrate that they could not have been authorised or committed by Umkhonto, I want to refer briefly to the roots and policy of the organisation.

I have already mentioned that I was one of the persons who helped to form Umkhonto. I, and the others who started the organisation, did so for two reasons. Firstly, we believed that as a result of Government policy, violence by the African people had become inevitable, and that unless responsible leadership was given to canalise and control the feelings of our people, there would be outbreaks of terrorism which would produce an intensity of bitterness and hostility between the various races of the country which is not produced even by war.

Secondly, we felt that without sabotage there would be no way open to the African people to succeed in their struggle against the principle of white supremacy. All lawful modes of expressing opposition to this principle had been closed by legislation, and we were placed in a position in which we had either to accept a permanent state of inferiority, or to defy the Government. We chose to defy the Government. We first broke the law in a way which avoided any recourse to violence; when this form was legislated against, and when the Government resorted to a show of force to crush opposition to its policies, only then did we decide to answer violence with violence.

But the violence which we chose to adopt was not terrorism. We who formed Umkhonto were all members of the African National Congress, and had behind us the ANC tradition of non-violence and negotiation as a means of solving political disputes. We believed that South Africa belonged to all the people who lived in it, and not to one group, be it black or white. We did not want an inter-racial war, and tried to avoid it to the last minute. If the Court is in doubt about this, it will be seen that the whole history of our organisation bears out what I have said, and what I will subsequently say, when I describe the tactics which Umkhonto decided to adopt. I want, therefore, to say something about the African National Congress.

The African National Congress was formed in 1912 to defend the rights of the African people which had been seriously curtailed by the South Africa Act, and which were then being threatened by the Native Land Act. For thirty-seven years—that is until 1949—it adhered strictly to a constitutional struggle. It put forward demands and resolutions; it sent delegations to the Government in the belief that African grievances could be settled through peaceful discussion and that Africans could advance gradually to full political rights. But white governments remained unmoved, and the rights of Africans became less instead of becoming greater. In the words of my leader, Chief Luthuli, who became President of the ANC, and who was later awarded the Nobel Peace Prize, I quote:

"Who will deny that thirty years of my life have been spent knocking in vain, patiently, moderately, and modestly at a closed and barred door? What have been the fruits of moderation? The past thirty years have seen the greatest number of laws restricting our rights and progress, until today we have reached a stage where we have almost no rights at all", unquote.

Even after 1949, the ANC remained determined to avoid violence. At this time, however, there was a change from the strictly constitutional means of protest which had been employed in the past. The change was embodied in a decision which was taken to protest against apartheid legislation by peaceful, but unlawful, demonstrations against certain laws. Pursuant to this policy the ANC launched the Defiance Campaign, in which I was placed in charge of volunteers. This campaign was based on the principles of passive resistance. More than 8,500 people defied apartheid laws and went to jail. Yet there was not a single instance of violence in the course of this campaign. I, and nineteen colleagues, were convicted for the role and this conviction was under the Suppression of Communism Act although our campaign had nothing to do with Communism, but our sentences were suspended, mainly because the Judge found that discipline and non-violence had been stressed throughout. This was the time when the volunteer section of the ANC was established, and when the word 'Amadelakufa' was first used; this was the time when the volunteers were asked to take a pledge to uphold certain principles. Evidence dealing with volunteers and their pledges has been introduced into this case, but completely out of context. The volunteers were not, and are not, the soldiers of a Black army pledged to fight a civil war against whites. They were, and are, dedicated workers who are prepared to lead campaigns initiated by the ANC to distribute leaflets, to organise strikes, or to do whatever the particular campaign required. They are called volunteers because they volunteer to face the penalties of imprisonment and whipping which are now prescribed by the legislature for such acts.

During the Defiance Campaign, the Public Safety Act and the Criminal Law Amendment Act were passed. These statutes provided harsher penalties for offences committed by way of protests against laws. Despite this, the protests continued and the ANC adhered to its policy of non-violence.

In 1956, 156 leading members of the Congress Alliance, including myself, were arrested on a charge of High Treason and charges under the Suppression of Communism Act. The non-violent policy of the ANC was put in issue by the State, but when the Court gave judgement some five years later, it found that the ANC did not have a policy of violence. We were acquitted on all counts, which included a count that the ANC sought to set up a Communist State in place of the existing regime. The Government has always sought to libel, to label all its opponents as communists. This allegation has been repeated in the present case, but as I will show, the ANC is not, and never has been, a communist organisation.

In 1960 there was the shooting at Sharpeville, which resulted in the proclamation of a State of Emergency and the declaration of the ANC as an unlawful organisation. My colleagues and I, after careful consideration, decided that we would not obey this decree. The African people were not part of the Government and did not make the laws by which they were governed. We believed in the words of the Universal Declaration of Human Rights, that "the will of the people shall be the basis of authority of the Government", and for us to accept the banning was equivalent to accepting the silencing of the African people for all time. The ANC refused to dissolve, but instead went underground. We believed it was our duty to preserve this organisation which had been built up with almost fifty years of unremitting toil. I have no doubt that no self-respecting white political organisation would disband itself if declared illegal by a government in which it had no say.

I now want to deal, My Lord, with evidence which misrepresents the true position in this case. In some of the evidence the M-Plan[1] has been completely misrepresented. It was nothing more than a method of organising planned in 1953, and put into operation with varying degrees of success thereafter. After April 1960 new methods had to be devised, for instance, by relying on smaller committees. The M-Plan was referred to in evidence at the Treason Trial but it had nothing whatsoever to do with sabotage or Umkhonto we Sizwe, and was never adopted by Umkhonto. The confusion, particularly by certain witnesses from the Eastern Cape is, I think, due to the use of the word or the phrase "High Command". This term was coined in Port Elizabeth during the Emergency, when most of the ANC leaders were gaoled, and the Gaol Committee set up to deal with complaints, was called the High Command. After the Emergency this phrase stuck, and was used to describe certain of the ANC Committees in that area. Thus we have had witnesses talking about the West Bank High Command, and the Port Elizabeth High Command. These so-called "High Commands" came into existence before Umkhonto was formed, and were not concerned in any way with sabotage. In fact, as I will subsequently explain, Umkhonto, as an organisation, was, as far as possible, kept separate from the ANC. This explains, My Lord, why persons like Bennett Mashiyane and Reginald Ndube heard nothing about sabotage at the meetings they attended. But, as has been mentioned the use of the phrase "High Command" caused some dissension in ANC circles in the Eastern Province.

I travelled there in 1961, because it was alleged that some of these so-called High Commands were using duress in order to enforce the new Plan. I did not find evidence of this but nevertheless forbade it, and also insisted that the term "High Command" should not be used to describe any ANC committee. My visit and the discussions which took place have been described by Zizi Njikelane, and I admit his evidence in so far as it relates to me. Although it does not seem to have much relevance, I deny that I was taken to the meeting by the taxi driver John Tshingane, and I also deny that I went to the sea with him.

My Lord, I would like now to deal with the immediate causes. In 1960 the government held a referendum which led to the establishment of the Republic. Africans, who constituted approximately 70 percent of the population of South Africa, were not entitled to vote, and were not even consulted about the proposed constitutional change. All of us were apprehensive of our future under the proposed white republic, and a resolution was taken to hold an All-In African Conference to call for a National Convention, and to organise mass demonstrations on the eve of the unwanted Republic, if the Government failed to call the Convention. The conference was attended by Africans of various political persuasions. I was the Honorary Secretary of the Conference, and undertook to be responsible for organising the national stay-at-home which was subsequently called to coincide with the declaration of the Republic. As all strikes by Africans are illegal, the person organising such a strike must avoid arrest. I was chosen to be this person, and consequently I had to leave my home and my family and my practice and go into hiding to avoid arrest.

The stay-at-home, in accordance with ANC policy, was to be a peaceful demonstration. Careful instructions were given to organisers and members to avoid any recourse to violence. The Government's answer was to introduce new and harsher laws, to mobilize its armed forces, and to send Saracens, armed vehicles, and soldiers into the townships in a massive show of force designed to intimidate the people. This was an indication that the Government had decided to rule by force alone, and this decision was a milestone on the road to Umkhonto.

---

1   *Editor's note*: M-Plan: The M was for Mandela.

Some of this may appear irrelevant to this trial. In fact, I believe none of it is irrelevant because it will, I hope, enable the Court to appreciate the attitude towards Umkhonto eventually adopted by the various persons and bodies concerned in the National Liberation Movement. When I went to gaol in 1962, the dominant idea was that loss of life should be avoided. I now know that this was still so in 1963.

I must return however, My Lord to June 1961. What were we, the leaders of our people, to do? Were we to give in to the show of force and the implied threat against future action, or were we to fight it out and, if so, how?

We had no doubt that we had to continue the fight. Anything else would have been abject surrender. Our problem, My Lord, was not whether to fight, but was how to continue the fight. We of the ANC had always stood for a non-racial democracy, and we shrank from any action which might drive the races further apart than they already were. But the hard facts were that fifty years of non-violence had brought the African people nothing but more and more repressive legislation, and fewer and fewer rights.

It may not be easy for this Court to understand, but it is a fact that for a long time the people had been talking of violence—of the day when they would fight the white man and win back their country, and we, the leaders of the ANC, had nevertheless always prevailed upon them to avoid violence and to pursue peaceful methods. When some of us discussed this in June of 1961, it could not be denied that our policy to achieve a non-racial state by non-violence had achieved nothing, and that our followers were beginning to lose confidence in this policy and were developing disturbing ideas of terrorism.

It must not be forgotten, My Lord, that by this time violence had, in fact, become a feature of the South African political scene. There had been violence in 1957 when the women of Zeerust were ordered to carry passes; there was violence in 1958 with the enforcement of Bantu Authorities and cattle culling in Sekhukhuneland; there was violence in 1959 when the people of Cato Manor protested against pass raids; there was violence in 1960 when the Government attempted to impose Bantu Authorities in Pondoland. Thirty-nine Africans died in these Pondoland disturbances. In 1961 there had been riots in Warmbaths, and all this time, My Lord, the Transkei had been a seething mass of unrest. Each disturbance pointed clearly to the inevitable growth amongst Africans of the belief that violence was the only way out—it showed that a Government which uses force to maintain its rule teaches the oppressed to use force to oppose it. Already small groups had arisen in the urban areas and were spontaneously making plans for violent forms of political struggle. There now arose a danger that these groups would adopt terrorism against Africans, as well as whites, if not properly directed. Particularly disturbing was the type of violence engendered in places such as Zeerust, Sekhukhuneland, and Pondoland amongst Africans. It was increasingly taking the form, not of struggle against the Government—though this is what prompted it—but of civil strife between pro-government chiefs and those opposed to them conducted in such a way that it could not hope to achieve anything other than a loss of life, and bitterness.

At the beginning of June 1961, after a long and anxious assessment of the South African situation, I, and some colleagues, came to the conclusion that as violence [in this country—inaudible] was inevitable, it would be unrealistic and wrong for African leaders to continue preaching peace and non-violence at a time when the Government met our peaceful demands with force.

This conclusion, My Lord, was not easily arrived at. It was when all, only when all else had failed, when all channels of peaceful protest had been barred to us, that the decision was made to embark on violent forms of struggle, and to form Umkhonto we Sizwe. We did so not because we desired such a course, but solely because the Government had left us with no other choice. In the Manifesto of Umkhonto published on the 16th of December 61, which is Exhibit AD, we said', I quote:

"The time comes in the life of any nation when there remain only two choices—submit or fight. That time has now come to South Africa. We shall not submit and we have no choice but to hit back by all means in our power in defence of our people, our future, and our freedom", unquote

This was our feeling in June of 1961, when we decided to press for a change in the policy of the National Liberation Movement. I can only say that I felt morally obliged to do what I did.

We, who had taken this decision, started to consult leaders of various organisations, including the ANC. I will not say whom we spoke to, or what they said, but I wish to deal with the role of the African National Congress in this phase of the struggle, and with the policy and objectives of Umkhonto we Sizwe.

As far as the ANC was concerned, it formed a clear view which can be summarised as follows:

a.   It was a mass political organisation with a political function to fulfil. Its members had joined on the express policy of non-violence.

b.   Because of all this, it could not and would not undertake violence. This must be stressed. One cannot turn such a body into the small, closely knit organisation required for sabotage. Nor would this be politically correct, because it would result in members ceasing to carry out this essential activity: political propaganda and organisation. Nor was it permissible to change the whole nature of the organisation.

c.   On the other hand, in view of this situation I have described, the ANC was prepared to depart from its fifty-year-old policy of non-violence to this extent that it would no longer disapprove of properly controlled sabotage. Hence members who undertook such activity would not be subject to disciplinary action by the ANC.

I say "properly controlled sabotage" because I made it clear that if I helped to form the organisation I would at all times subject it to the political guidance of the ANC and would not undertake any different form of activity from that contemplated without the consent of the ANC. And I shall now tell the Court how that form of violence came to be determined.

[Unidentified voice says, 'came to be determined']

As a result of this decision, Umkhonto was formed in 1961, in November 1961. When we took this decision, and subsequently formulated our plans, the ANC heritage of non-violence and racial harmony was very much with us. We felt that the country was drifting towards a civil war in which blacks and whites would fight each other. [tape seems to jump] [We viewed] the situation with alarm. Civil war would mean the destruction of what the ANC stood for; with civil war, racial peace would be more difficult than ever to achieve. We already had examples in South African history of the results of war. It has taken more than fifty years for the scars of the South African War to disappear. How much longer would it take to eradicate the scars of inter-racial civil war, which could not be fought without a great loss of life on both sides?

The avoidance of civil war had dominated our thinking for many years, but when we decided to adopt sabotage as part of our policy, we realised that we might one day have to face the prospect of such a war. This had to be taken into account in formulating our plans. We required a plan which was flexible, and which permitted us to act in accordance with the needs of the times; above all, the plan had to be one which recognized civil war as the last resort, and left the decision on this question to the future. We did not want to be committed to civil war, but we wanted to be ready if it became inevitable.

Four forms of violence are possible. There is sabotage, there is guerrilla warfare, there is terrorism, and there is open revolution. We chose to adopt the first method and to test it fully before taking any other decision.

In the light of our political background the choice was a logical one. Sabotage did not involve loss of life, and it offered the best hope for future race relations. Bitterness would be kept to a minimum and, if the policy bore fruit, democratic government could become a reality. This is what we felt at the time, and this is what we said in our Manifesto, Exhibit AD, I quote:

"We of Umkhonto we Sizwe have always sought to achieve liberation without bloodshed and civil clash. We hope, even at this late hour, that our first actions will awaken everyone to a realisation of the disastrous situation to which Nationalist policy is leading. We hope that we will bring the Government and its supporters to their senses before it is too late, so that both the Government and its policies can be changed before matters reach the desperate state of civil war", unquote

The initial plan was based on a careful analysis of the political and economic situation of our country. We believed that South Africa depended to a large extent on foreign capital and foreign trade. We felt that planned destruction of power plants, and interference with rail and telephone communications would tend to scare away capital from the country, make it more difficult for goods from the industrial areas to reach the seaports on schedule, and would in the long run be a heavy drain on the economic life of the country, thus compelling the voters of the country to reconsider their position.

Attacks on the economic life lines of the country were to be linked with sabotage on Government buildings and other symbols of apartheid. These attacks would serve as a source of inspiration to our people and encourage them to participate in non-violent mass action such as strikes. In addition, they would provide an outlet for those people who were urging the adoption of violent methods and would enable us to give concrete proof to our followers that we had adopted a stronger line, and we were fighting back against Government violence.

In addition, if mass action were successfully organised, and mass reprisals taken, we felt that sympathy for our cause would be roused in other countries, and that greater pressure would be brought to bear on the South African Government.

This then, My Lord was the plan. Umkhonto was to perform sabotage, and strict instructions were given to its members right from the start, that on no account were they to injure or kill people in planning or carrying out operations. These instructions have been referred to in the evidence of "X" and "Z".

The affairs of Umkhonto were controlled and directed by a National High Command, which had powers of co-option and which could, and did, appoint Regional Commands. The High Command was the body which determined tactics and targets and was in charge of training and finance. Under the High Command there were Regional Commands which were responsible for the direction of the local sabotage groups. Within the framework of the policy laid down by the National High Command, the Regional Commands had authority to select the targets to be attacked. They had no authority whatsoever to go beyond the prescribed framework and thus had no authority to embark upon acts which endangered lives, or which did not fit into the overall plan of sabotage. For instance, Umkhonto members were forbidden ever to go armed into operation. Incidentally, the terms High Command and Regional Command were an importation from the Jewish national underground organization the Irgun Zvai Leumi, which operated in Israel between 1944 and 1948.

Umkhonto had its first operation on the 16th of December 1961, when Government buildings in Johannesburg, Port Elizabeth and Durban were attacked. The selection of targets is proof of the policy to which I have referred. Had we intended to attack life, we would have selected targets where people congregated and not empty buildings and power stations. The sabotage which was committed before the 16th of December 1961 was the work of isolated groups and had no connection whatsoever with Umkhonto. In fact, My Lord, some of these and a number of later acts were claimed by other organisations.

Now My Lord, at this stage I would like to refer very briefly to a number of newspaper cuttings.

Justice De Wet: Yes well before you get there [inaudible] I will take the adjournment.

I was just about to refer Your Lordship to a number of newspaper cuttings. [Judge: Yes] It's not my intention, My Lord. to hand them in [Judge: Yes] but I merely wish to use them [Judge: Yes] to illustrate the point I had made, that before December 1961 it was common knowledge in the townships and throughout the country that there existed a number of bodies other than Umkhonto which planned and carried out acts of sabotage, and that some of the acts which took place during the period of the indictment were in fact claimed by some of these organisations.

The first newspaper cutting I wish to refer Your Lordship to is the Rand Daily Mail of the 22nd of December 1961. An article that appears on the front page—the caption, My Lord, reads as follows :

"We bombed two pylons, group claims"

And then I just wish to refer Your Lordship just to two passages:

"The bombing of two power pylons at Rembrandt Park, Johannesburg, on Wednesday night was claimed as the work of the National Committee for Liberation in a typewritten document on a sheet of common writing paper, put into the Rand Daily Mail Christmas Fund Jackpot box during Wednesday night or early yesterday."

And then the penultimate passage in the article reads as follows:

"The statement said that the NCL was not aligned with ["the Assegai of the Nation"— inaudible]—I presume My Lord, that it is the Spear of the Nation, which is the translation of Umkhonto we Sizwe.
"The group claims responsibility for the bomb outrages during the weekend, although both supported the liberatory movement, the NCL was non-racial, it was stated."

That's the first cutting I wish to refer to My Lord. Then the second one is also a copy of the Rand Daily Mail of 15th of April 1963, and the article I wish to refer to is on page 2. It's a very short article, My Lord, I will read it. The caption is:

"Forty-three held in petrol bomb incident. Forty-three Africans are now being held by Johannesburg police in connection with the petrol bomb attack last week on a store in

Pritchard Street, Johannesburg. Most of the Africans were arrested in Johannesburg's South-Western townships. They were alleged to have threatened a watchman, after telling him they wanted to steal garments from the shop. Police said that five more Africans had been arrested in the vicinity of King William's Town after last week's attack on the town's police station. This brings the total number of arrests to forty-one. Africans arrested after the two incidents are alleged members of the Poqo organisation. Although it is believed that a number of other Poqo members were arrested on the Reef and in other areas, no figures were available last night. The police [apparent jump in the recording] [are still continuing their investigation] and the final figure of the total number of Poqo suspects arrested yet so far cannot yet be given."

Then the third one, My Lord, is again a copy of the Rand Daily Mail of the 9th November 1963. And the particular article appears, My Lord, on page ten. Your Lordship will probably remember this matter. It was referred to during the argument on the second application to quash the indictment. Reference was made, both the State and the defence, to the judgment of Mr Justice van Heerden of the Cape Provincial Division. The accused in this case, My Lord, were arrested on the 12th of July 1963, according to the report and presumable for acts which are, were alleged to have been committed during the period prior to the 12th of July 1963. And I assume that that will cover the period of the indictment. This relates to what is known as the Yu Chi Chan[2] Guerilla Warfare Club. And according to this report, I will not read it My Lord, but just to mention that they were preparing a revolution and guerrilla warfare.

I wish to refer to a photostatic copy of the Rand Daily Mail of the 29th of November 1962. We couldn't get the actual copy of the Mail itself. And the article which I want to refer to appears on the first page. I just want to refer, again, just to two passages. The caption reads:

"Police put on strict guard after Rand blast. Security Police yesterday threw a light, tight cordon around an Eskom power pylon which was dynamited in the early hours of the morning disrupting train services in Germiston and Pretoria. A senior police spokesmen said, quote 'there is no doubt it was sabotage'", unquote.

Then the last paragraph read as follows:

"A woman telephoned the Rand Daily Mail last night and said, quote: "the explosion at Putfontein last night was the work of the National Committee of Liberation" unquote, then she put down the telephone".

In other words, My Lord, there were a number of bodies which, during the period of indictment planned and carried out acts of sabotage.

Now My Lord the Manifesto of Umkhonto was issued on the day that operations commenced. The response to our actions and Manifesto among the white population was characteristically violent. The Government threatened to take strong action, and called upon its supporters to stand firm and to ignore

---

2 *Editor's note*: Yu Chi Chan was of Maoist origins.

the demands of the Africans. The whites failed to respond by suggesting change; they responded to our call by retreating behind the laager.

In contrast, the response of the Africans was one of encouragement. Suddenly there was hope again. Things were happening. People in the townships became eager for political news. A great deal of enthusiasm was generated by the initial successes, and people began to speculate on how soon freedom would be obtained.

But we in Umkhonto weighed up the whites' response with anxiety. The lines were being drawn. The whites and blacks were moving into separate camps, and the prospects of avoiding a civil war were diminishing. The white newspapers carried reports that sabotage would be punished by death. If this was so, how could we continue to keep Africans away from terrorism?

I now wish, My Lord, to turn to the question of guerrilla warfare and how it came to be considered. By 1961 scores of Africans had died as a result of racial friction. In 1920 when the famous leader, Masabalala, was held in Port Elizabeth jail, twenty-four of a group of Africans who had gathered to demand his release were killed by the police and white civilians. More than one hundred Africans died in the Bulhoek affair. In 1924 over two hundred Africans were killed when the Administrator of South-West Africa led a force against a group which had rebelled against the imposition of dog tax. On the 1st of May 1950, eighteen Africans died as a result of police shootings during the strike. On the 21st of March 1960, sixty-nine unarmed Africans died at Sharpeville.

How many more Sharpevilles would there be in the history of our country? And how many more Sharpevilles could the country stand without violence and terror becoming the order of the day? And what would happen to our people when that stage was reached? In the long run we felt certain we must succeed, but at what cost to ourselves and the rest of the country? And if this happened, how could black and white ever live together again in peace and harmony? These were the problems that faced us, and these were our decisions.

Experience convinced us that rebellion would offer the Government limitless opportunities for the indiscriminate slaughter of our people. But it was precisely because the soil of South Africa is already drenched with the blood of innocent Africans that we felt it our duty to make preparations as a long-term undertaking to use force in order to defend ourselves against force. If war became inevitable, we wanted to be ready when the time came, and for the fight to be conducted on terms most favourable to our people. The fight which held out the best prospects for us and the least risk of life to both sides was guerrilla warfare. We decided, therefore, in our preparations for the future, to make provision for the possibility of guerrilla warfare.

All whites undergo compulsory military training, but no such training is given to Africans. It was in our view essential to build up a nucleus of trained men who would be able to provide the leadership which would be required if guerrilla warfare started. We had to prepare for such a situation before it became too late to make proper preparations. It was also necessary to build up a nucleus of men trained in civil administration and other professions, so that Africans would be equipped to participate in the government of this country as soon as they were allowed to do so.

At this stage, My Lord, the ANC decided that I should attend the Conference of the Pan-African Freedom Movement for Central, East, and Southern Africa, which was to be held in 1962 in Addis Ababa, and, it was also decided that, after the conference, I would undertake a tour of the African States with a view to soliciting support for our cause and obtaining scholarships for the higher education of matriculated Africans. At the same time the MK decided I should investigate whether facilities were available for the training of soldiers which was the first stage in the preparation for guerrilla warfare.

Training in both fields would be necessary, even if changes in South Africa came about by peaceful means. As I have just explained, administrators would be necessary who would be willing and able to administer a non-racial state and so men, and so would men be necessary to control the army and police force of such a state.

It was on this note that I left South Africa to proceed to Addis Ababa as a delegate of the ANC. My tour was successful beyond all our hopes. Wherever I went I met sympathy for our cause and promises of help. All Africa was united against the stand of white South Africa, and even in London I was received with great sympathy by political leaders, such as the late Mr. Hugh Gaitskell and Mr. Grimond. In Africa I was promised support by such men as Julius Nyerere, now President of Tanganyika; Mr. Kawawa, then Prime Minister of Tanganyika; Emperor Haile Selassie of Ethiopia; General Abboud, President of the Sudan; Habib Bourguiba, President of Tunisia; Ben Bella, now President of Algeria; Modibo Keita, President of Mali; Leopold Senghor, President of Senegal; Sekou Toure, President of Guinea; President Tubman of Liberia; and Milton Obote, Prime Minister of Uganda and Kenneth Kaunda, now Prime Minister of Northern Rhodesia. It was Ben Bella who invited me to visit Oujda, the Headquarters of the Algerian Army of National Liberation, the visit which is described in my diary, one of the exhibits.

I had already started to make a study of the art of war and revolution and, whilst abroad, underwent a course in military training. If there was to be guerrilla warfare, I wanted to be able to stand and fight with my people and to share the hazards of war with them. Notes of lectures which I received in Ethiopia and Algeria are contained in exhibits produced in evidence. Summaries of books on guerrilla warfare and military strategy have also been produced. I have already admitted that these documents are in my writing, and I acknowledge that I made these studies to equip myself for the role which I might have to play if the struggle drifted into guerrilla warfare. I approached this question as every African national-ist should do. I was completely objective. The Court will see that I attempted to examine all types of authority on the subject—from the East and from the West, going back to the classic work of Clausewitz, and covering such a variety as Mao Tse Tung, Che Guevara on the one hand, and the writings on the Anglo-Boer War on the other. Of course, these notes, My Lord, are merely summaries of the books I read and do not contain my personal views.

I also made arrangements for our recruits to undergo military training. But here, My Lord, it was impossible to organise any scheme without the co-operation of the ANC offices in Africa. I consequently obtained the permission of the ANC in South Africa to do this. To this extent then there was a departure from the original decision of the ANC that it would not take part in violent methods of struggle, but it applied outside South Africa only. The first batch of recruits actually arrived in Tanganyika when I was passing through that country on my way back to South Africa.

I returned to South Africa and reported to my colleagues on the results of my trip. On my return I found that there had been little alteration in the political scene save that the threat of a death penalty for sabotage had now become a fact. The attitude of my colleagues in Umkhonto was much the same as it had been before I left. They were feeling their way cautiously and felt that it would be a long time before the possibilities of sabotage were exhausted. The ANC had also not changed its attitude. In fact, My Lord, the view was expressed by some that the training of recruits was premature. This is recorded by me in the document which is Exhibit R14 which are very rough notes of comments made by others on my report back meeting after a full discussion, however, it was decided to go ahead with the plans for military training because of the fact that it would take many years to build up a sufficient nucleus of trained soldiers to start a guerrilla campaign, and whatever happened the training would be of value.

I want to deal now with some of the evidence of the Witness "X". Immediately before my arrest in August 1962, I met members of the Regional Command in Durban. This meeting has been referred to in "X"'s evidence. Much of his account is substantially correct, but much of it is slanted and is distorted, and in some important respects untruthful. I want to deal with the evidence as briefly as possible.

a. I did say that I had left the country early in the year to attend the PAFMECSA[3] Conference, that the Conference was opened by the Emperor Haile Selassie who attacked the racial policies of the South African government, and who pledged support to the African people in this country. I also informed them of the unanimous resolution condemning the ill treatment of the African people here and promising support. I did tell them that the Emperor sent his warmest felicitations to my leader Chief Luthuli.

b. But I never told them of any comparison made between Ghanaians and South African recruits, and could not have done so for very simple reasons. By the time I left Ethiopia the first South African recruits had not yet reached that country. And Ghanaian soldiers, as far as I am aware, received training in the United Kingdom. This being the fact and my understanding I could not possibly have thought of telling the Regional Command that the Emperor of Ethiopia thought our trainees were better than the Ghanaians.

c. These statements, therefore, are sheer invention unless they were suggested to "X" by someone wishing to create a false picture.

d. I did tell them of financial support received in Ethiopia and in other parts of Africa. I certainly did not tell him that certain African states had promised us one percent of their budgets. These suggestions of donating one percent never arose during my visit. It arose for the first time, as far as I am aware, at the Conference in May 1963 by which time I had been in jail for ten months.

e. Despite "X"'s alleged failure to remember this I did speak of scholarships promised in Ethiopia. Such general education of our people has always, as I have pointed out, been an important aspect of our plan.

f. I did tell them I had travelled through Africa and had been received by a number of Heads of State, mentioned them all by name. I also told them of President Ben Bella's invitation to me to go to Oujda where I met officers of the Algerian army including their Commander in Chief Colonel Boumediene. I also said that Algerians had promised assistance with training and arms. But I certainly did not say they must hide the fact that they were communists because I did not know whether they were communists or not. What I did say was that no communist should use his position in Umkhonto for communist propaganda, neither in South Africa nor beyond the borders because unity of purpose was essential for achieving freedom. What we aimed at was the vote for all and on this basis we could appeal to all

---

3   *Editor's note*: Pan-African Freedom Movement of East Central and South Africa.

social groups in South Africa, and expect the maximum support from the African states. "X" denies that I could not have suggested any other than the true objective nor could there have been any possible reason for hiding it.

g. It was in this context that I discussed New Age and its criticism of the Egyptian government. In speaking of my visit to Egypt, I said that my visit had coincided with that of Marshal Tito,[4] and that I had not been able to wait until General Nasser was free to interview me. I said that the officials whom I had seen had expressed criticism of articles appearing in New Age which had dealt with General Nasser's attacks on Communism. But that I told them that New Age did not necessarily express the policy of our movement, and that I will take up this complaint with New Age and try and use my influence to change their line because it was not our duty to say in what manner any state should achieve its freedom.

h. I told the Regional Committee that I had not visited Cuba but that I had met that country's ambassadors in Egypt, Morocco and Ghana. I spoke of the warm affection with which I was received at these embassies. And that we were offered all forms of assistance including scholarships for our youth. In dealing with the question of white and Asian recruits, I did say that as Cuba was a multi-racial country, it would be logical to send such persons to this country as these recruits would fit in more easily there than with black soldiers in African states.

i. But I never discussed Eric Mtshali[5] at the meeting for the simple reason that I did not know him until I heard his name mentioned by "X" in this case. On my return to Tanganyika after touring the African continent I met about thirty South African young men, who were on their way to Ethiopia for training. I addressed them on discipline and good behaviour while abroad. Eric Mtshali may have been amongst these young men, but in any event, if he was, this must have been before he visited any African state other than Tanganyika. And in Tanganyika he would not have starved or been in difficulties since our office there would have looked after him. It would be absurd to suggest that the South African office in Dar es Salaam would discriminate against him on the ground that he was a communist.

j. Of course, I referred to Umkhonto we Sizwe, but it cannot be true to say that they heard from me for the first time that this was the name or that it was the military wing of the ANC—a phrase much used by the State in this trial. A proclamation had been issued by Umkhonto on the 16th December 1961 announcing the existence of the body and its name had been known for seven months before the time of this meeting. And I had certainly never referred to it as the military wing of the ANC. I always regarded it as a separate organisation and endeavoured to keep it as such.

k. I did tell them that the activities of Umkhonto might go through two phases, namely: acts of sabotage and possible guerrilla warfare, if that became necessary. I dealt with the problems relating to each phase but I did not say that people were scouting out areas suitable for

---

4   *Editor's note*: Josef Tito was the post-war Communist and nationalist leader of Yugoslavia.
5   *Editor's note*: Anti-Apartheid activist.

guerrilla warfare because no such thing was being done at the time, at that time. I stressed, just as he said, that the most important thing was to study our history—our own history and our own situation. We must of course, study the experiences of other countries also. And in doing so we must study not only the cases where revolutions were victorious but also cases where revolutions were defeated. But I did not discuss the training of people in East Germany as testified by "X".

l.   I did not produce any photograph in Spark or New Age as testified to by "X". These photos were only published on the 21st of February 1963 after I was in jail. While referring to "X"'s evidence there is one other fact that I want to mention, "X" said that the sabotage which was committed on the 15th of October 1962 was in protest against my conviction and that the decision to commit such sabotage had been taken between the date of conviction and the date of sentence. He also said that the sabotage was held over for a few days because it was thought that the police would be on their watch on the day that I was sentenced. All this must be untrue. I was convicted, My Lord, on the 7th of November 1962, and was sentenced on the same day to five years imprisonment with hard labour. The sabotage in October 1962 could therefore not have had anything to do with my conviction and sentence.

My Lord, I wish now to turn to certain general allegations made in this case by the State. But before doing so, I wish to revert to certain occurrences said by witnesses to have happened in Port Elizabeth and East London. I am referring to the bombing of private houses of pro-government persons during December, during September, October and November 1962. I do not know what justification there was for these acts, nor what provocation had been given. But if what I have said already is accepted, then it is clear that these acts had nothing to do with the carrying out of the policy of Umkhonto.

One of the chief allegations in the indictment is that the ANC was a party to a general conspiracy to commit sabotage. I have already explained why this is incorrect but how externally there was a departure from the original principle laid down by the ANC. There have, of course, My Lord, been overlapping of functions internally as well because there is a difference between a resolution adopted in the atmosphere of a committee room and the complete difficulties that arise in the field of practical activity. At a later stage the position was further affected by bannings and house arrests and by persons leaving the country to take up political work abroad. This led to individuals having to do work in different capacities. But though this may have blurred the distinction between Umkhonto and the ANC, it by no means abolished that distinction. Great care was taken to keep the activities of the two organisations in South Africa distinct. The ANC remained a mass political body of Africans only carrying on the type of political work they have conducted prior to 1961. Umkhonto remained a small organisation recruiting its members from different races and organisations, and trying to achieve its own particular objectives. The fact that members of Umkhonto recruited from the ANC, and the fact that persons served both organisations, like Solomon Mbanjwa, did not in our view change the nature of the ANC or give it a policy of violence. This overlapping of officers, however, was more the exception than the rule. This is why, My Lord, persons such as "X" and "Z" who were on the Regional Command of their respective areas did not participate in any of the ANC committees or activities, and why people such as Bennett Mashiyane and Reginald Ndube did not hear of sabotage at their ANC meetings.

Another of the allegations in the indictment is that Rivonia was the headquarters of Umkhonto. This is not true of the time when I was there. I was told, of course, and knew that certain of the activities of the Communist Party were carried on there. But this was no reason, as I shall presently explain, why I should not use the place.

I came there in the following manner:

a. As already indicated, early in April 1961 I went underground to organise the May general strike. My work entailed travelling throughout the country, living now in African townships, then in country villages and again in cities. During the second half of the year I started visiting the Parktown home of Mr. Arthur Goldreich, where I used to meet my family privately. Although I had no direct political association with him, I had known Mr. Goldreich socially since 1958.

b. In October, Mr. Goldreich informed me that he was moving out of town and offered me a hiding place there. A few days thereafter, he arranged for Mr. Michael Harmel, another co-conspirator in this case, to take me to Rivonia. I naturally found Rivonia an ideal place for the man who lived the life of an outlaw. Up to that time I had been compelled to live indoors during the daytime and could only venture out under cover of darkness. But at Liliesleaf I could live differently and work far more efficiently.

c. For obvious reasons, I had to disguise myself and I assumed the fictitious name of David. In December, Mr. Goldreich and his family also moved in. I stayed there, My Lord, until I went abroad on the 11th January 1962. As already indicated, I returned in July 1962 and was arrested in Natal on the 5th August.

d. Up to the time of my arrest, Liliesleaf farm was the headquarters of neither the African National Congress nor Umkhonto. With the exception of myself, none of the officials or members of these bodies lived there, no meetings of the governing bodies were ever held there, and no activities connected with them were either organised or directed from there. On numerous occasions during my stay at Liliesleaf farm I met both the Executive Committee of the ANC, as well as the National High Command, but such meetings were held elsewhere and not on the farm.

e. Whilst staying at Liliesleaf farm, I frequently visited Mr. Goldreich in the main house and he also paid me visits in my room. We had numerous political discussions covering a variety of subjects. We discussed ideological and practical questions, the Congress Alliance, Umkhonto and its activities generally, and his experiences as a soldier in the Palmach, the military wing of the Haganah. Haganah was the political authority of the Jewish National Movement in Palestine.

f. Because of what I had got to know of Mr. Goldreich, I recommended on my return to South Africa that he should be recruited to Umkhonto. I do not know, of my personal knowledge whether this was done.

g. Before I went on my tour of Africa, I lived in the room marked twelve on Exhibit A. On my return in July 1962 I lived in the thatched cottage. The evidence of Joseph Mashefane that I lived in room number twelve during the period that he was there, at the farm, is incorrect.

Another of the allegations made by the State is that the aims and objects of the ANC and the Communist Party are the same. I wish to deal with this and with my own political position. The allegation as to the ANC is false. This is an old allegation which was disproved at the Treason Trial, and which has again reared its head. But since the allegation had been made again I shall deal with it as well as with the relationship between the ANC and the Communist Party and Umkhonto and that Party.

The ideological creed of the ANC is, and always has been, the creed of African Nationalism. It is not the concept of African Nationalism expressed in the cry, 'Drive the White man into the sea'. The African Nationalism for which the ANC stands is the concept of freedom and fulfilment for the African people in their own land. The most important political document ever adopted by the ANC is the Freedom Charter. It is by no means a blueprint for a socialist state. It calls for redistribution, but not nationalisation, of land; it provides for nationalisation of mines, banks, and monopoly industry, because monopolies, big monopolies are owned by one race only, and without such nationalisation racial domination would be perpetuated despite the spread of political power. It would be a hollow gesture to repeal the Gold Law prohibitions against Africans when all gold mines are owned by European companies. In this respect the ANC's policy corresponds with the old policy of the present Nationalist Party which, for many years, had as part of its programme the nationalisation of the gold mines which, at that time, were controlled by foreign capital. Under the Freedom Charter, nationalisation would take place in an economy based on private enterprise. The realisation of the Freedom Charter would open up fresh fields for a prosperous African population of all classes, including the middle class. The ANC has never at any period of its history advocated a revolutionary change in the economic structure of the country, nor has it, to the best of my recollection, ever condemned capitalist society.

As far as the Communist Party is concerned, and if I understand its policy correctly, it stands for the establishment of a State based on the principles of Marxism. Although it is prepared to work for the Freedom Charter, as a short term solution to the problems created by white supremacy, it regards the Freedom Charter as the beginning, and not the end, of its programme.

The ANC, unlike the Communist Party, admitted Africans only as members. Its chief goal was, and is, for the African people to win unity and full political rights. The Communist Party's main aim, on the other hand, was to remove the capitalists and to replace them with a working-class government. The Communist Party sought to emphasise class distinctions whilst the ANC seeks to harmonise them. This is, My Lord, a vital distinction.

It is true that there has often been close co-operation between the ANC and the Communist Party. But co-operation is merely proof of a common goal—in this case the removal of white supremacy—and is not proof of a complete community of interests.

My Lord, the history of the world is full of similar examples. Perhaps the most striking illustration is to be found in the co-operation between Great Britain, the United States of America, and the Soviet Union in the fight against Hitler. Nobody but Hitler would have dared to suggest that such co-operation turned Churchill or Roosevelt into communists or communist tools, or that Britain and America were working to bring about a communist world.

My Lord, I give these illustrations because they are relevant to the allegation that our sabotage was a communist plot or the work of so-called agitators. Because, My Lord, another instance of such co-operation is to be found precisely in Umkhonto. Shortly after Umkhonto was constituted, I was informed by some of its members that the Communist Party would support Umkhonto, and this then occurred. At a later stage the support was made openly.

I believe that communists have always played an active role in the fight by colonial countries for their freedom, because the short-term objects of Communism would always correspond with the long-term objects of freedom movements. Thus communists, My Lord, have played an important role in the freedom struggles fought in countries such as Malaya, Algeria, and Indonesia, yet none of these states today are communist countries. Similarly in the underground resistance movements which sprung up in Europe during the last World War, communists played an important role. Even General Chiang Kai-Shek, today one of the bitterest enemies of Communism, fought together with the communists against the ruling class in the struggle which led to his assumption of power in China in the 1930s.

This pattern of co-operation between communists and non-communists has been repeated in the National Liberation Movement of South Africa. Prior to the banning of the Communist Party, joint campaigns involving the Communist Party and the Congress movements were accepted practice. African communists could, and did, become members of the ANC, and some served on the National, Provincial, and local committees. Amongst those who served on the National Executive are Albert Nzula, a former Secretary of the Communist Party, another former Secretary, Edwin Mofutsanyana and J. B. Marks, a former member of the Central Committee of the Communist Party.

I joined the ANC in 1944, and in 1952 I became Transvaal President and Deputy National President. In my younger days I held the view that the policy of admitting communists to the ANC, and the close co-operation which existed at times on specific issues between the ANC and the Communist Party, would lead to a watering down of the concept of African Nationalism. At that stage I was a member of the African National Congress Youth League, and was one of a group which moved for the expulsion of communists from the ANC. This proposal was heavily defeated, and amongst those who voted against the proposal were some of the most conservative sections of African political opinion. They defended the policy on the ground that from its inception the ANC was formed and built up, not as a political party with one school of political thought, but as a Parliament of the African people accommodating people of various political views—convictions, all united by the common goal of national liberation. I was eventually won over to this point of view and I have upheld it ever since.

It is perhaps difficult for white South Africans, with an ingrained prejudice against Communism, to understand why experienced African politicians so readily accept communists as their friends. But to us the reason is obvious. Theoretical differences, amongst those fighting against oppression, is a luxury which cannot be afforded. What is more, for many decades communists were the only political group in South Africa who were prepared to treat Africans as human beings and as their equals; who were prepared to eat with us; talk with us, live with us, and work with us. They were the only political group which was prepared to work with the Africans for the attainment of political rights and a stake in society. Because of this, there are many Africans who today tend to equate freedom with Communism. They are supported in this belief by a legislature which brands all exponents of democratic government and African freedom as communists and banned many of them, who are not communists, under the Suppression of Communism Act. Although My Lord I am not a communist and I have never been a member of the Communist Party, I myself have been banned, have been named under that pernicious Act because of the role I played in the Defiance Campaign. I have also been banned and convicted under that Act.

It is not only in internal politics that we count communists as amongst those who support our cause. In the international field, communist countries have always come to our aid. In the United Nations and other Councils of the world the communist bloc has supported the Afro-Asian struggle against colonialism and often seems to be more sympathetic to our plight than some of the Western powers. Although there is a universal condemnation of apartheid, the communist bloc speaks out against it with a louder voice than most of the western world. In these circumstances, it would take a brash young politician, such as I was in 1949, to proclaim that the Communists are our enemies.

Judge: Well Mandela it is time for the court to adjourn.

My Lord, I wish now to turn to my own position. I have denied that I am a communist, and I think in the circumstances I am obliged to state exactly what my political beliefs are in order to explain what my position in Umkhonto was, and what my attitude towards the use of force is.

I have always regarded myself, in the first place, as an African patriot. After all, I was born in Umtata, forty-six years ago. My guardian was my cousin, who was the acting paramount chief of Thembuland, and I am related both to Sabata Dalindyebo, the present paramount chief, and to Kaiser Matanzima, the Chief Minister for the Transkei.

Today I am attracted by the idea of a classless society, an attraction which springs in part from Marxist reading and, in part, from my admiration of the structure and organisation of early African societies in this country. The land, then the main means of production, belonged to the tribe. There was no rich or poor and there was no exploitation.

It is true, as I have already stated that I have been influenced by Marxist thought. But this is also true of many of the leaders of the new independent states. Such widely different persons as Gandhi, Nehru, Nkrumah, and Nasser all acknowledge this fact. We all accept the need for some form of socialism to enable our people to catch up with the advanced countries of the world and to overcome their legacy of extreme poverty. But this does not mean we are Marxists.

Indeed, My Lord, for my own part, I believe it is open to debate whether the Communist Party has any specific role to play at this particular stage of our political struggle. The basic task at the present moment is the removal of race discrimination and the attainment of democratic rights on the basis of the Freedom Charter, and a struggle which can best be led by a strong ANC. In so far, My Lord, as that Party furthers this task, I welcome its assistance. I realise that it is one of the main means by which people of all races can be drawn into our struggle.

But from my reading of Marxist literature and from conversations with Marxists, I have gained the impression that communists regard the parliamentary system of the work - of the West as undemocratic and reactionary. But, on the contrary, I am an admirer of such a system.

The Magna Carta, the Petition of Rights, the Bill of Rights are documents which are held in veneration by democrats throughout the world.

I have great respect for British political institutions, and for the country's system of justice. I regard the British Parliament as the most democratic institution in the world, and the independence and impartiality of its judiciary never fail to arouse my admiration.

The American Congress, that country's doctrine of separation of powers, as well as the independence of its judiciary, arouse in me similar sentiments.

I have been influenced in my thinking by both West and East. All this has led me to feel that in my search for a political formula, I should be absolutely impartial and objective. I should tie myself to no particular system of society other than that of socialism. I must leave myself free to borrow the best from West and from the East.

I wish now to deal with some of the exhibits. Many of the exhibits are in my handwriting. It has always been my custom to reduce to writing the material which I have been studying.

Exhibits R20, 21 and 22 are lectures drafted in my own hand but they are not my original work. They came to be written in the following circumstances:

> For several years an old friend [unidentified person coughs] whom I worked very closely on ANC matters and who occupied senior positions both in the ANC and the Communist Party had been trying to get me to join the Communist Party. I had had many debates with him on the role the Communist Party can play at this stage of our struggle. And I advanced to him the same views in regard to my political beliefs which I have described earlier in my statement. In order to convince me that I should join the Communist Party, she from time to time gave me Marxist literature to read, thought I did not have—always find time to do this. Each of us always stuck to our guns in our arguments as to whether I should join the Communist Party. She [sic] maintained that on achieving freedom we would be unable to solve our problems of poverty and inequality without establishing a communist state and we would require trained Marxists to do this. I maintained my attitude that no ideological differences should be introduced until freedom had been achieved. I saw him on several occasions at Liliesleaf farm, and on one of the last of these occasions he was busy writing with books around him. When I asked him what he was doing he told me that he was busy writing lectures for use in the Communist Party, and suggested that I should read them. There were several lectures in draft form. After I had done so I told him that they seemed far too complicated for the ordinary reader.

Judge: I didn't catch the name—who do you say this man is you were talking to?
Mandela: I beg your pardon, My Lord
Judge: Who is the man you are referring to?
Mandela: My Lord, as a matter of principle
Judge: No, I thought you had mentioned his name
Mandela: I didn't mention his name
Judge: Well go on then Mandela: and that was done
Judge: Yes
Mandela: deliberately
Judge: Yes

Mandela: I was saying, My Lord, after I had read I told him that they seemed far too complicated for the ordinary reader in that the language was obtuse and they were full of usual communistic clichés and jargon. If the court will look at some of the standard works of Marxism, my point will be demonstrated. He said it was impossible to simplify the language without losing the effect of what the author was trying to stress. I disagreed with him and then he asked me to see whether I could redraft the lectures in the simplified form suggested by me. I agreed to help him and set to work in an endeavour to do this but I never finished the task as I later became occupied with other practical work which was more important. I never again saw the unfinished manuscript until it was produced at this trial. I wish to state that it is not my handwriting which appears on Exhibit R23 which was obviously drafted by the person who prepared the lectures.

My Lord, there are certain exhibits which suggest that we received financial support from abroad, and I wish now to deal with this question. [audio interference throughout the previous sentence] [audio interference] Our political struggle has always been financed from internal sources—from funds raised by our own people and by our own supporters. Whenever we had a special campaign or an important political case we received financial assistance from sympathetic individuals and organisations in the Western countries. We have never felt it necessary to go beyond these sources.

But when in 1961 the Umkhonto was formed, and a new phase of struggle introduced, we realised that these events would make a heavy call on our slender resources, and that the scale of our activities would be hampered by lack of funds. One of my instructions, as I went abroad in January 1962, was to raise funds from the African states.

I must add that whilst abroad, I had discussions with leaders of political movements in Africa and discovered that almost every single one of them, in areas which had still not attained independence, had received all forms of assistance from the socialist countries, as well as from the West, including that of financial support. I also discovered that some well-known African states, all of them non-communists, and even anti-communists, had received similar assistance.

On my return to the Republic, I made a strong recommendation to the ANC that we should not confine ourselves to Africa and the Western countries, but that we should also send a mission to the socialist countries to raise the funds which we so urgently needed.

I have been told that after I was convicted such a mission was sent.

As I understand the State case, and in particular the evidence of "X", Umkhonto was the inspiration of the Communist Party which sought, by playing upon imaginary grievances, to enrol the African people into an army which ostensibly was to fight for African freedom, but in reality was fighting for a communist state. Nothing could be further from the truth. In fact the suggestion is preposterous. Umkhonto was formed by Africans to further their struggle for freedom. Communists and others supported the movement, and we only wish that more sections of the community would join us.

Our fight is against real and not imaginary hardships or, to use the language of the State Prosecutor, 'so-called hardships'. Basically, My Lord, we fight against two features which are the hallmarks of African life in South Africa and which are entrenched by legislation which we seek to have repealed. These features are poverty and lack of human dignity, and we do not need communists or so-called 'agitators' to teach us about these things.

South Africa is the richest country in Africa, and could be one of the richest countries in the world. But it is a land of extremes and remarkable contrasts. [audio interference] The whites enjoy what may well be the highest standard of living in the world, whilst Africans live in poverty and misery. Forty percent of the Africans live in hopelessly overcrowded and, in some cases, drought-stricken reserves, where soil erosion and the overworking of the soil makes it impossible for them to live properly off the land. Thirty percent are labourers, labour tenants, and squatters on white farms and work and live under conditions similar to those of the serfs of the Middle Ages. The other thirty percent live in towns where they have developed economic and social habits which bring them closer in many respects to white standards. Yet most Africans, even in this group, are impoverished by low incomes and the high cost of living.

The highest-paid and the most prosperous section of urban African life is in Johannesburg. Yet their actual position is desperate. The latest figures were given on the 25th of March 1964 by Mr. Carr, Manager of the Johannesburg Non-European Affairs Department. The poverty datum line for the average African family in Johannesburg, according to Mr. Carr's department, is R42.84 per month. He showed that the average monthly wage is R32.24 and that forty-six percent of all African families in Johannesburg do not earn enough to keep them going.

Poverty goes hand in hand with malnutrition and disease. The incidence of malnutrition and deficiency diseases is very high amongst Africans. Tuberculosis, pellagra, kwashiorkor, gastro-enteritis, and scurvy bring death and destruction of health. The incidence of infant mortality is one of the highest in the world. According to the Medical Officer of Health for Pretoria, it is estimated that tuberculosis kills forty people a day, almost all Africans, and in 1961 there were 58,491 new cases reported. These diseases, My Lord, not only destroy the vital organs of the body, but they result in retarded mental conditions and lack of initiative, and reduce powers of concentration. The secondary results of such conditions affect the whole community and the standard of work performed by Africans.

The complaint of Africans, however, is not only that they are poor and whites are rich, but that the laws which are made by the whites are designed to preserve this situation.

There are two ways to break out of poverty. The first is by formal education, and the second is by the worker acquiring a greater skill at his work and thus higher wages. As far as Africans are concerned, both these avenues of advancement are deliberately curtailed by legislation.

I ask the Court to remember that the present Government has always sought to hamper Africans in their search for education. One of their early acts, after coming into power, was to stop subsidies for African school feeding. Many African children who attended schools depended on this supplement to their diet. This was a cruel act.

There is compulsory education for all white children at virtually no cost to their parents, be they rich or poor. Similar facilities are not provided for the African children, though there are some who receive such assistance. African children, however, generally have to pay more for their schooling than whites. According to figures quoted by the South African Institute of Race Relations in its 1963 journal, approximately forty percent of African children in the age group between seven and fourteen do not attend school. For those who do attend school, the standards are vastly different from those afforded to white children. In 1960–61 the per capita Government spending [someone coughs] on African students at State-aided schools was estimated at R12.46. In the same years, the per capita spending on white children in the Cape Province (which are the only figures available to me) was R144.57. Although there are no figures available to me, it can be stated, without doubt, that the white children on whom R144.57 per head was being spent all came from wealthier homes than African children on whom R12.46 per head was being spent.

The quality of education is also different. According to the Bantu Educational Journal, only 5,660 African children in the whole of South Africa passed their Junior Certificate in 1962, and in that year only 362 passed matric. This is presumably consistent with the policy of Bantu Education about which the present Prime Minister said, during the debate on the Bantu Education Bill in 1953 when he was Minister of Native Affairs, I quote:

> "When I have control of Native Education I will reform it so that Natives will be taught from childhood to realise that equality with Europeans is not for them. People who believe in equality are not desirable teachers for Natives. When my Department [audio interference] controls Native education it will know for what class of higher education a Native is fitted, and whether he will have a chance in life to use his knowledge," unquote.

The other main obstacle to the economic advancement of the African is the Industrial Colour Bar under which all the better paid, better jobs of industry are reserved for whites only. Moreover, [audio interference] Africans in the unskilled and semi-skilled occupations which are open to them are not allowed to form trade unions which have recognition under the Industrial Conciliation Act. This means that strikes of African workers are illegal, and that they are denied the right of collective bargaining which is permitted to the better-paid white workers. The discrimination in the policy of successive South African Governments towards African workers is demonstrated by the so-called 'civilized labour policy' under which sheltered, unskilled Government jobs are found for those white workers who cannot make the grade in industry, at wages far, which far exceed the earnings of the average African employee in industry.

The Government often answers its critics by saying that Africans in South Africa are economically better off than the inhabitants of the other countries in Africa. I do not know whether this statement is true and doubt whether any comparison can be made without having regard to the cost-of-living index in such countries. But even if it is true, as far as African people are concerned, it is irrelevant. Our complaint is not that we are poor by comparison with people in other countries, but that we are poor by comparison with white people in our own country, and that we are prevented by legislation from altering this imbalance.

The lack of human dignity experienced by Africans is the direct result of the policy of white supremacy. White supremacy implies black inferiority. Legislation designed to preserve white supremacy entrenches this notion. Menial tasks in South Africa are invariably performed by Africans. When anything has to be carried or cleaned the white man will look around for an African to do it for him, whether the African is employed by him or not. Because of this sort of attitude, whites tend to regard Africans as a separate breed. They do not look upon them as people with families of their own; they do not realise that we have emotions—that we fall in love like white people do; that we want to be with their wives and children like white people want to be with theirs; that we want to earn money, enough money to support our families properly, to feed and clothe them and send them to school. And what 'house-boy' or 'garden-boy' or labourer can ever hope to do this?

Pass laws, which to the Africans are among the most hated bits of legislation in South Africa, render any African liable to police surveillance at any time. I doubt whether there is a single African male in South Africa who has not at some stage had a brush with the police over his pass. Hundreds and thousands of Africans are thrown into jail each year under pass laws. Even worse than this is the fact that pass laws keep husband and wife apart and lead to the breakdown of family life.

Poverty and the breakdown of family life have secondary effects. Children wander about the streets of the townships because they have no schools to go to, or no money to enable them to go to school, or no parents at home to see that they go to school, because both parents, if there be two, have to work to keep the family alive. This leads to a breakdown in moral standards, to an alarming rise in illegitimacy, and to growing violence which erupts not only politically, but everywhere. Life in the townships is dangerous. There is not a day that goes by without somebody being stabbed or assaulted. And violence is carried out of the townships into the white living areas. People are afraid to walk alone in the streets after dark. Housebreakings and robberies are increasing, despite the fact that the death sentence can now be imposed for such offences. Death sentences cannot cure the festering sore.

The only cure is to alter the conditions under which Africans are forced to live and to meet their legitimate grievances. Africans want to be paid a living wage. Africans want to perform work which they are capable of doing, and not work which the Government declares them to be capable of. We want to be allowed to live where we obtain work, and not be endorsed out of an area because we were not born there. We want to be allowed and not to be obliged to live in rented houses which we can never call our own. We want to be part of the general population, and not confined to living in our ghettoes. African men want to have their wives and children to live with them where they work, and not to be forced into an unnatural existence in men's hostels. Our women want to be with their men folk and not to be left permanently widowed in the reserves. We want to be allowed out after eleven o'clock at night and not to be confined to our rooms like little children. We want to be allowed to travel in our own country and to seek work where we want to, where we want to and not where the Labour Bureau tells us to. We want a just share in the whole of South Africa; we want security and a stake in society.

Above all, My Lord, we want equal political rights, because without them our disabilities will be permanent. I know this sounds revolutionary to the whites in this country, because the majority of voters will be Africans. This makes the white man fear democracy.

But this fear cannot be allowed to stand in the way of the only solution which will guarantee racial harmony and freedom for all. It is not true that the enfranchisement of all will result in racial domination. Political division, based on colour, is entirely artificial and, when it disappears, so will the domination of one colour group by another. The ANC has spent half a century fighting against racialism. When it triumphs as it certainly must, it will not change that policy.

This then is what the ANC is fighting. Our struggle is a truly national one. It is a struggle of the African people, inspired by our own suffering and our own experience. It is a struggle for the right to live. [someone coughs]

During my lifetime I have dedicated my life to this struggle of the African people. I have fought against white domination, and I have fought against black domination. I have cherished the ideal of a democratic and free society in which all persons will live together in harmony and with equal opportunities. It is an ideal for which I hope to live for and to see realised. But, My Lord, if it needs be, it is an ideal for which I am prepared to die.

STUDY QUESTIONS

1. How does Mandela make his argument to the court?

2. What do you think is Mandela's message and legacy?

CPSIA information can be obtained
at www.ICGtesting.com
Printed in the USA
FSHW021741181121
86325FS

9 781793 521187